Henry Purcell and the London Stage

Henry Purcell
(portrait by John Closterman)

HENRY PURCELL
AND THE
LONDON STAGE

Curtis Alexander Price

Lecturer in Music
University of London King's College

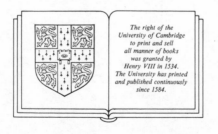

The right of the
University of Cambridge
to print and sell
all manner of books
was granted by
Henry VIII in 1534.
The University has printed
and published continuously
since 1584.

Cambridge University Press

Cambridge
London   New York   New Rochelle
Melbourne   Sydney

Published by the Press Syndicate of the University of Cambridge
The Pitt Building, Trumpington Street, Cambridge CB2 1RP
32 East 57th Street, New York, NY 10022, USA
296 Beaconsfield Parade, Middle Park, Melbourne 3206, Australia

First published 1984

Printed in Great Britain at
the University Press, Cambridge

Library of Congress catalogue card number: 83-15170

British Library Cataloguing in Publication Data

Price, Curtis A.
Henry Purcell and the London stage.
1. Purcell, Henry   2. Music in theatres - History
I. Title
782.8'09421   ML410.P93

ISBN 0 521 23831 5

ME

for
MY PARENTS

Contents

Part I: The Plays

Contents

Part II: The Operas

Plates

Preface

The idea for this book grew from a performance of *King Arthur* given by the English Opera Group at Sadler's Wells Theatre in 1971. This bizarre introduction to Purcell on the stage has coloured my view of his theatre works ever since. The producer, Colin Graham, had arrived at a rather drastic solution to what has been called the 'problem' of Purcell's semi-operas, namely, that the main characters do not sing. Dryden's dialogue was heavily cut, and Arthur, Merlin, Emmeline, and other speaking characters were allotted lyrics originally sung by Saxon priests and Kentish shepherds, the singing roles augmented with music borrowed from other Purcell stage works.

During the interval, a friend of mine offered a defence of Graham's radical alteration, noting that *King Arthur* presented the producer with two dilemmas, one aesthetic, since it is not enough like a 'real opera' to be appealing to modern audiences, and the other practical: the English Opera Group could hardly have engaged an artist of Benjamin Luxon's stature to sing three or four incidental songs, only to have him stand silently by while under-employed actors hammered their way through pages of spoken dialogue. Why, I mused, had the producer not taken the plunge and hired someone to convert what little remained of the dialogue into recitative? Would not Purcell, had he not died at the lamentably early age of thirty-six, soon have seen his countrymen outgrow their dislike of dramatis personae conversing in recitative? Was not the English opera already laden with so much music that it was only a matter of time before it blossomed into the real thing? I have since learned that Purcell and his contemporaries were not inching towards all-sung opera, that they did not deem the native semi-opera an imperfect form to be improved by adopting continental practices. And while writing this book, I gradually came to understand that the most disturbing aspect of the 1971 adaptation of *King Arthur* was not that Graham had tried to make it more like an opera, but that in tipping the balance steeply in favour of music, he had destroyed the structure of Dryden's play itself.

Purcell was a brilliant music dramatist, but he was not an opera composer. His major works for the professional stage, *Dioclesian*, *King Arthur*, and *The Fairy-Queen*, are essentially plays to which a great deal of music is added. My method in writing this book has been to examine the music strictly in terms of its attendant spoken drama, being as much concerned with the late seventeenth-century London theatre world as with the composer himself. While Purcell needs no advocate for his genius, the playwrights whom he faithfully served – Dryden, Lee, Durfey, Southerne, and others – certainly do, if for no other reason than to acquit them of the fallacious charge of conspiracy to subvert the emergence of true opera in English. The reader may be surprised to discover that I devote so much space to Purcell's music for ordinary plays, works for which he typically contributed only a song or two and perhaps a suite of incidental tunes. This repertoire is almost wholly neglected by musicologists, yet it includes some of his best compositions. To understand the function of music in the semi-operas, indeed to appreciate England's apparent reluctance to step into the mainstream of operatic evolution, one must begin with these 'mere plays', in which speaking characters sing and musical episodes advance plots.

While this book primarily addresses musicologists and – perhaps too ambitiously – drama historians, I should be most pleased if performers of Purcell's theatre music also find it useful. Many of the works discussed on the following pages have a secure place in the modern concert repertoire, but musicians are not always aware of the role favourites such as 'Sweeter than roses' and 'Let the dreadful engines' have in the original plays. That the former was sung as an aphrodisiac for a concubine and the latter performed by a spurned lover who is conscious of his own madness are facts that might conceivably influence interpretation. And for those works that are not so well known, perhaps because they are too exotic, I attempt to show how carefully Purcell tailored his music to the drama. My fondest hope is that this book will contribute in some small way to unadulterated revivals of the semi-operas and plays with music.

Robert D. Hume, who has done much to make late seventeenth-century English drama a legitimate subject for modern criticism, encouraged me to undertake this project and provided invaluable help at every stage. That his works are cited so frequently in the following pages reflects both their sheer quantity and my admiration for them. I have also to thank Judith Milhous, who read the entire typescript and made innumerable corrections and improvements. To Rhian Samuel goes deepest gratitude for teaching me so much about the music of Purcell.

I owe special thanks to A. Margaret Laurie, whose doctoral thesis on Purcell's theatre music provides the foundation for this book. In reading the first draft, she saved me from several blunders and has since graciously allowed me to incorporate many of her ideas. Neither Dr Laurie nor any of those scholars mentioned above is, however, responsible for the errors that may have crept into the following pages.

The research for this study was done primarily at the British Library, the Bodleian, the libraries of the Royal Academy of Music and the Royal College of Music, the University Library and the Fitzwilliam Museum,

Cambridge, and the Guildhall Library, London, whose staffs I thank for much assistance. I should also like to thank Mr Barrie Iliffe for allowing me to consult the Purcell manuscripts at the British Council. I am grateful to the American Council of Learned Societies and the John Simon Guggenheim Memorial Foundation for generous fellowships enabling me to complete this book.

December 1982

This book went to press before the publication of Eric Walter White's *A History of English Opera* (London: Faber, 1983). Chapters 1–6 of that study provide a clear and accurate background to Restoration theatre music. It is gratifying to learn that regarding several of the more controversial aspects of Purcell's stage career (the disputed authorship of the *Tempest* music, for example) we are in substantial agreement.

London
October 1983

Note on the Music Examples

Unless otherwise indicated, all music examples are taken from *The Works of Henry Purcell*, 32 vols. (London: Novello, 1878–), hereinafter cited as the Purcell Society Edition. Minor emendations to excerpts drawn from unrevised volumes (XVI, XIX, XX, and XXI) are supplied silently from the earliest printed or manuscript source. In no instance are sources conflated. Some excerpts are condensed and, where indicated, parts occasionally omitted.

Titles of vocal pieces cited in the text and words underlaid in the music examples are modernized where the setting is by Purcell, but follow the earliest source where it is by another composer. Spoken or sung texts quoted at length follow the earliest source in all cases, including those set by Purcell.

Part I
THE PLAYS

1 Music in the Late Seventeenth-Century English Theatre

Purcell's admirers have long lamented his ill luck. The master dramatist composed for a theatre in which music played second fiddle to spoken drama, and at a time when the term 'opera' was proudly applied to comedies and tragicomedies abridged to make room for incidental entertainments and masques. In the mid-1670s the Restoration play with music, like the sixteenth-century *intermedio* and the seventeenth-century *comédie-ballet*, seemed to stagger on the brink of true opera, but twenty years later when Purcell was in his prime, opera in the Italian manner seemed as remote to the English taste as ever. Had he lived only ten years longer, the Orpheus Britannicus would have seen his rational audience finally accept the convention of actors conversing in recitative and could have shared in Handel's victory over English sensibility.

This traditional view of Purcell's 'unlucky' role in the non-development of English opera does him a great disservice. To understand his theatre music one must begin by questioning the assumption that opera in the Italian style is the apex of music drama and that those hybrids which mix song and speech are necessarily inferior. Many music historians are enthusiastically opera-centric, believing that what seems to have happened so naturally in Florence and Mantua about 1600 was destined to be repeated all over the rest of Europe, that Lully's achievement in France and Steffani's in Germany were inevitable 'improvements' on the anaemic and impure stage types native to those countries. England's failure to develop its own opera tradition has been viewed as an aberration; and most studies of Purcell's theatre works are in some measure apologies for his not having travelled in the mainstream of operatic evolution. Even the two pioneering chronicles of dramatic music in England in the seventeenth century, Edward J. Dent's *Foundations of English Opera* (1928) and Dennis Arundell's *The Critic at the Opera* (1957), attempt to judge Purcell's stage works by continental standards, assessing, for example, to what extent *Dido and Aeneas* resembles an Italian chamber cantata or a *tragédie lyrique*. The period produced only two works that a foreign traveller of the time would have recognized as operas: Dryden's *Albion and Albanius* of 1685, composed by the French-trained Spaniard Louis Grabu and a *tragédie lyrique* in all but language, and Congreve's *Semele*, a *sui generis* music drama set by John Eccles in 1706-7 but unperformed until this century. My main purpose here is not to explain why England failed to produce true opera during the baroque period but rather to show why the English felt no compelling need to have it.

What is English Opera?

Alfred Einstein wrote that music 'is not the natural means of expression for the Englishman to the same extent as it is for the Italian'.[1] Before condemning a non-Briton for such a breezy judgement, one should know that Dent also laid the blame for a lack of native baroque opera on national character: 'Music for the Italian is the exaggeration of personality – for the Englishman its annihilation.'[2] Jack Westrup argued more dispassionately that England's slowness to follow continental developments in opera was partly due to its strong tradition of plays.[3] Indeed, the hottest objection to the successful importation of foreign opera into London about 1700 came from actors and playwrights, who had the most to lose. Both explanations are undoubtedly valid in part, each seeking to account for a certain uneasiness that Restoration audiences felt at the very idea of opera: namely, that human actions and emotions be conveyed by vocal music rather than speech. We may suppose that a late seventeenth-century Englishman would have found Italianate opera in his language distasteful not simply because singers rather than actors delivered all the lines written by the poet, but because the singers represented real human beings and would thus, as Roger North says, 'break unity'.[4] The issue was not whether a story could be told in music, but whether this could be done as autonomous drama. Most playwrights of the period were willing to allow practically any amount of singing in their works, provided the protagonists conducted the main 'business' in spoken dialogue. The aesthetic is well illustrated by *Albion and Albanius*. With this super-masque Dryden, an experienced playwright and arguably England's greatest drama theorist, blithely unveiled a full-length, all-sung opera.[5] It has no spoken dialogue and each member of the cast sings. *Albion and Albanius* was not much of a success, but this was owing more to political circumstances than to artistic shortcomings (see Chapter 6). Why, then, did no critic stand up and declare it another suit of the emperor's new clothes? Was it not the very annihilation of dramatic unity? The opera did not violate the English ideal of music drama for the following reasons. It was conceived, Dryden claimed, as a French-style prologue to a musical play – *King Arthur*, as it

---

[1] *A Short History of Music*, rev. edn (New York: Vintage, 1954), p. 81.
[2] *Foundations of English Opera* (1928; rpt New York: Da Capo, 1965), p. 2.
[3] *Purcell*, rev. Nigel Fortune (London: Dent, 1980), pp. 104–14.
[4] *Roger North on Music*, ed. John Wilson (London: Novello, 1959), p. 307.
[5] The only true English opera to pre-date *Albion and Albanius* is Sir William Davenant's *The Siege of Rhodes*, of which no music survives. But see John Buttrey, 'The Evolution of English Opera between 1656 and 1695: A Re-investigation', Diss. Cambridge 1967, pp. ii, 22–55; and Chapter 2 below.

happens – and not as an autonomous work. And much more important, it was a well-advertised allegory. The singers who took the roles of Albion and Albanius were known to be surrogates for Charles II and the Duke of York; they were not actors personating the royal brothers themselves. There is not the slightest inconsistency in Dryden's having these figures converse entirely in recitative and air in *Albion and Albanius*, while limiting King Arthur and Merlin to speech and mime in his next major musical work, a semi-opera. Arthur and his magician were thought to be historical personages, and in a rational world, even one represented on the stage, mortals do not converse exclusively in music.

King Arthur was not the first dramatic opera (called variously 'semi-opera', 'ambigue entertainment', or 'English opera'). From the Restoration of Charles II in 1660 until about 1705, English plays were performed with substantial amounts of music. Some historians have assumed incorrectly that the semi-opera is a transitional stage in an incomplete development, with early playwrights insidiously increasing the amount of music in their works in order to soften up a recalcitrant audience for the eventual introduction of all-sung opera. Yet many productions of new and revamped dramas in the sixties, such as Stapylton's *The Step-mother*, included considerable music; and several large-scale works of the next decade lie somewhere between play and dramatic opera – *Circe*, *The Libertine*, and *Oedipus*, to name but three. Two extraordinary productions are frequently cited as the earliest semi-operas, because they contained more than enough music to distinguish them from run-of-the-mill plays: the 1674 alteration of *The Tempest*, with music by several composers, and Thomas Shadwell's tragedy *Psyche* of 1675, with music by Matthew Locke and G. B. Draghi. Regardless of quality, these works came much closer to pushing England into the operatic mainstream than did Purcell's major stage compositions, which represent a marked retrenchment. In *Psyche*, for instance, Venus, the antagonist, sings as often as she speaks, and the musical episodes do almost as much to advance the plot as the spoken dialogue. This cannot be said of any of Purcell's dramatic operas. In these later works considerable care is taken to keep the music and speech on different planes. The protagonists do not sing and the masques rarely impel the action.

Purcell's semi-operas have been misunderstood by historians who view them as teetering between masque and true opera. Allardyce Nicoll's high-falutin notion that they contain 'prose or blank verse dialogue breaking into song' is particularly misleading.[6] This view implies that *King Arthur*, for instance, could have been coaxed into becoming pure *dramma per musica* simply by converting its spoken dialogue into recitative, much the way Ernest Guiraud changed *Carmen* from an *opéra comique* into a grand

[6] *A History of English Drama 1660–1900*, rev. edn (Cambridge: Cambridge Univ. Press, 1952–9), II, 225.

opera for the 1875 Vienna production. This is far from the truth. Even after Purcell's death, the dramatic opera never threatened to shed its spoken dialogue and metamorphose into an independent form. To the very end it remained essentially a tragicomedy with interpolated episodes of music and dancing and more than the usual amount of scenic spectacle. Furthermore, I can find no evidence to support the perverse theory advanced by some drama historians that such works were conspiratorial. Michael Alssid, for example, claims that Dryden purposely tried to maintain a separation of music and drama in *King Arthur* in order to 'sabotage' England's attempt to move 'toward the Handelian achievement'.[7] But *Albion and Albanius* makes nonsense of this argument. The dramatic opera may have been only a play with knobs on, yet as Richard Luckett and others have recently shown, the 'ambigues' were stable, rational, and financially successful works that had simply run their course by the time Giovanni Bononcini's *Camilla* arrived in London in 1706.[8]

Critics who would study *King Arthur* and *Dioclesian* in order to gauge how closely such works moved towards true opera will look in vain for Arundell's 'missing link between dramas, masques, and operas', because Dryden and Purcell did not strive to create pieces modelled after continental forms. When Romain Rolland concludes that 'le malheureux Purcell dépensait son génie avec fièvre dans une quantité d'oeuvres où la musique jouait un rôle secondaire', he is echoing, perhaps too closely, Burney's famous epitaph: 'Unluckily for Purcell! he built his fame with such perishable materials, that his worth and works are daily diminishing.'[9] Both writers were only adding their voices to the chorus of lamentation that this composer never wrote a true national opera. One of the myths of modern musicology, which is rooted directly in Burney's view of an opera-centred musical world, is that any great composer who has an interest in the theatre will sooner or later write an opera; since Purcell, clearly a good composer, dabbled in music drama but failed to come up with a real opera, he may not, therefore, be a great composer. Not only is this faulty logic, but it assumes arrogantly that opera is the monarch of the stage. This may have been true for Italy during the last 350 years, but in Restoration England the play was Protean enough to accommodate native operatic proclivities.

---

[7] 'The Impossible Form of Art: Dryden, Purcell and *King Arthur*', *Studies in the Literary Imagination*, 10 (Spring 1977), 126.

[8] 'Exotick but Rational Entertainments: The English Dramatick Operas', in *English Drama: Forms and Development*, ed. Marie Axton and Raymond Williams (Cambridge: Cambridge Univ. Press, 1977), pp. 123–41, 232–4. See also Robert D. Hume, 'Opera in London, 1695–1706', forthcoming in *British Theatre and the Other Arts*, ed. Shirley Strum Kenny.

[9] Rolland, 'L'Opéra anglais au xviie siècle', *Encyclopédie de la musique*, ed. Albert Lavignac (Paris: Delagrave, 1913), I, 1894; Charles Burney, *A General History of Music* (1776–89; rpt New York: Dover, 1957), II, 380.

Plays with Music

Most studies of Purcell's theatre music have concentrated on the three semi-operas and *Dido and Aeneas*, a not unreasonable deployment of effort considering their quality. Almost wholly neglected is the music for ordinary dramas, which represents more than half his total output for the theatre. Paradoxically, some of these comedies, tragedies, and heroic plays include musical scenes far more significant dramatically than any of the masques of the better known semi-operas. Many of Purcell's songs in plays, for example, are not only integral, in that their omission would leave a gap in the plot, but 'operatic' as well. By the latter term I mean that the music itself supplies emotions, characterizations, or foreshadowings not apparent from the verse alone. Even more remarkable is that such songs are occasionally sung by important speaking characters, something that never happens in his semi-operas. Purcell inherited a rich legacy of music in spoken drama, and his achievement in the less extravagant works is solidly in this tradition. Beginning with the earliest tragedies and tragicomedies of the Restoration, one can often detect the same close links between music and action – the very wellsprings of opera – that Nino Pirrotta finds not in the *intermedi*, but within late fifteenth- and sixteenth-century Italian plays themselves.[10] Two of these modest English dramas, Stapylton's *The Step-mother* and Settle's *The Empress of Morocco*, are landmark precursors of the type of play in which music and spoken dialogue work together as equal partners. Purcell brought this form to fruition in several works, perhaps most magnificently in the 1695 alteration of *The Indian Queen*.

Sir Robert Stapylton wrote two plays for the Duke's Theatre in Lincoln's Inn Fields, *The Slighted Maid* (February 1663) and *The Step-mother* (October 1663), both of which have deservedly escaped much critical commentary but are nonetheless remarkable for their lengthy musical scenes.[11] Arundell points to *The Slighted Maid* as the elusive missing link between spoken drama and opera. So important does he consider this work that he devotes the greater part of an enthusiastic chapter to it in *The Critic at the Opera*. He is amazed to find that its 'masques and entertainments . . . are not mere excrescences, but are integral parts of the drama: while at the end a musical scene directly brings about the denouement'.[12] He looks less favourably on *The Step-mother*, which he describes as 'dully unreal', not 'saved by the musical scenes'; 'though the chief characters all appear as actors in the masques, that fails to make them an integral part of the play'

[10] See *Music and Theatre from Poliziano to Monteverdi*, trans. Karen Eales (Cambridge: Cambridge Univ. Press, 1982), pp. x, 49, 78–82, 102.
[11] Hume, for example, devotes one sentence to both in *The Development of English Drama in the Late Seventeenth Century* (Oxford: Clarendon, 1976), p. 241.
[12] *The Critic at the Opera* (1957; rpt New York: Da Capo, 1980), p. 76.

(p. 90). I admire Arundell's iconoclastic audacity in giving a mere play a central position in his history of opera criticism but disagree with his assessment, viewing *The Step-mother* as a quasi-opera and *The Slighted Maid*, admittedly an ingenious drama, as wholly conventional in its musical entertainments.

The Step-mother's three masques, composed by Locke though the music is not extant, are the pivots on which the gangling plot turns. Later playwrights preferred to treat shows of music and dancing as incidental entertainments for the speaking cast, who sit mute 'hearkening to' the music. But Stapylton is careful to give his masques trenchant roles. The play is set in ancient Britain a few years after the Roman decampment. Sylvanus is struggling to keep his principality intact while his villainous wife, Pontia, plots against him. His son, Filamor, though greatly distrusting his stepmother, nevertheless desires her daughter, Caesarina. The first two acts require large amounts of music, but only in the third does Stapylton's originality begin to surface. The centrepiece is a masque of Ovid's huntsmen, during which Caesarina tries to lure Filamor towards assassins. Daphne, singing in the hollow tree, is reluctant to emerge, uncertain of Apollo's intentions. The allegory is plain enough to put Filamor on his guard, but his sister, the poor Violinda, is set upon. She screams 'Murder, murder', which evokes a droll response from her assailant: 'No faith, tis but a Rape'. Filamor comes to the rescue and shortly thereafter convinces his father that something must be done about his stepmother. The prince finally agrees, but delays her death sentence until after yet another masque, an apologue to persuade his wife to confess her crimes.

The fourth-act masque is extremely important. The previous entertainments, while neatly inserted into the plot, have done little to alter the course of events. But with this climactic masque, the playwright asks us to suspend disbelief, to allow music to effect an improbable change of behaviour in an important speaking character. Most remarkable of all, the dramatis personae themselves, except Filamor, will act their mythological counterparts. Stapylton thereby puts considerable distance between this scene and its obvious model, the play-within-the-play of *Hamlet*. The masque of Diana and the Hawthorn Tree is a metaphor of the rape in the preceding act. Flora, sung by Caesarina, is under the control of Diana, who is portrayed by the arrogant Pontia herself. Violinda plays Philomel, who can only sing like a nightingale since her tongue was cut out. She blames Diana for her misfortune. The rape is mimed by a satyr, who leaps out from behind a bush to catch the hem of Philomel's vest. At the end of the masque, Pontia, half in the character of Diana and half as herself, makes a long confessional *speech*, sparing no detail of her wrong-doing. All the other courtiers remain masked during this remarkable scene, and Prince Sylvanus, who has just danced the role of his namesake the wood

8

god, removes his vizard only after his wife's *mea culpa* to order her execution. Pontia's contrition is thus prompted by the allegorical representation of her real transgressions. In *The Step-mother* Stapylton made a bold attempt to create a novel genre for the English stage, one in which a significant portion of the drama is borne by protagonist, antagonist, and supporting characters who express themselves in vocal music and ballet: an opera by any other name. But, alas, the force of the final masque is deflected when Pontia, having gained the upper hand and promptly condemned her husband and his faction, recants and promises to be a virtuous and obedient wife. Stapylton has, however, proven himself a skilled dramatist throughout the four previous acts, and the banality of the final one is a pardonable bow to convention.

How different is the fifth-act entertainment in *The Slighted Maid*, the one for which Arundell claims a seminal role. The masque of Vulcan, Venus, and Mars, like Diana's in the later play, is an allegory of the main plot, with two or three important differences.[13] First, no member of the speaking cast sings or dances. Second, the masque, which recounts Venus's cuckolding of Vulcan with Mars, clearly parallels Iberio and Pyramena's supposed adultery, especially when these 'real' characters, rather than their masqueing counterparts Mars and Venus, are discovered *in flagrante delicto* at the end of the masque. But only Vulcan is cuckolded: when Pyramena's 'husband', Decio, is revealed as a woman, the allegory collapses. The masque has thus added little to the plot, and the startling appearance of Iberio and Pyramena brings the music to a jolting halt.

Music was not called upon again to take such an important role until ten years later in Elkanah Settle's drama *The Empress of Morocco* (1673). The fourth-act masque of Orpheus was also set by Locke and fortunately survives. The play is well known in literary circles because it drew a savage attack from Crowne, Shadwell, and Dryden in their *Notes and Observations on the Empress of Morocco*, where it is labelled a 'confus'd heap of false Grammar, improper English, strain'd Hyperboles, and downright Bulls' (from the preface). In an equally stinging reply, Settle parries these thrusts by showing that Dryden's rhymed plays are no less nonsensical. But it was an internecine squabble, since, as Maximillian Novak notes, the controversy signalled the demise of the heroic drama.[14] While Settle's debating skills did little to acquit him of writing doggerel, *The Empress of Morocco* is blessed for being powerfully dramatic, the climax occurring during a musical scene.

The plot is stock heroic stuff: the young King of Morocco, Muly Labas,

---

[13] In New York Public Library, Drexel MS 3849, p. 104, is an anonymous dance called 'Vulcans' that was perhaps used in the masque. But note that Vulcan also appears in III.i of Shadwell's *Psyche*.

[14] See his introduction to the collection of the relevant documents reprinted in facsimile (Los Angeles: Augustan Reprint Society, 1968), pp. ii-iv.

and his wife are held captive by the villain, Crimalhaz. The Queen Mother pretends to offer a plan for her son's escape, but she is Crimalhaz's secret lover and wants only to betray her son. The gaoler–host, in a display of Restoration good manners, has prepared a fourth-act masque to entertain his royal 'guests'; the argument is Orpheus's descent into Hades to fetch Euridice. The Queen Mother tells her son that she has privately arranged with the masquers for the young king himself to play Orpheus, and his queen, Morena, Euridice. After Orpheus retrieves his bride from the Stygian shores and the happy pair have marched out of Hell, they may continue past the guards and out of Crimalhaz's hellish camp to safety. A good plan and good drama, but not the whole story.

After instructing her son in the intricacies of the masque, the Queen Mother gives Morena false stage directions: Crimalhaz will act Orpheus, who will carry off 'Euridice' and ravish her during the last scene. To save herself and her king, Morena must stab 'Orpheus' at the appropriate moment. With the deceptive plot thus laid, the entertainment begins with 'all the Court in Masquerade'.

The masque, though hardly riveting musically or dramatically, nevertheless has a complex double meaning. Orpheus makes his usual plea for the return of his beloved. Pluto scoffs at the mere mortal's request. Proserpine intervenes and touches a sentimental nerve in her husband, who finally releases the fair Euridice. Rejoicing follows and Orpheus is spared the usual test of faith. Crowne, Shadwell, and Dryden objected particularly to Orpheus's weak response to Pluto's first question: 'Whence Mortal does thy Courage grow, / To dare to take a Walk so Low?' He answers, 'To Tell thee God, thou art a Ravisher' who commits 'Rapes on Souls'. The critics observe disparagingly that 'Orpheus came a long Journey to tell Pluto very great news, viz. that he was a Ravisher, as if he did not know that before' (p. 45). But they have missed the point. King Muly Labas masquerades as Orpheus; his fears that Morena may be ravished indeed by her real captor are creeping into his lines. Unfortunately, Settle did not complete the irony by having Crimalhaz act Pluto, but this felicitous arrangement may have been rendered impossible because the villain was portrayed by Thomas Betterton, who did not sing.[15] At the end of the masque after a dance of celebration by infernal spirits, Orpheus advances to claim his bride. Thinking he is Crimalhaz about to abduct her, Morena stabs him. Treachery is discovered when the masks are removed, and Muly Labas dies as the deceitful Crimalhaz sends for doctors. Though unremitting in their attacks on Settle's poetry, the niggling critics are silent about the *coup de théâtre*.

Is this *dramma per musica*? The masque is an allegorical setting of the

---

[15] This might explain why Filamor, also played by Betterton, does not sing in *The Step-mother*.

concluding catastrophe, but the music is static, neither recalling nor presaging events. In this respect it is like the ballet in Act V of *The Revenger's Tragedy* (1607). The two entertainments have similar functions, namely to disguise those bent on murder and to provide a ritualistic confrontation of victim and assailant. And the similarity between the plays extends beyond their masques. In the earlier tragedy Gratiana is bribed to pimp for her own daughter, while in *The Empress of Morocco* the Queen Mother will go to any lengths to usurp her son's throne. But here the comparison ends. In *The Revenger's Tragedy* the masqued murder of Lussurioso is brilliantly ironic, because at the height of an earlier revels his youngest brother had raped and killed Antonio's daughter.[16] The masque in Settle's play, however, is contrived, an unnecessarily complicated means of escape for Muly Labas. In neither work is the completion of the action dependent upon the music. Locke's score,[17] which is on the whole bland and archaic compared to the later *Psyche*, is remarkable only for its characterization of Orpheus, who shuns the traditional display of virtuosity and moves the intransigent Pluto with yearning simplicity instead. The masque is only a play-within-the-play; and the young queen's stabbing of her husband, for example, could have been accomplished as surely, though not as strikingly, in dumb show as in recitative. Locke illuminates the character of Orpheus, but not Muly Labas *as* Orpheus.[18]

Here, then, was the principal limitation of the musical play before Purcell. Even when masque and spoken dialogue were as finely integrated as in *The Step-mother* and *The Empress of Morocco*, the music did little to develop the psyches of the dramatis personae. The main speaking characters could react to the music and, occasionally, sing. But they do not live through the music. In the plays for which Purcell composed, no protagonist delivers his own songs, but secondary characters frequently do, repeatedly underscoring irony, pathos and humour, foreshadowing dread events, and, most important, revealing personal traits unexplored in the spoken dialogue. The music may seem only a small part of some of the works discussed in the following chapters, but it is nevertheless operatic.

---

[16] A similar episode is found in a scene that the Earl of Rochester added to his adaptation of Beaumont and Fletcher's *Valentinian* (written c. 1677, performed February 1684); in IV[ii] Lucina's rape is drowned out by music for the rehearsal of a masque. During the Restoration *The Revenger's Tragedy* was not reprinted and is not known to have been revived, so it was probably not the direct model for either this scene or the masque in *The Empress of Morocco*.

[17] In Oxford, Christ Church Mus. MS 692, lacking only the final dance.

[18] Settle may not have intended the actor playing Muly Labas to sing. Earlier in Act IV, the Queen Mother tells her son that he should 'in dumb show enter in *Orpheus* Roome'. But Henry Harris, who created the role, was something of a singer. See my essay 'Music as Drama', in *The London Theatre World, 1660–1800*, ed. Robert D. Hume (Carbondale: Southern Illinois Univ. Press, 1980), p. 219.

The Plays

Purcell and the Theatre Companies

The first half of the seventies was a heady time for London music lovers. During these years the semi-opera was invented, and audiences could sample a French opera of sorts, Pierre Perrin and Robert Cambert's *Ariane ou le Mariage de Baccus* (March 1674, with additions by Grabu), and perhaps even an Italian one in January 1674, if we can believe John Evelyn.[19] The troupe that produced Settle's *The Empress of Morocco* (July 1673), the operatic *Tempest* (April 1674), Shadwell's *Psyche* (February 1675), and Charles Davenant's *Circe* (May 1677) was called the Duke's Company. Established in 1660 as an hereditary monopoly granted by the king to Sir William Davenant, it was managed, after the playwright's death in 1668, by the actors Betterton and Henry Harris.[20] Beginning in November 1671, its home was the Dorset Garden theatre, equipped to mount standard repertoire plays as well as machine dramas and operas. Most of the important theatre composers, including Locke, Grabu, and John Banister, worked for this playhouse. The only other patent granted in 1660 was to Thomas Killigrew's unfortunate King's Company, frequently penurious, its older actors plagued with perpetual bad luck. In 1674 they played host to a visiting troupe which mounted Perrin's *Ariane* and other French entertainments, part of Charles II's abortive attempt to establish a Lully-like royal academy.[21] Except for Thomas Duffett's devastating parodies *The Empress of Morocco*, *The Mock-Tempest*, and *Psyche Debauch'd*, brought out shortly after their originals, the King's Company lost interest in plays with music after mounting *Ariane*; it employed the Master of the King's Music, Nicholas Staggins, a composer of mean ability. Throughout the decade the Duke's Company was dominant, but by the late seventies both houses were struggling, and *Circe* proved to be the last semi-opera until the form was resuscitated in the early nineties.

After Locke died in 1677, Thomas Farmer was Dorset Garden's principal composer, with Francis Forcer and John Blow contributing an occasional song. The young Henry Purcell, who replaced Blow as organist of Westminster Abbey in 1679, wrote his first dramatic music for Nathaniel Lee's heroic play *Theodosius*, which probably had its première at Dorset Garden in the spring or early summer of 1680 (see Chapter 2). It was an

[19] *Diary*, 5 January 1674. Unless otherwise stated, all performance dates are taken from *The London Stage 1600–1800*, Part 1 (1660–1700), ed. William Van Lennep, Emmett L. Avery, and Arthur H. Scouten (Carbondale: Southern Illinois Univ. Press, 1965).
[20] The best summary of the organization and management of the late seventeenth-century London theatres is found in Judith Milhous, *Thomas Betterton and the Management of Lincoln's Inn Fields 1695–1708* (Carbondale: Southern Illinois Univ. Press, 1979), pp. 3–88.
[21] The 'English' royal academy of music was dissolved following a scandal; for a detailed discussion, see Pierre Danchin's forthcoming article in *Theatre Survey*.

12

auspicious beginning. The play required more music than any new drama since *Circe*, and some of Purcell's songs were published in the play-book itself. This was only the second time music and dialogue had been printed together in an English quarto, Locke's songs for Durfey's *The Fool Turn'd Critick* (November 1676) being the first. With *Theodosius* Purcell declared himself the obvious successor to the late Matthew Locke as Dorset Garden's chief composer. Strangely, however, the 1680–1 season found him employed instead by the rival King's Company at Drury Lane, leaving Farmer, Simon Pack, and Draghi to supply most of the music for the Duke's Theatre.

The mutinous and nearly bankrupt King's Company was in its death-throes. Yet it rallied enough in its last two seasons to produce some note-worthy plays. And, more important from our point of view, the managers hired the Westminster Abbey organist to write songs for two of their new productions. The first, Nahum Tate's *The History of King Richard the Second* (December 1680), twice banned for its parallels to the Exclusion Crisis, contains Purcell's 'Retir'd from any mortal's sight'. In October of the next season, he wrote the robustious storm song 'Blow, Boreas, blow' for Durfey's comedy *Sir Barnaby Whigg*, probably as a reply to Mother Demdike's 'Now the winds roar' in the first scene of Shadwell's popular *The Lancashire Witches*, which had its première a month before at Dorset Garden. The bubble finally burst for the King's Company at the end of the 1681–2 season, and in November 1682 the two theatres united under a single patent and continued to use both the Dorset Garden and Drury Lane playhouses until the end of the century.

In this union may lie the reasons for Purcell's virtual absence from the stage between autumn 1681 and April 1688. Perhaps his leaving Dorset Garden after *Theodosius* shut him out from working for the United Company, which turned instead to Pack for most of the music in its new productions. The amalgamation produced a more stable company than London had known since the Restoration, but the lack of competition did little to encourage playwrights, and performance records show that the United Company concentrated on revivals rather than new works. The union seems to have had little effect on music in the first season or two; but beginning in early 1684 the government became directly involved in the company's affairs. Charles II, who had long admired French music, desired to hear a *tragédie lyrique* and, accordingly, dispatched the acknowledged authority on musical extravagance, Betterton, to France to bring back a suitable opera. Instead, the actor returned with Louis Grabu, who had left England four or five years before. The would-be Frenchman was afforded considerable preferment upon his return, first composing the music for a production of the late Earl of Rochester's altered version of *Valentinian* in February 1684, and then, later in the year, setting Dryden's

Albion and Albanius. The complex circumstances of the second production are discussed in Chapters 6 and 7; but we may note here that its apparent failure owed more to political events – the untimely death of Charles II, the accession of the Roman Catholic James II, and the Duke of Monmouth's Rebellion – than to Grabu's limitations as a composer. The United Company reeled from the opera's failure, but, except for the period of mourning for the king, production never faltered. In fact, a month after the June 1685 première of *Albion and Albanius*, Tate's farce *Cuckolds-Haven* opened; this included a song between acts by Purcell, an indication that Grabu had not entirely eliminated the competition. But during the brief reign of James II, English composers did not fare well. The United Company favoured Draghi for songs and commissioned Grabu to write the instrumental music for a revival of Massinger and Fletcher's *The Double Marriage* in February 1688.[22]

Purcell's big break came two months later, with the songs for Durfey's smutty comedy *A Fool's Preferment*, which show an unmistakable genius for the dramatic. They were sung by the versatile actor William Mountfort as Lyonel, a character who speaks like a madman while delivering unvarnished, ironic truths in his songs. Had it not been for the Glorious Revolution, which all but stopped the production of new works during much of the 1688–9 season, the play, though not especially successful, would surely have established Purcell as the principal composer of the United Company.

Sometime in the spring of 1689, perhaps in conjunction with the installation of William and Mary, Purcell and Tate's opera *Dido and Aeneas* was given at Josias Priest's boarding school for girls in Chelsea. Questions abound. Who sang in it? Was it ever revived at the Theatre Royal or at court during Purcell's lifetime? Who constituted the audience and what did they make of the miniature? Of course, it was not entirely unnoticed. Priest was a dancer and choreographer at the Theatre Royal, and Durfey, who wrote the spoken epilogue for *Dido*, was one of the most popular playwrights of the era. A year later when Betterton and the United Company managers asked Purcell to compose the first semi-opera since *Circe*, they were taking a calculated risk. With the première of *Dioclesian* (June 1690) English opera was reborn, and Dryden publicly acknowledged its composer's rare gift. Moreover, all the new plays produced during the first

---

[22] Franklin B. Zimmerman includes this set of act music in Purcell's canon (z 593), though noting that the ascription in Royal College of Music MS 1144, fols. 38–9, is doubtful: *Henry Purcell 1659–1695: An Analytical Catalogue of His Music* (New York: St Martin's Press, 1963), p. 269. For a reliable attribution to Grabu, see Yale University, Filmer MS 9, pp. 26–8. Grabu left for Paris on 3 December 1685 but may have returned to London in 1687; see Philip H. Highfill, Jr, Kalman A. Burnim, and Edward A. Langhans, *A Biographical Dictionary of Actors, Actresses, Musicians . . . in London, 1660–1800* (Carbondale: Southern Illinois Univ. Press, 1973–), VI, 293.

three months of the 1690–1 season had music by Purcell: Southerne's *Sir Anthony Love* in late September, Dryden's *Amphitryon* and Settle's *Distress'd Innocence* in October, and the lost comedy *The Gordian Knot Untied*, probably in November. In the winter and early spring Purcell withdrew from the stage to work on his first unmitigated triumph, *King Arthur* (May 1691). The 1691–2 season followed the same pattern, again culminating in a dramatic opera, *The Fairy-Queen* (May 1692). During the next year Purcell continued to provide most of the music for new productions, but instead of a May première of another opera, *Dioclesian* and *The Fairy-Queen* were revived, the season's large work being the Ode for St Cecilia's Day *Hail bright Cecilia*, in late November. In early 1694 Purcell threw his energies into providing much of the music for the first two parts of Durfey's *Don Quixote* trilogy (May 1694), thus signalling a major change in the musical establishment of the Theatre Royal, as he was forced to share the limelight with a relative newcomer, John Eccles.

Now Eccles, regardless of how neglected his music may be, is no Purcell. But his initial popularity, following on the heels of Purcell's being acclaimed a truly great musician 'equal with the best abroad', must not be taken lightly. In the early nineties a new breed of actors found their way onto the London stage. Thomas Doggett, Charlotte Butler, Anne Bracegirdle, Mountfort, and others had respectable singing voices and frequently delivered songs in character. Purcell wrote for nearly all the special performers, but with the re-emergence of the dramatic opera and its segregation of actors and singers, he preferred to compose more challenging music for the professionals. Eccles, in contrast, concentrated on supplying songs for the singing actors. A moment of truth seems to have been the April 1693 première of Durfey's *The Richmond Heiress*. Purcell wrote a splendidly difficult mad dialogue, 'Behold the man that with gigantic might', for singers who do not speak in the play, while Eccles composed a simple piece for Doggett and Bracegirdle, who also had important speaking roles. According to Dryden, who attended a performance, the actor-singers stole the show, being 'wonderfully good' and clearly better than Reading and Ayliff, 'whose trade it was to sing'.[23] Regrettably, Purcell never wrote a song for Mrs Bracegirdle and, except for Letitia Cross and John Bowman, avoided the actor–singers after Mountfort died in late 1692 and Mrs Butler left for Dublin in the following year. Eccles's easy and tuneful songs were ideal for Mrs Bracegirdle, who never sang in public a piece by another composer. All evidence points to this having been an amicable arrangement, and certain plays – Crowne's *The Married Beau* (April 1694) and Durfey's *1 and 2 Don Quixote*, for example – seem to have benefited from the composers' collaboration.

[23] Dryden to William Walsh, 9 May 1693, *The Letters of John Dryden*, ed. Charles E. Ward (Durham, N. C.: Duke Univ. Press, 1942), p. 53.

While Purcell's career at the Theatre Royal flourished after the success of *Dioclesian* in 1690, the actors grew ever more dissatisfied with the fiscal management of the United Company, especially after the notorious Christopher Rich assumed control in December 1693. Betterton and several other experienced players gradually realized that their only recourse was to secede from the Patent Company and set up a second house, the two factions coming to loggerheads at the end of 1694. Queen Mary died on 28 December and the theatre closed for a three-month mourning period during which the Lord Chamberlain tried unsuccessfully to reconcile the feuding parties. In March 1695 Betterton and his cohorts were finally issued with a permit to act plays at the hastily refurbished theatre in Lincoln's Inn Fields, which opened at the end of April with Congreve's comedy *Love for Love*, a great hit for the new company.

The reorganization had far-reaching implications for Purcell, who remained with Rich at Drury Lane. Nearly all the best players, including the singing actors Doggett, Mrs Bracegirdle, and Purcell's favourite, Bowman, sided with Betterton. Even more devastating for the composer was the loss of several professional singers: Pate and Reading, and the sopranos Ayliff and Hodgson.[24] The Lincoln's Inn Fields troupe hired Eccles as its main composer of vocal music. Purcell's former colleague was very busy during the next few seasons writing songs, choruses, and occasional instrumental pieces for a host of new plays. But the scores of Purcell's major stage works remained with Drury Lane after the composer died in November 1695, and Rich milked them for all their worth in the following years. Given the virtual annihilation of the Theatre Royal's musical staff after Betterton's departure, Purcell's final creative burst at the beginning of the 1695-6 season is truly astonishing. In addition to act tunes and songs for several summer and autumn plays, he composed substantial scores for *Bonduca*, *The Libertine*, *Timon of Athens*, and perhaps *The Indian Queen*. His last months must have been hectic.

Following the 1695 actors' rebellion, Purcell's best singers were the boy treble Jemmy Bowen, Letitia Cross, also a mere child to whom were entrusted 'From rosy bowers', 'I attempt from Love's sickness to fly', and other masterful songs, and the bass Richard Leveridge, by all indications a better singer than actor, though not particularly outstanding as either.[25] Purcell's decision to remain with the Patent Company – if indeed he had a choice – when all the best singers and even the father of the dramatic opera himself, Betterton, left for Lincoln's Inn Fields, is the final puzzle of the composer's stage career. Perhaps Rich, knowing that the loss of so many experienced actors would make competition with Betterton very difficult,

[24] Pate later returned to the Patent Company, as did Doggett and Mrs Ayliff, but apparently not before Purcell's death in November. See Milhous, *Thomas Betterton*, p. 87.
[25] See the discussion of *The Indian Queen* in Chapter 3.

threw his support and money behind Purcell to induce the composer to remain at Drury Lane and Dorset Garden in order to write more operas. How could Purcell have refused? The small, ramshackle Lincoln's Inn Fields theatre was not a suitable house in which to mount a musical extravaganza.

Theatre politics, disgruntled actors, petty jealousies, and embezzled funds are mundane subjects, but these nagging details directly influenced Purcell's music for the London stage. Few if any theatre composers have ever worked under ideal conditions, but he had more than his share of frustration: the *Theodosius* music seems to have made little impression on the Duke's Company in 1680; in 1684 he was passed over in favour of Grabu for *Albion and Albanius*; *Dido and Aeneas* may have opened some doors for him in 1689, but the masque itself left no mark; the three successful semi-operas of 1690–2 led to the dubious privilege of collaborating with Eccles on the slapstick *Don Quixote* trilogy; finally, the much-hailed actors' rebellion of 1695 deprived Purcell of the finest singers but, paradoxically, released a flood of music, performed mostly by children, for the revivals of several well-worn tragedies.

Purcell's Musical Style

In the following chapters I attempt to establish links between musical gestures and dramatic action – to discover the language the music speaks. Such an approach must obviously take into account the evolution of Purcell's style of composition. The secular vocal music underwent a gradual transformation from mostly syllabic text settings, in rhythms closely tied to the metre of the poetry, to the luxuriant melodies of the late works, in which expressible words are set to a catalogue of rhetorical figures, none of which appears twice in quite the same form. In the instrumental music the ingenious counterpoint of the early works, suffused with dissonances and harmonic 'irregularities', gives way to the infectious tunefulness of the later symphonies, overtures, and dances, in whose inner parts the old contrapuntal daring churns just beneath the surface. Music historians have felt the need to account for this remarkable change by weighing lines of influence. Three strands are often mentioned. The first is the 'English' style of Locke and Blow, the rough edges of which were allegedly smoothed down during the early eighties to bring it into line with more refined continental practices. The second, the French influence, felt most strongly, it is claimed, in *Circe* and *Dido and Aeneas*, has been detected in Purcell's formal designs, in the 'Gayety and Fashion' of his melodies, and in the withdrawal from rigorous counterpoint during the middle period. Routing both the French elegance and the antiquated part-writing is the third major influence, that of the 'fam'd Italian masters', which supposedly swept across the vocal music in the last three or four years of Purcell's life, having already caused a profound change in the instrumental style more than ten years before.

This unnecessary apologia for Purcell's rugged individualism is not always easy to reconcile with the theatre music, even that dating from the early eighties in which one would expect to see the clear influence of his teachers. The brief pieces for *Theodosius* (mid-1680), his first for the London stage, are simple, mostly strophic settings, even the most expressive of which show little melismatic treatment of individual words, the hallmark of his later style. Except for strong, purposeful bass lines and two or three memorable tunes, these songs and ensembles are hardly distinguishable from the best of Thomas Farmer, Samuel Ackeroyde, or Simon Pack. And none is as graphic in conveying joy or mordancy as Locke's angular songs in *Psyche*, though Purcell was still standing in his shadow, as is apparent from the odd moments of boldly dissonant part-writing injected into an otherwise lacklustre texture. Yet 'Retir'd from any mortal's sight', written a few months after *Theodosius* for Tate's *The History of King Richard the Second* (December 1680), shows a pronounced break with his first effort and could almost have been composed ten years later. It crystallizes the meaning of the text and enhances the atmosphere of the dialogue round it through purely musical means. The graphic setting of emotive words such as 'cursed' and 'smiling' and the descending chromatics underscoring its morbid message are characteristic of many later songs for tragedies.

Despite the striking 'advances' of 'Retir'd from any mortal's sight', the Purcell who emerges at the end of the disruptive eighties in *Dido and Aeneas* and *Dioclesian* is quite another composer. Besides having reached intellectual maturity by 1689, he had obviously been exposed to much Italian music. Yet *Dido* bears Blow's stamp throughout, except perhaps in the choruses, while relying heavily on French forms for its structure. And *Dioclesian*, a far more important work in the evolution of his style, is as grand as *Dido* is modest and attempts at once to parody the French operatic style, to acknowledge the debt owed to French music, and to re-establish the English semi-opera tradition begun by *The Tempest* and *Psyche*. The metamorphosis was effected, one might suppose, by exposure to Grabu's *Albion and Albanius* and the 1686 London première of Lully's *Cadmus et Hermione*, though tempered by a love of Italian instrumental music and a persistent nostalgia for the Stuart masque. But this is dangerous speculation. Students of Purcell's theatre music sorely lack two or three major works to fill the virtual silence between 1680 and 1688. The score for *Circe*, traditionally dated 1685, would seem to fit neatly into the proposed pattern of development. The graceful triple-metre melodies such as 'Circe, the daughter of the sun', *en rondeau* with chorus, seem very French. Yet *Circe* cannot be dated precisely; even the most recent suggestion of 1690 is only a guess.[26] And the commonly held belief that harmonic blandness, rhythmic flexibility, a fondness for triple-metre airs, and a heavy reliance on rondeau forms were the sole prerogatives of the Lully school is absurd. The most striking feature of *Circe* is how much its ensembles owe to the verse anthem.

Although authorities have disagreed over the forces shaping Purcell's mature style, which I believe begins to emerge in the songs for Durfey's *A Fool's Preferment* (April 1688), nearly all writers on the composer have acknowledged that in the truly remarkable music of the final four or five years of his life the Italian manner gradually supplants the archaic English part-writing and the affected French airiness. Purcell, like most northern European composers, was 'learning Italian'; to chronicle such a fundamental and pervasive change of style is outside the scope of this book. Yet advocates of southern influence point to the late recitatives as confirmation that his music had finally shaken off its 'barbarities'. But are the declamatory songs really Italianate? Composers had long before learned to set their native language in a speech-like manner. And beginning as early as 1663, dramatists occasionally wanted certain lyrics in their plays to be 'in recitative musick'.[27] I know of only one Purcell song characterized by a contemporary as being in the Italian style: 'Ah me! to many deaths decreed', from Crowne's *Regulus* (June 1692), which Peter Motteux says is 'set by *Mr*. Purcell the *Italian* way' (*The Gentleman's Journal*, August 1692, p. 28). Like a dozen others, it opens with an expansive recitative, but the bass, instead of simply sustaining long notes, begins with a hidden point of imitation. Is Motteux referring to the declamatory style, the imitative counterpoint, or to the way that the second half is constructed entirely of a repeated anapaestic motif, when he dubs this 'Italian'? How, I wonder, would he have described 'Ingrateful Love thus every hour', composed a few months earlier for the music-meeting scene of Southerne's *The Wives Excuse* (December 1691)? This piece, which includes almost as much recitative as 'Ah me! to many deaths decreed', is performed in response to a request for 'an English song' that a listener can understand without first having to see 'an *Opera* at *Venice*'. One should always bear in mind Westrup's dry observation that 'the just setting of English words will naturally have a flavour different from that of French or Italian song' (*Purcell*, p. 240). If Purcell's manner of humouring a lyric was significantly affected by contact with foreign music, this surely happened long before 1691.

The best argument I can advance for not taking too seriously the claims that Purcell's late music was greatly influenced by the Italian style is to

[26] Westrup, *Purcell*, rev. Fortune, p. 151.
[27] See my article 'The Songs for Katherine Philips' *Pompey* (1663)', *Theatre Notebook*, 33 (1979), 63.

recount the controversy surrounding *The Tempest*. Several authorities consider this to be his last and most Italianate work; and little wonder, with the string of *da capo* arias in Act V and the Corelli-like vocal figuration throughout. Westrup, for example, writes that it exhibits a 'complete absorption of the Italian style . . . and an unfaltering technical facility' (*Purcell*, p. 145). Robert E. Moore wrestles with Arundell's scorn for the score, concedes that the composer has, puzzlingly, allowed a few gaucheries to slip by, but concludes that 'no one can seriously doubt that *The Tempest* is predominantly Purcell's', because none of 'his contemporaries could possibly have produced the great concluding masque of Neptune. It is as simple as that.'[28]

It is not simple, however. In the early 1960s Margaret Laurie began to assemble bibliographic data to support a suspicion shared by Arundell, Thurston Dart, and a few others that Purcell did not compose the version of *The Tempest* included in Vol. xix of the Purcell Society Edition. Her argument (set forth in a paper delivered to the Royal Musical Association in 1963) that he composed only 'Dear pretty youth' and not the rest of the score came as a considerable shock to those who held this music close to their hearts.[29] The documentary evidence by itself was sufficient to cast doubt on Purcell's authorship, but in order to answer those who would claim, like Moore, that the music is too good to have been composed by anyone else, Dr Laurie also demonstrated that John Weldon was *capable* of having written the bulk of the music. Discussion after the paper centred on the relative value of musical style and bibliographic evidence in making attributions, and the authorship of *The Tempest* is still being debated twenty years on. For those who have come to know 'Full fathom five', 'Come unto these yellow sands', and 'Halcyon days' as Purcell's and whose knowledge of turn-of-the-century theatre music is limited to that which is available in modern editions, Dr Laurie's argument is not convincing. But for those who have taken the trouble to learn something of English theatre history, who are familiar with all of Purcell's dramatic works, and who are steeped in the style prevailing among the early eighteenth-century epigones, the question has been answered beyond a reasonable doubt. No, Purcell did not set *The Tempest*, except for a song added to the fourth act in 1695. But Westrup's discussion of this lovely music is so enthusiastic that, with Dr Laurie's article pushed to the back of our minds, we want to believe Purcell purified his style in his last year, produced clear, Italianate melodies and solidly regular harmonic progressions, and finally surrendered to the *da capo* aria. It is a soothing story – the Orpheus Britan-

[28] *Henry Purcell & the Restoration Theatre* (Cambridge, Mass.: Harvard Univ. Press, 1961), pp. 191–2.
[29] 'Did Purcell Set *The Tempest*?', *Proceedings of the Royal Musical Association*, 90 (1963–4), 43–57.

nicus reaching from beyond the grave to welcome *il sassone* and the 'perfect' opera to England – but it is fiction.

The fallacy of tracing a stylistic development through such a large repertoire composed in so brief a span of time is that one will inevitably make comparisons between pieces carefully chosen to support one's thesis. That Purcell decided, for example, to set the lyric 'Thy genius, lo!' from Lee's *The Massacre of Paris* first as a rousing baritone 'cantata' and later as a mysterious declamatory air for soprano probably had more to do with the singers available to him in 1689 and 1695 than with his possible exposure to genuine Italian recitative during the interim. On balance, one may find less quirky part-writing, smoother bass lines, and stronger, more conventional chord progressions in the late music than in that written around 1690, but Purcell's basic manner of setting English words seems to have changed little during his last five years; and he never completely purged his music of certain archaisms. A cavalier approach to counterpoint, with clashes, cross-relations and angular melodies, as well as solo-choral scenes drawn from the verse-anthem tradition, are found in abundance even in the latest works, *Bonduca* and *The Indian Queen*.

A final word about Purcell's development as a composer: 1690 is pivotal. This year marked his first major success in the theatre – the music for Betterton's alteration of *Dioclesian* followed shortly by that for Dryden's *Amphitryon*. No overture or act tune known to have been composed before 1690 is found in the posthumous *Collection of Ayres for the Theatre* (1697), and even *Orpheus Britannicus* contains very few songs from before this year. He did not burst upon the London stage, Athena-like, after a ten-year apprenticeship frustrated by a revolution and Monsieur Grabu; but the young composer of *Dioclesian* was nonetheless a complete master of his art.

Meanings of Keys in the Theatre Music

W. Gillies Whittaker limits his eccentric survey of Purcell's 'harmonic surprises' to instrumental pieces, excluding the theatre works because 'absolute music reveals the composer's habits of thought perhaps more surely than when special demands call him to depart from the normal'.[30] For its time, this is a radical statement, as Whittaker admits that 'some daring departure from convention', an especially pungent cross-relation, for instance, might have been elicited by a word, a phrase of text, or even a dramatic event. Purcell was clearly fond of rhetorical gestures, such as melismas of dotted rhythms to express joy and descending chromatic lines to depict grief. But did Whittaker also believe that basic choices, such as key, mode, even harmonic progressions, might acquire specific meanings in the dramatic music? Had he noticed, for example, that Purcell nearly

---

[30] 'Some Observations of Purcell's Harmony', *The Musical Times*, 75 (1934), 887–94.

always sets lyrics treating of death in the key of G minor? Is it mere co-incidence that in the comedies and semi-operas almost every song whose principal subject is eroticism is in either D minor or A minor?

That a composer should attach meanings to certain keys is nothing new. From the beginning of the sixteenth century musicians tried to rekindle the Classical ties between rhetoric and music, and several late Renaissance theorists wrote at length about the different emotional qualities of the modes. In Purcell's time these ideas were taken up again, perhaps most passionately by Johann Mattheson of Hamburg. In *Das neu-eröffnete Orchestre* (1713), he attempts to broaden the doctrine of the affects to include tonality. For the sixteen keys in common use at the time, he describes the emotional state that each produces in him. The affects are sometimes complex: A minor, for example, is agreeably sleep-inducing; E minor can depict grief, but with some chance of consolation.[31] If this were all Mattheson had to say about the affects of keys, then we could thank him for his opinions and dismiss him as another crank theorist. But he admits that simply because he associates a key with a particular emotion there is no reason to assume it will produce the same affect in someone else. He only recommends that some tonalities are more suitable for conveying certain emotions than others. Simply put, Mattheson, the composer, has worked out a system of key associations for himself. Anyone wishing to do serious analysis of his music would, of course, be foolish not to arm himself with a knowledge of the composer's own code of affects for the various keys, even if he considers them utter nonsense.

Purcell did not leave us with such a catalogue. But he did use certain keys in the theatre music with remarkable consistency. Some of these – G minor for death, F minor for horror, witches, and the like, and F major and B♭ major for pastoral scenes – are also evident, to a lesser degree, in the dramatic works of his predecessors and contemporaries. Other correspondences seem to have been encouraged by the exigencies of performance. C major and D major, for example, are often linked with triumph, ceremonies, and monarchs sitting in state, an association undoubtedly reinforced by the royal and military use of trumpets, which normally played in those keys. Beyond these common affects, Purcell often used C minor to depict melancholy, seriousness, mystery, or a feeling of awe; E minor might be called his key of fate; and, as mentioned above, D minor and A minor are often linked with sexual ardour.

This is not a static system, wherein one key evokes a single emotion or conceit throughout a piece. Modulation can signal a shift of mood not

---

[31] Summarized in Hans Lenneberg, 'Johann Mattheson on Affect and Rhetoric in Music (II)', *Journal of Music Theory*, 2 (1958), 234–6, and George J. Buelow, 'An Evaluation of Johann Mattheson's Opera *Cleopatra* (Hamburg, 1704)', in *Studies in Eighteenth-Century Music*, ed. H. C. Robbins Landon and Roger E. Chapman (New York: Oxford Univ. Press, 1970), pp. 98–104.

immediately apparent in the text; passages that mix major and minor modes often graphically symbolize struggle or ambivalence barely hinted at in the lyric; a tonality seemingly at variance with the usual scheme – G minor in a pastoral scene, for example – can presage an otherwise unexpected horrific event. Purcell also refined the traditional connotations. For example, G minor, the harbinger of death in tragedies, often suggests *le petit mort* in pastoral dialogues. (One should allow, of course, that the two conditions have had a long and hackneyed duality among poets and composers, especially the stage-struck.) Purcell's C major ceremonial music is often purposefully pompous and overblown, while D major is favoured for pieces of untainted celebration.

This theory is easily abused. I can find no evidence that Purcell intended any of these relationships to serve a rhetorical function, in the way that Johann David Heinichen, for example, believed that certain styles of composition could stir particular emotions, 'even when employing texts that fail to contain an easily discernible emotional substratum'.[32] When Moore refers to F minor as Purcell's horror key (p. 52) or, for that matter, when Winton Dean calls E major Handel's key of sleep, they do not mean that these keys alone will induce fright or drowsiness in the listener;[33] only that in the composers' private or even subconscious thoughts about their dramatic music the choice of key was a means of achieving cohesion.

Why some keys should have assumed representational functions is difficult to fathom, though one, G minor, seems to have had a traditional association with death for at least two generations of English theatre composers. Since gamma-ut was still theoretically the lowest note of the scale, one can easily understand how its minor key came to symbolize the grave, the lowest point to which all must sink. Another possible bond is the so-called lament bass, the descending minor tetrachord. Its extra-musical connotations were well established in Italy by the 1640s.[34] Late seventeenth-century English composers often place this pattern in G minor, whether stated once or treated as a ground (note the interlocking play on words).

Although much of the theatre music from the early years of the Restoration is lost, the few surviving scores suggest that Purcell's predecessors also attached a special meaning to G minor. Its morbid affect is even detectable in Shirley's Commonwealth masque *Cupid and Death*, with music by Christopher Gibbons and Matthew Locke. The plot would have taxed even Richard Strauss's powers of differentiating the various emotional layers

[32] George J. Buelow, 'The *Loci Topici* and Affect in Late Baroque Music: Heinichen's Practical Demonstration', *The Music Review*, 27 (1966), 176.
[33] For a discussion of some of Handel's common key associations, see Dean, *Handel's Dramatic Oratorios and Masques* (London: Oxford Univ. Press, 1972), p. 60.
[34] See Ellen Rosand, 'The Descending Tetrachord: An Emblem of Lament', *The Musical Quarterly*, 65 (1979), 346–59.

caused by inverted relationships. Cupid and Death, who put up in the same inn during bad weather, unknowingly exchange arrows. Cupid then wreaks havoc on young lovers, while Death stirs the passions of the old and infirm. This delightful confusion lends itself well to what Dent calls 'the unsettled nature of Locke's tonality in recitative' (*Foundations*, p. 86). I read even more significance than he does into the harmonic progressions at the appearance of Death in the fourth entry. Nature narrates, horrified, as Cupid's arrow kills an innocent lover. Locke's recitative reaches an imperfect cadence in A minor, then shifts abruptly to G minor (Example 1, bar 4), the first sounding of this key in the masque, as the grim reaper enters. A few bars later when Death looses a shaft at two old couples who then behave contrary to his expectation, Nature moves just as suddenly to G major, then E major again (bar 15). Death's transformation is thus

Example 1. *Cupid and Death*: Matthew Locke, from the fourth entry

reflected in Locke's music. The polarities of key established in this brief passage are not strictly adhered to in the rest of the work, especially in Gibbons's part, but some later composers are consistent in their tonal schemes.

One of the earliest pieces for a Restoration play is John Banister's 'From lasting and unclouded day' for Katherine Philips's translation of *Pompey* (1663). It is sung by the protagonist's ghost between Acts III and IV to comfort the sleeping Cornelia, his distraught widow.[35] But it quickly turns to a nightmarish description of his own murder and a call for revenge. The lengthy piece is in G minor, modulating freely, with a cadence in E♭ major at the end of the lines

> . . . *Pompey* now shall bleed no more.
> By Death my glory I resume;
> For 'twould have been a harsher Doom
> T'outlive the Liberty of Rome.

But it returns to the tonic for Pompey's prophecy that Caesar 'shall fall an offring at my shrine, / As I was his, he must be mine'. This is a poor effort by a mediocre composer, but later songs serving similar functions show it to be of seminal importance.[36]

The largest theatre score published in England before Grabu's *Albion and Albanius* is Locke's *Psyche*. The overall tonal organization is a model of balance and variety, and Locke's choice of keys for the major dramatic units is remarkably like Purcell's for the later semi-operas. In the first scene of Act II, for instance, the choral procession to the temple of Apollo, where Psyche's destiny is to be prophesied, is in G minor, perhaps in anticipation of the pronouncement that she must marry a poisonous serpent and thus be killed by it. The key of death is heard again in the following scene, the rocky desert, where two pairs of despairing lovers are waiting to be sacrificed to the serpent. Impatient at the delay, they sing the G minor duet 'Break distracted heart', and all four commit mass suicide.

The choice of tonality for a single piece or even a group of pieces in a work as large as *Psyche* was determined by a wide range of musical and dramatic considerations. Hence, the key for Act II may have been dictated by the grand plan, which is framed by ceremonial music in D major, a trumpet key. So perhaps G minor in the second act simply balances the A minor symphony at the end of Act I. Purcell's dramatic operas also have carefully controlled key schemes favouring large-scale cohesiveness over the slavish application of the usual affective tonal relationships. Like Locke, he prefers to remain in the same key and its close neighbours for an

[35] In Oxford, Christ Church, Mus. MS 350. For a brief discussion, see my article 'The Songs for Katherine Philips' *Pompey*', pp. 63–4.

[36] See, for example, Pack's 'Tell me Thyrsis, tell your anguish' in Dryden and Lee's *The Duke of Guise* (1683), discussed in my essay 'Music as Drama', pp. 213–15.

entire act. Therefore, if a hypothetical scene were to include three lyrics in succession, the first sung by a witch, the second by a condemned prisoner, and the third by an amorous shepherdess, the airs would certainly not be in F minor, G minor, and A minor, respectively. The tonal connotations outlined above and Purcell's desire for a smooth succession of keys coincide beautifully in *Dido and Aeneas, Dioclesian, Bonduca,* and *The Indian Queen*, with only an occasional compromise. In *Dido*, for example, at the beginning of Act II when the Sorceress makes her first appearance the key is the conventional F minor. But when she returns to gloat over Aeneas's imminent departure in Act III, her music is in B♭ major to conform to the overall plan of the final scene.

In the following chapters I try to reconcile the dichotomy between Purcell's style and the tone of the plays for which he wrote music. He was a composer in whom the passions ran high. His response to a lyric or a dramatic event was unflinchingly direct; the music almost always declares an unequivocal point of view. But most of the plays discussed below are shot through with double meanings, irony, and plots embroidered with extended metaphors, all of which make the question of tone very problematical. Are Dryden's heroic plays, for instance, high-minded dramas of love and honour, or are they self-satiric, with no serious content, as some critics claim? Are the comedies of Durfey simply cobbled-together scenes of unremitting bawdry, or is there a sober side to all the banter and slapstick? Are we meant to take an 'exuberant bloodbath' of a play such as Shadwell's *The Libertine* seriously, or is it a spoof of profligacy? Purcell is extremely sensitive to such ambiguities and rarely leaves any doubt about his interpretation of them.

2 The Serious Dramas

While musicologists have slighted Purcell's theatre works for not being enough like true opera, drama historians have largely regarded the music for Restoration plays as an annoyance, to be mentioned in passing, then forgotten when faced with the task of neatly categorizing the works. The old straitening labels – comedy of manners, comedy of humours, rhymed heroic play, and so forth – cut across chronological development and fail to take into account a nasty tangle of mutables – actors, theatres, public taste, foreign influences, and political circumstances. Recent scholarly reappraisal of this huge body of plays has begun to acknowledge its enormous diversity and to appreciate the full importance of performance.[1] But even the revisionists usually treat the musical scenes as eccentricities.

Purcell did not write one style of music for tragedies and another for comedies. Rather, his works are carefully designed to fit specific dramatic events and emotional states. That a humorous dialogue found its way into Dryden's *Tyrannick Love*, an heroic play, and a remorseful lament was composed for Crowne's *The Married Beau*, a bedroom farce, only underscores the fact that few Restoration plays are monolithic in tone. Even the semi-opera is difficult to classify. It has long been viewed as a sub-species of heroic drama, the one genre with which Purcell's operas, at least, have little in common.[2] *Dioclesian*, *King Arthur*, and *The Fairy-Queen* do not fit into the serious category at all but are, like most of the earlier and later works of this type, essentially comedic. The tragedies for which Purcell wrote music fall into two general groups: those requiring only modest amounts of music, from heroic plays such as Dryden's *The Indian Emperour* to domestic dramas such as Southerne's *The Fatal Marriage*; and the tragic extravaganzas, notably *Bonduca* and *The Indian Queen*, both adaptations of old plays into which is woven a considerable amount of music, though much less than in the semi-operas. A similar division applies to the comedies: those which require only a song or two, like Congreve's *The Old Batchelour*; and those for which music is the main attraction, for instance Durfey's *Don Quixote*. Critics have somehow accepted the infusion of music into the lighter forms, much as modern audiences

---

[1] For an assessment of two recent major studies, see Laura Brown, 'Restoration Drama Criticism: Revisions and Orthodoxies', in *Drama, Dance and Music* (Themes in Drama, 3), ed. James Redmond (Cambridge: Cambridge Univ. Press, 1981), pp. 191–201.

[2] For example, Hazelton Spencer describes them as 'the bastard offspring of tragedy', in *Shakespeare Improved* (Cambridge, Mass.: Harvard Univ. Press, 1927), pp. 93–4.

seem to be able to tolerate the so-called musical comedy, but the songs, dialogues, choruses and ballets in the serious dramas – plays already diffi- cult to defend – have proved a stumbling-block to most drama historians.

The nineties saw a considerable resurgence of interest in tragedies, a marked change of taste away from the political dramas of the eighties. From 1688 through the end of 1694, the Theatre Royal produced a flurry of new works of rather dubious quality, revisions of old Jacobean tra- gedies and tragicomedies, as well as revivals of most of the heroic plays written in the sixties and seventies. The adaptations are now considered to be the low point of late seventeenth-century English drama. In rewriting Shirley or Beaumont and Fletcher, hack playwrights filed down irony, sharpened up sex and horror, and laid on a thick coating of pathos. The new works of the period cannot be summarized so easily. Some dramatists attempted to mix the old heroic mode with comic or pathetic sub-plots, while others tried to write domestic tragedies. Robert Hume, one of the few critics to have dirtied his hands with them, concludes that sentimen- tality is their major achievement. Though the stage was perhaps a waste- land for serious drama, Purcell happened to be drawn to it at an auspici- ous moment. Most of the old heroic plays already required considerable music, and the new sentimental tragedies, while needing less, relied heavily on songs to intensify the pathetic qualities of tragic heroines.

The resurrection of the heroic plays of Dryden and Lee in the early nineties has never been adequately explained. These highly stylized por- trayals of extravagant behaviour – surely the least approachable of all seventeenth-century English stage works – had not quite lain in oblivion since the seventies, but neither had they fully recovered from the Duke of Buckingham's jolting satire in *The Rehearsal* (December 1671). This famous parody was frequently revived during the period, as if to quash any residual enthusiasm. Even Dryden, the finest master of the style and its staunchest defender in the essays 'Of Heroique Playes' and 'A Defence of an Essay of Dramatique Poesie', bade good riddance to the dramatic couplet after 1675. By 1690, the rhymed heroic play had long been out of fashion. It is tempting to link the revivals with Purcell's emergence as a stage composer. In their generally tepid advocacy of heroic drama, modern critics are fond of pointing to certain ironic similarities between these plays and all-sung opera. John Loftis, for example, offers grudging approval of *The Indian Emperour*, which he describes as 'less notable for its thematic coherence than for the rhetoric of its isolated scenes, which at their best achieve a kind of operatic formality'.[3] Robert Moore has more sympathy for the heroic plays in the first chapter of *Henry Purcell & the Restoration Theatre*, extolling Dryden's *Aureng-Zebe* as belonging 'to a

---

[3] *The Works of John Dryden* (Berkeley and Los Angeles: Univ. of California Press, 1966), IX, 318.

world peculiarly suited to operatic treatment'. On the face of it, then, these old plays could have provided Purcell with the necessary framework in which to develop the genius for opera which he so ably demonstrated in *Dido and Aeneas*. Yet, except for *The Indian Queen*, which is a special case, he did not attempt to alter the basic design of the heroic play, but simply replaced the music of his less distinguished predecessors.

In the classic rhymed drama, as established by Davenant and Dryden and emulated by Settle, Lee, and others, the characters are led through a maze of stock crises, choosing painfully between love and honour at each turn. Since the dramatis personae are exalted and the action often fabulous, the language is elevated into heroic rhymed couplets. To relieve the melodramatic tedium and the mesmerizing regularity of the poetry, music is injected into basically two kinds of scenes. (1) Dramatically static temple or other ceremonial processions are found early in the play (often at the beginning of the second act) or near the end. Little of the original music for these episodes survives from plays of the sixties and early seventies; it was probably not very elaborate. But Locke's for the scene in the Temple of Apollo in Act II of *Psyche* (1675) set a new standard for these spectacles, and the later ones by Purcell are undoubtedly grander in scope than the originals. (2) Conjurations are important in many heroic plays, introduced sparingly and almost never as easy escapes from the complications of the plot. Typically, the protagonist seeks the services of a necromancer on matters of love only to be given unexpected bad news by spirits who are called forth to prognosticate. In some plays the apparitions simply entertain the troubled character; in others, they make specific prophecies. Purcell lavished some of his finest music on such scenes. Yet Montague Summers, usually a perceptive critic, remarks querulously that 'Wizards, witches, and incantation scenes are frequent in heroic tragedies. They were largely introduced for scenic purposes.'[4] I am surprised that Summers, who happened also to be a notorious expert on witchcraft and demonology, did not recognize the extraordinary dramatic potential of such fantastical elements in the hands of an inventive composer. The likeliest reason for the remarkable popularity of the heroic plays in the nineties – indeed, for their being revived at all – is Purcell's resuscitation of the conjuration scenes.

The new tragedies require much less music than the heroic plays, but it is more closely associated with the main speaking characters: in Dryden's *Cleomenes* (April 1692) a musical episode underlines Ptolomy's decadence; in Crowne's *Regulus* (June 1692) a song presages Fulvia's heroism and eventual madness; in *Henry the Second* (November 1692) music captures Rosamond's ambivalence about losing her innocence; and in

---

[4] In the commentary to his edition of Buckingham's *The Rehearsal* (Stratford-upon-Avon: The Shakespeare Head Press, 1914), p. 139.

Southerne's *The Fatal Marriage* (February 1694) Purcell wrote an ironic epithalamium for the heroine, who unknowingly commits adultery on her wedding night. And so for the rest of the new tragedies music is almost always associated with important individuals rather than events.

Few of the serious plays for which Purcell wrote music are likely to be revived by professional companies in the near future. In the heroic plays, the rhyme itself is a bane to stage-worthiness, despite Dryden's flowing dialogue, achieved with remarkably little enjambement to break the suffocating chains of closed couplets. What modern audience would sit through a performance of *The Indian Emperour*, let alone Lee's *Sophonisba*, unless it were acted *Tom Thumb* fashion? Yet Purcell's songs for the serious dramas do not bear excerption well. A concert performance of 'Ah cruel bloody fate', for example, from the fifth act of *Theodosius*, would almost certainly produce music-hall guffaws; the closing lines are sung to an innocent, lilting tune:

> *Philander*! ah, *Philander*! still
> The bleeding *Phillis* cry'd,
> She wept a while,
> And she forc'd a smile;
> Then clos'd her eyes and dy'd.

But for the tolerant listener who had recently read Lee's wild tragedy, Purcell's song could be heart-rending. One need not see full-blown productions of the plays discussed on the following pages to admire Purcell's music for them, but some familiarity with plots and characters, the theatre companies, and the actors and singers is necessary to understand how faithfully the composer served the playwrights.

1. Early Works

Theodosius

Nathaniel Lee's *Theodosius* had its première in the spring or summer of 1680 at Dorset Garden.[5] The prompter of the Duke's Company, John Downes, reports that it was a great success, noting also the 'several Entertainments of Singing; Compos'd by the Famous Master Mr. *Henry Purcell*, (being the first he e'er Compos'd for the Stage)'.[6] The 1680 quarto includes 'The Musick betwixt the Acts', without naming a composer. Of these songs, only 'Ah cruel bloody fate' (z 606/9) is attributed to Purcell in the contemporary song-books, though most bibliographers assign the rest

---

[5] *The London Stage,* Part 1, p. 291, suggests September or October; but see Judith Milhous and Robert D. Hume, 'Dating Play Premières from Publication Data, 1660–1700', *Harvard Library Bulletin,* 22 (1974), 391.

[6] *Roscius Anglicanus* (1708), p. 38.

to him as well.[7] The music for the temple scene in Act I, however, is clearly ascribed to Purcell in an early manuscript.[8]

Lee's early tragedies are unabashedly Drydenesque, and he even collaborated with his mentor on *Oedipus* in 1678. But his mad individualism soon led him to explore 'the hard and rocky paths of existence' which Dryden would have considered indecorous in the world of exalted heroes.[9] Lee admits in the dedication to *Theodosius* that his early works 'abound in ungovern'd Fancy'; though he tried to rein in his fustian dialogue in later plays, most sprawl into a tangle of barely related sub-plots, and *Sophonisba* and *The Massacre of Paris*, in particular, leave an amazing number of loose ends.

At first reading, the directions for music in *Theodosius* appear squarely conventional: the temple ceremonies in the opening scene and III.ii and the lyrics to be sung during the intervals are hardly innovative; music is performed to comfort the protagonist and tragic heroine in Acts IV and V, as happens in many other plays of the genre. But each of these devices has a twist. The temple music sets a cynical tone for the whole play; the incidental songs are actually woven tightly into the action; and the comforting tune in Act V is warped into a wrenching climax. Purcell's first experience in the theatre was a trial by fire, but his simple, direct settings work a wonderful counterpoint to Lee's unbridled imagination.

The play opens in a temple at Constantinople in the early days of the Christian era. The emperor Theodosius has become pensive and feckless after falling deeply in love with an unknown nymph he glimpsed bathing in a river, and he will not be dissuaded from taking holy orders and abdicating in favour of his sister, Pulcheria. The priest Atticus sings the invocation 'Prepare, the rites begin', answered by two attendants accompanied by recorders. Various speaking characters are then overheard gossiping about the emperor's withdrawal from public life. The versatile Atticus twice chides the gathered courtiers for their irreverent language in a place of worship, then asks for silence as the cloistering ceremony begins. Hoping the novel Christian faith will cool his lust for the river nymph, Theodosius has invited the royal maidens Marina and Flavilla to accompany him on his retreat, requiring that they join a convent. When the emperor later encounters the 'river nymph', he throws off his piety as easily as an old coat, leaving the two maidens to attain Heaven by pain and suffering. Thus the ceremony in Act I is really for them. Flavilla firmly renounces all

---

[7] 'Hail to the myrtle shade', for example, is unascribed in John Playford's *Choice Ayres and Songs*, III (1681), p. 22, and is sandwiched between pieces by John Reading and William Turner; yet several other songs elsewhere in the volume are attributed to 'Mr. Henry Pursell'.

[8] Oxford, Bodleian MS Mus. c.27, fols. 33–6. The air and chorus for the procession in III.ii as well as the song for Theodosius in IV.ii, 'Happy day! ah happy day!', do not survive.

[9] Nicoll, *A History of English Drama*, I, 121.

worldly pleasures, though Marina is more circumspect about taking the veil.

The solemn music befits the occasion yet seems also to reflect contempt for Theodosius's hypocrisy. In the trio for Atticus and the other priests, 'Canst thou, Marina', one notices a high concentration of cross-relations, admittedly common in seventeenth-century English part-writing, but here arrayed in a striking manner. The dissonance is particularly pungent near the beginning (see Example 1),[10] and just before the chorus the bass slides into a leading-note F♯ at the last moment, forming an oblique chromaticism with the preceding F♮ (Example 2).[11] The latter might be de-

Example 1. *Theodosius*: 'Canst thou, Marina', bars 1–4

Example 2. *Theodosius*: 'Canst thou, Marina', bars 29–33

scribed as a dislocated 'English' cadence. In its commonest form, this is produced when an inner voice descends by step through the lowered seventh degree, making a cross-relation with the leading-note, which sounds the next moment in the treble. Purcell and his contemporaries, notably Blow, frequently use this close, often evoking pathos. One of the most memorable instances is shown in Example 3, from the Funeral Sen-

Example 3. Funeral Sentences: 'Man that is born of a woman', bars 22–3

[10] Examples 1, 2, 4, and 5 are taken from Oxford, Bodleian MS Mus. c.27.
[11] Bodleian MS Mus. c.27 lacks the bass part of this passage.

tences (z 27). The cross-relations in 'Canst thou, Marina' can hardly be mere accidents of part-writing, 'in which the logical progress of independent parts was considered more important than euphony' (Westrup, *Purcell*, p. 251). Atticus and the priests ask Marina if she can bear the loss of worldly ornaments, to suffer affliction to attain Heaven. The composer thereby establishes a connection between this dissonance and the sacrifice the maidens are about to make. The symbolism is carried into the following air, 'The gate to bliss does open stand', in which Marina challenges Atticus to discover in her any traces of secular 'Pomp and Pride'. Purcell sets off Temptation's plea, 'O do not bid adieu!', as a moment of angular recitative. The G minor melody, briefly imitated in the bass at the beginning, is never allowed to reach high F♯, perhaps to symbolize the yet-to-be-attained bliss. This design produces a striking cross-relation in bar 2 and, then, one of the oddest cadences in all of Purcell (see Example 4). With

Example 4. *Theodosius*: 'The gate to bliss does open stand', bars 24–6

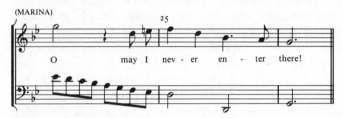

this double dissonance, the clash of E♮ and E♭ in bar 24 and the high F♮ in the voice followed by the leading-note the continuo demands, Purcell seems to imply that Marina, like Theodosius, will never achieve Heaven because she lacks conviction. Though the lyric says just the opposite, the music reveals a struggle of conscience.

Flavilla's air 'What! what can pomp or glory do?' follows without pause, the first four bars of the melody being identical to those of the preceding song. But, importantly, the bass line avoids the dissonance-producing F♯, and the rest of the piece lacks the dramatic declamation and cross-relations that punctuate Marina's. Purcell thus gives Lee's indistinguishable virgins different personalities, despite a shared predicament. Flavilla is clearly the more complacent. They join voices in the chorus, asking the priests to shield them from future sin. At the moment of renunciation – 'And let us see the world no more' – Purcell introduces an extraordinary harmonic surprise that I can interpret only as a final, panicky gasp at the loss of worldly charms (Example 5). Such hair-raising progressions abound in the music of Locke; Purcell shows more restraint, but even in the later works he occasionally relies on similar harmonic extravagance to intensify dramatic extremes.

The Plays

Example 5. *Theodosius*: 'What! what can pomp or glory do?', bars 30–3

The scene concludes with a solo for Atticus, flanked by a symphony of recorders and a perfunctory chorus, all very proper and tame compared to the maidens' songs. The rest of the extant music for the tragedy is that 'betwixt the Acts', except the final song. But these vocal pieces are by no means incidental. At the end of the first act is heard the bellicose 'Now the fight's done' in C major: after years of strife, the God of War turns to matters of love. Commenting on Theodosius's withdrawal from politics, the song also prepares for the entrance of Marcian. One of Lee's finest-made characters, the crusty old general is disgusted by the emperor's softness; he longs for the golden days of Roman might and despises the new religion sweeping across the empire.

In the second act we learn that the emperor's boyhood friend, Prince Varanes, loves one Athenais, the daughter of a poor philosopher who proudly refuses to allow the match because of her lowly station. Nothing in this act prepares us for the gloomy songs following it. 'Sad as death at dead of night', which tells of a wretched, abandoned Caelia whose chastity is nearly violated, obviously pertains to Athenais, but the key of G minor and the 'lament bass' would seem to be over-reactions to her not-yet-fatal predicament. The message of the second, 'Dream no more of pleasures past', in the same key, is even clearer: Athenais will be condemned to suffer endless shame; 'the false forsworn alas is gone' is a direct reference to Varanes, who has given up his pursuit without much protest. The chorus for soprano and alto includes a passage (Example 6), somewhat garbled in

Example 6. *Theodosius*: 'Dream no more of pleasures past', bars 47–52

the original version, that recalls the cross-relations of Marina's song in Act I.[12] With this crushing attack on 'trust' Purcell links Varanes's cowardly surrender of Athenais to Theodosius's Christian 'seduction' and abandonment of Marina and Flavilla in Act I, a subtle intertwining of these seemingly unrelated sub-plots: the royal maidens are betrayed by Atticus's promise of heavenly bliss; Athenais is betrayed by a fair-weather lover, by a slothful emperor, and finally by her father, who forces her to marry Theodosius and thus betray Varanes.

Act III continues to focus on the innocent Athenais, who, like Theodosius in Act I, decides to take vows in order to escape the temptation of love. At her clothing ceremony in III.ii the world-weary emperor discovers that the 'river nymph' of his obsession is Athenais. Discarding his newly acquired religion, he immediately asks her to become his queen. The old philosopher again protests that his daughter is unworthy, but Theodosius scoffs, 'O thou *Atheist* to perfection!', a line reminiscent of the earlier, unfettered Lee. The song following the third act evokes pathos rather than doom. 'Hail to the myrtle shade', in B♭ major, praises Athenais's virtue and provides a respite from the threnodic drone.[13] With a simplicity and grace anticipating 'Fairest isle', the swaying, wistful tune will haunt the memory.

In the fourth act the emperor, showing belated deference to his old friend Varanes, allows Athenais to choose between them. Near the end of the touching second scene, she confesses her love for the prince but accedes to her father's wish that she marry Theodosius secretly at midnight. The final act knits the plots into a double catastrophe. Athenais pretends to prepare for the wedding, but then asks her maid to 'Go fetch thy Lute, and sing those lines I gave thee'. Unhesitatingly, she drinks poison: ''Tis done, haste, *Delia*, haste! come bring thy Lute, / And sing my wastage to immortal Joys'. With the lyric that follows, 'Ah cruel bloody fate', Lee stands convention on its head.[14] In several earlier tragedies, the final acts open with fated heroines awash with melancholy, as songs are sung to divert the dumps. The lull in the drama is then shattered by a clamour of events: daggers flash, bowls of hemlock are drained, battles rage, and actors begin their rants. But here in *Theodosius* the culminating tragic act slips in unexpectedly; the dramatist forces us to pause, to reflect during a most remarkable song. Who could have anticipated Purcell's stroke of

---

[12] In the critical notes to the Purcell Society Edition, xxi, xviii, the editor simply remarks that 'Several obvious misprints in this song have been corrected.' Example 6 is taken from the 1680 quarto, changing only the crotchet in the alto part of bar 48 from F to G and the quaver in the bass on the third beat of bar 50 from G to F.

[13] In the play-book this is printed between scenes i and ii, while the rubric for the song states that it was performed 'after the Third Act'.

[14] In the 1680 quarto the music for this lyric is headed 'SONG after the Fourth ACT', but it is clearly to be performed in the fifth.

genius? He surveyed Athenais's own account of her most vile fate and set the vividly morbid lines to a Scotch air of extreme simplicity (Example 7).[15] This is an apotheosis. These are *her* words, *her* melody. There is nothing left to foreshadow ("tis now too late, *Philander* to restore'). The G minor songs at the end of Act II foretell her death, while this one transcends it. With a ballad-like tune in a painless G major Purcell conveys more irony and pathos than with a hundred artificial melismas or obstinate descending tetrachords.

Were it not for this and the songs at the ends of Acts II and III, Athenais would pale badly next to the powerful Pulcheria, 'one of the few really

Example 7. *Theodosius*: 'Ah cruel bloody Fate'

Ah cru - el blood-y fate, what canst thou now do more? A -

- las! 'tis now too late Phi - lan - der to re - store: Why should the heav'n-ly

pow'rs per-suade poor mor - tals to be - lieve That they

guard us here, and re-ward us there, yet all our joys de-ceive.

[15] From *Choice Ayres and Songs*, III (1681).

artistically-drawn women figures of Restoration tragedy, a character that inestimably raises in our eyes the worth of Lee as a dramatic poet'.[16] Purcell ennobles this heroine as he later does Bonduca and the Indian Queen. With the composer's help, Lee achieved a rare thing in *Theodosius*: melodrama without sentimental overtones.

King Richard the Second

Purcell's second opportunity to write for the stage came in late 1680, when he set one of the lyrics for Nahum Tate's adaptation of Shakespeare's *The History of King Richard the Second*, produced by the King's Company at the Theatre Royal in Drury Lane. Although the exact date of the première is unknown, the work was apparently scheduled for mid-December but was refused a licence because of its supposed parallels with the Exclusion Crisis; in an attempt to slip it by the censors, it was retitled *The Sicilian Usurper*. As Tate reports in the dedication, the plot was thereby 'render'd obscure and incoherent'. In fact, it bore only a slim resemblance to political events, but during those troubled times, any play dealing with the deposition of an English king, even a vile and unsuccessful one, was highly sensitive.

The subject of Restoration adaptations of Shakespeare is discussed at length in Chapter 8; here I need say only that the 1680 version of *King Richard the Second* has little to recommend it. Nicoll is probably too generous in suggesting that Tate 'thought a good deal of and about Shakespeare and was prepared honestly to like or to dislike . . . not swayed by sudden fancies but basing his ideas on definite critical precepts'.[17] In this adaptation he softened Shakespeare's characters with ruthless zeal, leaving only husks to shuffle round the Drury Lane stage. This is especially apparent in the penultimate scene, which depicts Richard's imprisonment at Pomfret Castle. The adapter transmutes the king's inner torment into a gastronomic hallucination. He approaches a table laid with a feast only to see it sink and disappear.[18] This is followed shortly by Purcell's song 'Retir'd from any mortal's sight' (z 581), which Tate's King Richard describes as yet another form of torture.[19] The lyric was probably spawned by Shakespeare's stage direction 'The music plays' inserted about midway through the famous soliloquy to coincide with the extended metaphor beginning:

[16] Nicoll, *A History of English Drama*, I, 146–7.
[17] *A History of English Drama*, I, 172.
[18] Probably inspired by similar flummery in the 1674 version of *The Tempest*.
[19] W. Barclay Squire, in 'Purcell's Dramatic Music', *Sammelbände der Internationalen Musikgesellschaft*, 5 (1903–4), 532, states that there is no evidence that the song 'was sung at the original production'; however, it was published in *Choice Ayres and Songs*, IV (1683), and the verse is included in the 1681 play-book, being 'For the Prison SCENE in the last ACT'. Squire's error is repeated by Alan Gray in the Purcell Society Edition, XX, ix.

> . . . How sour sweet music is
> When time is broke, and no proportion kept!
> So is it in the music of men's lives.
> And here have I the daintiness of ear
> To check time broke in a disordered string;
> But for the concord of my state and time
> Had not an ear to hear my true time broke.

Tate dispenses with this speech, but obviously wants to retain some of its emotional weight. For all the havoc he wreaks on Shakespeare, the new verses for Purcell include some fine images. The poem is pastoral, but the cause of the shepherd's melancholy – in nearly every other lyric of the genre, the pain of love – is undisclosed. Damon is 'too much distrest to Live, / And yet forbid to Dye'. The moving lines of the first stanza,

> The tender sharers of his Pain,
> His Flocks no longer Graze,
> But sadly fixt around the Swain,
> Like silent Mourners gaze,

poignantly recall John of Gaunt's remark to Bullingbrook before his exile (I.iii):

> O to what purpose dost thou hoard thy words,
> When thou shouldst breath[e] farewels to thy Friends
> That round thee, all like silent Mourners gaze.

Shortly after the song, Sir Pierce of Exton enters and kills Richard; the music is thus a harbinger of the king's passing-bell.

Although composed within a few months of the similarly threnodic music for *Theodosius*, this song is in a markedly different style. More sophisticated harmonically with expressible words set to distinctive melodic figures, it is nevertheless strophic. In the mature music Purcell almost always avoids overtly expressive prolixity in strophic settings, for the obvious reason that figures depicting words such as 'drooping' or 'triumph' in the first verse might fall on inappropriate ones in subsequent stanzas. Assuming he intended all the words of 'Retir'd from any mortal's sight' to be sung, one can see that even the long melisma of the final phrase fits well with the corresponding lines of the second and third stanzas, though this is hardly Purcell's most characteristic way of setting the word 'sigh' (see Example 8).[20] The descending chromatics at the end of the bass part only add to the gathering gloom. With so remarkable a gift for capturing the essence of tragedy, it is a great pity that Purcell composed no other song for a serious play until nearly ten years after the abortive première of Tate's *King Richard the Second*.

[20] In *Choice Ayres and Songs*, IV (1683), all three verses are given.

Example 8. *King Richard the Second*: 'Retir'd from any mortal's sight', bars 11–15

graze;   But sad - ly fix'd   around _____ the swain, Like
swain,   Like au - tumn winds   was heard _____ to groan, Out -
lay;   At last ___ so deep   a sigh _____ he drew, As

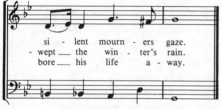

si - lent mourn - ers gaze.
- wept ___ the win - ter's rain.
bore ___ his life a - way.

II.   The Revivals of Dryden's Heroic Plays

Purcell was too young to have written music for the first productions of any of Dryden's rhymed tragedies, the last of which, *Aureng-Zebe*, was mounted in the autumn of 1675. All the revivals discussed below – *The Indian Emperour*, *Aureng-Zebe*, and *The Indian Queen* (Chapter 3) – occurred after Dryden and Purcell had collaborated on *King Arthur* in the spring of 1691. These productions were probably encouraged by the partnership. The plays were twenty years old or more, their original music lost, out of fashion, or forgotten. Dusting them off was an easy way to help satisfy the increased demand for serious drama in the early nineties.

The commonly held belief that the origins of the heroic play lie in the world of opera is a red herring. Dryden had a very clear idea about the evolution of the genre, tracing its beginnings in England directly to *The Siege of Rhodes* of 1656. He was convinced that Davenant's 'opera' had been 'perform'd in *Recitative Musique*' to circumvent the Puritan ban on acting plays, but attributed the 'heightening of Characters' and its theme of moral virtue not to *The Siege*'s having been set completely to music, but to the influence of '*Corneille* and some *French Poets*'. In fact Dryden made no connection at all between the purported operatic nature of the work and the later full development of the heroic mode, except to point out that *The Siege*, when revived after the Restoration, was 'acted as a just *Drama*' – that is, spoken instead of sung.[21] Dryden's own heroic dramas require

---

[21] Dent, *Foundations of English Opera*, p. 65, argues reasonably that *The Siege* was originally written as a play.

less music than most of the conventional tragedies written in the sixties and seventies, and he was even compelled to defend his 'use of Drums and Trumpets' during battle scenes by noting that 'Shakespear us'd them frequently'.[22] Some critics may find the lofty poetry in which Dryden's characters converse too rich for spoken drama, but for all their exoticism the rhymed couplets are not recitative; his protagonists may express 'operatic solitude', but they do not sing.

The Indian Emperour

This heroic play, first performed at Bridges Street in February or March 1665 as the sequel to Dryden and Sir Robert Howard's *The Indian Queen*, continues the saga of Montezuma and treats specifically Cortez's conquest of Mexico. Purcell composed only one song for *The Indian Emperour*, whereas the adaptation of *The Indian Queen* is a major musical work. But the sequel is much more dramatic than the original, the action more credible, and the main characters far more complex. Twenty years have elapsed since Montezuma witnessed the suicide of the usurping queen of Mexico, Zempoalla, at the end of the earlier play. The only character to survive from it, he has ascended the throne. In Act I he invites Almeria, the late queen's daughter, to become his bride. She still resents Montezuma's passive role in the death of her mother, not to mention his active dispatching of Traxalla, her father, and finds his advances distasteful. The emperor, preoccupied with Almeria's aloofness, is remarkably unperturbed by the invading Spaniards' demands for his abdication and the country's conversion to Christianity. Brushing aside his political troubles, he prepares to consult the spirits.

Act II opens in the '*Magitians Cave*', apparently an old scene first used in *The Indian Queen*, since no conjurer appears here.[23] The High Priest calls up an earthy spirit. Complaining that the usual channels of precognition are being disrupted by a powerful foreign god, it expresses the fear that 'A Nation loving Gold must rule this place, / Our Temples Ruine, and our Rites Deface'. The priest, embarrassed by such a bald prediction, meekly explains that earthy spirits are always pessimistic. He hastily invokes other gods 'of form more fair: / Who Visions dress in pleasing Colours still, / Set all the good to show, and hide the ill'. Kalib then appears clothed in white and '*in the shape of a Woman*'.[24] Dryden provides him with the first lyric, 'I look'd and saw within the book of Fate', the original setting of which does not survive. Kalib puts the best face on it,

---

[22] 'Of Heroique Playes An Essay', in *1 The Conquest of Granada* (published 1672).

[23] In fact the prologue warns the audience that the scenes and costumes are old.

[24] Loftis believes the playwright was thinking of *The Tempest* when choosing names for the dramatis personae (*The Works of John Dryden*, IX, 308). As the manuscript of the play shows, the High Priest was originally called 'Callib[an?]'.

telling Montezuma that a time will come when he will have his foes at a disadvantage. The fair spirit urges him to seize that opportunity, 'Which once refus'd will never come again'. The emperor, exasperated by all this arcane advice, asks again about Almeria. Nearly at the end of his tether, the priest promises to produce spirits specializing in predictions about love. But he has now lost all control over his conjurations, and the ghosts of slaughtered characters from *The Indian Queen* arise to threaten Montezuma, who laughs in their faces, until that of Zempoalla herself appears, claiming his affections forever. This scene, which began with a sedate incantation addressed to the good spirits, ends in dismal confusion.

Purcell set 'I look'd and saw within the book of Fate' (z 598) for a revival of Dryden's play mounted at Drury Lane sometime in 1692.[25] The composer divided the lyric into rather arbitrary sections for recitative and aria. Such words as 'smiled' and 'sinking' are treated in his typically graphic manner. The key is G minor, but the music does more than simply foreshadow Montezuma's death, for Kalib neither explicitly predicts dire events, as the earthy spirit does earlier, nor hints at Zempoalla's subsequent message. It begins with a firmly declaimed line rising over a tonic pedal (see Example 9). Kalib has peered into the future and is about to relate what he sees. The five-bar invocation has an ominous ring to it, but Montezuma receives qualified good news. The fifth bar is curious because of the abandoned imperfect cadence. In Purcell's music of this period dominant chords approached in a forthright manner are seldom left unresolved (this is commoner in the works of Pelham Humfrey, for example), and rarely are leading-notes cancelled in the same part, expecially in solo vocal music. Just when Kalib seems poised to tell the worst – and Purcell to affirm G minor in the plainest possible way – the key of foreboding dissolves into Bb major. But one must wait until the end of the song for confirmation of the significance of the F♯/F♮ juxtaposition in bar 5.

The aria proper begins at the words 'A day shall come', from which Montezuma learns that he must strike his foes when he has the chance. The odd final cadence is remarkably like that of Marina's air 'The gate to bliss' in *Theodosius*, because a cross-relation is created between F♮ in the voice and the following leading-note required by the continuo (see Example 10, and Example 4 above). The climactic 'never' in the next-to-last bar miraculously lessens the blow of the G minor cadence, and at the same time the falling Bb major triad recalls the 'happy hour' of the preceding recitative. The tonality of this piece symbolizes our common fate, but Purcell's guarded message to Montezuma, a much more sympathetic, human character in this play than in *The Indian Queen*, is gentle and compassionate. The music perfectly captures the ambivalence of the lyric.

[25] See *The London Stage*, Part 1, p. 402.

Example 9. *The Indian Emperour*: 'I look'd and saw within the book of Fate', bars 1–9

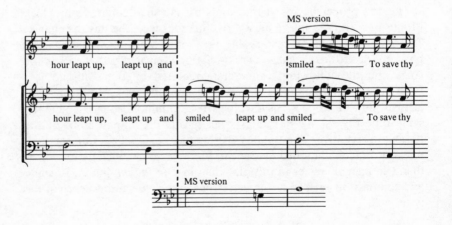

Example 10. *The Indian Emperour*: 'I look'd and saw within the book of Fate', bars 32–5

nev-er,   nev-er,   nev-er,   nev-er, nev-er,   nev-er, nev-er come   a   -   gain.

Two versions survive (see Example 9), one published in *The Banquet of Musick*, VI (1692), probably a few months after the play was revived, and another in Purcell's autograph song-book, London Guildhall Library, MS Safe 3.[26] The version in the print is more austere and mysterious than that in the manuscript. In the latter (shown in Example 9 as alternative readings) the bleak opening harmonies are softened by feinting at the dominant of the subdominant in bar 3 with a B♮ at the final quaver, while a diminished-seventh chord is substituted for the clash in the next bar. Perhaps because the E♭ in the bass helps to rob bar 5 of its harmonic surprise, Purcell strips the voice part of its ornaments in the Guildhall manuscript, having the singer rise directly to the B♭. A prudent editor would naturally prefer an autograph to a print, but I find the version in *The Banquet of Musick* more theatrical.

Significantly, the only other music of *The Indian Emperour* is linked directly to Kalib's prophecy in Act II. The fourth act finds the 'passion-ridden' emperor besieged by Cortez's men, who are content to lie about carelessly, enjoying idle pleasures, until the Aztecs starve to death. But Montezuma's son, Guyomar, who emerges victorious from a sub-plot in which he has vied with his elder brother for Alibech's hand, decides to launch a surprise attack against the complacent invaders. The third scene of Act IV represents a grotto in which the unarmed Spaniards are entertained by Indian women, one of whom sings the beautiful 'Ah fading joy, how quickly art thou past?' The chorus, especially, drifts over the soldiers like an opiate, and after a sarabande with castanets, Guyomar and his band burst in, gaining an easy victory. When Montezuma learns of this shift of fortune, he recalls Kalib's prophecy, but procrastinates. Purcell is not known to have set 'Ah fading joy'. I am tempted to guess that Humfrey's version, probably written for an earlier revival, was still held in high esteem, and Purcell left well enough alone.[27] It too is in G minor, and

---

[26] For a description and list of contents of the latter, see W. Barclay Squire, 'An Unknown Autograph of Henry Purcell', *The Musical Antiquary*, 3 (1911–12), 5–17. Peter Dennison believes that the manuscript 'is to be dated probably closer to 1695 than to 1692...': see the Purcell Society Edition, VIII (rev.), xi.

[27] Composed before 1674, the year of Humfrey's death. The song first appeared in *Choice Ayres, Songs, & Dialogues*, 1 (1676).

though not as froward as 'I look'd and saw within the book of Fate', it treats the seventh scale degree with similar sensitivity. For instance, the bass moves from F♮ to F♯ in bars 15–16 (see Example 11a), but when a parallel passage later changes direction (Example 11b), attention is drawn

Example 11. *The Indian Emperour*: Pelham Humfrey, 'Ah fading joy', bars 12–17 and 23–8

to the text. 'Pevish Mortals' tread as inexorably to their doom as the first passage does to G minor, while the happy wild creatures who put their trust in Mother Nature are 'Not anxious how to get or spare', and Humfrey's music deftly steps away into a brighter key.[28]

The music for this play, though appearing to support my thesis about G minor, raises a troublesome question: is such symbolism at all remarkable if most of the principal characters are to die in Act V? A cynic might argue that G minor in the music for tragedies is like background radiation, always present, undoubtedly potent, but of no significance because it affects all of us equally. An aspect of Purcell's genius is that he turned this cliché to his advantage. The key is conventionally gloomy, but 'I look'd and saw' does far more than simply presage Montezuma's demise; it takes the sting from Kalib's prophecy. For a fleeting moment we believe the emperor *can* escape destruction.

Tyrannick Love

D. W. Jefferson and his followers argue that Dryden created the extravagant heroic mode as a vehicle 'for his powers of wit and rhetoric', never intending all the rant and bombast to be taken completely seriously.[29]

---

[28] The song is reprinted and discussed by Ian Spink, *English Song Dowland to Purcell* (London: Batsford, 1974), pp. 187–8. Note that the lyric Humfrey set is considerably different from that printed in Dryden's play-book.

[29] For a bibliography of works in this school of criticism, see L. Brown, 'Restoration Drama Criticism: Revisions and Orthodoxies', p. 201, n. 8.

Other scholars counter that had Dryden written the heroic plays with a twinkle in his eye, they would not have been so brutally burlesqued in *The Rehearsal*; and if the protagonists' absurd hyperboles were sometimes greeted with 'laughs of approbation', the genuinely comic moments would be superfluous.[30] Purcell's music for the conjuration scenes sheds some light on this controversy, but from a surprising angle. Did Dryden intend the earthy spirit in the second act of *The Indian Emperour* to put the fear of God into his audience, or was he meant to be a blundering acolyte who takes his job too seriously? Was the High Priest supposed to remain dignified while all his attempts to please Montezuma backfired, or were his faint excuses meant to be comical, like those of an amateur magician who fails to make the rabbit appear? Although we know nothing of the original music, Purcell's song suggests that this episode was deadly serious, at least when revived in 1692. This is not the case, however, with the much more elaborate incantation scene in *Tyrannick Love*, a play with a complicated stage history. Here the supporters of Jefferson's unfashionable theory may take heart from Purcell's music.

Dryden's third heroic play, which was a great success, is celebrated as much for the circumstances of its first production as for the famous 'Scaene of an Elysium' in Act IV. We even know something about the scenery itself from a lawsuit filed against its painter, Isaac Fuller; and Nell Gwyn's uncharacteristic acting of a serious role – righted in the end by her delivery of 'the most amusing [epilogue] ever written' – is said to have endeared her to Charles II.[31]

As in *The Indian Emperour*, the music is introduced into the main sub-plot, the martyrdom of St Catharine at the hands of the Roman Emperor Maximin. For the first four acts this plot is nearly as important as the central story (a study of Maximin's increasing cruelty to his subjects and his own family in mad defiance of a rebellion), but it peters out rather badly in the last. Some critics see Dryden's failure to sustain the secondary plot as a weakness, an inability to reconcile the usual theme of love and honour with the viler intrigues of tyranny and proselytism.[32] But *Tyrannick Love* is a different kind of heroic tragedy from *The Indian Emperour*, *The Conquest of Granada,* and *Aureng-Zebe*, because it has the added ingredient of show, elaborate musical and scenic display that includes the spectacular destruction of the wheel of torture in Act V. For experimenting with these operatic elements, Dryden himself was soon to suffer upon the Duke of Buckingham's rack of satire.

The scene in the '*Indian Cave*' in Act IV is reminiscent of Montezuma's

---

[30] See Hume, *The Development*, p. 191, and Novak, introduction to Settle, *The Empress of Morocco*, p. vi.

[31] See *The Works of John Dryden*, x, ed. Novak, 380 ff.

[32] See, for example, *The Works of John Dryden*, VIII, 296; x, 392–9.

consultation with the High Priest in *The Indian Emperour*.[33] Maximin is also enamoured of an unreceptive woman, St Catharine. Both repelled and fascinated by her power to convert the staunchest disbelievers and fearing that he, too, may fall under her spell, he engages the obedient and much-abused Placidius to act as a kind of spiritual pimp to learn the workings of her Christian heart. The 'tribune and conjurer' Nigrinus, on learning of Placidius's errand, complains, like the High Priest in *The Indian Emperour*, of love's unpredictability; he is much better with 'Wars, and Bloodshed, and . . . dire Events'. After trying unsuccessfully to dissuade Placidius, he agrees to call up an earthy fiend, who he fears will be angry to be disturbed about such a trifling matter. The appearance of the tipsy Nakar and his mate Damilcar (who *'descend in Clouds'* despite being 'earthy fiends') must have come as a surprise to an audience bred on Dryden's earlier incantation scenes. The high-spirited dialogue, rich in fantastic images, would be more at home in a Spanish romance. Nakar announces that he must return to his battles in the air, leaving the timid Damilcar 'to perform what the man will have done'. At the end of the duet, he flies up and she descends to answer in speech Nigrinus's questions about Catharine. The conjurer, finding Damilcar's enigmatic aphorisms unsatisfactory, commands the spirit to enter the saint's dreams, drive out all thoughts of Heaven, and replace them with images of profane delights. This invasion of the subconscious begins as *'the Bed arises with S. Catharine in it'*, revealing *'A Scene of a Paradise'*. But the vision is violently dispersed by Catharine's guardian angel, Amariel, who descends with a flaming sword, dispatching Damilcar amid pleas for mercy. Dryden's earlier incantation scenes in *The Indian Queen* and *The Indian Emperour* are designed to illuminate the character flaws of protagonist and antagonist and to forecast the results of their follies. From 'I look'd and saw', for example, one discovers more about Montezuma than Kalib. The purpose of the corresponding scene in *Tyrannick Love*, however, is diversion. One learns nothing about Maximin or Placidius, and of Catharine, only what one already knows: that she is pure of heart and mind. Nor is the future explicitly revealed.

At the première on 24 June 1669, both spirits were sung by women.[34] Epicene casting of antimasque-like characters was common during the period, but perhaps Dryden also wanted to show that spirits are neuter and lack human emotions.[35] The earliest surviving setting of the dialogue,

---

[33] Summers says in *Dryden: The Dramatic Works* (London: Nonesuch, 1931–2), II, 527, that 'No doubt [this] scene . . . had already been used for Ismeron in *The Indian Queen*, III, and for the incantation scene in *The Indian Emperour*, II.i, "the Magician's Cave".'

[34] According to Downes, *Roscius Anglicanus*, p. 10, Mrs James played Damilcar and Mrs Knepp, a favourite of Pepys, sang Nakar.

[35] See *Notes and Observations on the Empress of Morocco* (1674), p. 44: 'it is non sense to say Women-Spirits, as if Spirits had Sexes'.

'Hark, my Damilcar, we are called below', anonymous in a manuscript copied in the early eighties, is written entirely in the treble clef.[36] Barclay Squire suggests that this is the original 1669 setting;[37] but I believe it was composed not for the première but for a revival. After fire had destroyed the Bridges Street theatre on 25 January 1672, the play was presented at Lincoln's Inn Fields in a version that eliminated the machines needed for the temptation scene in Act IV. A prompt copy used for the production shows that this episode was cut, except for an unidentified song and a scaled-down representation of the attempt to invade Catharine's dreams.[38] The anonymous setting of 'Hark, my Damilcar' has minor changes in the verse to suggest that it was probably adapted especially for this production. While suspended in air, Dryden's spirits sing 'we mount and we fly' (IV. i. 50), whereas in the song the tense is altered to 'wee'l mount and wee'l fly' and later 'wee'l slide' instead of 'we slide'. This implies a future action that the 1672 audience were not to enjoy. Also the anonymous composer redistributed the dialogue, though the manuscript does not specify who sings what. For example, Nakar's line 'But their men lye securely intrench'd in a Cloud', becomes '*Your* men lye securly intencht in a Cloud', obviously to be sung by Damilcar. Later the opposite happens, when Damilcar's line 'Then call me again when the Battel is won' is changed to read 'Ile call the[e] againe . . .'[39] In general, the composer of the 1672 version simplified Dryden's allocation of the verse between the two singers, giving each longer, uninterrupted chunks, thus largely eliminating their contentiousness.

Purcell's resetting of 'Hark, my Damilcar' (z 613/1) is usually assigned to a 1694 revival of *Tyrannick Love*.[40] The dialogue begins in the rollicking style of the more famous one for Coridon and Mopsa, 'Now the maids and the men are making of hay', in *The Fairy-Queen*. After a rather conventional page or two, Purcell infuses Dryden's sexless spirits with human passions by restoring the original distribution of the text, as well as dividing some 'speeches' and even adding a line or two, thereby tightening the exchanges. (In light of his close association with Purcell in the early nineties, one should not rule out the poet's direct participation in the revision.)

[36] British Library, Add. MS 19759, fols. 29v–30. This belonged to Charles Campelman and is dated 9 June 1681, presumably when the copying began. A facsimile of these pages is given in Cyrus L. Day, *The Songs of John Dryden* (Cambridge, Mass.: Harvard Univ. Press, 1932), pp. 19–20.

[37] 'Purcell's Dramatic Music', p. 559.

[38] For a description, see Henry Hitch Adams, 'A Prompt Copy of Dryden's *Tyrannick Love*', *Studies in Bibliography*, 4 (1951–2), 170–4.

[39] Following Squire, Laurie also believes the dialogue in Add. MS 19759 to be the original setting ('Purcell's Stage Works', Diss. Cambridge 1961, pp. 12, 210). In her transcription she alters without comment the text of the British Library manuscript version to agree with the 1670 play-book.

[40] See *The London Stage*, Part 1, p. 441. Because it was sung by Mrs Ayliff and Bowman, the revival must have occurred before the company divided in early 1695.

The most important change was to give Nakar's part to a man. Purcell seems to have been aware of the earlier setting, or, to put it more cautiously, Dryden's verse elicited similar musical responses from the two composers: for the most part the different sections have the same metres; both versions shift to the minor mode at the line 'But now the Sun's down, and the Element's red', and Dryden's bellicose phrase 'a Trumpeter-Hornet to battel sounds loud' is set to similar C major fanfares.[41] But Purcell's genius was for the dramatic. When Nakar announces that he must leave to do battle against the spirits of fire, a moment of reluctant parting interrupts the banter. In the exchange shown in Example 12, Damilcar's pleading motif, 'Oh stay!', contrasts sharply with Nakar's jolly dotted rhythm. Distress at the prospect of his departure is registered by her very obstinacy. And in bar 113, when Nakar tries to soften the blow with a warm cadence in E♭ major, she refuses to join him in the new key, and the unexpected F♯ is a jab of intense pain.

This duet is not as important structurally as 'I look'd and saw within the book of Fate' in *The Indian Emperour*, because the spirits, however kindred, do not intersect the plot of the 'real' characters. But 'Hark, my Damilcar' is nevertheless operatic, because it expresses emotions and even implies actions not present in Dryden's verse. Purcell brings the spirits down to earth. Damilcar, whom the playwright portrays as nothing more than a flighty elf called upon to make obscure predictions, is transformed into an insecure lover, left wretched on her own to perform a hopelessly difficult and, as it happens, dangerous task that leaves her begging for mercy at the feet of an avenging angel. Why the composer did not also set the continuation of the scene between Damilcar and Nigrinus, surely the ripest episode for operatic exploitation in all heroic drama, is a mystery on which I shall presently try to shed a little light.

A reasonably accurate secondary source of Purcell's dialogue is British Library Add. MS 22099, which dates from about 1705. The volume is a whole book, beautifully copied, and though not systematically organized it includes a meticulous table of contents by the principal scribe. The gatherings of songs from plays were compiled almost entirely from the widely available printed collections of Playford and Pearson as well as from single-sheets. One is puzzled, therefore, to find that the dialogue from *Tyrannick Love* (on fols. 38v–40v) has a completely different text, which begins 'Haste, brother King, we're sent from above'. To my knowledge no one has recognized that this is the line-for-line parody of Dryden's verse that Buckingham provided for the Kings of Brentford in Act V of his celebrated farce.

The Rehearsal, which was first performed on 7 December 1671, is of course a general satire on Dryden and his heroic plays, and its dialogue an

---

[41] Changed to 'the trumpetts and Hornetts to battle sound loud' in the 1672 version.

Example 12. *Tyrannick Love*: 'Hark, my Damilcar', bars 99–118

ingenious web of paraphrases of passages from nearly every tragedy produced during the first decade of the Restoration. It is probably the single most discussed play of the period, but most *Rehearsal* scholars, in their tireless searches for Buckingham's sources and targets, are tentative in their adumbration of his satirical treatment of music and musicians. One notices, for example, some confusion in the explications of the attempt to raise the dead men with music in II.v. Bayes says that the melodious resurrection will happen at the sounding of a piece in '*Effaut flat*'. G. G. Falle thinks the 'correct designation would be E'.[42] In the late seventeenth century, however, 'F fa ut flat' meant simply the key of 'F with a flat third', that is F minor, the favourite for ghosts, witches, and the like, and not at all inappropriate for this bizarre dance. The point is not that Bayes is ignorant of music theory, but that the dance, which he has composed himself, is rhythmically confusing; one of the dancers says, "'tis impossible to do any thing in time, to this Tune'. In yet another way the pantomime playwright is shown to be a competent, even learned, theoretician and a bungling practitioner.

The song of the rightful Kings of Brentford, a vivid discourse on food, seems to have been inspired by Nakar's unfortunate suggestion that he and Damilcar 'drop from above, / In a Gelly of Love'.[43] One must admit that Dryden left himself vulnerable with this obscure allusion, but too much has been made of the language of Buckingham's parody, which is only slightly more extravagant than its model, and not enough of the *reges ex machina* themselves. The monarchs 'descend in the Clouds, singing in white garments'; one should recall Kalib's costume in *The Indian Emperour*. Sitting in the machine with them as accompanists are three fiddlers dressed in green. The purpose of the colourful habits becomes clear when in the middle of the duet (see Example 13) the first king sings 'the Ladies have all inclination to dance, / And the green Frogs croak out a Coranto of *France*'. At this point, the immortal Bayes stops the music to explain the jest to his friends Smith and Johnson. The slur is clearly against French-trained musicians, who came to London in their numbers after the Restoration and one of whom, Louis Grabu, was even master of the King's Violins at the time; I cannot, however, offer an exegesis of Smith's pun on the words 'no Coranto', which causes Bayes much amusement. Again, the main thrust, a backhanded one, is at a larger target: Dryden's practice of interspersing spoken dialogue with music, here cleverly satirized by its inversion.

The original setting of 'Haste, brother King', if there ever was one, is lost. Buckingham almost certainly made his paraphrase so that it could be

[42] *Three Restoration Comedies* (Toronto: Macmillan, 1964), II.v.
[43] For an explication, see *The Works of John Dryden*, x, 423.

Example 13. *Tyrannick Love*: 'Hark, my Damilcar', bars 146–163

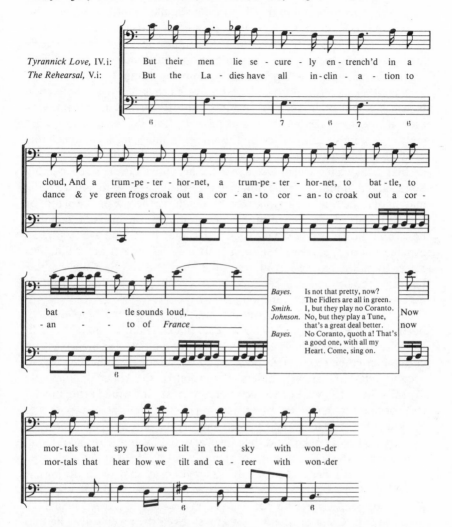

Tyrannick Love, IV.i:
But their men lie se - cure - ly en - trench'd in a

The Rehearsal, V.i:
But the La - dies have all in - clin - a - tion to

cloud, And a trum-pe - ter - hor-net, a trum-pe - ter - hor-net, to bat - tle, to

dance & ye green frogs croak out a cor - an - to cor - an - to croak out a cor -

bat - - tle sounds loud,_____

- an - - to of *France*_____

Now

Bayes. Is not that pretty, now?
The Fidlers are all in green.
Smith. I, but they play no Coranto.
Johnson. No, but they play a Tune,
that's a great deal better.
Bayes. No Coranto, quoth a! That's
a good one, with all my
Heart. Come, sing on.

mor-tals that spy How we tilt in the sky with won-der

mor-tals that hear how we tilt and ca - reer with won-der

sung to the original duet;[44] to use this music as the vehicle for its own
ridicule would certainly be in keeping with *The Rehearsal*'s own parasitic
verse. The borrowing could also explain how Purcell's version came to be
pressed into service for a later revival, probably the one in 1699.[45] That

[44] See Dent, *Foundations*, p. 145, n. 4: 'Whether the parody was sung to the music of an
anonymous setting [in British Library Add. MS 19759] cannot be definitely ascertained.'
[45] The famous 18 November 1709 revival at the Haymarket would seem to be a *terminus ante
quem* for the Purcell *contrafactum*, since the two kings were played then by Messrs Bul-
lock and Bowen, neither known for his singing, unless of course the latter was the former
boy treble Jemmy Bowen.

Nakar and Damilcar were both sung by women in the first production of *Tyrannick Love* was surely the inspiration for the Brentford Kings, who enter hand in hand in Act II, calling each other 'sweetheart'. Bayes says, 'take notice of their stile: 'twas never yet upon the Stage'. But Purcell's dialogue *and* its parody are for soprano and baritone. Was the adapter willing to sacrifice the off-colour humour by using Purcell's music? Perhaps, because the portrayal of one or both kings by a woman in breeches would be in keeping with the travesty casting that began very early in the stage history of *The Rehearsal*. Colley Cibber reports that audiences were so fond of seeing Susannah Mountfort play a man's role 'that when the Part of *Bays* . . . had, for some time, lain dormant, she was desired to take it up, which I have seen her act with all the true, coxcombly Spirit, and Humour, that the Sufficiency of the Character required'.[46] She may have done this as early as 1687.[47] Whatever the sex of the actors or singers in this forerunner of modern pantomimes, the question remains: how could Purcell's music have been interrupted in mid-phrase by Bayes's explanation of the 'green frog' pun? Nakar is enthusiastically calling his forces to battle, having just arrived on a long-held top E, while the bass line moves continuously in semiquavers (see Example 13). An interruption here would be ludicrous – and very funny.

Yet something rings false about this pat chronology for *The Rehearsal*'s borrowing of music from *Tyrannick Love*. Buckingham's words seem to fit Purcell's music too well. The prosody is nearly faultless; the melismas and chromatics come at the right places; and the minor rhythmic changes to accommodate the slightly different scansion of the kings' dialogue are skilfully done. Unaware of Dryden's original text, one would probably not suspect that the *Rehearsal* verses were affixed to the music by a poetaster working after the fact. Could Purcell have set the parody first, say in 1692 or even as early as 1689, and then later adapted his music to the *original* words for a 1694–5 revival of *Tyrannick Love*? He was certainly well acquainted with *The Rehearsal*. It was revived at least twice during his tenure at Drury Lane, and was likely performed by many of the same players and musicians who participated in his musical plays. Finally, the dialogue is in C major, the 'key of kings'. Even if Purcell's duet had no direct connection with *The Rehearsal* in performance, perhaps he could not resist a wry acknowledgement of the Brentford monarchs.

But I have heaped speculation upon speculation. The calendar of recorded performances for this period is extremely scanty, and one must resist equally the urge to use it as an excuse to invent complex chronologies or to employ it to support simplistic ones. We shall probably never know

[46] *An Apology for the Life of Colley Cibber*, ed. B. R. S. Fone (Ann Arbor: Univ. of Michigan Press, 1968), pp. 95–6.
[47] See *The London Stage*, Part 1, pp. 354–5.

which version came first, only that *The Rehearsal* sent a tremor through the entire heroic play repertoire, changing *Tyrannick Love* forever. The temptation scene may have been abridged for the 1672 revival not because the Lincoln's Inn Fields theatre lacked the stage machines destroyed by the fire at Bridges Street, but because the duke's wicked parody, which had appeared a year before, rendered impossible a serious mounting of the original. How can we distinguish between the descent of the spirits in *Tyrannick Love* and the arrival of the Brentford Kings in *The Rehearsal*, if Purcell's music can serve both equally well? I am reminded of the fabled Restoration version of *Romeo and Juliet*, which James Howard provided with a happy ending in order to preserve the lovers alive. Downes reports that "twas Play'd Alternately, Tragical one Day, and Tragicomical another; for several Days together' (*Roscius Anglicanus*, p. 22). I wonder not why audiences thronged to such a curiosity but whether the actors played Shakespeare's original scenes variously, according to the ending selected for a given performance. Similarly, was the temptation scene in *Tyrannick Love* acted any differently from its parody in *The Rehearsal* by 1694? Had it become, in fact, self-satiric, a parody of itself?

Purcell omitted to set the one truly operatic sequence in *Tyrannick Love*: after Nakar exits, Damilcar is supposed to sing 'You pleasing dreams of Love', with which she conjures a vision of the sleeping Catharine. Perhaps the composer felt that this was too serious and dramatically sensitive an invocation to be delivered by the flighty Damilcar of the preceding dialogue. He did, however, set the later lyric 'Ah how sweet it is to love', a pedestrian concatenation of clichés. The lovelorn spirit could easily perform this in the character of 'Hark, my Damilcar'. A hauntingly beautiful piece with restless counterpoint and hypnotic rhythm, it anticipates Amariel's vengeful descent to stop the unholy conjuration and perhaps even Catharine's fiery martyrdom. The lines that seem so commonplace here – 'And what pleasing pains we prove / When first we feel a lover's fire' – assume an awful irony in Act V.[48]

Although Purcell's self-parodying dialogue does not necessarily support Jefferson's claim for the mock seriousness of Dryden's heroic plays, it does suggest that when the rhymed tragedies were revived in the early nineties, they were acted in a camped-up manner. But to describe 'Hark, my Damilcar' as simply humorous is to miss the point. Like so much of Purcell's dramatic music, it runs the gamut of a wide range of emotions, making Dryden's fanciful verses the utterances of passionate beings.

---

[48] An alteration of Dryden's original couplet: 'And what pleasing pains we prove, / When we first approach Loves fire!'

The Conquest of Granada

The two parts of *The Conquest of Granada* (published together in 1672) include a prefatory essay in which Dryden reaffirms the principles of heroic drama, defends his old mistress rhyme, and rationalizes the introduction of supernatural characters and magic. But he largely overhauled the heroic formula in this pair of plays, drastically reducing the role of music. Almanzor is a protagonist brazen and crafty enough not to need the assistance of spirits or soothsayers, and no masque or conjuration scene is found here. Nevertheless, Dryden handled what little music there is in his last two heroic plays very skilfully.

The first part of *The Conquest of Granada* (December 1670) is a full-length play but not autonomous, since it only plants the seeds for the conquest depicted in Part 2. (What other heroic drama has no violence in its final four acts?) The weak Moorish king, Mahomet Boabdelin, fails to parry the abuse he receives from the Montezuma-like hero, Almanzor, brought from northern Africa to rally the defence of Granada but fighting in turn for whichever side or woman he thinks the nobler. The villainess, Lyndaraxa, left unpunished save for banishment in Part 2, is driven purely by her ambition for the throne: she loves the king; fortune need only name the man. Much of the action of the first half of the play culminates in a special entertainment called the zambra, prepared by the queen-to-be, Almahide, to ease the tension between the temporarily reconciled Zegrys and Abencerrages.[49] Although announced in the opening scene, the entertainment is delayed until III.ii, by which time Almanzor has nearly succeeded in rekindling the feud. The centrally placed zambra includes John Banister's 'Beneath a myrtle shade', which tells of a nymph who resists the singer's advances, yet admits her desire 'with a smile'.[50] The lyric pertains directly to Lyndaraxa, who conquers nearly all the men in the play (save Almanzor) with her smile. The long strophic song is no masterpiece, but the main internal cadence in a seductive F major supports the key word of the fourth verse (in italics): 'for all the while / She bid me not believe her, with a *smile*'. Like the Spaniards' dance with castanets in *The Indian Emperour*, the zambra ends abruptly with the Zegrys in violent revolt. The only other song of the tragedy, in IV.ii, is addressed to Lyndaraxa.

[49] In the preface to *Albion and Albanius*, Dryden conjectures that the zambras of 'the *Spanish* Moores' may have influenced the Italians in the evolution of opera. Though he retracts this in a postscript ('possibly the *Italians* went not so far as *Spain*, for the Invention of their *Opera's*'), this half-baked theory gives some idea of the significance he may have attached to the zambra in *1 Conquest of Granada*.

[50] For the sources of this song, see Cyrus L. Day and Eleanore Boswell Murrie, *English Song-Books 1651–1702* (London: Bibliographical Society, 1940), hereinafter cited as 'D&M', No. 357. The lyric is printed at the end of the 1672 quarto with a note that it should be 'Sung at the dance, or Zambra *in the third Act*'.

'Wherever I am, and whatever I doe', arranged by her suitor, Abdalla, the traitorous brother of King Boabdelin, is closely tied to the drama. Alphonso Marsh's setting (see D&M No. 3853) is in G minor and opens with the 'lament bass', here without any sinister connotation.

The second instalment of *The Conquest of Granada* (January 1671) spins out the permutations of the Moorish factionalism and Almanzor's impudent treason. The only music required is Nicholas Staggins's dialogue 'How unhappy a Lover am I', commissioned by the protagonist as a serenade for Queen Almahide in IV.iii.[51] It also presages the single super-natural event of the tragedy. When the music stops, Almanzor feels cold and frightened. His mother's ghost appears (without benefit of a conjuration), declaring the hero's Christian birth and royal lineage, a revelation that prepares him for his final defection to the victorious forces of King Ferdinand.

When *The Conquest of Granada* was revived in the early nineties, Purcell set none of the three original lyrics. Yet a single-sheet engraving of the dialogue 'Celemene, pray tell me' (z 584), dating from 'before 1704', records that it was performed 'in the Second Part of the Conquest of Granada. The Words by Thomas D'Urfey'. Zimmerman suggests that it probably replaced Staggins's 'How unhappy a Lover am I' in the fourth act of Part 2.[52] But Purcell's dialogue would be an inappropriate serenade for Queen Almahide; as explained below, 'Celemene, pray tell me' has a much stronger connection with Southerne's tragedy *Oroonoko* (November 1695), and this salacious dialogue would be a hideous substitute for the song which prepares the arrival of a ghost. If it had any connection at all with *The Conquest of Granada*, it probably replaced 'Beneath a myrtle shade' in Part 1, III.ii. Both songs are in D minor and have sexual overtones.

Aureng-Zebe

Dryden's last and finest rhymed tragedy, *Aureng-Zebe* (November 1675), is based on a true story about events in mid-seventeenth-century India. It has no lyric and only requires instrumental music in two places. But the laconic stage directions reveal the playwright's continued interest in music to enhance dramatic effect. Between Acts II and III 'a Warlike Tune is plaid, shooting off Guns and shouts of Souldiers are heard, as in an assault'. In no other play does Dryden mention the obligatory music between the acts, even though unseen battles rage during several intervals. He probably included the stage direction here because the warlike tune (which does not survive) unconventionally anticipates the mood of the following

---

[51] See D&M No. 1466. For thoughts about how it was performed, see my *Music in the Restoration Theatre* (Ann Arbor, Mich.: UMI Research Press, 1979), p. 42.
[52] *An Analytical Catalogue*, pp. 261–2.

scene, rather than reflecting that which has just transpired.[53] The first act ends with Aureng-Zebe being rebuffed by his father, the emperor, whose other sons are trying to gain the throne by force. The reason for the king's coldness is that he desires Indamora, Aureng-Zebe's betrothed. Between the acts, Morat, the blackest sheep of the family, is supposed to storm the city walls, being repulsed by his brother; hence the expectant warlike tune. The other occasion for music is in the fourth act, when the hero's father condemns him to be poisoned at the hand of the empress Nourmahal, his stepmother. Aureng-Zebe's soliloquy is accompanied by '*Soft Music*' probably meant to tug at the heartstrings.

Purcell's fine song 'I see she flies me' (z 573) is described in an undated single-sheet edition (British Library k.7.i.2[19]) as sung by Mrs Ayliff 'in the Play call'd *Oranzebe*', though it appears in both *Comes Amoris*, v (1694) and *Orpheus Britannicus*, i (1698) without mention of any play. I can find no place within the drama where it would not disrupt the plot. It might have been sung during an interval, perhaps in place of the warlike tune after the first act. Although intended for soprano, the song expresses the sentiments of a man spurned by a scornful woman. Indamora is very cool to Aureng-Zebe at the close of Act I, and the air might well reflect his feelings:

> But what's her scorn or my despair
> Since 'tis my fate to love her
> Were she but kind whom I adore,
> I might live longer but not love more.

Flight from adversity, suggested in the first line of the lyric, is an image evoked several times in the play (see, for instance, II.i.272–7).

The song is in two sharply contrasting parts. The first is a fiery rant. The excited vocal line is supported by a nervous rhythmic ostinato of ascending semiquavers reversing direction at the word 'despair'. The second part, in triple metre, shifts to a much less agitated extension of the word 'longer'. Except for remaining in G minor, the two halves seem worlds apart. This striking dichotomy apparently prompted Alan Gray, editor of Vol. xvi of the Purcell Society, to make this a *da capo* aria, a licence endorsed by later authorities.[54] But none of the sources, including Purcell's autograph (London, Guildhall Library, MS Safe 3, fols. 34v–35v), shows a return to the opening. This two-part design, quite common in Purcell's solo vocal music, is often used paradoxically for lyrics that appear to have no strong internal contrasts. The tone of each section is set by focussing on words suggestive of powerful emotions or actions, often taken out of syntactic context. In the first part these are 'she flies' and 'her scorn'; in the second,

---

[53] For a discussion of the role of act tunes, see my *Music in the Restoration Theatre*, pp. 58–61.

[54] See, for example, Spink, *English Song Dowland to Purcell*, p. 230.

Plate 1. John Dryden
(portrait by Godfrey Kneller)

Plate 2. Nathaniel Lee
(engraving by William Dobson)

'kind' and 'I adore'. But the two sections are in fact subtly related in several ways. Even the melodies shown in Example 14 have similar contours when reduced to their bare bones.

Example 14. *Aureng-Zebe*: 'I see, she flies me', bars 2–5 and 22–7

One other piece survives for this play, an undated choral setting by John Eccles of a limping couplet not found in Dryden's original:[55]

> She hear'd summonds w.th a chearfull face
> Made hast to welcome Death & met him half ye Race.

This was obviously sung in the fifth act when Melesinda, Morat's widow, is led off by priests, stoically complying with the Indian custom that a wife be burned on her husband's funeral pyre. The sacrifice is all the more unjust because her husband has been thoroughly unfaithful to her. Eccles's A major dirge is almost jaunty, the imitative counterpoint of the opening phrase giving way to a dance-like setting of the second line. No music is called for here in the original play, and the chorus spreads an unwanted layer of sickly sweet sentimentality over this bitter irony. Such 'Hollywood' touches are common in the serious plays of the nineties.

III. Two Tragedies of Nathaniel Lee

Besides *Theodosius* in 1680, Purcell had two other opportunities to write songs for the brilliantly unpredictable Lee. Both *Sophonisba* and *The Massacre of Paris* have stock musical scenes – an elaborate conjuration in a pagan temple in the first, and the appearance of a spirit warning a

---

[55] In British Library, Add. MS 29378, fols. 140v-141.

protagonist of trouble in the second – but Lee avoids the conventional consequences of these episodes, requiring Purcell to supply music that is functionally quite different from that in Dryden's heroic dramas.

Sophonisba

The conjuration scene in *Sophonisba, or Hannibal's Overthrow* (April 1675) is closely modelled on those in *The Indian Queen* and *The Indian Emperour*, but extravagance and complexity almost cause its collapse. Hannibal, like Dryden's heroes, is worried more about his affair with Rosalinda than about the uphill struggle he faces against Scipio and the Roman legions. In the second scene of Act III he becomes jealous when his beloved appears to dote on the youth Massina. Her rejection of the love-struck boy and his precipitous suicide do nothing to quell the general's doubts, and Hannibal resolves to consult the gods. Act IV is devoted largely to a rhapsody of prognostication featuring flagellation, music, dance, and scenic spectacle, all of which could be held together only by a herculean performance from the priestess Cumana. She and her acolyte, Aglave, have just sacrificed a soldier and are purifying the Temple of Bellona. Departing from Dryden's formula, Lee treats Hannibal's request for a prognosis of his chances against Scipio almost whimsically, perhaps because the outcome has already been prophesied. Earlier in the third scene of Act II, Hannibal witnessed a grim vision: '*The* SCENE *drawn, discovers a Heaven of blood, two Suns, Spirits in Battle, Arrows shot to and fro in the Air: Cryes of yielding Persons, &c. Cryes of* Carthage *is fal'n,* Carthage, *etc.*' Despite this, the fourth-act 'entertainment' forges ahead when Cumana re-enters '*scratching her face, stabbing a Dagger into her Armes: Spirits following her*'. She sings 'Beneath the poplar's shadow lay me', designed to induce a trance. Continuing in speech, she instructs Hannibal on the defeat of Scipio. To drive home the lesson, she sings a vivid battle song, 'Hark, hark, the drums rattle'. Her energy spent, the priestess gives way to a dance of spirits, but before leaving mutters some enigmatic lines about 'A poyson'd General' who 'rules upon the sand'. (Is this Scipio, Syphax, or Hannibal?) Hannibal responds with a flurry of questions, chief among them: what will become of Rosalinda? Her assistant, Aglave, replies with a pair of Drydenesque couplets:

> Too curious mortal, seek not what once known,
> May snatch your sleep, and make you ever groan.
> Your fate crowds back, and would not come in view,
> Do not too far th'unwilling Gods pursue.

This is remarkably like a passage spoken by the God of Dreams in III.ii of *The Indian Queen*, lines that Purcell would later set as the famous air with oboe obbligato 'Seek not to know what must not be reveal'd' (see Chapter

3). But the couplets are left unsung in *Sophonisba*. Hannibal demands to know the future, and Lee obliges tastelessly: 'Rosalinda *rises in a Chaire pale with a wound on her breast.*' For all its 'slovenly construction and vague motivation', this episode is perfectly operatic.[56] The two lyrics frame the scene grandly, one subdued and mysterious, the other fast, violent, and wildly descriptive, with the flourish of an exit aria; the spoken dialogue resembles linking recitative.

The original music is lost, and Purcell set only 'Beneath the poplar's shadow' (z 590), presumably for an early nineties revival.[57] This composition did not appear in print until 1702, in the second book of *Orpheus Britannicus*, where it is called '*A Mad* SONG', with no indication that the lyric was drawn from *Sophonisba*. Though risking a paradox, I think this piece is a rather routine mad song. It is constructed along the lines of the better-known examples of the genre, 'Let the dreadful engines' and 'From silent shades and the Elysian groves' (*Bess of Bedlam*), namely with a series of sharply contrasting melodies in different metres, interrupted by a central outburst in *secco* recitative. Colourful words such as 'raging', 'swell', and 'fury' are given characteristic roulades. But it is almost too brief to support so many violent shifts of mood. Why did Purcell not set the other lyrics in this scene? Cumana's strategic advice to Hannibal is redundant, because the vision of Act II has already foretold Scipio's victory. And why should he have lavished a musical *double entendre* on Aglave's 'Too curious mortal' speech when its hidden meaning is immediately revealed by the grisly apparition of Rosalinda dead? In this instance Purcell can be exonerated from the criticism that he failed to take advantage of truly operatic moments in the heroic dramas. Hannibal, while at the centre of this episode, is not the tragic hero of this 'grand but sloppy' play (Hume). In Act V Rosalinda, dressed as a man, dies in battle, while the Carthaginian general simply withdraws dejectedly from the action, never to speak again. Gripping as the ceremony in Bellona's Temple may be, it is sealed off at both ends from the drama around it, the rapacious musical scene lacking operatic vision.

The Massacre of Paris

This particularly gruesome tragedy has a complicated early history, much of which is conjectural. About 1680 Lee's politics changed radically from a fiercely Whiggish stance, reflected by *The Massacre of Paris*, to a full endorsement of the Tory view of the succession, zealously alluded to in *The Duke of Guise*. Although the date of composition is uncertain, *The Massacre of Paris* was probably banned in 1681. Lee then used parts of it

---

[56] See Hume, *The Development*, p. 313.

[57] The first edition of the play-book was reprinted several times, including 1693, the likeliest year for the revival with Purcell's song.

in later plays, including *The Duke of Guise*, which reached the stage in November 1682. During much of the mid-eighties, the playwright was in and out of Bedlam, and a few months after his final release in the spring of 1689 *The Massacre of Paris* was finally acted.[58]

The play dramatizes the extermination of the Huguenots during the reign of Charles IX. Its final scenes of mayhem acquire a documentary realism, and only with difficulty can one elevate the Admiral of France to a tragic hero, since he and his followers die without much ceremony in Act V. Nor is there occasion to foreshadow these horrors. One might expect a ghost or conjurer to forewarn the admiral of his fate at the end of Act II. Instead, his wife, Antramont, in a beautiful speech lacking any hint of Drydenesque heroics, recounts a premonition engendered 'not by Visions, Fantoms of the Night, / But by day Arguments, and certain Reason'.

What place has music in such a rock-hard drama? Lee's original script calls for none. Yet Purcell transformed the speech of the Genius in Act V into a song, 'Thy genius, lo!' (z 604A), probably heard at the première in 1689, when Bowman acted this minor role.[59] The king, weak-willed and torn with guilt, tries to oppose his mother's plan to annihilate the Huguenots but realizes after a sleepless night that he can no longer stop the massive conspiracy. While he delivers the play's first sustained passage of rhymed couplets, a certain sign in many post-*Aureng-Zebe* tragedies that the drama is moving into the realm of the supernatural, a genius appears, assuring Charles that a divine power will intervene to save him if he repents. The apparition will travel to Heaven as 'swift as thought' to plead the king's case before the angels, but it concludes, '*Charles* beware, oh dally not with Heav'n, / For after this no Pardon shall be giv'n'. Purcell responded with a grand 'set piece' for baritone, which opens with an expansive recitative in C major, an appropriate key in which to address a king. The poetically insignificant phrase 'And swift as thought' triggers a virtuoso aria in A minor on a modulating ground bass. A recitative then exploits the words 'sad' and 'groan' with an unexpected shift to F minor, while the Genius's parting warning (the beginning of which is given in Example 15) is set to a triple-metre air in C minor, which in its fourth bar begins an ominous descending tetrachord. Armed with the knowledge of Purcell's favourite key associations, could one not predict the outcome of the play from the song? The massacre is accomplished despite the spirit's warning. Though horrified by the Queen Mother's blood-bath, Charles survives, cursing his religion as the play ends. One might, therefore, glance at 'Thy genius, lo!' with the smugness of hindsight and declare that Purcell

---

[58] Hume offers a careful analysis of the relationship between these plays in 'The Satiric Design of Nat. Lee's *The Princess of Cleve*', *Journal of English and Germanic Philology*, 75 (1976), 118–23.

[59] One will recall that he took the part of Atticus in *Theodosius* nearly ten years earlier.

Example 15. *The Massacre of Paris*: 'Thy genius, lo!', first setting, bars 39–47

presages the horror with F minor and the royal torment with the C minor tetrachord, but *not* the king's death, since this piece completely avoids G minor.

In 1695 Purcell made another setting of 'Thy genius, lo!', an eerie, unsettling recitative for the boy Jemmy Bowen, that could hardly be more different from the piece for Bowman. While the baritone gives the troubled king robust, forthright advice sealed with a hearty warning, the later version is detached from Charles's nightmare. But by far the most surprising difference between the settings is that the treble recitative is in G minor. One writer recommends that Purcell's choice of tonalities for these pieces 'should be a matter for reflection by any student of the idea that key and mode should be linked to the affect of the text'.[60] But this apparent weakening of the death-key theory will become in fact a strong confirmation.

The later version is remarkable in several respects, besides being one of the few single lyrics Purcell set entirely in recitative. The dominant is treated equivocally and the avoidance of strong cadences in G minor borders on obsession. The feeling of tonic is already dissipated by the second bar (see Example 16), and despite the six-bar dominant pedal beginning in bar 5, the voice part drifts off into airy F major filigree. At the next cadence in the tonic (Example 17, bars 13–14), the voice eschews the leading-note, though it is supplied on the fourth beat by a continuo figure accidentally omitted in the Purcell Society Edition (xx, 106). Purcell made a curious spoonerism in the third couplet. The original reads:

> So soon as born, she made her self a Shroud,
> The *weeping* Mantle of a *Fleecy* Cloud.

---

[60] Katherine T. Rohrer, 'Interactions of Phonology and Music in Purcell's Two Settings of "Thy Genius, lo"', forthcoming in *Studies in the History of Music*.

Example 16. *The Massacre of Paris*: 'Thy genius, lo!', second setting, bars 1–11

Example 17. *The Massacre of Paris*: 'Thy genius, lo!', second setting, bars 13–14

For the baritone setting in *Orpheus Britannicus*, this is rendered as 'the *fleecy* mantel of a *weeping* cloud', with a brief melisma on 'weeping' (Example 18a). In the later version (Example 18b), Lee's contrasting adjectives are restored to their original places, with 'weeping' being set to ascending chromatics, which is unusual for Purcell, while 'fleecy' receives

Example 18. *The Massacre of Paris*: 'Thy genius, lo!', (a) first setting, bars 15–17, and (b) second setting, bars 18–21 (bass omitted)

an elaborate grace. Either form of the couplet could be sung to the soprano version, but only Purcell's alteration of the original line works well with the baritone setting.

The most striking feature of the soprano song is the avoidance of the tonic minor near the end (see Example 19). The weak cadence in bars 33–4 is immediately raised to G major, and this mode reigns until the close,

Example 19. *The Massacre of Paris*: 'Thy genius, lo!', second setting, bars 33–43

except in bar 40, where the absence of a bass figure implies a G minor chord. The shimmering clashes between B♭ and B♮ in these final bars imbue the recitative with an unsettled feeling. The persistent chromaticism, the cancelled dominant chords, and the modal ambivalence signal unfinished business, thus mirroring the lack of any dramatic resolution in the final scene of the play itself. The baritone setting of 'Thy genius, lo!' would make the better concert piece. Though it begins in C major and ends in the parallel minor, this is a common design for Purcell, and the final section provides a balance for the more remote excursion into flats during the second recitative, 'She told thy story in so sad a tone'. A concert performance of the soprano version, on the other hand, might leave the listener expecting an aria or at least a resolution of the modal conflict. Because it barely ventures into the realm of the dominant, the emphasis on G major in the closing bars causes an unwarranted shift towards the subdominant. And the ascending chromaticism throughout is hardly recompensed by opposite motion.

The appearance of the spirit in the last act of *The Massacre of Paris* is far removed from the conjuration scenes of Dryden's heroic plays. Kalib and Damilcar, though supernatural characters, interact with the protagonists and are thus allowed to alter the course of events, if only slightly. In Lee's drama, the Genius is meant to represent Charles's guilty conscience; it is a theatrical materialization of an uncontrite soul. The second version of 'Thy genius, lo!' captures this torment, while the first merely transmutes it into a *scena*.

iv. New Plays of the Nineties

A tabulation of Purcell's compositions for serious plays produced in the early nineties reveals no predilection for a particular kind of drama, except of course for the semi-opera, of which he was the sole master. He appears to have accepted whatever work came his way, supplying music for a cross-section of good, bad, and mediocre plays, only a few of which – all revivals – require substantial amounts of music. One wonders why the managers and authors of serious drama, with so demonstrably gifted a composer in their midst, demanded so little of him. The answer lies partly in the kinds of tragedies being written at the time. Hume identifies three main types, with much overlapping and many exceptions (*The Development*, p. 397): the heroic, the pathetic, and the classic–stoic. The first group is quite different from the heroic dramas of Dryden and Lee. As far as music is concerned, the most important change is that the plots of the new tragedies are more plausible, less fantastical, following the example of *Aureng-Zebe* rather than *Tyrannick Love*. Ceremonies and conjurations are eased out in favour of violence and comic sub-plots. In the other types – the pathetic and classic–stoic – music fares little better, as songs are typically employed for maudlin effect. But Purcell charges his music with a strain of cynicism that spills over into the surrounding scenes of spoken dialogue, and thereby saves them from excruciating banality.

Distress'd Innocence

After the great success of *Dioclesian* in spring 1690, the Theatre Royal commissioned Purcell to compose most of the music in the new plays produced in the following autumn. One of these, Elkanah Settle's *Distress'd Innocence: or, the Princess of Persia* (October 1690), includes no lyric, but the composer provided an overture and a set of incidental tunes.[61] Luckily, their performance order is known, so it is possible to suggest dramatic roles for at least the act tunes, because in several other plays of the period such pieces, which were performed immediately after each of the first four acts, sometimes reflect the action or mood of the preceding scene.[62]

Settle, who had help from the actor Mountfort in writing the final scene of Act V, attempted to create a tragedy to suit current tastes: heroic pathos is grafted onto a stoic theme. Although the dramatic high points are no more bombastic than those in the better examples of the genre, the plot is meandering and at times incoherent, especially in IV.i. And Settle seems to have allowed the most exciting moments to happen off stage. The story concerns the accession of the princess of Persia to her father's throne. To discredit General Hormidas, a Christian stoic and supporter of the lawful succession, villains put the pagan royal temple to the torch. The innocent Christians' attempt to quench the blaze is regarded as proof of their complicity. This might have been compelling action, but Settle chooses to have it occur between Acts I and II. Whether the first act tune (z 577/2), a C minor air with rather turgid imitation between treble and bass, is meant to depict the temple fire is difficult to say.

During the second interval, time passes to a plaintive slow air, allowing the audience to reflect on Hormidas's fall from general of the armies to camel waterer, punishment for being falsely named as the perpetrator of the temple holocaust. Near the end of Act III, Prince Theodosius recounts witnessing a hunter catch a milk-white stag that mysteriously turned jet-black. Hormidas supposes this a bad omen, and his friend replies with this typically Settlesque verse at the end of the act:

> But hark.
> So loud a Storm my Young Ears never heard,
> Unless these Roarers of the Sky are only
> The Revellers of Heaven, and Tune for Pleasure;
> Some more than Common Cause leads this rough Dance.

[61] In Tenbury MS 785, now on deposit at the Bodleian Library. The first section of this manuscript (fols. 1–24) is perhaps the earliest source of Purcell's act music, since all the pieces recorded here are for plays mounted before 1691: *Amphitryon*, *Distress'd Innocence*, and *The Gordian Knot Untied*.
[62] For a discussion of the function of act tunes, see my *Music in the Restoration Theatre*, pp. 52–61.

Purcell's C minor air (z 577/4) with its agitated bass line of continuous quavers surely depicts the violent storm raging during the interval.

In the fourth act, Hormidas's wife, the rightful heiress to the throne, is drugged and raped by Otrantes. In a scene heavy with pathos, she and Hormidas plan to kill the villain, knowing that this act will seal their own ruin. True to form, Settle defers to Purcell when his dialogue fails him. But the fourth act tune, a jerky hornpipe with a rest on the fifth crotchet of every bar (z 577/5), seems to want too lively a performance for Hormidas's desolation, though one should note that hornpipes were sometimes played slowly.[63]

The incidental music for *Distress'd Innocence* is typical in that the act tunes do not really carry the drama through the intervals, except when special effects are desired, such as the magical storm after Act III. Nor does Purcell make an overt attempt to presage later action in overtures, save possibly those for *Dido and Aeneas* and *Bonduca*. He took the task of writing act music very seriously, however, and during the last five years it provided him with a necessary outlet for his instrumental muse. One can hardly find a single lacklustre piece in the entire *Collection of Ayres*.

Cleomenes

The music for Dryden's stoic tragedy *Cleomenes, the Spartan-Heroe* (April 1692) is meant to connote decadence and corruption. The plot, unbroken by comedy or machines, is the playwright's simplest. Cleomenes, King of Sparta, humiliated in battle against the Macedonians, has fled to Alexandria with his family to seek Egyptian support. But deprived of his kingdom and even of a battlefield upon which to prove his courage, he must repress his heroic tendencies and flail away at his hosts with unquiet diplomacy and sordid bargaining. The focus of his frustration is the slothful Egyptian King Ptolomy, who keeps the Spartan waiting three months for an audience, while doting on the ambitious Cassandra. In an ironic forestalling of Cleomenes's desire to regain power and Ptolomy's haste to make love to his toying mistress, Dryden delays the monarchs' first meeting (II[iii]) while an entertainment of singing and dancing is presented in Cassandra's apartment. The Spartan is sickened by Ptolomy's preoccupation with sex and music.

Purcell's only contribution to this 'exceedingly sober play' is a setting of the lyric 'No, no, poor suff'ring heart' (z 576), the centrepiece of this scene. Though sung by a soprano (Charlotte Butler, in the first production), it clearly expresses Ptolomy's bilious passion for Cassandrà in an extended metaphor on the double meaning of 'death'. Puzzlingly, Purcell gives the lyric a simple strophic setting in D minor, skipping over his favourite musical words ('languish', 'anguish', 'pain' and 'bliss') as if they formed a

---

[63] See my article 'Restoration Stage Fiddlers and Their Music', *Early Music*, 7 (1979), 320.

secular doxology. When he copied it into the Guildhall Library song-book (fol. 15v), the composer made a few minor changes in the rhythm and harmony to add a dash more expression, but this remains one of the few serious songs not to declare its message openly. The memorable though emotionally neutral melody was an ideal vehicle for the ballad mongers, and after the composer's death it enjoyed some popularity.[64]

Only one other episode requires music. In Act III, during an old-fashioned temple scene, Ptolomy and Cassandra have their fortunes told while soft 'instrumental and vocal' music is heard. This does not survive. Perhaps the composer was preoccupied with putting the final touches on *The Fairy-Queen*, which had its première a month after that of *Cleomenes*. For him even to have found time to set 'No, no, poor suff'ring heart' suggests a strong loyalty to Dryden.

Regulus

A month after the gala production of *The Fairy-Queen* opened, Purcell set a song for John Crowne's *Regulus* (June 1692), which resembles *Cleomenes* in its classical theme. But unlike Dryden's play, its plot has a tasteless, low comic thread and two serious ones, both of which are contrived to put the protagonist through various self-induced difficulties that he endures with implausible stoicism. While Carthage is under siege by the invading Roman army, several of the city's most disloyal citizens seek ways to capitalize on the expected conquest. A senator encourages Prince Asdrubal to overthrow the government while it is distracted by the invasion; and Batto lines his pockets by selling arms and supplies to the enemy. For nearly two acts Crowne paints a lurid picture of a corrupt society inviting extermination.

The appearance of the Roman invaders is delayed until the third scene of the second act, which opens with Purcell's song 'Ah me! to many deaths decreed' (z 586), sung to entertain Regulus's mistress, Fulvia. On the surface, the lyric conveys only the mixed pain and joy of being a soldier's consort. She dies many deaths while waiting for him to return from battle, yet would hate him should he prove a coward. Near the end of the song, she tries to disavow its message, commanding a servant to 'bid the Musick cease, I find it vain'. It has an integral role in the drama, presaging Fulvia's behaviour, and even her madness in later acts. Purcell set the pompous, over-passionate lyric strophically, which is all the more remarkable since it is also in his vivid, declamatory style. Though both the early sources of the piece – *The Gentleman's Journal* (August 1692) and *Orpheus Britannicus*, 1 (1698) – print the second verse, the abundant fiorituras might suggest that

---

[64] See Claude M. Simpson, *The British Broadside Ballad and Its Music* (New Brunswick, N.J.: Rutgers Univ. Press, 1966), pp. 513–14.

he did not want it sung.[65] But both verses have the same opening line, and melisma-strewn words appear in the same locations in each stanza, making a strophic performance possible. Still, some adjustment to the underlay of the second verse would be necessary for the passage shown in Example 20. And the oft-repeated words of the final line, 'He kills me', fit the music rather awkwardly. But the cleverness of setting an oxymoronic text strophically is seen in the rhythmically active closing section. The final lines of each verse express exactly opposite sentiments: to paraphrase, 'if my lover stays, I shall hate him' in the first; 'when he is with me, I am overcome with joy' in the second. This anticipates Fulvia's mad scene in Act V. After seeing Regulus die happily under torture, she alternates between sane, rational observation and pathetic raving.

Other noteworthy aspects of the song include its opening 'Ah me!' (shown in Example 21) which is imitated by the accompaniment in an

Example 20. *Regulus*: 'Ah me! to many deaths decreed', bars 15–19 (bass omitted)

Example 21. *Regulus*: 'Ah me! to many deaths decreed', bars 1–5

[65] That he normally took all the verses of his strophic songs seriously may be seen in the Guildhall Library autograph, in which he carefully wrote out the additional stanzas at the end of the music.

undecorated form. In the Purcell Society Edition (XXI, 51) the first bass note is tied over into the second bar, thus obscuring the point of imitation. The tie is found in neither of the early sources and should be removed. A few bars later, the brave roulades on 'war', which Crowne neatly works into the same position in each stanza, foreshadow Fulvia's otherwise unexpected transformation into a 'virgin warrior' in Act V. The obsessive anapaestic rhythm of the final section is probably meant to suggest her eventual insanity, since this repetitive figure is often heard in the fast sections of other mad songs (for example, in 'From rosy bowers').

That Fulvia survives at the end of the play may account for the avoidance of G minor in a song concerned chiefly with death. The music even shuns the tonic note itself. In the first five bars the bass descends an octave, touching each diatonic degree except G (see Example 21). And later in bars 15–17 an ascending scale bolts as it approaches the note of doom, plunging to an A just as the word 'die' is uttered. Fulvia will suffer many deaths during the course of the drama, but only figuratively.

After hearing Mrs Ayliff sing 'Ah me! to many deaths decreed', Motteux, the editor of *The Gentleman's Journal*, remarked 'there is no pleasure like that which good Notes, when so divinely sung, can create'. He also describes it as being set 'the *Italian* way'. In Chapter 1 I expressed the doubt that we shall ever know exactly what Motteux meant by 'Italian' and whether it applies specifically to this song or generally to Purcell's vocal style in the early nineties. I should guess, however, that he was referring to the ornamented vocal line of the declamatory section. Consider Tope's less polite remarks in Thomas Shadwell's contemporary comedy *The Scowrers* (*c.* December 1690), III.i: 'I hate these melancholy, foolish love Madrigals, with damn'd imitation of the Italians quavering and division.' A century later Burney describes this style as 'only *recitative* graced, or embellished with the fashionable *volate*, or *flourishes* of the times', with no implication that it was particularly Italianate.[66]

Henry the Second

In the autumn of 1692 Purcell was hard at work on his Ode for St Cecilia's Day (22 November) but also found time to set a song for a new play, *Henry the Second, King of England*, which had its première in early November. The author is unknown, but the actor William Mountfort, whom Purcell had known since at least 1688, probably brought it to the stage.[67] Historical plays, especially new ones, were not particularly fashionable in the early nineties. But *Henry the Second* is a surprisingly fine drama with exciting, realistic action, workmanlike verse, carefully developed characters, a

---

[66] *A General History of Music*, II, 392.
[67] For a discussion of the authorship, see Judith Milhous and Robert D. Hume, 'Attribution Problems in English Drama, 1660–1700', *Harvard Library Bulletin*, 31 (1983), 19.

biting, timely satire on the clergy, and a comic sub-plot beautifully dovetailed with the tragic catastrophe. The story centres on Rosamond, Henry II's mistress, victim of the king's lust and Queen Eleanore's jealousy, fanned into vengeance by a traitorous abbot. The anonymous playwright portrays Rosamond as a virtuous heroine, drawn unwillingly into an affair with a king who cowers at his wife's aggressive attempts to preserve the royal marriage. The plotting abbot is blamed for Rosamond's destruction, but her anguish is clearly caused by the king.

'In vain 'gainst Love I strove' (z 580) is not printed in the 1693 play-book, but the earliest source for the music, *Comes Amoris*, IV (1693), describes it as 'A New Song, Sung by Mrs. *Dyer* in the new Play call'd *Henry* the 2^{d}'. Barclay Squire was uncertain about its location in the drama, but the song was obviously performed in the second scene of Act III.[68] Rosamond, acted by Mrs Bracegirdle, who often portrayed sympathetic maidens whose virtue is under constant assault, is lamenting her plight.[69] She resolves to resist the king's advances and preserve her honour, even though she loves him:

> Oh! could Men guess the terror we endure,
> What 'twixt our Honour and our Love we suffer,
> They sure would prize each generous Maid much more,
> And, as their Souls, indulge them to the last.

She then asks an attendant to sing 'that Song I gave thee th'other day, / And if thou canst, charm me into a slumber'. Here then should follow Purcell's 'In vain 'gainst Love', which in fact continues the love-versus-honour debate, but tipping the balance firmly in favour of love. In the first quatrain, the singer weighs the strong objections to her desire posed by reason; in the second, she acknowledges the superior strength of the heart. The song opens stolidly in C minor (see Example 22).[70] The easy move to the relative major in bar 6 is of course an obligatory gesture, but the following five bars of tonal ambivalence capture perfectly Rosamond's studied indecision, as the music rocks back and forth between the two keys. By the cadence in E♭ in bar 11, coming at the end of one of Purcell's most felicitous melismas, Rosamond has completely succumbed to love. The second part, a brisk triple-metre air, moves gradually upward to confirm the decision already made in the first half, achieving high F at the word 'louder'. The song is not difficult and Mrs Bracegirdle could probably have performed it herself. But *Henry the Second* was produced a few seasons before this leading lady felt confident enough to deliver her own songs. Even though this one was left to an attendant, it is still the turning point of the main plot.

[68] 'Purcell's Dramatic Music', p. 528.
[69] For a discussion of type-casting in the serious plays of the eighties and nineties, see Eric Rothstein, *Restoration Tragedy* (Madison: Univ. of Wisconsin Press, 1967), pp. 141–4.
[70] Source: Guildhall Library autograph.

Example 22. *Henry the Second*: 'In vain 'gainst Love I strove', bars 1–11

The Fatal Marriage

Southerne's *The Fatal Marriage: or, the Innocent Adultery* (February 1694), a domestic tragedy set in seventeenth-century Brussels, is one of the best plays of the period. The plot is taken from a novel by Aphra Behn, a skilled spinner of sentimental tales on whose contrived pathos Southerne puts a hard edge. Purcell's music, which lies at the heart of the drama, would almost certainly be misinterpreted without some knowledge of the plot. Isabella, a former nun and a woman of low station, is married to Biron, who has been missing for several years, presumably killed in battle. Destitute and with a young child to support, she mourns for her husband and stubbornly rejects the entreaties of honest Villeroy, who wants to marry the 'widow'. Her father-in-law, the wealthy Count Baldwin, cruelly refuses to relieve her poverty, while her brother-in-law, Carlos, a wolf in sheep's clothing, harbours the knowledge that his brother, Isabella's husband, is alive but in bondage. If Biron buys his freedom and returns to Brussels, Carlos plans to murder him for his inheritance, first seeing his sister-in-law married safely out of the family. Isabella is finally left no choice but to marry Villeroy.

The Fatal Marriage is a 'hip-hop' play. Interpolated between the scenes of the tragic plot is a seemingly unrelated comedy, a lantern-and-mask affair in which Fernando is tricked into letting his daughter marry against his will. After a couple of acts jumping from one story to the other, one realizes that the plots are simply 'parallel tales told in different keys' (Hume, *The Development*, p. 403), and Southerne makes certain that no one will miss the irony. The only scene in which characters from the two stories intermingle is the wedding celebration in III.ii, a dramatic *tour de force*. Villeroy is truly happy, but the guilt-ridden Isabella is barely able to conceal her melancholy. The musicians and servants sense this undercurrent, and the bridegroom is forced to buy their mirth. But Carlos, the evil matchmaker and jubilant best man, has much to celebrate now that Isabella's disinheritance is assured. For their epithalamium, he provides the newly-weds with a waggish sonnet 'pretty well to the purpose':

> The danger is over, the Battle is past,
> The Nymph had her fears, but she ventur'd at last.
> . . .
> By her Eyes we discover that she has been pleas'd,
> Her blushes become her, her feelings are eas'd,
> She dissembles her joy, and affects to look down:
> If she Sighs, 'tis for sorrow 'tis ended so soon.[71]

And so the song continues with a string of tasteless ironies. Later in the nuptial scene, after an entertainment of dancing, 'I sigh'd and own'd my love' is heard. Though a conventional love song, it also takes note of the emotional undertow.

Following the psychological maelstrom of the wedding party, Southerne lets events propel the rest of the drama. Biron returns to Brussels not knowing that his wife has committed 'innocent adultery' the night before. Isabella's agony, so convincingly conveyed at the première by Elizabeth Barry that she 'forc'd Tears from the Eyes of her Auditory', ends in madness and suicide. Biron discovers Carlos's treachery but is killed by him. Villeroy rants and Count Baldwin repents.

A champion of the play has to admit that 'we may be left tearful, but we are never deeply moved', because 'there is almost no internal conflict; this

---

[71] In the 1694 quarto the penultimate couplet reads: 'By her Eyes we discover the Bride has been pleas'd; / Her blushes become her, her passion is eas'd'.

is a tragedy almost entirely of circumstances . . .' (Hume, *The Development*, pp. 402–3). One may not be moved by the music either, but Purcell's songs avoid the excessive pathos of the final scene. The first, Carlos's impertinent epithalamium 'The danger is over' (z 595/1), is cast as a bustling D minor jig (sung by the soprano Mrs Hudson). The setting is routine, but the second verse does not fit comfortably with the tune, especially the opening line: the F major trumpet-call for 'the battle is past' awkwardly bears the words 'both aged and young'.

'I sigh'd and own'd my love' (z 595/2) is a long lyric of ecstatic love that turns sour. It opens with aspirated off-beat sighs that are obviously meant to give voice to Villeroy's emotions. The teeth-rattling clash in bar 7 of Example 23[72] is perhaps intended to reflect the underlying irony of the

Example 23. *The Fatal Marriage*: 'I sigh'd and own'd my love', bars 1–8

celebration. A casual listener would surely think the continuo player had made a mistake, but one familiar with the play might argue that this is Purcell's acknowledgement of Villeroy's dreadfully misguided love for Isabella, an interpretation that places a great burden on the quaver F♮ in bar 7. Clashes between the leading-note and the lowered seventh degree are fairly common in English music of the period, though not in pieces in G major. In fact, these grinding dissonances occur most often in G minor

[72] Source: *Thesaurus Musicus*, III (1695).

(see, for instance, Example 6 above). Regardless of key, leading-note con-
flicts need not necessarily have unpleasant connotations. Blow, for example, occasionally treats them as delicate ornaments.[73] And even in the
written-out continuo realization for Purcell's 'How pleasant is this flow'ry
plain' (z 543/2) that Ian Spink found in the Bodleian Library's copy of
The Banquet of Musick, I (1688), an anonymous harpsichordist invented
an embellishment whose dissonance would make most modern players
wince.[74] Even though the F♮ in bar 7 of Example 23 is thus dramatically
efficacious and stylistically possible, I must report that the blue note,
which is found in the earliest printed source, is not included in Purcell's
autograph, the Guildhall Library song-book (fol. 53v). Yet I cannot believe that it is an error. Perhaps Purcell simply found that what had seemed
an appropriate theatrical gesture later became an unwanted distraction.
Interpretation of the rest of 'I sigh'd and own'd my love' need be less
speculative. The music shifts to G minor for the lines 'But, Oh, her change
destroys / The Charming prospect of my promis'd Joys'. The new key and
the angular, widely disjointed lines of both treble and bass produce a
sombreness that is hardly dispelled by the warbling G major jig that ends
the piece.

The last scene of *The Fatal Marriage* is so charged with pathos and
blood-stained irony that a modern audience, however captivated by four
and a half acts of gripping drama, would feel little more for Isabella than
they would for the Princess Huncamunca in Fielding's *Tom Thumb*. But
Purcell's great song in Act III avoids all sentimentalism. It is both a bitter
harbinger of Isabella's fate and 'a soft engaging air'.

The Rival Sisters

With the secession of Betterton and the other veteran actors from the
Theatre Royal in spring 1695 (see Chapter 1), competition once again influenced the kinds of dramas the companies produced. The rebel troupe
decided to concentrate on new plays, while the young actors who remained
with Rich at Drury Lane struck out in several directions – musicals, new
tragedies and comedies, as well as adaptations. Robert Gould's tragedy
The Rival Sisters: or, the Violence of Love (October 1695) belongs to the
last group. Though it is based on James Shirley's *The Maid's Revenge,*
the two plays are barely comparable: both are blood-baths, but the catalyst
of the violence is quite different in each work. Gould has not simply
grafted 'pathos and sentiment onto an old play' (Hume, *The Development*, p. 424) but has created a substantially novel drama in which music

[73] See, for example, Cupid's recitative 'Come, all ye Graces!', near the end of Act II of *Venus
and Adonis*.
[74] See *English Song Dowland to Purcell*, pp. 216–17, and Peter Holman, 'Continuo Realizations in a Playford Songbook', *Early Music*, 6 (1978), 268–9.

takes an important part. He was obviously encouraged to fashion a work to exploit the Theatre Royal's most valuable asset in the autumn of 1695: its chief composer, Purcell.

The play, which is set in Portugal, examines the tragic consequences of the custom that the eldest daughter must be the first to marry. Vilarezo, a wealthy landowner, has promised his daughter Catalina that she may wed the dashing Spaniard Antonio, who has already fallen in love with her younger sister, Berinthia, thus fostering a vicious sibling rivalry. In keeping with the Restoration theatre's predilection for pairs of star-crossed lovers, Gould provides Antonio with a sister, Alphanta, a flighty, promiscuous adolescent whom Antonio suggests as a lover for Berinthia's brother, Sebastian. This tangle of liaisons is further complicated by Alphanta's betrothed, Alonzo, a character not found in Shirley's play. The spurned lover's bizarre attempt to reclaim the perfidious Alphanta's affections provides a raison d'être for much of the music.

Even though they are delivered by attendants, the lyrics are designed to reveal the unspoken thoughts of the principal characters. In Act I Catalina, who emerges as an arch-villainess, is indignant when her sister claims Antonio's heart. But instead of lashing out at Berinthia, she turns to her maid for consolation, asking her to have someone 'sing that Song I gave thee, / For 'tis a Glass where I may see my Folly'. No setting of the pathetic lyric 'Not tho' I know he fondly lies' is known.

The second act opens in a grove where Sebastian is resting after the hunt. Alonzo arrives in search of his unfaithful fiancée, Alphanta. Disguised and behaving like a lunatic, he is travelling with a little boy, a role apparently created for Jemmy Bowen, to whom he occasionally turns for music. Alonzo's speech is extravagant babble, but the boy's coherent songs are meant to convey his master's true emotions. The first is 'Celia has a thousand charms' (z 609/10): to lie in his beloved's arms is ecstasy; but he is on his guard, for 'she is more false than fair'. The work received pride of place in the first book of *Orpheus Britannicus*, and Burney reports that during his youth it was one of Purcell's most admired songs. Of the abundant embellishments of the opening recitative, the critic writes that they 'are now as antiquated as the curls of [Purcell's] own peruque, or the furbelows and flounces of Queen Elizabeth' (*A General History*, II, 392). Burney rarely pulls his punches, even when discussing the music of composers he admires, and his sneer at the frilly pomposity of the first section of 'Celia has a thousand charms' should not be entirely dismissed. With these exaggerated *passaggi* Purcell suggests Alonzo's purposely overstated passion for Alphanta. In the air proper, which Burney concedes is 'plaintive and graceful', are expressed simpler, more direct emotions ungarnished with 'fashionable *volate*'. The 'broken-record' setting of 'wretched' with its sinuous cross-relations is as stylized as the antiquated

curls depicting 'thousand', but Burney considers the passage shown in Example 24 'still new and pathetic'. The key of G minor is not particularly gloomy in this piece, though in the opening recitative the descent of the bass line through nearly three octaves (with register displacements) is awe-inspiring.

Example 24. *The Rival Sisters*: 'Celia has a thousand charms', bars 34–9

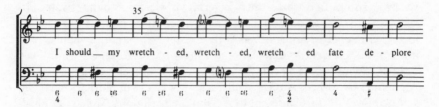

Burney may have misunderstood this recitative in part because he was ignorant of its dramatic context. But he also misleads the reader by calling Purcell's ornaments 'fashionable . . . *flourishes* of the times'. Except for Blow, no other late seventeenth-century English composer was writing anything remotely like Purcell's embellished declamatory airs. They were fashionable only to him, yet quintessentially baroque. Why he should have favoured Jemmy Bowen with such opulent music is puzzling. Sir John Hawkins, who was no champion of English vocalists, sought to document the shortcomings of theatre singers such as Miss Cross, Mrs Bracegirdle, and Miss Campion by citing Purcell's songs in which one 'will find the graces written at length, a manifest proof that in the performance of them little was meant to be trusted to the singer'.[75] By contrast, Anthony Aston's oft-quoted anecdote about the boy seems to contradict Hawkins's claim that Purcell could not trust his singers to invent embellishments:

. . . when practising a Song set by Mr. *Purcell*, some of the Music told him to grace and run a Division in such a Place. *O let him alone*, said Mr. *Purcell*; *he will grace it more naturally than you, or I, can teach him.*[76]

I should think that the 'division' mentioned by the musicians trying to help young Bowen was not the kind of grand melisma found in 'Celia has a thousand charms', but rather a simple grace such as a shake or slide.

Purcell set two other lyrics for *The Rival Sisters*. 'Take not a woman's anger ill' (z 609/11) is a boisterous song meant to be sung in Act IV by Gerardo, a comic servant first portrayed by Benjamin Johnson, but apparently sung for him by Richard Leveridge.[77] The other is 'How happy is

[75] *A General History of the Science and Practice of Music* (1776; rpt New York: Dover, 1963), II, 815–16. Note that Mrs Bracegirdle sang exclusively the music of Eccles, and Miss Campion did not take the stage until after Purcell's death.

[76] *A Brief Supplement to Colley Cibber, An Apology*, ed. Robert W. Lowe (1889; rpt New York: AMS, 1966), II, 312.   [77] See *Deliciae Musicae*, III (1696).

she' (z 609/12), which was not printed in the 1696 quarto. Although sung by Miss Cross (then aged thirteen), who acted Alphanta, its location in the drama is uncertain. It is a mild bit of child pornography, this form of which was enjoying some vogue at the time.

Purcell did not set the most important lyric in the play. After Alonzo and the boy leave the grove in Act II, Antonio enters lamenting his predicament: he loves Berinthia but must marry her elder sister. To ease his melancholy, Sebastian has arranged an antic dance of woodsmen and a dialogue between a nymph and a shepherd. The lyric 'To me y'ave made a thousand vows' shows some stock Arcadiana: a shepherdess fears that her swain loves another; he confesses a desire for one 'Caelia', asking his mate, 'how cou'd my Passion injure you?' She reminds him that marriage is a sacred vow. The not-so-innocent dialogue looks forward to Antonio's being tricked into marrying Catalina. John Blow transformed this banter into a long, elaborate piece published in his *Amphion Anglicus* (1700) and presumably included in the October 1695 première of *The Rival Sisters*. It is called *'A Dialogue between a Man and his Wife'*, thereby fixing a rather plainer connection with Antonio's dilemma than perhaps Gould intended. Blow chose F major, the traditional pastoral key, but exercised considerable licence in adding a verse to the original lyric. For these lines, the 'wife' is joined by a second soprano:

> Away then all Fondness, I find tis in vain;
> For Wives when neglected to sigh and complain,
> We raise the loose Wishes we strive to restrain.

The added singer probably represents Catalina, and the 'wife', Berinthia, both of whom reject Antonio in Act V – the former because she knows he loves another, the latter because he has married her sister. This fine piece would never be mistaken for Purcell, but in the chorus Blow paints the conflicting emotions of the shepherd and shepherdess with persistent touches of F minor (the horror key), which intrudes in this scene of sylvan repose (see Example 25). As Tovey says of Beethoven's piano sonata Op. 28, the dialogue is 'on the whole, about as pastoral as Jane Austen'.

Blow did not compose much theatre music during the nineties, and I should guess he set the dialogue in an emergency as a favour to his former pupil, who was under great pressure at the Theatre Royal during the last months of his life. Purcell's haste is also reflected by the act music for *The Rival Sisters*. For the curtain tune he borrowed the overture to *Love's goddess sure was blind*, the 1692 Ode for Queen Mary's Birthday (z 331/1). The rest of the incidental music survives in two manuscripts whose ascriptions are not trustworthy. Zimmerman believes that these eight tunes, of which only treble and bass parts survive, are not up to the composer's usual standard (*An Analytical Catalogue*, p. 288); they cer-

Example 25. John Blow, *Amphion Anglicus*, 'To me you made a thousand vows', chorus,
bars 1-9

tainly have a few awkward passages. But without the inner voices, which
more than anything else distinguish Purcell's four-part orchestral writing
from that of his contemporaries, the question of authorship must remain
open.

Oroonoko

For its second new tragedy of the 1695–6 season, the Theatre Royal turned
to Southerne, the author of the fine domestic drama *The Fatal Marriage*,
which the company had produced two years before. Again the playwright
drew upon a novel by Aphra Behn, another 'hip-hop' story; but in *Oroonoko* (November 1695) the nearly autonomous comic and serious plots are
brought together at various points to give different perspectives on the
tragic action. Purcell's contribution to this very successful play, mounted
during the final month of his life, is a pornographic dialogue for children.
'Celemene, pray tell me' (z 584) is discussed here in the chapter on serious
dramas instead of later in the one on the music for comedies because
Southerne, always the innovator, introduces this erotic entertainment not
into the comic plot, as one might expect, but into the tragic one.

The play, set in the West Indies, is a vigorous attack on slavery, but the stratification within the slave and master societies is borrowed from contemporary drama. The evil lieutenant governor of colonial Surinam is like the tyrant of an heroic play. In the comic plot, the Welldon sisters have immigrated to the island to search for husbands because they have become notorious and shopworn in London. These clever characters from a Covent Garden comedy make fools of the Widow Lackitt and her booby son Daniel. Below them is the vile slave-trader Captain Driver. A similar pecking order exists among the slaves. Oroonoko, an African prince and, ironically, a slave-trader himself before his capture, is every inch a tragic protagonist, even speaking heroic verse. Hottman, Aboan, and the other blacks are of a much lower station, and it is Hottman who betrays Oroonoko's noble rebellion. As Novak and Rodes remark, the other singing and dancing slaves appearing in Act II are like the shepherds and shepherdesses of the pastoral or the Incas and Aztecs of the heroic tragedy.[78] Occupying the bottom of the heap, and thereby weakening Southerne's righteous indignation, are the natives of Surinam, the Indians, who try to plunder the plantations only to be butchered by the hero.

The character on whom the plot centres and to whom the music in the second act is offered is Clemene, a beautiful slave girl desired by the lieutenant governor. She is in fact Imoinda, Oroonoko's bride, sold into slavery by the hero's father when she refused to join his harem. In yet another twist, Imoinda, who has not seen her husband since their wedding day, is white, a condition that presumably added to her troubles with her black father-in-law. Since her arrival in Surinam, she has been gripped with melancholy. In an attempt to lift her spirits, the governor orders some slaves to perform a proto-minstrel show (II.iii).

The lyrics printed in the play-book, neither of which is by Southerne, are not particularly apropos. Both are pastoral love songs that stay well within the bounds of good taste. Sir Harry Sheer's 'A Lass there lives upon the Green' was set by Ralph Courteville and sung by Jemmy Bowen (D&M No. 1925); Thomas Cheek's 'Bright Cynthia's Pow'r' (D&M No. 418), from the same composer, was sung by Leveridge. Courteville, who also collaborated with Purcell on *3 Don Quixote* at about this time, is a happy discovery. Both songs are melodious and harmonically secure, and the word-setting is decidedly Purcellian. In fact no other composer of his generation comes quite so close to the master's melodic style, not just in the profusion of ornaments but, more important, in the choice of words on which the extended graces fall. Courteville is also the only other composer known to have written for the boy before Purcell died.

The text of Purcell's dialogue, which is by Durfey, is not printed in

[78] *Oroonoko*, ed. Maximillian E. Novak and David Stuart Rodes (Lincoln: Univ. of Nebraska Press, 1976), p. xxxiv.

Southerne's 1696 quarto but is linked with the play in all the printed sources of the music, except the single-sheet engraving mentioned above in connection with *The Conquest of Granada*.[79] Unlike Courteville's songs, 'Celemene, pray tell me' is closely related to the drama. (Note the similarity between 'Celemene' and Imoinda's slave name, 'Clemene'.) The purposely tasteless text underscores the governor's boorishness and confirms his sexual interest in Oroonoko's wife. The dialogue, performed by Bowen and the teen-aged Miss Cross, describes the sexual awakening of a pubescent boy and girl. Their arousal is essentially innocent and the verse avoids the prurient vein, but it proved too erotic for the editor of Vol. XXI of the Purcell Society Edition, Alan Gray, who asked R. A. Streatfeild to supply some polite Edwardian phrases in a few sensitive places. The censorship tells more about the censor than about the objectionable work itself, and Gray obviously ordered the alterations because of the delicate age of the singers. As mentioned earlier, children were often exploited in plays of the period, and, like Dryden in *Cleomenes*, some playwrights relied on a starving or wounded child to bring out the handkerchiefs. Perhaps the dialogue is a cynical comment on the over-use of young actors in creating pathetic effects. Several simple musical devices suggest the boy's incipient desire, chief among them a quick rising three-note figure. The most explicit word-

Example 26. *Oroonoko*: 'Celemene, pray tell me', bars 85–102

79 See Zimmerman, *An Analytical Catalogue*, pp. 261–2.

painting occurs in the boy's solo just after Celemene has allowed him a first kiss. The unsettling abandonment of the dominant in bar 93 of Example 26 and the undulating cross-relations soon thereafter reflect the singer's growing frustration. At the end of the piece, when Celemene joins the boy in a lithe duet shown in Example 27, the composer sets the closing line to a beguiling harmonic formula. Purcell achieves so much passion here by such simple means that analysis almost spoils the effect.

Example 27. *Oroonoko*: 'Celemene, pray tell me', bars 150–4

Most of James Paisible's act music for the play survives, and fortunately the order of the tunes is known.[80] Because the play exhibits 'mirth in one scene and distress in another', the composer seems to have made some attempt to tailor the incidental tunes to the mood of the action they follow, especially the fourth act tune.[81] In the last scene of Act IV, Oroonoko is persuaded to abandon his rebellion and surrender in consideration of Imoinda, who is now pregnant. But this is a ploy by the lieutenant governor to separate the couple so he may ravish the hero's wife. Their wrenching scene of parting is punctuated by Paisible's G minor tune, the only one of the suite marked 'slow'. Its dissonant inner parts and prominent 'lament bass' would seem to have their usual functions, since both Oroonoko and Imoinda die in the next act.

Pausanias

Among Purcell's last works are two vocal pieces for the tragedy *Pausanias*, probably by the insignificant playwright Richard Norton. The flood of theatre music produced during the composer's final summer and autumn lacks nothing in quality, and the forgotten play includes one of his greatest songs, 'Sweeter than roses' (z 585/1). The publication of the play-book was not advertised until May 1696, but the première may have taken place earlier. Laurie believes that a reference in the prologue to hot weather suggests a summer production – June or early July 1695.[82] But the opening couplet ('New Plays have been so frequent, all this Season; / We must be-

[80] See my *Music in the Restoration Theatre*, pp. 208–9.
[81] For discussions of the play's sudden changes of mood, see *Oroonoko*, ed. Novak and Rodes, pp. xix ff, and Rothstein, *Restoration Tragedy*, pp. 146–7.
[82] 'Purcell's Stage Works', pp. 223–4.

lieve You'r tir'd, and you have Reason') seems more appropriate to spring 1696 than to the preceding summer.

The author of *Pausanias* attempted to follow the neo-heroic formula, even mixing in a vaguely parallel comic plot, but his plan went terribly wrong in the last act. Pausanias, the regent of Sparta, is enticed by the prospect of marrying a Persian princess, a favour promised if he will plot to overthrow his own government. He is betrayed by his mistress, Pandora, even after his friend and counsellor Argilius has warned him of the double-cross. Norton pays out too much of the plot too soon: Pandora quits the action in IV.iii, and the comic sub-plot dries up almost as soon as it begins. He is then forced to set Act V entirely in Neptune's temple, conveying thither reports of the culminating catastrophes, all of which happen off stage. The only character worthy of note is Pandora, whose Poppea-like ambition and total lack of sentimentality set her apart from the other leading women in the classic–heroic plays of the early nineties. She and Pausanias are nearing the end of a stormy affair; their first scene together (II.ii) is a well-drawn sketch of a couple whose past quarrels have left them able only to reiterate intransigent positions. She now has designs on Argilius, both for passion's sake and in order to blackmail him into conspiring with the Persians.

The lyrics at the beginning of Act III have only one purpose: to fire Pandora's sexual desire while she awaits the arrival of her intended lover, Argilius. The first describes the effects of a 'dear kiss', and the second is an amorous dialogue in which the singers promise to be ever true. The utter passion, not to mention the masterful construction, of 'Sweeter than roses' suggest that Purcell did not realize that it was intended merely as an aphrodisiac for the treacherous Pandora. Despite the serious shortcomings of the plot, Norton concentrates in the lyric an astounding variety of those words and images that Purcell had often singled out for special treatment in earlier songs. The ones in the opening quatrain are shown in italics:

> *Sweeter* than *Roses*, or *cool Evening's breeze*,
> On a *warm Flowery* Shore,
> Was the *dear Kiss*, first *trembling* made me *freeze*,
> Then *shot* like *Fire all o're*.

The characteristic melismas, the exotic harmony, and the liberal chromaticism meld into an unforgettable evocation of suspended ecstasy. This is partly achieved by an economy of motif and rhythm, in contrast with the abundance of poetic riches. The rising semiquavers of 'sweeter' in bar 8 are inverted for 'warm' in bar 12 and used again later for 'trembling'. When the opening line is repeated, the melismas on 'roses' and 'cool' are trimmed down, whereas 'evening', set syllabically the first time, is given a full bar.

The most attention is lavished on 'dear', repeated four times, first to a syncopated slide heard earlier with 'cool', and finally to a falling diminished fifth used before in the 'evening' melisma. The central importance of this passage is confirmed in the second part of the song. The brief foray into Eb minor at the word 'freeze' can still shock modern listeners, and it stands in sharpest possible relief to the leaping triads of the closing flourish. Burney would not have described this declamatory air as a *recitative* grac'd', because the fiorituras are not mere decorations; they are the words themselves.

The virtuoso C major strain that follows, 'What magic has victorious Love', is comprised of long, exuberant phrases. The rhythm hurries the song to a conclusion, interrupted only when the singer mentions the 'dear kiss' (see Example 28). The striding music pauses to recall the passionate moment depicted in the recitative.

While this song transforms Norton's cliché-strewn lyric into something noble, the following duet returns to Pandora's erotic reverie. Ascribed to Daniel Purcell in one early manuscript, 'My dearest, my fairest' (z 585/2) is an anticlimax, but is admirable for its lilting rhythms and delicious supensions at the phrase 'I languish for thee.'[83] The duetting lovers ask why love's rapture is so short and sweet. Despite their mutual promises, the woman finally voices her fear of abandonment, thereby presaging Argilius's steadfast refusal to be ensnared by Pandora's charms. The

Example 28. *Pausanias*: 'Sweeter than roses', bars 55–9

Example 29. *Pausanias*: 'My dearest, my fairest', bars 41–4

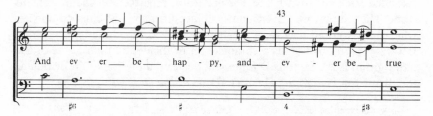

[83] This passage is garbled in the Purcell Society Edition, XXI, 47: bar 8 should be omitted. The attribution to Daniel Purcell is in Nanki MS 3/27, which dates from about 1700.

setting of the singers' pledge, shown in Example 29, is especially cynical. Parallel sevenths before cadences – what Morley calls 'exasperating the close' – are common in Purcell's part-songs, and the prodigious string of dissonances in bar 43 is an ironical aside to the text, but it hardly proves his authorship.[84]

The music for the ceremony in Neptune's temple in Act V is certainly Daniel Purcell's, and surprisingly good, though I fail to see the point of the scene itself.[85] The solemn C minor symphony begins with a majestic point of imitation and, except for a nasty set of consecutives in the sixth bar, is a skilful bit of part-writing. The baritone solos for the presiding priest are highly ornamented but seem to rise and fall to little purpose. The choral responds are similarly workmanlike. After the death of Henry Purcell, the production of music at the Theatre Royal seems barely to have missed a beat. Daniel's initial reception was enthusiastic, and he was entrusted with all his late brother's responsibilities, including composing new semi-operas. The devastating effect of the loss on the course of English dramatic music would not be felt for another ten years.

v. Patent Company Revivals of 1695

The new tragedies produced at Drury Lane in the months following the 1695 establishment of the rival company occupied relatively little of Purcell's time. His chief task was to supply music for revivals. Like the major shows of this season, *Bonduca* and *The Indian Queen*, the less ambitious serious dramas restaged in the spring and early autumn appear to have been chosen largely with an eye to musical scenes. They are a motley assortment with nothing in common save Purcell's rejuvenating music.

Abdelazer

The first play produced at Drury Lane after the actors' rebellion and the state mourning for Queen Mary was Aphra Behn's twenty-year-old *Abdelazer, or the Moor's Revenge*, probably on 1 April 1695. It clearly signalled Rich's plans for the Theatre Royal repertoire in the months to come. The old play was given a musical face-lifting by the chief composer, who wrote a grand new song for Jemmy Bowen, 'Lucinda is bewitching fair' (z 570/10), as well as a complete set of incidental tunes. One of the latter group is the famous D minor rondeau used by Benjamin Britten as the theme for *The Young Person's Guide to the Orchestra*, Op. 34.

---

[84] On 'exasperated cadences', see Peter Dennison, '[Purcell:] The Stylistic Origins of the Early Church Music', in *Essays on Opera and English Music* (Oxford: Blackwell, 1975), p. 55.

[85] In Tenbury MS 1175, pp. 71-9.

Abdelazer is perhaps the bloodiest of all Restoration plays. To call it a tragedy is to dignify the protagonist's crimes: he commits adultery with Queen Isabella of Spain, poisons her husband, solicits lovers for his own wife, deceives everyone, and utters unremitting contumely. His Julius Caesar-like assassination in Act V is long overdue. Mrs Behn so exaggerates horrific event that the dramatis personae seem like caricatures and the action little more than black humour. The music is meant to torment Abdelazer. As the drama opens the ruthless Moorish warrior, who later professes to hate 'all softness', is forced to listen to an effeminate song, 'Love in Phantastique Triumph sat' (which does not survive). Later in the scene when Queen Isabella tries to seduce him, she unknowingly insults his masculinity by having the musicians 'Play all your sweetest Notes, such as inspire / The active Soul with new and soft desire, / Whilst we from Eyes – thus – dying, fan the fire.' The most important scene with music is the banquet in II.ii. Fernando, who has ascended the throne upon the suspicious death of his father, is celebrating his coronation. Yet he is despondent because his beloved, Florella, has married Abdelazer. The king's entertainment is thus intended to nettle the villain, and its centrepiece, the long pastoral dialogue 'Make haste Amintas', is a veiled allegory of the love triangle. The shepherd represents King Fernando and the nymph, Florella. After the music, Abdelazer, disgusted by the underhanded attack on his virility, orders Florella home to bed with him. Francis Forcer's setting of the dialogue (D&M No. 2158) leaves much to be desired, but even a great composer would have difficulty with Mrs Behn's lengthy, undifferentiated verse. The F major air begins bravely, but stumbles at least once in each of the four sections, adding support to Spink's harsh judgement that Forcer's songs 'are among the feeblest written by any composer of the period' (*English Song Dowland to Purcell*, p. 178).

Barclay Squire argues that Purcell's 'Lucinda is bewitching fair' replaced 'Love in Phantastique Triumph sat' in Act I ('Purcell's Dramatic Music', p. 495), but I believe it substituted for the pastorale in the second act. Not only does it retain Forcer's refrain structure, but in the later song Philander and Strephon are rivals for the fair Lucinda, a barefaced reference to the love triangle. Furthermore, Purcell's anonymous lyricist puts the rivals on an equal footing for the shepherdess's affection and thereby foreshadows the power Abdelazer will soon acquire through treachery. 'Lucinda is bewitching fair' is cool and detached, with none of the pathos or passion of the other great pieces for Jemmy Bowen. Purcell seems more concerned with faultless technique, and the measured graces draped on almost every expressible word smell faintly of the lamp. This is not the only time he retreated into stilted formality when confronted with characters in which he saw little potential for musical elucidation (see the discussion of *The Libertine* in Chapter 3). Collective expression of pathos, irony, jealousy, grief, eroticism, and so on was not Purcell's strong suit. His most moving music is almost always focussed on individuals.

The Spanish Fryar

That Purcell's setting of 'Whilst I with grief did on you look' (z 610) was sung in a revival of Dryden's tragicomedy is known only from an undated single-sheet edition: '*A new Song in the Play call'd the* Spanish *Fryer . . . sung by a boy*'.[86] The lyric is not found in any edition of the play; nor does *Deliciae Musicae*, 1 (1695), or *Orpheus Britannicus*, 1 (1698), in which it also appears, mention Dryden's drama. It was, however, almost certainly performed in the first week or two after the Drury Lane theatre reopened in April 1695.

Purcell's text is an altered and abridged version of a poem set by Godfrey Finger and published contemporaneously in the fourth book of *Thesaurus Musicus* (1695).[87]

I.

> While I with wounding grief did look,
>   When Love had turn'd your brain;
> From you the dire Disease I took,
>   And bore my self your pain.
>
> *Marcella* then your Lover prize,
>   And be not too severe;
> Use well the conquests of your Eyes,
>   For Pride has lost your Deare.

II.

> *Ambrosio* treats your flames with scorn,
>   And rakes your tender mind;
> Withdraw your Frowns, and Smiles return,
>   And pay him in his kind.
>
> Yet Smiles again where Smiles are due,
>   And my true Love esteem:
> For I much more doe rage for you
>   Than you can burn for him.

Finger's air is described as 'A Song upon Mrs. *Brace-girdle*'s Acting *Marcella*, in *Don-Quixote*', and the poem clearly refers to her appearance in Act V of the second part of Durfey's trilogy (May 1694), in which she sang John Eccles's 'I burn, I burn, my brain consumes to ashes', perhaps the most celebrated 'mad song' of the era (discussed in Chapter 4). Marcella has fallen in love with Ambrosio, who secretly blames her for a

---

[86] Copy in British Library H.1601.c(4). A later, more corrupt version was engraved by Walsh – in British Library G.304(182).
[87] The verse, by Durfey, is published in *Wit and Mirth, or Pills to Purge Melancholy*.

friend's suicide. When she realizes that he is only toying with her, she goes insane, expressing her malady in Eccles's famous song. In Durfey's tribute to Mrs Bracegirdle's moving performance quoted above, the line 'for Pride has lost your Deare' is therefore a reference to Marcella's singing ''Twas Pride, hot as Hell, that first made me Rebell'. And the suggestion that she simply shrug off Ambrosio's cruelty with a sarcastic smile reflects the generally brittle humour of the final scene of 2 Don Quixote. Her madness, like everything else about this unruly comedy, is slightly off-colour. But Mrs Bracegirdle was apparently able to convey Marcella's pathetic side with great power. Even if one allows that he is touting his own play, Durfey writes in the preface that 'I burn, I burn' was 'so incomparably well sung, and acted by Mrs. Bracegirdle, that the most envious do allow . . . 'tis the best of that kind ever done before'.

Finger's 'While I with wounding grief' is simple, strophic, and syllabic, the jolly G major tune apparently taking its lead from the second verse ('Yet Smiles again where Smiles are due'). Purcell's is a completely different reading of the poem. Besides omitting the upbeat second quatrain of the second verse and making several significant changes in diction throughout the opening stanza, he altered the line 'Withdraw your Frowns, and Smiles return' to read oppositely: 'Withdraw your smiles and frowns return'. Even the composer's own rubric in the Guildhall Library manuscript shows a subtle shift of emphasis. Whereas Finger's is a song upon Mrs Bracegirdle's *acting* Marcella, Purcell's is upon her '*Singing* (I Burn &c)'. I suspect that far more lies behind these two settings than the documents will permit us to know. Both songs were composed about the time Mrs Bracegirdle and her mentor Eccles left the Patent Company. Why did Purcell immortalize the actress's singing when he never wrote for her? 'Whilst I with grief' was performed by young Bowen, whom Purcell had probably trained during the months the theatres were dark. Was the composer telling the world that he and Drury Lane could manage well enough without the seasoned professionals who had just decamped for Lincoln's Inn Fields? Was the song also a sharp reply to Finger's mediocre effort, a broad hint to the Moravian to leave the English language alone and stick to writing instrumental music? Interestingly, Finger, an important musician on the London scene who even gained the honour of setting the 1693 Ode for St Cecilia's Day, became the main composer of incidental tunes at Lincoln's Inn Fields for the next five years, while Eccles wrote almost all the songs required by the new company.

Regardless of what prompted Purcell to dedicate his setting of 'Whilst I with grief' to Mrs Bracegirdle, most of the textual alterations can be explained by its dramatic context, namely Dryden's *The Spanish Fryar* (première November 1680). Only two scenes require music, both involving Queen Leonora. In Act I a choral procession of priests escorts her to the cathedral. The role of the song in Act V is more important. Torrismond, having married the queen, is informed falsely that she is responsible for the death of his father. He rants in private, 'Is she mine? My Father's Murtherer mine?' The queen does not know why her new husband recoils from her 'as if he touch'd a Serpent', and to ease her distress she asks an attendant to sing 'Farewell ungratefull Traytor', a poem 'which poor *Olympia* made / When false *Bireno* left her'. This was set by Simon Pack (D&M No. 974) and, though not published until 1706, was almost certainly composed for the première. Purcell's 'Whilst I with grief' obviously replaced it, since the lyrics convey essentially the same message. But the later one had to be altered to bear more directly on Leonora's predicament. For example, the original line, 'from you the dire Disease I took', which invites a double meaning anyway and would have surely raised eyebrows in its new context, was changed to the more poetic 'from you I the contagion took'. In *2 Don Quixote* Ambrosio abandons Marcella, while in *The Spanish Fryar* Torrismond remains with the queen; Purcell had thus to change two words in the second quatrain of the first stanza (shown in italics):

Finger	Purcell
Use well the conquest of your Eyes,	Use well the conquest of your eyes,
For Pride has *lost your* Deare.	For pride has *cost you* dear.

All but one of the opening four lines of 'Whilst I with grief' are immediately repeated at different pitch levels, thereby giving considerable weight to what at first hearing might be interpreted as mere graces. The simple, cohesive design is not found in any of the other declamatory songs from Purcell's final year. Furthermore, the recitative and air are clearly related. Not only do the bass lines of each section progress steadily downward, but the climaxes (shown in Example 30) are achieved by inching upward to the tonic note.

Eccles's 'Sylvia, how could you e're mistrust' is probably yet another replacement for the original song in Act V, perhaps included in a Lincoln's Inn Fields revival mounted after Purcell's death.[88] Eccles's setting of

Example 30. *The Spanish Fryar*: 'Whilst I with grief', bars 15-18 and 45-9 (voice only)

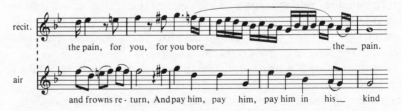

[88] In *A Collection of Songs* (1704), sung by Mrs Hodgson, and reprinted in *Eight Songs by John Eccles*, ed. Michael Pilkington (London: Stainer & Bell, 1978), pp. 12-15.

'Look down, ye bless'd above' in Act I may have been used for the same production.[89] This chorus is a miniature masterpiece, marred only by one or two easily correctable errors of part-writing. Was Eccles familiar with the dramatic context? The priests are praying for success in a battle already won: the cynical Pedro remarks that 'By my computation now, the Victory was gain'd before the Procession was made for it; and yet it will go hard, but the Priests will make a Miracle on't.' Elizabeth Barry's portrayal of the dissembling Leonora is mentioned in Durfey's *The Richmond Heiress* (1693), I.i. Sir Quibble Quere remarks that she plays 'the Queen in the *Spanish Fryar* better than any Woman in *England*: I'll say't, I had rather see her wag after the Fidlers in the Procession there, than see another Coronation, ad'sniggers'. One wonders whether Eccles, with his earnest, pathetic appoggiaturas, miscalculated the tone of the scene, or whether he wanted to comment ironically on the priests' hypocrisy. No such ambiguity surrounds Purcell's 'Whilst I with grief'. In later acts the tables of deceit are turned against the queen, and the song, especially the opening declamatory section, is an extension of her heroic anguish. Lesser composers and playwrights may well have brought in 'their Musick by head and shoulders', making it 'serve in one Play as well as another';[90] but Purcell's overriding desire was to have the music fit the drama.

Timon of Athens

Shadwell's adaptation of Shakespeare's *Timon of Athens*, first acted in early 1678, was very popular and was frequently revived. Louis Grabu composed the original music for the masque in Act II, and in spring 1693 Peter Motteux wrote some verses that later found their way into the version that included Purcell's music. This was mounted at Drury Lane probably in May or June 1695.[91] Shadwell's rendering of the 'Misanthropus' story is generally faithful to its model, but as Hume remarks, comparison 'is simply a needless distraction', since the adapter's main purpose was to attack the late seventeenth-century moral code. Timon is 'made a test case for the libertine ethic, with two women to choose between: the good Evandra and the hypocritical Melissa' (*The Development*, pp. 327–8). Shakespeare's dance of Amazons performed at the banquet in I.ii and Shadwell's more elaborate pastoral confrontation of shepherds and bacchants in II.ii have a common purpose: to show the good-natured Timon, generous to a fault, squandering his wealth on fair-weather friends. As the feast is served up in Shadwell's version, the stoic philosopher Apemantus, who chooses to dine on roots and water, carps that the masque is 'all leaf

---

[89] In British Library Add. MS 29378, fols. 140–140v.

[90] Edward Ravenscroft, *The Italian Husband* (1697), 'The Prelude'.

[91] The date is suggested by one of Purcell's songs, 'The cares of lovers', first published in *Deliciae Musicae*, II, which was issued in the third week of July. Other evidence is presented below.

gold [with] no weight in it'. By having the masquers sing instead of dance, Shadwell is better able to fashion an allegory of the rivalry between Timon's mistresses, characters that do not appear in Shakespeare.

In the new sub-plot Timon is anxious to marry Melissa, but has scruples about casting off Evandra, his erstwhile lover. The former is beautiful, vain, hedonistic, mercenary, and sometimes humorous. Evandra is plain, faithful, and pathetic, offering to kill herself after she catches a glimpse of Timon and Melissa gambolling at the masque. Shadwell places the entertainment an act later than does Shakespeare, and raises the audience's expectation with several references to it during the first two scenes, thereby giving it more weight. Its function is to bring together the themes of hedonism *versus* stoicism and platonic love *versus* sexual passion. The masque opens with a 'Symphony of Pipes imitating the chirping of Birds', after which nymphs and shepherds extol the power of love. As in *The Libertine*, Shadwell shows the disruption of Arcadia by vulgar intruders; when the bacchants burst in to ridicule the effeminate adoration, the nymphs reply in kind, dropping their pretentious dialogue to deliver pugnacious and indelicate lines replaced in 1695 by conventionally frilly ones. The debate is settled near the end of the entertainment when Cupid and Bacchus enter to declare that 'by Love and good Drinking, all the World is our own' – more a truce than a reconciliation. The allegory is plain: Bacchus represents Melissa and the hedonistic side of Timon; Cupid is Evandra, devotion, and compassion. After the masque, when the protagonist is confronted by his tearful former mistress, he offers to love both women equally, a reflection of the imperfect agreement reached in the entertainment, since Evandra does not view bigamy as a satisfactory solution.

The masque was revised for the 1695 production, and though Shadwell's exposition of the combatants (somewhat less than half the total text) is preserved, Bacchus is introduced much earlier and Cupid is transformed into a solo singing role. The brisk debate between these familiar characters is more focussed and dramatic than Shadwell's meandering succession of tableaux for nameless nymphs and bacchants. Of the original music, there survives only Grabu's strophic setting of the first two verses, 'Hark how the songsters' and 'Love in their little veins inspires'.[92] The light, gay song, which inexplicably changes from triple to duple metre midway through each strain, would invite an invidious comparison with Purcell's inspired handling of the same verses, if one were to forget that nearly two decades and a considerable change of musical style separate them. Grabu's piece is preserved in *Choice Ayres & Songs*, II (1679), omitting the 'Symphony of Pipes' mentioned in the stage directions; but the song-books rarely print

---

[92] D&M No. 1256. The first few bars of the voice part are given in Moore, *Henry Purcell & the Restoration Theatre*, p. 198.

ritornels, and Grabu, a skilled instrumental composer, probably supplied the symphony as well as the rest of the music in the masque.

The new verses set by Purcell in the masque were first mentioned by their author, Motteux, in the May 1693 issue of *The Gentleman's Journal*, as being hastily penned for 'a Consort of Music'. Therefore, the lyrics may not have been intended for the stage at all. Motteux claims they were sung to the music of J. W. Franck, admitting that 'some of the Words were fitted to the Tunes'. In any case, the 1693 'settings' do not survive nor is it certain that Motteux was responsible for the patchwork masque included in the summer 1695 production of the play.

The masque of Cupid and Bacchus (z 632) is Purcell at his best, transforming the static, trite verses into a miniature drama. The opening F major duet, 'Hark how the songsters', evokes the pleasures of the grove with gentle, rocking quavers in the bass and sweet Italianate figuration shared between voices and recorders. This piece and the following treble solo, 'Love in their little veins', are almost completely devoid of dissonance, a purity rare in either Purcell's vocal or instrumental music. For a moment one might assume he had finally 'shaken off his barbarities' and had embraced the supposed regularity of the Italian style. But he is simply painting a picture of the harmony enjoyed by the plants and animals of the grove. With the trio 'But ah! how much are our delights more dear' attention shifts to 'human kind' and key to sombre C minor. The halting exclamations and, later, the sophisticated counterpoint contrast strongly with the uncomplicated birdsong opening the scene. That the trio is unaccompanied by recorders or even basso continuo further emphasizes the human element.[93] One can assume that the following solo, 'Hence! with your trifling deity', a boisterous, triadic attack on love that turns to chromatic sneers, is sung by Bacchus, though he is not mentioned in the manuscripts. The piece, with obbligato oboes, is in B♭ major, changing to G minor at the mention of 'that blind childish pow'r', while a perfunctory chorus repeats the soloist's last two lines in the first key. Cupid's solo 'Come all, come all to me' is introduced by a jerky symphony for violins in D minor. He sings of 'the joys of love without its pain', but the oily imitation between treble and bass and the frequent diminished fourths give the song a deliberately laboured quality that contradicts the literal meaning of the lyric. The chorus that follows is the masterpiece of the *Timon* score:

> Who can resist such mighty charms?
>   Victorious love,
> Whose pow'r controls the Gods above,
> And even the Thunderer disarms!

---

[93] The continuo part in the Purcell Society Edition, II (rev. Westrup), 12–13, is not found in the primary sources.

Example 31. *Timon of Athens*: 'Who can resist such mighty charms?', bars 38–58 (strings partly omitted)

Example 31 (cont.)

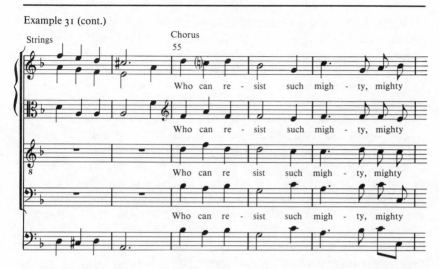

Purcell cast this as a quasi-rondeau in which the resistance to love is depicted by the inevitable return to D minor, the tonic, and Cupid's victory by the intervening modulations to a softer F major. At the mention of Jupiter (the 'Thunderer') the measured, stately music acquires an awesome sweep, moving swiftly from C major, a royal key, to A minor. The disarming of Jove, shown in Example 31, is a stroke of genius: the return of the rondeau theme 'Who can resist' feints at D minor, then bends gracefully to the relative major.

In the *da capo* aria 'Return revolting rebels', Bacchus reassumes B♭ major and the oboes are heard again. Purcell once more couples the portentous descending chromatics of G minor to the pain of love in the *B* section, whose text concerns the grief caused by 'barbarous jealousy'. Of course, any *da capo* aria in B♭ major might well modulate to the relative minor in the middle section, but the choice of the 'death key' here seems to have more than just local significance. Its linkage with Cupid, who represents the spurned mistress Evandra, symbolizes her continuing loyalty to Timon, a devotion that will destroy her in Act V.

'The cares of lovers' is known to have been sung by 'the boy', who may therefore have performed the rest of Cupid's airs.[94] One of Purcell's few independent songs to be set entirely as '*recitative* graced', the long melismas and slow-moving bass line avoid the morbid chromaticism of the previous air. The masque concludes in B♭ major with a solo for an alto bacchant, and an unremarkable duet for Cupid and Bacchus which is repeated as a chorus.

[94] In British Library Royal Music MS 24.e.13 Cupid's part is labelled 'George', an unknown treble who apparently sang the role in a later revival. Olive Baldwin and Thelma Wilson believe Bowen did not sing Cupid (*The Musical Times*, 116 [1975], 890). Cf. the Purcell Society Edition, II (rev. Westrup), xii.

On the surface, the miniature libretto is only a tedious debate about the pleasures of love and wine. But Purcell strengthens the masque's tenuous allegorical connection with the sub-plot by underscoring the pains of abiding love – jealousy and loss. Timon's profligacy, represented by the bacchanal, leads to his ruin but also to a belated appreciation of Evandra's constancy. Her devotion, reflected in Cupid's joyless music and Bacchus's cynicism, is also her downfall. The masque will probably never hold a place among Purcell's great stage works, largely because the finale is rather flat. Moore describes it as 'the least individual number of the score . . . Purcell simply could not think of a mood that would suggest a combination of these rival qualities', that is, love and wine (*Henry Purcell & the Restoration Theatre*, p. 199). For a composer with as unerring a feeling for the dramatic as Purcell, one must make pejorative judgements with great caution. I would argue that the limp, unenthusiastic quality of the final numbers is precisely what the composer wanted. The reconciliation of the opposing parties is not only unsatisfactory but will prove fatal.

Of Purcell's act music only a D major trumpet overture survives, and it is a transposition of the C major symphony for the Duke of Gloucester's Birthday Song, *Who can from joy refrain* (z 342).[95] The remainder of the incidental music was apparently supplied by James Paisible, a French composer and wind player long resident in London.[96] The two men later collaborated similarly on Southerne's *Oroonoko* (November 1695).

One other piece certain to be Purcell's is assigned to *Timon of Athens* in its only complete source, London, Royal College of Music MS 1172: the G minor ground for orchestra (z 632/20), which is labelled 'Courtin Tune', that is, overture. The rubrics in this important manuscript are generally accurate, but if Purcell designed the piece as an overture to the play, it would be his only mature composition with this title not patterned after the French introduction–canzona type. I believe that it was used in *Timon of Athens* as background music in the third scene of Act IV and not as the curtain tune before the play began. Timon, having lost his fortune and thus his friends, has taken refuge in the wilderness and shuns all human contact. But he has accidentally dug up some buried treasure while grubbing for roots, and word of this has reached Athens. The first to arrive

---

[95] The only source to assign the D major version to Shadwell's drama is British Library Add. MS 35043, fol. 70, a 'fiddler's book' that gives only the first violin part, with two different canzonas.

[96] Given as appendices to Westrup's revised edition, the eight-movement suite lacks an overture, though the first tune, in two sections – duple then triple metre – could have served the purpose. All the pieces are found in manuscripts dating from the late nineties; Westrup believes the ones in D major are anonymous, but three are ascribed to Paisible in Walsh's early print *The Compleat Flute-Master*, issued in mid-August 1695. In British Library, Royal Music MS 24.e.13, pp. 53–6, are the viola and bass parts of an 'Overture in Timon of Athens' for which I have been unable to locate the upper parts, though the fragment does not seem to be by Purcell.

to share his good fortune are the three sycophants who appeared in Act I, a painter, a poet, and a musician. Before confronting the misanthrope, they prudently test his mood by having a symphony played at a distance, but Timon hurls stones at the 'flattering Rogues'. Purcell's ground, with its slashing quavers and progressive agitation, displays the most audacious concentration of cross-relations of any of his instrumental pieces, with the possible exception of the four-part Fantazia in C minor (z 738). The bass itself invites insidious dissonance, especially in its third bar, where Purcell surely wanted the first note to be the F♮ shown in the Royal College manuscript, even though Westrup opts to sharpen it (see Example 32).[97] The E♭/E♮ and F♮/F♯ cross-relations flash from part to part until the climactic, frenzied eighth division, in which the chromatics ascend in the same voices, with the second violin increasing the tension with an implied cross between B♭ and B♮ on the first beat of bar 65 and a real one between C♮ and C♯ in the next bar. Purcell further highlights this variation by avoiding cross-relations in the preceding one, in which dissonance is

Example 32. *Timon of Athens*: Curtain tune on a ground, bars 61–82

[97] In British Library Add. MS 35043, fol. 56v, this is given as F♯, but the E♮ of the preceding bar is lacking.

Example 32 (cont.)

generated by oblique augmented fifths instead (see Example 32, bars 62–4). To slow the tremendous momentum created by the relentless rhythm and excruciating chromaticism, Purcell eliminates all dissonance in the final variation except for a few gentle suspensions. The cross-relations have disappeared.

3 The Tragic Extravaganzas

Five serious plays required substantially more music of Purcell than any of the tragedies and heroic dramas discussed in the preceding chapter. The five, all revivals, are *Circe, Oedipus, The Libertine, Bonduca,* and *The Indian Queen*. I make a distinction between these 'tragic extravaganzas' and the semi-operas *Dioclesian, King Arthur,* and *The Fairy-Queen*, because the latter three are comedic rather than tragic, contain even more music, and were scenically much more spectacular. Though Purcell's major stage works are of the lighter genre, English playwrights seem not to have purposely avoided tragic endings in the dramatic operas, as did Lully and Quinault in the *tragédie lyrique*. Shadwell's *Psyche*, for instance, is a classicized tragedy with apotheosis. And about the turn of the century, several genuine tragic semi-operas were produced.[1] Only *The Indian Queen* falls somewhere between serious play and dramatic opera; it was in fact planned as the major spring musical for 1695, but had to be postponed and scaled down because of the disruptive actors' rebellion. Yet in this, Purcell's last large-scale theatre work, the masques, like those of the other tragic extravaganzas, are handled quite differently from ones in the true semi-operas. In the five plays discussed in this chapter, the protagonists named in the titles do not die *through* music but are nevertheless ingeniously encircled by it.

Circe

Charles Davenant's rhymed drama *Circe* (May 1677) is contemptuously dismissed by many critics for its execrable verse and its rapinous treatment of the story of Iphigenia in Tauris. It must be defended, however, as one of the boldest and most imaginative plays of the era, requiring more music than the 1674 version of *The Tempest* and nearly as much as *Psyche*. For a revival of uncertain date, Purcell wrote music for only one scene, but if he had set all five masques he might have created a nonpareil: a tragic dramatic opera in which the musical episodes are highly integrated allegories of the main action.

---

[1] John Dennis's *Rinaldo and Armida* (November 1698), music by Eccles, described as a 'tragedy' on the quarto title-page and characterized by Hume (*Development*, p. 457) as a 'pocket-opera'; John Oldmixon's and Daniel Purcell's *The Grove* (February 1700), which the playwright says began as 'a Pastoral, tho in the three last Acts, the Dignity of the Characters rais'd it into the form of a Tragedy' (from the preface); an anonymous adaptation of Lee's *The Rival Queens* (February 1700), music by Daniel Purcell and Finger; and Settle's *The Virgin Prophetess* (May 1701), music by Finger.

The plot of *Circe* is an orderly rotation of three interlocking love triangles (see Figure 1). Circe is the queen of Scythia and consort of King Thoas, while Iphigenia, a captive priestess, is beloved by the king. Circe's son, Ithacus, also loves the virtuous Iphigenia, which is a source of consternation to Princess Osmida, Thoas's daughter, who is betrothed to Ithacus, her stepbrother. Circe is naturally threatened by her husband's illicit *amour*, and in the fourth scene of Act I the web of relationships has grown so intricate that she is forced to consult the gods of the underworld for a prognosis. Pluto arises '*in a Chariot drawn by Black Horses*' to reveal that both King Thoas and Ithacus will perish unless one of two noble youths soon to arrive from Argos is sacrificed.

Fig. 1

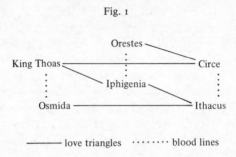

——— love triangles   · · · · · · · blood lines

As Act II opens, Circe is working her musical charms on Orestes and Pylades, the Greek youths of Pluto's prophecy. In a scene reminiscent of Ariel's tormenting of Ferdinand in the first act of *The Tempest*, furies play 'horrid Musick' and sing of Orestes's dead mother. Circe then applies the balm, a song of comfort performed by Iris, 'Cease valiant Hero! cease to grieve' (D&M No. 499). Though unascribed, it is almost certainly by John Banister, who, according to Downes, wrote all the music for the 1677 production (*Roscius Anglicanus*, pp. 36–7). Banister was not a gifted composer but had nevertheless a flair for the dramatic. The brief air begins tortuously in A minor, perhaps to reflect Orestes's guilty conscience, and ends smoothly in C major, absolving him of alleged matricide. The rest of the music for this scene does not survive. The ensuing action establishes the third love triangle, which puts Iphigenia in an appalling dilemma. Circe lusts after Orestes, while Iphigenia falls in love with his travelling companion Pylades. The priestess is forced to choose one of the Greeks for the sacrifice. To Circe's dismay, she names Orestes, who is then revealed as Iphigenia's long-lost brother. Ceremonial music (not extant) accompanies the '*entry of Priests*' in III[v] but is interrupted when Circe's dragons arise and carry the designated victim away.

The second scene of Act IV, in Circe's palace, is one of the most extraordinary in any drama of the period. The queen charms Orestes to the accompaniment of Banister's 'Young Phaon strove the bliss to taste' (D&M No. 4132), a most explicit song of seduction. While the illicit couple dally in dumb show, a little masque is performed in which Orpheus sings 'Give me my Lute' (D&M No. 1123), a bitter lament for his dead Euridice. Banister's G minor setting includes the usual clichés of the key – a descending chromatic tetrachord, a cross-relation in conjunction with the word 'dead', and sevenths on the strong beats at 'false' (see Example 1).[2] The two verses are set to essentially the same music, but by juggling the fourth bar in the second strophe and thereby throwing the music off by three crotchets, the composer makes the striking cross-relation at 'dead' in the first part (bar 4) fall on 'darts' in the second. The reason for this slight adjustment will soon become clear. After a '*Soft Symphony*', the heavens open and Cupid sings 'How dull is all the world' (not extant), chiding Orpheus for his spoil-sport mourning and abstinence. In an astonishing violation of the usual baroque redaction of the legend, several bacchants kill Orpheus with arrows during an entry dance: hence Banister's ominous setting of the preceding lines 'Lay by your useless darts, for all the Young will guard their hearts'. This obscure scene can be added to the tiny handful of musical settings of the Orpheus tale that end with the violent death of the protagonist. It is, of course, a savage allegory of Circe's seduction of Orestes, cleverly enhanced by Banister's song. Most unfortunately, Purcell either did not reset this scene, or if he did, his version does not survive. This was not his only brush with the Orpheus legend (see the discussions of *A Fool's Preferment* and *The Richmond Heiress* in Chapter 4). The rest of the plot need not be recounted in detail. All the main characters named in Figure 1 die in Act V. Orestes's madness is depicted in a long dream sequence in V.vi. Though the music does not survive, it was apparently the grandest of all the masques, and included an echo chorus of three spirits in the clouds. No mere entertainment, it recalls the youth's seduction in Act IV.

The conjuration of Pluto near the end of Act I, the only episode for which Purcell wrote music (z 575), is the least dramatic of the lyrical scenes. Almost all the pieces are separated or interrupted by Circe's spoken invocations and instructions to her acolytes. But the composer imposed a tight organization on the various choruses, recitatives, and airs, thereby giving them a cohesion lacking in Davenant's verse. The music is remarkably suave and refined, contrasting with that of the temple and conjuration scenes in *The Indian Emperour*, *Bonduca*, and *The Indian Queen*. An air of formality, even stiffness, prevails, and words such as 'poisonous', 'wound', 'famine', 'pestilence', and 'torments' are handled

[2] Note Banister's 'English' pronunciation of Eu´ri•dice (bar 3), and compare with Locke's somewhat more Italianate Eu•ri´di•ce in the masque of Orpheus in *The Empress of Morocco*, Oxford, Christ Church Mus. MS 692.

Example 1. *Circe*: John Banister, 'Give me my Lute', bars 1–8 and 18–23

with kid gloves. One might suppose the elegant restraint is an indication that *Circe* was composed in the mid- or late eighties while Purcell was under the sway of Grabu's *Albion and Albanius* (1685) and of Lully's *Cadmus et Hermione*, which had its London première in 1686.[3] But as explained below, the date of composition is open to considerable question. A likelier reason for the score's unusual character is the ecclesiastical aura of

---

[3] See Westrup, *Purcell*, pp. 110–11.

the scene. In these alternating solos and choruses Westrup catches 'a glimpse of the relationship between Purcell's stage music and his anthems' (*Purcell*, p. 152), a quality that might well account for the absence of the usual theatrical gargoyles.

The ceremony opens in C major with a stately, four-square bass solo and chorus, 'We must assemble by a sacrifice', preceded by a symphony for strings. Much of the immediately felt expansiveness is imparted by a shift towards the subdominant with the I-IV$^6_4$-I progression in bars 1 and 2 and the B♭s heard two beats later. The former gesture is found almost exclusively at the beginning of long pieces, especially songs conveying a feeling of awe or hugeness, such as 'Let the dreadful engines of eternal will' of *1 Don Quixote*. But in *Circe* the persistent sliding towards flat keys has an ominous meaning. The ensuing tenor recitative, 'Their necessary aid you use', begins with the same progression (see Example 2), and the B♭ tied

Example 2. *Circe*: 'Their necessary aid you use', bars 1–4

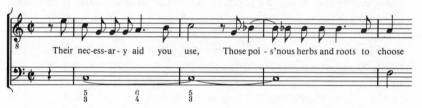

over from the second to the third bar, as in the preceding symphony, falls on the word 'poisonous', thereby establishing a sinister connotation. The key changes to C minor for the first invocation, 'The air with music gently wound', sung by a tenor over a four-bar ground that shifts briefly to the subdominant, then to B♭ major, the key of the lowered seventh, during the sixth variation. This is an unusual tonal arrangement but one well prepared by previous flat-side tendencies. The text is repeated by the chorus, but the ground is discarded and the tenor's melody is only suggested for a bar or two.[4] The sedate diatonic spell of the surrounding pieces is then broken by richly dissonant part-writing, particularly at the important words 'every pleasing sound', where an apparent movement towards E♭ major is wrested back to the tonic (see Example 3).

A sure sign of the surprisingly light-hearted tone of this scene is the next set of airs and choruses. One should recall that Circe consults the spirits to learn the outcome of unrequited illicit love. Like Montezuma in *The Indian Emperour*, Placidius in *Tyrannick Love*, and Hannibal in *Sophonisba*, she and her priests try to cajole the augurs into rosy predictions. Despite the threatening text, the mood of the tenor air and chorus 'Come every demon'

---

[4] In *Henry Purcell & the Restoration Theatre*, p. 176, Moore remarks misleadingly that the chorus enters with 'the same melody'.

Example 3. *Circe*: 'The air with music gently wound', chorus, bars 25–30 (strings omitted)

is gay and carefree. The opening duple-metre section is followed by the elegant, flowing 'Circe, the daughter of the sun' in triple time, which is echoed by the chorus. The tenor then repeats the first air to new words, 'You who hatch factions in the court'. This is an unusual form for Purcell, and he alters the tune in several places to make it fit the second verse, as Example 4 shows. Such close attention to melodic detail is rare in the strophic songs. The group of pieces concludes with a repetition of the chorus 'Circe, the daughter of the sun'. This is wonderful, stylish music, but not quite in touch with the drama. The Lulliesque aloofness from the seamier side of the action, not to mention the rondeau-like form, contributes to the apparent Frenchness.

The declamatory air 'Lovers, who to their first embraces go', sung by one of Circe's women, is the more familiar Purcell of the early nineties. The elaborate graces and the quick change to imitative counterpoint at the line 'In speed you can out-do the winged wind', as well as the chromaticism shown in Example 5, stand out from the rest of the *Circe* music. This passage is descriptive. Here *'A Spirit rises, and layes a Jarre at* Circe's *feet'*, an encouraging signal from the underworld that allows the conjuration to begin in earnest with the chorus 'Great minister of fate'. But even the potent line 'Famine and pestilence about you wait' is set in a dignified, Old-Testament manner. Most of the staggered entries pull towards the subdominant (see Example 6). The chorus is followed by a Magicians' Dance in G minor, a transposition from D minor of the Slow Air (z 603/2) used in the act music for *The Married Beau* (April 1694). The latter version has more melodic embellishment, but one should not assume that it is a variation of the *Circe* dance and therefore a later arrangement. Most of the ornaments complement the slow tempo of the act tune.

The final piece is the accompanied bass recitative 'Pluto, arise!' This serves the same function – namely, to call forth a spirit – as 'You twice ten hundred deities' in *The Indian Queen*, which it resembles in several points of melodic detail. But the two pieces are radically different in intensity.

Example 4. *Circe*: 'Come every demon', bars 8–12, and 'You who hatch factions', bars 8–12

Example 5. *Circe*: 'Lovers, who to their first embraces go', bars 14–17 (bass omitted)

'You twice ten hundred deities' is gloomy and portentous, whereas 'Pluto, arise!' is sedate like most of the rest of the *Circe* music. It opens with the same harmonic shift to the subdominant, now almost a motto. The unexpected C minor chord in bar 4 of Example 7 is an ominous touch, but it is immediately dispelled. This piece is an anticlimax both in the concert hall and on the stage, since Pluto, after ascending in a machine, speaks without musical accompaniment.

Example 6. *Circe*: 'Great minister of fate', bars 11–18 (strings omitted)

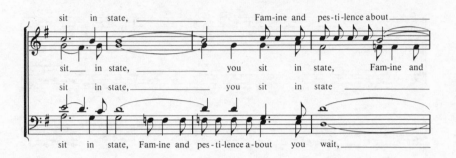

Example 7. *Circe*: 'Pluto, arise!', bars 1–5

The date of the revival that included this music is unknown. Zimmerman (*An Analytical Catalogue*, p. 251) follows Squire's suggestion of 1685 ('Purcell's Dramatic Music', p. 505) but admits that it could have been written as late as 1690. 'On the evidence of style', Westrup is inclined to place it 'several years later' than 1685, and a recent editor of his book suggets 1690 (*Purcell*, rev. N. Fortune, p. 151 n.). Some of the pitfalls of attempting to date Purcell's stage music by style alone are discussed in Chapter 1, but the usual bibliographic tools also fail us with *Circe*. Charles Davenant's tragedy was revived in the summer of 1689 and in late 1690 (*The London Stage*, Part 1, pp. 371 and 391), but performance records for the period are scanty, particularly for revivals. No part of the score was published in the early song-books or in the first volume of *Orpheus Britannicus*; this omission suggests that it was composed before 1690, since both Purcell and his early editors largely turned their backs on the theatre music written before *Dioclesian* (1690). Yet almost none of the solos in *Circe* were suitable for inclusion in the song-books, most being accompanied recitatives and airs interspersed with choruses.

The music survives in six manuscripts, the earliest of which dates from after 1700.[5] The company it keeps in these collections suggests that the compilers and copyists regarded it as a major work; *Circe* is found among *Bonduca*, *Timon of Athens*, *Oedipus*, *The Indian Queen*, and *The Libertine*, all but one composed in 1695.[6] The style of the *Circe* music is somewhat pale, and the composer's typical theatrics are muted by an enigmatic formality. If someone were lucky enough to find proof of the year of its creation, no date between 1685 and 1695 would surprise me.

Oedipus

The most memorable necromantic scene in a Restoration tragedy is in the third act of Dryden and Lee's *Oedipus*, where the ghost of Laius is raised with the help of Purcell's beautiful countertenor air 'Music for a while' (z 583/2). This is the second of three lyrics in the scene that are '*set through*', that is, set to continuous music. While bearing excerption well, it makes

---

[5] Laurie believes Oxford, Oriel College Mus. MS Ua 36 to be the earliest, with the other important scores (British Library Add. MS 31447 and Cambridge, Fitzwilliam Museum MS 87) having been copied from it, since they miss out the first bar and a half of 'You who hatch factions in the court' ('Purcell's Stage Works', p. 173). But the Oriel College manuscript also lacks the second violin and viola parts of the first eleven bars of the chorus 'Great minister of fate' (the Purcell Society Edition, Vol. XVI, simply reproduces the alto and tenor parts of the chorus an octave higher to fill the gap). British Library Add. MS 31447 and another score, Royal College of Music MS 996, supply instrumental parts for this passage different from the choral ones. On this evidence, Add. MS 31447 and Royal College MS 996 seem to have been copied not from the Oriel College score but from a fourth one, now lost.

[6] North twice refers to *Circe* as one of Purcell's major semi-operas; see *Roger North on Music*, pp. 307, 353.

much more sense when coupled with its flanking trios; and just once I should like to hear it performed in Dryden and Lee's enchanted grove with 'the Stage wholly darkn'd'.

Oedipus (September 1678) was one of the most admired dramas of its day. Hume believes that 'had we not Sophocles's version to compare, this play would be accounted far better than it has been' (*The Development*, p. 325). Anyone reasonably familiar with the collaborating playwrights' quite different dramatic styles can detect their division of labour: Dryden wrote Acts I and III and Lee the rest.[7] Thus the laureate is responsible for the scene that includes Purcell's celebrated music. Perhaps it was composed for a revival mounted sometime after their first joint effort, *Amphitryon*, in October 1690; 1692 is often proposed, but this is only a guess. 'Music for a while' was first published in the second book of *Orpheus Britannicus* (1702).

None of the original vocal music survives, but Grabu wrote a set of act tunes, the only copy of which is in an undated manuscript in the Leeds Public Library (MS Q784.21 1969). This is conceivably the music for the first production, since Grabu did not leave England until March or April 1679, eight months after the première.[8] But its style and the music surrounding it in the Leeds manuscript, much of which was composed about 1700, suggest a later date.[9] Grabu returned to London in late 1683 to begin work on *Albion and Albanius* and left again for Paris in December 1685. Though Lafontaine supposes that he was 'in 1687 already regarded as dead', he is known to have written music for a revival of *The Double Marriage* in early 1688, and in November 1694 *The London Gazette* announced a concert of music 'composed by Mr Grabue', though this could be another member of the family.[10] The *Oedipus* act music, an overture and six incidental tunes all in C major, is not unworthy, and the *menuet en rondeau* is a wonderfully noble piece.

Dryden and Lee treat the revelation of Oedipus's parricide and incest not as the climax but as a ritualistic discovery in which music plays an important part. Dramatic irony is screwed to the breaking point; for example, at the end of Act I when Jocasta suggests that her brother Creon marry their niece Eurydice, Oedipus warns that they are too closely related by blood. The playwrights' most flagrant alteration of Sophocles, whom

[7] See Dryden, 'The Vindication of the Duke of Guise', in *The Dramatic Works*, ed. M. Summers, v, 325.

[8] See *The Works of John Dryden*, xv, ed. Earl Miner, 341.

[9] In addition to some arrangements of instrumental music by Lully, the part-books include pieces by Finger for Congreve's *The Mourning Bride* (1697) and Dennis's *Iphigenia* (1700); by Paisible for Cibber's *Love's Last Shift* (1696); and by John Barrett for Vanbrugh's *The Pilgrim* (1700).

[10] See Lafontaine, *The King's Musick* (1909; rpt New York: Da Capo, 1973), p. 455; Highfill, *A Biographical Dictionary*, vi, 293; and *The London Stage*, Part 1, p. 443.

they claim to have followed closely, is the addition of a love-and-honour sub-plot drawn from the heroic play tradition.

A sombre mood is set by a 'plaintive' curtain tune accompanying the discovery of a prospect of Thebes in the grip of the plague: *'Dead Bodies appear at a distance in the Streets; Some faintly go over the Stage, others drop.'* None of Grabu's act pieces seems severe enough for this effect. Later in Act I an oracle tells the rabble that King Laius's unavenged murder is the cause of the city's present woes, and much of the next two acts is devoted to divining the name of the regicide. The first musical scene, II.i, takes place at midnight while a magical tempest rages. Lee's wild, unbridled verse is well suited to the air of fantasy.[11] Prodigies appear in the heavens with the names 'Oedipus' and 'Jocasta' emblazoned in their crowns. But the protagonist is puzzled by this sign and asks the blind soothsayer Tiresias to reveal the identity of the murderer. The prophet turns to his daughter:

> Thou hast a voice that might have sav'd the Bard
> Of *Thrace*, and forc'd the raging Bacchanals,
> With lifted Prongs, to listen to thy airs:
> O Charm this God, this Fury in my Bosom,
> Lull him with tuneful notes, and artful strings,
> With pow'rful strains; *Manto*, my lovely Child,
> Sooth the unruly God-head to be mild.

She then sings 'Phoebus, God belov'd by men', no setting of which survives. Tiresias, now in a trance, reports plainly that 'the first of *Lajus* blood his life did seize . . . ' Assuming Eurydice to be the late king's eldest child, Creon accuses her of the evil deed. The ensuing family squabble is quelled only when Tiresias offers to go directly to the grove of furies, Laius's burial place, to attempt a definitive conjuration.

Was Dryden's scene in the grove in Act III simply a routine spectacle, or was the audience meant to shudder as thunder pealed, lightning flashed, and the ghost of Laius rose *'arm'd in his Chariot, as he was slain'*? Despite the sacrifice of a calf and the disinterment of the late king's bones in the 'darkest part o'th' Grove', the ghost is reluctant to rise, and complaining groans are heard below. After the stage is completely darkened, Tiresias asks, 'Must you have Musick too? [to the priests] then tune your voices, / And let 'em have such sounds as Hell ne're heard / Since *Orpheus* brib'd the Shades'. It is exceedingly important to notice, then, that the soothsayer calls for wondrous not horrid music. Laius's spirit must be coaxed up in the same manner that Orpheus moved Charon at the River Styx. Ignorance of the dramatic context has led to many a misguided performance of 'Music for a while'. Even the trio for alto, tenor, and bass that precedes it,

[11] Cf. *Sophonisba* (April 1675), II.iii.

'Hear ye sullen powers', is restrained and smooth-edged, despite such vivid invocations as 'You that boiling cauldrons blow, you that scum the molten lead', which are declaimed with a minimum of melodic enlivening. Only the tenor soloist is allowed the odd extravagance, such as the augmented-sixth chord at the words 'Of poor ghosts'. The scarcity of this sonority in Purcell's dramatic music suggests a grotesque touch here.[12] The magnificent concluding section, 'Down, ten thousand fathoms low', is set to a free canon of descending C minor scales, each voice dropping more than four octaves (allowing for displacements of register). Significantly, the falling lines combine both forms of the harmonic minor scale, thereby juxtaposing the raised and lowered sixth and seventh degrees. These pairs, A♭/A♮ and B♭/B♮, become the principal chromatics of the ostinato bass in 'Music for a while'.

The opening trio invokes the attention of the gods of the underworld, while the air on a ground is designed to charm the ghost of Laius, to release it from the 'eternal bands' long enough for the slain king to proclaim Eurydice's innocence and to name Oedipus as his killer. Therefore, the ground itself represents the close confines of death, its ascending chromatics the wonderment of a spirit rising from its own bones, and the alterations and extensions of the repeating bass the actual release from the grave. The bass in fact comprises two voices, a stepwise ascending fifth overlaid with the chromatic tetrachord, which in defiance of tradition moves upwards to the tonic rather than downwards to the dominant. These strands (shown separately in Example 8) are knit together by the voice, which enters with the first three notes heard in the bass.[13]

Example 8. *Oedipus*: 'Music for a while', bars 1–6

The release of Laius's spirit begins, fittingly, after a modulation to G minor. As Alecto, one of the furies, frees the dead, the bass line rises from the key of doom to cadence first in B♭ major and then triumphantly in E♭ major four bars later. Purcell depicts 'eternal' in two ways: with a long melisma reminiscent of the one at 'trembling' in the preceding trio; and with an ever-ascending extension of the bass pattern. The 'premature' return of the ostinato in C minor in bar 23 of Example 9 complements the

[12] Cf. 'By the croaking of the toad' in *The Indian Queen*.

[13] Purcell wrote other two-voice grounds, the most notable being that for 'Here the deities approve' in the 1683 St Cecilia's Day Ode (z 339/3). A keyboard arrangement in *The Second Part of Musick's Hand Maid* (1689) makes clear the two-part character of the bass. Though called 'A New Ground', it is the familiar chromatic passacaglia.

Example 9. *Oedipus*: 'Music for a while', bars 19–30

out-of-joint setting of 'drop' in the voice.[14] And the unexpected shift to G minor just before the *da capo* is a reminder that Laius's release from the underworld is only a brief reprieve.

It is a fitting irony that this perfect song should be so imperfectly preserved, and not for want of sources. Besides the version in the second book of *Orpheus Britannicus*, 'Music for a while' and the rest of the *Oedipus* music is found in more than a dozen eighteenth-century manuscripts. Most of the questionable readings arise from the high concentration of chromatics and the inherent ambiguity of the sixth degree. In the late seventeenth century, music in the flat minor keys (D, G, C, and F) did not normally include an accidental for the sixth degree in the key signature. Thus in C minor, if an A♭ was required, the copyist either added it or relied

[14] Cf. John Danyel's treatment of this word in 'Mrs. M. E. her Funerall teares'.

on the performer to supply it according to the harmonic context and melodic direction. (Before about 1690, one even notices the application of the old rule 'una nota super la, semper est canendum fa'.) Accidentals were not automatically cancelled by the bar-line, nor did they necessarily hold throughout the bar. But some meticulous copyists – and Purcell was one of them – showed every accidental unequivocally, the only exception being the cancellation of a chromatically altered note implied by melodic and harmonic direction.[15] For instance, in Example 10, an excerpt from 'In

Example 10. *Henry the Second*: 'In vain 'gainst Love', bars 24–5

more   strong

vain 'gainst Love', the dotted quaver A on the third beat of the bar should be A♮ even though Purcell did not show it.[16] These conventions are adequate for most music of the period but cannot cope with the complexities of 'Music for a while', and the *Orpheus Britannicus* version especially is a notational nightmare. Not only is it plagued with misprints, but the key signature has only two flats and almost no accidentals are cancelled. On the other hand, the copy in British Library Add. MS 31447, an unusually reliable source dating from the first years of the eighteenth century, has a modern key signature and shows every accidental.[17] All works fairly well until the music begins to modulate, and then even this exceptionally clear manuscript falters. A sampling of readings for the problematic shift to G minor is shown in Example 11. Any of these versions is preferable to the fictitious conflation in the Purcell Society Edition. The song has even survived the abominable addition of C♭s at the word 'eternal', which are found in none of the reputable sources.

The concluding trio, 'Come away, do not stay', suffers the curse of being an anticlimax, memorable only for the central invocation addressed to Laius ('Hear and appear!'). Of course, Dryden's lyric offers the composer

---

[15] Further discussion of Purcell's own practice is found in Chapter 8.
[16] Source: Guildhall Library MS Safe 3, fol. 17.
[17] As with the sources of the *Circe* music, Add. MS 31447 is central to the stemma. Several other manuscripts, such as Tenbury 338, appear to have been copied from it or from a closely related source. This relationship is signalled by a deficiency: Add. MS 31447 is compactly written, often with more than one part per staff. Though the copyist was careful to distinguish between, for instance, first and second violins by making the stems go in opposite directions, the cramped format sometimes led others to confuse the two parts. The accidental exchange of parts in several manuscripts can thus be traced back to Add. MS 31447.

Example 11. *Oedipus*: 'Music for a while', bars 13–15

little to work with: 'Come away, Do not stay, But obey, While we play, For hell's broke up, and ghosts have holiday'. The piece is also musically superfluous; it is intended to raise the spirit of Laius, but this has already happened – figuratively at least.

'Music for a while' holds a special place in Purcell's *oeuvre*. Much admired for its technique, it is also well suited to the drama. The song was meant to be beautiful, not bizarre. As old Tiresias implies, it is Purcell's 'Possente spirto', a calculated, formal display of his art and not an impassioned, personal appeal to the gods.

The Libertine

For the reader whose knowledge of the Don Juan legend comes mainly from Mozart's *dramma giocoso*, Shadwell's *The Libertine* (June 1675) will probably be disturbing and bewildering, perhaps confirming one's worst suspicions about Restoration art and morality. Except for the stone-guest episode and the immolation, Shadwell's Don John is largely home-grown, a complete perversion of Molière's libertine and even of its immediate source, Dorimon's *Le Festin de pierre* (1659). The English Don has raped nuns, committed dozens of murders including those of his own father and the governor of Seville, and indulged in other atrocities before the play begins. In the first two acts alone he kills a rival serenader as well as the brother of a woman he tries to seduce, and allows his fourth wife to commit suicide while he makes a crude jest about becoming a widower. Before being brought to justice in Act V, he murders a cast-off mistress, Leonora, 'the onely Creature living that cou'd love' him, and encourages his rakish companions Antonio and Lopez to burn a nunnery, then massacre a band of shepherds.

This 'exuberant bloodbath' has permitted few reactions beyond astonishment. In the mid-eighteenth century, David Erskine Baker wrote

that the Incidents are so cramm'd together in it, without any Consideration of Time or Place as to make it highly unnatural, that the villainy of Don *John*'s Character is worked up to such an Height, as to exceed even the Limits of Possibility, and that the Catastrophe is so very horrid, as to render it little less than Impiety to represent it on the Stage.[18]

Modern critics have made more tentative assessments, viewing the protagonist uneasily as a tragic rake and the play in general as a glancing attack on seventeenth-century moral values. Hume, however, cautiously asks whether it is a burlesque of 'both horror tragedy and the ethic of libertine comedy' (*The Development*, p. 312). This interpretation would solve a lot of problems, if only Shadwell himself had been less defensive in the preface:

I hope the Readers will excuse the Irregularities of the Play, when they consider, that the Extravagance of the Subject forced me to it . . . I hope that the severest Reader will not be offended at the representation of those Vices, on which they will see a dreadful punishment inflicted.

The question of tone is vexing, but no critic has entertained the possibility that the play is first and foremost a novel vehicle for music and dance.[19] It was produced shortly after Shadwell's semi-opera *Psyche*, during the musically rich mid-seventies. I would stop short of dubbing *The Libertine* simply a burlesque, because its music – both the original by William Turner and Purcell's for a nineties revival – seems to take itself much too seriously for that.

Most of the musical scenes are superficially conventional. The rival serenades of Act I are common in Spanish romances, the immediate inspiration probably coming from Dryden's *An Evening's Love* (June 1668), II.i. Don John's fiddlers perform 'Thou joy of all hearts'. Maria comes to the balcony window, thinking the music is offered by her lover Octavio, and throws down a note which the Don intercepts. When Octavio's tardy musicians enter to sing 'When you dispense your Influence', she wonders what mischief is afoot. Turner's settings of both lyrics survive (D&M Nos. 3298 and 563) and the first, supposedly prepared by Don John himself, is an especially beautiful piece. The sarcastic epithalamium in Act II to celebrate the protagonist's sextuple polygamy is a forerunner of Durfey's witty

[18] *The Companion to the Play-House* (London: T. Becket, 1764), Vol. 1, s.v. 'The Libertine'.
[19] Dent, in *Mozart's Operas*, 2nd edn (London: Oxford Univ. Press, 1947), p. 123, is uncharacteristically muted in his judgement of this work: 'Shadwell's play is of interest to us now only for the fact that Purcell wrote incidental music for it.'

ballads. The lyric, no setting of which survives, also introduces an important theme: the libertine as a repugnant but essentially innocent beast completely controlled by the forces of nature and therefore, like all animals of prey, not morally accountable for his savage behaviour. This idea bears fruit in Act III, when the Don and his friends confront the hermit with whom they debate naturalistic philosophy, a fine scene showing no trace of the burlesque.

The Libertine amusingly modifies other stock musical scenes. The song performed in the third act by Clara and Flavia, the Lorcaesque daughters of Don Francisco, is a wry twisting of the convention wherein a lyric ornaments and reflects a woman's chastity. The wanton verses of 'Woman who is by Nature wild' reveal the sisters to be repressed libertines themselves, as debased in spirit as Don John is in action.[20] The pastoral masque in Act IV, the first setting of which is not extant, is the least important dramatically of all the musical scenes. The full-blown display of rustic merriment is rudely interrupted by the villains who crash in and ravish the shepherdesses.

In the final scene, Shadwell preserves the traditional damnation. The ghosts of the brigand's victims have assembled in a church, calling loudly for revenge. Yet the climax is more whimsical than horrible, and the playwright, as if in last-minute desperation, turns to singing devils to punish the Don's gleeful sins. Turner's original Song of Devils, 'Prepare, prepare, new guests draw near', a dialogue for alto, tenor, and baritone, with two brief four-part choruses, is preserved in British Library Add. MS 22100. Too little of Turner's dramatic music survives to determine where within his emotional spectrum the composition lies, nor does the dialogue include enough melismatic pictorialism to give a firm indication of how seriously he interpreted Shadwell's gloomy text. Turner was not a particularly imaginative composer; his songs are simple and strophic, the very antithesis of Locke's flamboyant theatre pieces.[21] Yet his text setting is natural and flowing, and his strong, balanced harmonic progressions are far more 'regular' than those of most of his contemporaries, especially Blow. The Song of Devils is in C minor, with conventional modulations to E♭ major, F minor, and G minor. Although barred in triple metre throughout, the rhythm is plastic, and only the tenor's second solo, 'In vain they shall here their past mischiefs bewail', moves in regular aria-like phrases. One detects but few touches of word-painting: when the alto sings

20 No setting survives. That it was sung by the actresses portraying Clara and Flavia rather than by surrogates is suggested by manuscript cast lists for a revival, showing that Flavia was played by Mrs Butler, a popular singer. See The London Stage, Part 1, p. 368, and Hume, 'Manuscript Casts for Revivals of Shadwell's The Libertine and Epsom-Wells', Theatre Notebook, 31 (1977), 19–22.

21 Spink calls him an 'agreeable melodist', but remarks that his 'simpering quavers pall after a time' (English Song Dowland to Purcell, pp. 172, 174).

'Here they shall weep', an F♯ in the voice clashes with an F♮ in the bass at 'weep', and later a descending chromatic tetrachord supports the phrase 'Eternal darkness they shall find'. But the poetry is uniformly vivid, and other lines ('Here they shall howl, and make eternal moan', for instance) bear sweet, consonant cadences in E♭ major. Turner creates a feeling of sombre awe largely through a distinctive tonal plan. Though the music moves away from the tonic in an ordered way, it returns abruptly after every modulation. A cloud of 'eternal dreadful doom' thus hangs heavy in the air. Purcell's resetting of this scene owes much to the original.

The exact date of the revival that included Purcell's music is not known. The play-book was reprinted in 1692, but there is no record of a performance at that time. The second volume of *Deliciae Musicae* (1695) contains Purcell's 'To arms, heroic prince' (z 600/3), a trumpet song performed by 'the Boy, in the (*Libertine destroy'd*)'. The lyric is found in no early edition of the play, and the song is included in none of the reliable manuscripts of the rest of the *Libertine* music, which suggests that 'To arms, heroic prince' may not have been heard in the same revival for which Purcell composed the bulk of the music discussed below. 'The boy' is probably Jemmy Bowen, who began his professional career with the re-opening of Drury Lane in April 1695. How the 'admirable military song' with trumpet obbligato came to be associated with the play is a puzzle, but it was apparently designed to show off young Bowen's voice. The 'frivolous and unmeaning melody' (Burney, *A General History*, II, 396) contains not the slightest trace of the irony necessary for it to have been introduced into the play's scenes of violence. It was probably sung between acts.

None of the manuscripts of the rest of the *Libertine* music is a theatre score, and even the earliest is probably several stages removed from the original. But the large number of early eighteenth-century copies suggests that it was one of Purcell's most popular compositions, and parts of it have remained so. The main sources show a virtual absence of significant variant readings, which is not the case with most of the other late dramatic works. Only one manuscript, British Library Royal Music MS 24.e.13 (fols. 1–25), felt an editor's hand. It is typical of several other scores of the period in which an attempt is made to 'smooth out' what was then perceived as a certain choppiness in Purcell's music, especially the instrumental pieces. Repeated notes are lengthened from quavers to crotchets and from crotchets to minims, or are tied across bar-lines; slurs are added willy-nilly, and silences are filled in by aimless bass notes. Such changes are especially evident in the symphony preceding 'Nymphs and shepherds'.

Purcell is known to have supplied music for only a portion of the pastoral masque in Act IV. The soprano air 'Nymphs and shepherds' (z 600/1) has become in this century a hackneyed emblem of schoolboy innocence, a particularly sweet irony considering its dramatic origins. But Purcell's flouncing jollity is on purpose, a faithful representation of the all-too-precious revels of Shadwell's stilted Arcadians, whose celebration is about to be squashed by the rake-hells. The shepherds honour Flora, the goddess of flowers; this also happens to be the name of Maria's servant, whom Don John has killed in Act II, an unsubtle hint of what awaits the country folk. After the bouncing chorus 'We come', also in G major, Purcell omitted several verses and moved directly to 'In these delightful pleasant groves', a madrigal-like 'general chorus' in G minor.[22] This piece could be offered as a prime exhibit in a case against the threnodic symbolism of G minor, since it pipes merrily along in the old-fashioned 'fa-la-la' manner. But the shepherds are celebrating their own demise, for they will be caught up in the massacre at the beginning of Act V. The earliest printed version of this piece, the second edition of *Orpheus Britannicus*, II (1706), is an arrangement for bass solo with the upper parts apparently given to instruments. In it the top part has an F♮ for the first two beats of bar 6, but all the manuscripts preserve the reading shown in Example 12. The arrival on and immediate abandonment of the dominant conveys a feeling of alarm lacking in *Orpheus Britannicus*.

Example 12. *The Libertine*: 'In these delightful pleasant groves', bars 1–7

The music for the immolation scene is in C minor, the key of Turner's dialogue. But Purcell made several basic design changes. While the first and third devils are still portrayed by a bass and an alto respectively, the second is now a soprano rather than a tenor as before. The most important alteration is the greater role given the chorus, even though Purcell reduced it to three parts by omitting the tenor. This suggests that the ensembles

---

[22] The original text begins, 'In these delightful fragrant groves'.

may have been performed by the soloists rather than by a separate group of singers. In Purcell's version the chorus interjects the opening 'Prepare, prepare' at frequent intervals during the recitatives, thereby tempering the devils' outrageously expressive declamations with decorous solemnity, an effect enhanced by the quick returns to the tonic from the secondary keys of the recitatives (see Example 13). Turner's setting also repeatedly leaps

Example 13. *The Libertine*: 'Prepare, prepare', bars 11–15

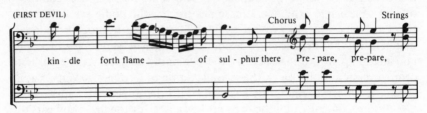

back to C minor, though not quite so abruptly. Another sign that Purcell may have been influenced by the earlier setting is the descending chromatic tetrachord at the phrase 'Here they shall weep and shall unpitied groan', which echoes Turner's similar underpinning of the line 'Eternal darkness they shall find'. But for such a scene one would be surprised only if Purcell had not included descending chromatics.

Though Purcell was perfectly capable of eliciting pity for otherwise detestable villains (witness Zempoalla in *The Indian Queen*), his obvious lack of compassion for Don John produced music which attempts nothing like pathos or ennoblement, the Don's behaviour being beyond the pale of good taste. In fact, Shadwell prevented the protagonist's being perceived as a tragic hero, since the devils' threats are directed collectively at all three rakes ('*they* shall weep . . . *they* shall howl . . . *they* shall feel the hottest flames of hell'). Before the demons enter, Don Lopez asks, 'What's here? Musick to treat us with?' Purcell's reply is of course ironical, but the song of devils is as much an entertainment as it is a glimpse of the abyss.

The composer's ambivalence towards this scene is further suggested by the 'Flourish' played at the beginning. This is the solemn prelude for 'flat trumpets' (that is, sackbuts) also heard during Queen Mary's funeral procession on 5 March 1695. Considering Purcell's great sensitivity to music and dramatic event, one wonders how a symphony designed to prepare a damnation could have been thought an appropriate accompaniment for the final progress of a beloved monarch. Laurie argues convincingly that *The Libertine* revival probably occurred after the royal funeral.[23] But I should hesitate to endorse her opinion that Purcell was able to get away with this dubious borrowing because the prelude 'was not sufficiently distinctive to be recognised'. Its stark simplicity and bold movement from major to minor chords, punctuated by bars of rest, are searingly memorable, and also anticipate the inexorable return to C minor in the trio that follows. Rather than hoping the audience would not recognize the funeral music, Purcell perhaps relied on this association for its effect. The burlesque has finally turned 'sober-faced'.

Bonduca

The Indian Queen, in many respects the crowning achievement of Purcell's brief stage career, has overshadowed another important work written at about the same time: music for the October 1695 adaptation of John Fletcher's tragedy *Bonduca* (z 574). This late score, which is remarkably free of Italianate traits, ranks among Purcell's finest. At first it may appear simply reactionary in style, the solo–choral numbers reminiscent of the verse anthems of the early eighties, and the declamatory airs a bit stiff and austere. But closer study reveals that Purcell was moving in a new direction: the contrapuntal technique is acutely heightened; traditional English dissonances abound, but are handled in an orderly fashion. Clashes no longer seem to be produced by a devil-may-care approach to part-writing, but by painstaking suspensions, anticipations, and other suavities. And one can rationalize most of the dissonant notes as ninths, elevenths, and thirteenths, often difficult to do in the earlier music. Even Burney senses a freshness about *Bonduca*: 'there are new harmonies hazarded, which I do not recollect having seen in anterior contrapuntists, at least of our own country' (*A General History*, ii, 396). Perhaps the most striking feature of the score is its unity, present to such an extent only in *Dido and Aeneas* and *The Fairy-Queen*. Almost all the numbers are linked by characteristic figures, the most audible being the ascending diminished fourth and the augmented triad. Even the act tunes are patently related to the rest of the music.

Bonduca was obviously rushed into production at the beginning of the 1695-6 season in response to the generally successful offerings of the renegade company at Lincoln's Inn Fields. In the preface to the 1696 playbook, the Drury Lane actor George Powell writes that he 'prompted a

---

[23] 'Purcell's Stage Works', pp. 214–15. Zimmerman, however, believes the events happened the other way round: see *An Analytical Catalogue*, p. 275, and *Henry Purcell* (New York: Macmillan, 1967), p. 219.

Friend of mine, a much abler Hand than my own', to adapt Fletcher's old tragedy. Its hasty execution is reflected by a flood of misprints, incorrect and contradictory stage directions and speech prefixes. A piece of hack work this may be, but the choice of *Bonduca* for transformation into a musical was sound, since the original requires more songs than most Jacobean plays. In fact, Powell (or his friend) did not take advantage of all the scenes with music (see IV.i and V.i), preferring instead to expand the sacrifice in Act III. Purcell's experience with such episodes may well have prompted the play's revival.

Fletcher's drama is an uncompromisingly objective study of enemies. Both the Romans and the Britons have among them men of honour, the magnanimous invading General Swetonius and the defending Caratacke, an admirer of his opponents' valour. Both camps have self-destructive leaders, Penius, a fair-weather ally of the Romans, and Bonduca (or Boadicea), the fatally flawed 'British heroine'. And Judas, the Roman who bites the hand that feeds him, is balanced by Bonvica, a crafty British princess. In Fletcher's play the invaders are ultimately victorious because Swetonius is compassionate, noble, and gracious, while Bonduca is brash and crude, especially in speeches to her daughter. Powell's scribbling friend attempted to shift the favourable light from Swetonius and the Romans to Bonduca and the Britons, but failed.[24] By retaining the outlines of the story, he was forced to depict Bonduca as being unfit to lead the defence of the nation, and her battlefield blunder in the third act still results in a humiliating defeat. Another grave disfigurement of the original is the adapter's marring the subtly drawn Bonvica, a thoroughly believable mixture of wickedness and adolescent innocence. She is all but removed from the first four acts of the 1695 version and, in an awkward attempt to pour on sentimentality, is required to sing her own truly touching lyric in Act V. Members of the audience unfamiliar with the original must have wondered why an insignificant character was suddenly and belatedly allowed to reveal so much of herself immediately before committing suicide. By far the most serious dramatic imbalance is the new sacrifice scene in the third act. Fletcher treats the druid incantation as a brief entertainment. But the adapter, probably under orders to write something substantial for Purcell, tried to make the temple scene the central pillar of the tragedy.

The drama begins, I believe, with the overture, scored for trumpet and strings.[25] Only the most liberal of modern music historians would claim that any of Purcell's continental contemporaries imagined the action of

---

[24] The two versions are discussed at length by Arthur C. Sprague, *Beaumont and Fletcher on the Restoration Stage* (Cambridge, Mass.: Harvard Univ. Press, 1926), pp. 160–5.

[25] The only source for the trumpet part is the set of part-books in Cambridge, Magdalene College MS F.4.35 (1–5), fol. 83v. It largely duplicates the first violin, but its authenticity is strongly suggested by bars 49–56, where the trumpet holds an E for eight bars while the violin moves to another point of imitation. See also Laurie, 'Purcell's Stage Works', p. 241.

their operas to commence with the overture. But the idea was not unknown in late seventeenth-century English theatre circles. John Dennis states matter-of-factly that the drama of his tragedy *Rinaldo and Armida* (November 1698) 'begins with the Beginning of the Overture, which is a Trumpet-Tune, supposed to be Play'd by the Good Spirits who have the Conduct and Care of Action, and the Guardianship of the Persons concern'd in it'.[26] Purcell's C major overture begins with rushing French roulades that soon abate to less agitated rhythms. As early as the fifth bar, the music moves to G minor, an unexpected turn for a piece begun so bravely.[27] The steady descent of the bass line is arrested in bar 9, and the pall cast by the death key is swept away at the return to sprightly rhythms in C major. This brief sally may be simply the composer's acknowledgement of the tragedy to follow, but the wrenching C minor close of the overture (Example 14) is clearly linked to later pieces. The bouncing canzona

Example 14. *Bonduca*: final section of overture

ends in the tonic major, but immediately the second violin ascends a diminished fourth, an interval later to acquire pathetic connotations, producing an augmented chord, C-E-Ab, a sonority that recurs time and again in the rest of the score. The bias towards F minor and the descending chromatics evoke a strong feeling of lamentation; even the sounding of G major in bar 3, perhaps an atonement for the G minor passage near the

[26] *The Musical Entertainments in the Tragedy of Rinaldo and Armida* (1699), ed. Herbert Davis, rpt in *Theatre Miscellany*, ed. C. H. Wilkinson (Oxford: Blackwell, 1953), p. 107. See also my *Music in the Restoration Theatre*, pp. 57–8, 60.

[27] *A Collection of Ayres for the Theatre* (1697), the most important source for the act music, does not give the Bbs in the second violin part in bar 6, though they are found in all the early manuscripts.

beginning, is coloured by an E♭, producing the characteristic triad. Bonduca's C major glory is shattered even before the play begins.[28]

The temple scene in III.ii depicts a crumbling monarchy, a queen
doomed by her shortcomings as a soldier, and the senselessness of continuing a hopeless war. Having just won a battle against the under-
nourished and bedraggled Romans, she asks the druid priests to petition
the gods for another, more decisive victory. But the augurs are unrespon-
sive and the scene falls embarrassingly flat. Purcell, obviously aware that
the gods are unco-operative because the Britons are about to be soundly
defeated, alludes to the disaster in several ways and also lays the ground-
work for the intense pathos of Bonvica's song in Act V. The drama of this
scene is propelled mainly by the conflict between C major and C minor, as
the royal key is under constant attack from its sinister parallel. Adding a
layer of irony to the struggle is G minor, which serves its traditional
function. The symphony preceding the invocation 'Hear us, great
Rugwith' recalls the close of the overture, beginning with similar rhythms
and descending chromatic lines. Purcell wastes little time in establishing
the prominence of E♭ itself. In bar 7 of Example 15a, the perfect cadence
in G minor is spoilt by the viola's deflection to the contentious pitch, and
later during the chorus (Example 15b) a cadence in C minor is blurred by

Example 15. *Bonduca*: 'Hear us, great Rugwith', bars 6–7 and 24–5 (strings omitted)

an anticipatory E♭ and the 'irregular' resolution to A♭ major. Clashes
between E♮ and E♭ are sprinkled throughout, but nowhere more strikingly
than near the end of this chorus (shown in Example 16), where the druids'
plea 'O save us' slips helplessly downward.

The chorus is followed by 'Hear, ye gods of Britain', a magnificent bass
song mentioned by Burney for its ingenious transition from recitative *à
pedale* to a 'spiritedly accompanied' air. He admires 'the true dramatic cast
of this composition', as well as its 'new harmonies', citing the fifth bar in
which 'we have a 2d, 4th, flat 6th, and sharp 7th, which, prepared by a 4th
with a 6th and melted into a common chord, have a very fine effect' (*A
Géneral History*, II, 396–7). This 'new' harmony is simply a diminished-

---

[28] Westrup admires this close, 'where we may suppose Purcell to have been stirred by the suggestion of the tragic theme' (*Purcell*, p. 152).

Example 16. *Bonduca*: 'Hear us, great Rugwith', bars 53–5 (strings omitted)

O save us,   O save us,   save__ us,

O save us,   O save us,

seventh chord sounded over a tonic pedal, a device that Purcell had already used to eerie effect in the witches' music in *Dido and Aeneas* and the Frost Scene in *King Arthur*. That Burney singles out this rather commonplace sonority and ignores a later extraordinary one generated by the uncompromising counterpoint (Example 17) gives a rare glimpse of the critic's usually well-hidden naïveté.

Example 17. *Bonduca*: 'Hear, ye gods of Britain', bars 8–9

Violins

Viola

Druid

Clip, clip their wings, clip, clip their wings,   clip,clip their wings, __ or chase__

B.C.

The G minor duet and chorus for sopranos and recorders, 'Sing, sing ye druids' (originally a speech for Caratacke), is a hypnotic, muted call for celebration that seems far too long; the problem is aggravated by the Purcell Society Edition's inexplicable addition of four bars of ritornel not found in any of the sources (XVI, 69, bars 20–4). The piece is built over a ground, one of the most malleable of all Purcell's modulating ostinato basses. The duet conveys much the same feeling as the similarly accompanied countertenor air in Act II of *Dioclesian*, 'With dances and songs', which is also on a ground. Each is an ill-timed Te Deum, which perhaps explains its restraint, even lugubriousness.[29]

[29] See Dent, *Foundations*, p. 221, for a more charitable analysis.

The music ceases and Bonduca and the princesses offer prayers, but the altar does not smoke with a good omen. According to the 1696 play-book, General Caratach, acted by Powell at the première, is supposed to deliver a spoken invocation, which begins 'Divine *Andate*! President of War'. But Purcell elevated the six-line speech into a vivid tenor recitative (given complete in Example 18),[30] thereby reducing Powell's role in the scene. The

Example 18. *Bonduca*: 'Divine Andate!'

Di-vine Anda-te! pres-i-dent of war, The for-tune of the day de-

- clare. Shall we, shall we to the Ro-mans yield, Or shall each arm that wields a

spear, Strike it through a mass - y shield, And dye with Roman blood— the

field, dye with Ro -   -   -

-                -   man blood the— field?

[30] Source: British Library Add. MS 5337.

solo recalls the earlier conflict between E♮ and E♭. The rising opening line
reaches E♭ at the word 'war'; and in the midst of the important question
asked in the invocation comes a truly stunning passage. The leaping
diminished octave in bar 9 is echoed three bars later by the simultaneous sounding of the two notes. For Purcell, a melodic major seventh or
diminished octave is a passionate exclamation at the threat of impending
death.[31] The tenor priest thus answers his own question, yet the oracle
responds: 'Much [blood] will be spill'd'. The Britons, collectively misinter-
preting the all-purpose prophecy, launch into a confident call to battle, first
with the duet for countertenor and bass 'To arms, to arms', then with the
ever-popular, if slightly vacuous, 'Britons strike home'. In the trumpet
symphony preceding the duet (see Example 19), Purcell presages the out-

Example 19. *Bonduca*: 'To arms', bars 1–3

come of the drama. After the obligatory move to the dominant, the music
shifts without warning to G minor – a terrible irony. The chilling B♭ in the
second violin part is not found in *A Collection of Ayres*, nor do the bass
figures of the following duet show the G minor chord in the corresponding
location, but nearly all the early manuscript scores include it. This small
touch, in which one hears the sanguine Britons tumbling headlong into
oblivion, is the work of a master dramatist.

Act V finds Bonduca and her family trapped in their castle, besieged by
the vanquishing Romans and refusing to surrender. Claudia, the older
princess, rants at the death of her lover, Venutius; then follows a pathetic
vignette for young Bonvica, who has hardly appeared at all in the first four
acts of the 1695 version. Probably because she was portrayed by the teen-
aged singer Letitia Cross, the anonymous adapter gave Bonvica her own
swan song. As is detectable in her spoken charge to a maid, the scene
panders to the sentimental:

> Where shall the wretched Off spring of *Bonduca* fly,
> To escape those dismal Screams of Horror,
> That fill the *Britains* Ears? Oh wretched Mother!
> Unhappy Sister! More unhappy I!
> Their Courage makes th'approach of Death

[31] See the discussion of 'From rosy bowers' in *3 Don Quixote*, Chapter 4.

> Seem pleasing: But I have the true fearful
> Soul of Woman; and wou'd not quit the World.
> *Julia*, call *Lucius*, and bid him bring his Lute;
> Fain wou'd I leave this dire consuming Melancholy.
> [*Enter* Lucius *with a Lute*.]

Miss Cross then sang 'O lead me to some peaceful gloom'. Since Bonvica had conquered no one with love or arms in the 1695 version, the final couplet requires some explanation: 'What glory can a lover have, / To conquer yet be still a slave?'[32] This, a reference to Fletcher's Bonvica, who plays a full and active role in the earlier play, both as lover and warrior, is yet another sign of the adapter's haste. Moore is troubled by the extreme contrast between the warlike setting of the lines quoted above and the stalking loneliness of the opening section, labelling the song 'one of Purcell's rare failures', largely because of its incongruous bravura passages (*Henry Purcell & the Restoration Theatre*, p. 154). But as in many of his great vocal works, the opening bars set a mood for the whole piece, even though the style changes radically and often throughout. It is laced with the 'pathetic' diminished fourth B♮/E♭ heard prominently in the overture and act tunes (see Example 20). And the leap upwards of a major seventh in the

Example 20. *Bonduca*: 'O lead me to some peaceful gloom', bars 61–7

penultimate bar recalls the threnodic gasp in the tenor recitative shown in Example 18. This is the only song in the serious dramas that relies on a child and on contrived pathos for its effect. But unlike Bonduca's nephew, Hengo, who bravely endures starvation only to be slain by a heartless Roman soldier near the end of the act, Bonvica expresses genuine fear. The song conveys her sinking spirits and her panicky attempt to summon heroic courage.

[32] In British Library Add. MS 22099, fol. 62, this reads 'What glory can a Souldier have'.

Bonduca is a cheap and careless revision of Fletcher's tragedy. Onto the original theme of honour among enemies is grafted brassy patriotism and mindless bloodshed. One of Purcell's greatest theatrical achievements is the reconciliation of these disparate themes through music: the patriotism is treated cynically, and from the bloodshed emerges tragedy.

The Indian Queen

Purcell's last major stage work is *The Indian Queen* of 1695 (z 630). Although it contains much less music than the semi-operas – even when Daniel Purcell's lengthy afterpiece is included – and bears the wounds inflicted by a slipshod first production, the score is of the highest quality throughout. The composer has, in truth, contributed as much to the drama as the poet.

The Indian Queen is a collaboration of Dryden and his brother-in-law Sir Robert Howard, but authorities have hotly debated the division of labour. Axe grinding has defined the camps. Dryden editors John Harrington Smith and Dougald MacMillan allow 'that the second and third scenes of Act II may contain some writing by Howard', whereas in 'other parts of the play Dryden's hand would seem to predominate or to be exclusively present'.[33] They are joined by George McFadden, who theorizes 'that Dryden "wrote" practically all of *The Indian Queen*, making some use of a prose plot outline contributed by Sir Robert Howard'.[34] On the other side, H. J. Oliver argues that the play is really Howard's, 'while recognizing the probability that Dryden showed an interest in it and contributed to its success in some indefinable but not major way'.[35] This is a classic conflict between bibliographers and critics. Oliver simply points out that *The Indian Queen*, whose earliest recorded performance was on 25 January 1664, was published in Howard's *Four New Plays* of 1665 and republished in his *Five New Plays* of 1692. He adds that Dryden did not include it in a list of his works compiled in 1691, though he did stake a claim to *The Tempest* (which he and Davenant adapted in the late sixties); only once did the laureate mention that part of *The Indian Queen* 'was wrote by me'. J. H. Smith, however, *feels* that Dryden wrote some of the scenes because the verse is so fluent. McFadden seconds him, adding that 'It is beyond reasonable doubt, I think, though no one seems to have appreciated it, that in Dryden's relationship with Sir Robert Howard the rift in the lute was Howard's printing of *The Indian Queen*, without any mention of a collaborator . . .' (*Dryden the Public Writer*, p. 72). The 1695 alteration on which Purcell worked is significantly different from the original, especially in the musical scenes. As is shown below, Betterton can

---

[33] *The Works of John Dryden*, VIII, 283.
[34] *Dryden the Public Writer* (Princeton: Princeton Univ. Press, 1978), p. 49 n.
[35] *Sir Robert Howard* (Durham, N.C.: Duke Univ. Press, 1963), p. 67.

The Plays

be ruled out as the adapter, and Dryden, who had many dealings with Purcell in the early nineties, may have undertaken the revision himself, since it is so expertly made.

This dusty old play has the catalytic ingredients of the later, grander heroic dramas: the theme of love and honour, battles, an usurping monarch, a hero who insults the king, a visit to a soothsayer, and a climactic, ironic suicide. But the work is only a *Rheingold* to its larger successors and would probably have been completely forgotten if not for its sequel, *The Indian Emperour*. The plot is simpler than those of the later heroic plays, yet beautifully balanced and well paced, and opulent scenes helped to make the first production a great success. It required little music: a curtain tune before the prologue; a warlike dance in III.i; a duet for aerial spirits in III.ii; and a song of sacrifice for a priest in V.i.[36] In short, *The Indian Queen* seems an unlikely candidate for transformation into one of the great music dramas of the era.

The month of the première of the 1695 adaptation is the subject of much speculation, ranging from early April, shortly after Rich's company resumed acting, to well into the next season, even after Henry Purcell's death in November. I shall first state the facts and summarize various authorities' interpretations of them, and then offer my own scenario based on evidence provided by the main sources of the music. Sometime in 1694 the patentees of the Theatre Royal paid Betterton £50 in advance to 'gett up ye Indian Queen'.[37] The doyen of English actors had been the driving force behind almost all the dramatic operas. As with *Dioclesian* in 1690, he was probably to prepare the play as the company's major spring musical attraction by trimming the original dialogue, adding musical scenes, devising some stage 'business', contracting a composer and choreographer, and holding rehearsals.[38] But by 10 December 1694 he had not yet begun the project, undoubtedly because of the bitter dispute with the company managers.[39] Buttrey believes the operatic *Indian Queen* was to have honoured Queen Mary on her birthday, 30 April, and that Daniel's masque of Hymen was attached to Act V in order to conclude with a celebration.[40] But the queen died in late December 1694, and when the Theatre Royal reopened after three months of mourning, the play had to be given without the final entertainment. Buttrey cites as primary evidence for a spring 1695 première British Library Add. MS 31449, the earliest

---

[36] Some instrumental music by John Banister from an early production survives, but whether or not this dates from 1664 is uncertain. See my *Music in the Restoration Theatre*, pp. 181–2.

[37] The full 'Reply of the Patentees' (Public Record Office LC 7/3) is printed by Milhous in *Thomas Betterton*, pp. 230–46 (see esp. p. 240).

[38] For a discussion of Betterton's role in other dramatic operas, see Luckett, 'Exotick but Rational Entertainments', p. 133.

[39] See *The Works of John Dryden*, VIII, 325.

[40] 'The Evolution of English Opera between 1659 and 1695', pp. 290–5.

manuscript, which he erroneously claims lacks the fifth-act masque, while Add. MS 31453, which is of a later date, includes it. Yet April 1695 is the earliest date that the operatic *Indian Queen* could have been performed, since a partial cast-list copied into Add. MS 31449 (fol. 1) includes only the names of actors left behind at Drury Lane after the rebels set up the theatre in Lincoln's Inn Fields. Several scholars – the editors of *The London Stage*, Part 1, among them – join Buttrey in believing that the play was mounted shortly after the beginning of April, when acting resumed.[41]

Other authorities favour late autumn for the revival, about the time Henry Purcell died. The chief evidence for this is that Daniel's afterpiece is included in several of the early manuscripts. One of them, British Library Add. MS 31453, even has a suggestive note: 'Last Act by Mr Daniel Purcell, (Mr Henery Purcell being dead)'.[42] A logical assumption, but one unsupported by other evidence, is that during the final stages of composition Henry fell ill and his brother was brought down from Oxford to finish the last act. Hume posits a date 'sometime between late October and December 1695', giving considerable weight to Heptinstall's pirated edition, *The Songs in the Indian Queen*, which appeared in late 1695 with a dedication to 'Mr. *Henry Purcell*'.[43] If taken at face value, the publisher's note (reprinted in full by Squire, 'Purcell's Dramatic Music', pp. 529–30) clearly implies that the composer was still alive. With the outpouring of genuine affection for the Orpheus Britannicus after his death, Heptinstall would hardly have owned publicly to having acquired Purcell's score 'of your Incomparable Essay of Musick' by less than honest means. That he was in possession of the 'Original Draught' might suggest, however, that the composer was in no condition to protest against its improper distribution.[44]

An early spring première does not accord well with the musical sources, which point to the following series of events. Betterton's dispute with the patent-company managers was so bitter that he could never have agreed to 'gett up the Indian Queen' after reading 'The Reply of the Patentees' in December 1694. But they still wanted to produce the play in the spring after the period of state mourning and therefore probably engaged someone loyal to the company, perhaps even Dryden himself, to carry out the job Betterton refused to do. I believe Purcell had finished most of the vocal music before the Lord Chamberlain announced the establishment of Betterton's new company on 25 March, because the score appears to have

[41] Laurie suggests the slightly later date of May or June 1695 ('Purcell's Stage Works', p. 124).
[42] Fol. 69. The phrase in brackets was added by a later hand.
[43] 'Opera in London, 1695–1706', forthcoming in *British Theatre and the Other Arts*.
[44] Zimmerman (*An Analytical Catalogue*, p. 332) says 'the fact that Heptinstall, May and Hudgebutt had the temerity to bring out an edition unauthorized by Purcell suggests that they might have taken courage to do so during his last illness, or after his death'.

been written for the Theatre Royal's seasoned singers: the baritone Bowman, the sopranos Ayliff and Hodgson, the countertenor Freeman, and perhaps even Mrs Bracegirdle. But when most of these veterans joined Betterton's group, *The Indian Queen* had to be shelved while Drury Lane recruited and trained new singers.

That the company reorganization was an unexpected and crippling blow to Purcell is reflected by the makeshift casting of *The Indian Queen* when it was finally mounted. The prologue was meant to be sung by a boy and girl, countertenor and soprano, respectively. John Freeman, who was one of the few singers to remain with the patent company after the split, took the boy's part, while the demanding song for Quevira, the Indian girl, had to be sung by Jemmy Bowen; confusingly, 'the boy' was the girl.[45] The long aria in Act III for the God of Dreams, 'Seek not to know', was also performed by Bowen, though one early eighteenth-century score, Tenbury MS 338, states that it is 'for the tenor'. And neither of the celebrated songs known to have been sung by Letitia Cross seems at all right for this notorious ingénue. As explained below, 'I attempt from Love's sickness to fly', was probably designed originally for Queen Zempoalla herself, who would perhaps have been portrayed by Mrs Bracegirdle (now with Betterton), and the other, 'They tell us that you mighty powers above', fits Princess Orazia perfectly, except that she was acted by Mrs Rogers, who was not known for her singing.

The two versions of Ismeron's famous recitative 'You twice ten hundred deities' also indicate that the operatic *Indian Queen* had a complicated gestation. The first print, *Deliciae Musicae*, IV (1696), and the earliest manuscript, British Library Add. MS 31449, which dates from about 1698 or 1699, give a significantly different reading (version A) from the one found in three other important early manuscripts, British Library Add. MS 31447, Add. MS 31453, and Oriel College Mus. MS Ua 36 (version B). Example 21 shows the complete recitative, with both forms of the penultimate phrase. The variant is particularly noteworthy considering the high degree of unanimity among all the sources in other respects. One could simply dismiss version B for its directionless bass in bars 13–16, except that the Oriel College manuscript, the main source for this reading, is the most accurate and otherwise least problematic of all the scores, though perhaps slightly later than Add. MS 31449. Two questions arise: which version is earlier? and did Purcell make the dubious changes in B? Laurie approaches the disputed passage cautiously. While noting that version A is pasted over the other in Add. MS 31453, she argues that A is in fact earlier, because it is found in the earliest dated sources, *Deliciae Musicae*, IV, and *Orpheus Britannicus*, I; therefore, she suggests that someone tampered with the original after Purcell died ('Purcell's Stage Works', p. 129). If,

[45] See *The Songs in the Indian Queen* (1695), and *Orpheus Britannicus*, II (1702).

Example 21. *The Indian Queen*: 'You twice ten hundred deities'

however, one accepts for the moment that the bulk of the score was composed before March 1695, another explanation can be offered.

For a singer, the crucial difference between the two readings is that B goes a major third higher. 'You twice ten hundred deities' was first sung by Richard Leveridge, the young bass who probably joined the Theatre Royal sometime after the April split.[46] A survey of the dramatic music that he is known to have sung in ensuing years, including that which he wrote for himself, shows the upper limit of his range to be E or E♭, occasionally touching F.[47] Bowman, by contrast, was a baritone able to manage high G, as may be seen in his aria 'Let the dreadful engines' in *1 Don Quixote* and other pieces. Thus Purcell may have composed version B with him in mind. When he learned that Bowman was to be lost to the Lincoln's Inn Fields company in the March reshuffle and that Leveridge was to take the role of Ismeron, he then produced the lower version, which does not exceed high E♭.

Leveridge has become celebrated for his long and varied career, but I think a recent assessment of his skills goes too far in claiming that before he joined the Theatre Royal in mid-1695 'Purcell had not previously had a virtuoso bass singer available for his stage music' and that Ismeron's air is therefore 'more elaborate' than the bass songs he had written earlier.[48] Purcell's airs for Bowman require no less technical prowess than any of the pieces later sung by Leveridge. Furthermore, I wonder if the bass was altogether successful as Ismeron. His own part for *The Indian Queen* is preserved in Tenbury MS 1278, now in the Bodleian Library. It reveals that at some performance *after* the 1695 première he sang the roles of the high priest at the sacrifice in Act V and Hymen in Daniel's afterpiece; he also joined in the choruses 'We come to sing great Zempoalla's story' and 'We the spirits of the air'. But, curiously, he did *not* sing Ismeron in Act III nor Envy in Act II, two of the choicest roles Purcell ever created for a bass.

The first performance remains hidden by the disruptive events of 1695. Daniel Purcell's masque, discussed below, would appear to have been a part of the original conception of the whole work. But since we do not know exactly when he began to compose for the Theatre Royal, and because all the manuscripts that include his afterpiece were copied after his brother died, the masque of Hymen does not help solve the dating problem. In fact, nothing in the sources of the music would rule out a première well after Henry's death, except perhaps Hudgebutt's curious dedication to *The Songs in the Indian Queen*. What is important to recognize in this

---

[46] For an account of his early career, see Olive Baldwin and Thelma Wilson, 'Richard Leveridge, 1670–1758, 1: Purcell and the Dramatic Operas', *The Musical Times*, 111 (1970), 592–4.

[47] See, for example, the 'Enthusiastic Song' in *The Island Princes* (February 1699), British Library Add. MS 15318, fols. 41–4.

[48] Baldwin and Wilson, 'Richard Leveridge', p. 593.

welter of speculation is that the elder Purcell's part may have been composed in the spring of 1695, perhaps even in late autumn 1694, much
earlier than has hitherto been suggested. This hypothesis helps to explain
many anomalies in the various scores.

Fortunately, the earliest manuscript, Add. MS 31449, includes the full
text of the abridged play as well as most of the music in *partitura*, inserted
at the appropriate places. No other source of any of Purcell's major stage
works is nearly so complete. The Dryden editors Smith and MacMillan
contend that it 'represents the opera in an early form', that is, before April
1695 (*The Works of John Dryden*, VIII, 325, n.2). They believe that its cast
list was tentative, because the song in the fourth act, 'They tell us that you
mighty powers', was sung by Miss Cross, not Mrs Rogers, who is named as
having portrayed Orazia. But nothing suggests that Orazia would have performed her own song. Laurie argues that since the score is virtually complete in both spoken dialogue and music, it is probably a theatre copy used
for the first performance ('Purcell's Stage Works', p. 126). Add. MS 31449
is the work of two scribes. The spoken dialogue is in the hand of a professional scrivener, bold, regular, and highly stylized. The music hand is the
practised scrawl of one in haste; pitch errors are frequent and accidentals
unreliably recorded. The same hands appear in the full score of Motteux's
1699 adaptation of *The Island Princess* (British Library Add. MS 15318),
a volume identical in format to *The Indian Queen*. The music hand is also
found in Royal College MS 1172, an important collection of incidental
music for plays produced at Drury Lane between 1691 and 1699, and is
responsible for copying Purcell's masque for *Timon of Athens* in British
Library Royal Music MS 24.e.13 (fols. 62ff) and some of his theatre songs
in Tenbury MS 345 (fols. 11v–19).[49] These manuscripts appear to date
from about 1698–1700, thus suggesting that Add. MS 31449 may have
been written well after Purcell's death. I am tempted to guess that it was
prepared by one of the Theatre Royal's house copyists.

Though faulty as a musical document, Add. MS 31449 shows precisely
how the play was transformed into a tragic extravaganza. The original is
none too long, but the insertion of the Purcells' music required extensive
cuts. Of a total of 1404 lines, 640½ have been eliminated or reduced by
combination, including the songs, which were replaced with the new verses
set by Henry. To appreciate the adapter's taste and skill in making the
abridgement and to understand how Purcell strengthened the character of
Zempoalla, one must know something of the main plot as it stands in the
1664 version.

In defiance of history and geography, the play opens with the Mexicans
(Aztecs) engaged in a losing battle with the Incas. The Peruvian success is

---

[49] The same hand is also responsible for the table of contents and fols. 82v–100 of Add. MS
31452.

owing almost entirely to the skill and bravery of Montezuma, who came as a youth to the Incan court from parts unknown. When the Inca of Peru allows the brash young warrior to name his own reward, Montezuma asks for the hand of his daughter, Orazia. But the Inca vetoes the match because the suitor is of 'unknown Race'; Montezuma then angrily decamps to the Mexican side to avenge this insult on the battlefield. The Aztecs' is a sordid court. The queen, Zempoalla, has gained the throne by collaborating with the villain Traxalla in the murder of her brother. When she learns that the turncoat Montezuma has led her beleaguered army to victory against the Peruvian invaders, she is envious of his power and shocked to hear that the 'private man' has taken the Inca as a slave. Like nearly all of Dryden's later tragic antagonists, she falls in love with her nemesis, who remains arrogant and steadfastly devoted to Orazia. This unrequited love leads her to seek the help of a conjurer, who, being unable to divine her future, defers to aerial spirits to ease the queen's melancholy. The last two acts embroider this simple story. Zempoalla's son, Acacis, who voluntarily remained the Inca's prisoner, becomes a serious rival for Orazia's favour. And the Indian queen tries various ways to exploit this triangle to gain Montezuma's affection. The main plot and its sub-plots are brought crashing together in the last act when Acacis kills himself, Montezuma disposes of Traxalla, and Zempoalla, under the weight of these misfortunes and the imminent return of the banished queen (who is revealed to be Montezuma's mother), takes her own life.

The original Montezuma of 1664 is an unsavoury hero. He is unmoved by Zempoalla's distress, even by her death, and has little regard for Acacis's honour and self-sacrifice, until too late. In his impudence to kings and queens, he anticipates Dryden's greatest regi-clast, Almanzor of *The Conquest of Granada*. The Montezuma of *The Indian Emperour* is a far more sympathetic character who treats his enemy Cortez as an equal (see Chapter 2). The adapter of *The Indian Queen* perhaps had the less contumelious Montezuma of the sequel in mind when he began the extensive pruning of the 1664 version, for many of the passages that depict the darker side of the protagonist are deleted. For instance, in I.i when he demands Orazia's hand in marriage, the Inca's scornful reaction to the request is cut (lines 37–43), along with the key reference to Montezuma as a 'Young man of unknown Race'. Even stronger evidence of the adapter's plan is the removal of lines 66–87 of the opening scene: gone are Montezuma's decision to kill the Inca and his rationale for joining the Mexican side. Also thrown out is the passage showing Acacis's refusal to accept a traitor's offer of freedom. In all, a little more than a third of this scene is cut, but here, as in each of the shortened passages, the anonymous redactor carefully retains those closing speeches summarizing or alluding to the deleted action; thus, one learns why Montezuma bolts to the enemy camp, but his nastier side is concealed.

As Moore points out, the weakest character is Zempoalla (*Henry Purcell & the Restoration Theatre*, p. 163). Her jealousy of the hero is not fully explained, and her vacillation over the fate of her captives in the last two acts seems contrived to fill space. The adapter cleverly prepared the way for Purcell's strengthening of her character by reducing the role of her rival, Orazia, on whose plight much of the action turns. In general, the Inca's daughter is whitewashed, isolated from the gore and turmoil surrounding her in the 1664 version. This design is most apparent in her removal from the squabble between Acacis and Montezuma in Act IV. Zempoalla is also elevated by various other omissions. For example, Montezuma's callous reaction to her suicide, epitomized by the line 'How equally our joyes and sorrows move!' (in which 'sorrows' refers to the dead Acacis), is deleted.[50] And we are also spared his hollow moralizing. I cannot stress too much the care taken in the cutting of the play. The drama historian may be appalled by how much is removed, but the loss is recovered many-fold by the music. As in the libretto for Verdi's *Otello*, theme, action, and characterization of the original are distilled into compact units for the composer to expand.

The 1664 tragedy was preceded by a spoken dialogue between an Indian boy and girl rather than by the usual topical prologue. It refers to events in the drama itself and even looks ahead to *The Indian Emperour*: 'By ancient Prophesies we have been told / Our World shall be subdu'd by one more old'. Omitting only one couplet, Purcell set the prologue as a series of related but sharply contrasting pieces: three arias for the boy, a countertenor; one for the girl Quevira, a soprano; and two duets. The prologue opens and closes with the same C major trumpet tune, a liberal interpretation of the original stage direction, 'the Musick plays a soft Air [which] turns into a Tune expressing an Alarm'. The first two airs, settings of the poet's rather rambling discourse on native innocence, have repeating but variable bass patterns, both of which descend, the first in a steep plunge and the second in graceful curls. The long stretches of leisurely imitation in 'Wake, Quevira' and the tight motivic construction of 'Why should men quarrel?' reveal the heightened concern for counterpoint noticed earlier in *Bonduca*. The second song handles obsessive details masterfully, the generating spark being the word 'quarrel'. Quevira's anxiety is conveyed by the quarrelsome interplay of the accompanying recorders and the frequent clashes of A♭ and A♮. The rest of the prologue continues the relentless exposition of new and apparently unrelated melodic ideas. The open-

---

[50] Moore discusses the plot in detail (*Henry Purcell & the Restoration Theatre*, pp. 156–9), without mentioning that his analysis applies to the 1664 version and not to the one found in British Library Add. MS 31449, which is quite a different play. And the statement that 'at the end the entire dramatis personae, or at least those who are permitted still to live, praise her extravagantly' (p. 163) is misleading, since this does not happen even in the uncut version.

ing collection of pieces presents in miniature the tonal scheme of the entire work. The Indian girl is awakened by C major, the brash disturber of her 'Country's Peace', a key later to be linked to Fame and the imperious Zempoalla herself. The girl's querulous C minor will soon become associated with Envy. The duet 'If these be they, we welcome then our doom', though not an especially ominous line in context, is nonetheless in G minor, which will serve its conventional function in Act III. The return to C major through C minor also foreshadows larger events.

The second scene of Act II begins with a masque of Fame and Envy, Henry Purcell's only major interpolation into the drama.[51] In the original throne-room scene, devoid of music, an icy Zempoalla railed at her attendants for proclaiming Montezuma's victory over the Incas more loudly than the liberation of her phlegmatic son Acacis. The added verses, which at first seem incongruous to the action, pit Fame, a countertenor (Freeman), against Envy, a bass. The former bravely sings Zempoalla's praises in glittering C major, but the pompous chain of tonic and dominant harmonies pales when the chorus repeats the panegyric.[52] The music then shifts to a darker C minor, a relationship prepared by the prologue, for the engaging trio of Envy and his sibilant assistants, 'What flatt'ring noise is this, at which my snakes all hiss'. With its sinuous violin parts, active bass line, and clashes between A♭ and A♮, it recalls Quevira's song 'Why should men quarrel?' Throughout the exchange, Envy, like the Sorceress in the second act of *Dido and Aeneas*, is always accompanied by violins. While Fame lauds Zempoalla, Envy alludes to Montezuma: 'I hate to See fond Tongues advance / High as the Gods ye Slaves of Chance'. When Fame's chorus is repeated at the end of the scene, the victory sounds hollow indeed. The music transforms Zempoalla's external problems, represented in the original as a tableau, into an extended inner conflict – the erosion of glory by envy and guilt. In a sense the masque replaces II.iii, cut from the operatic version, in which Acacis wallows in the shame he feels about his mother's ruthless *coup d'état*.

An instrumental version of the chorus 'I come to sing great Zempoalla's story' serves as the second act tune. The large number of variant readings among the sources of the symphony suggests that it is not the work of the composer himself but was casually drawn from the chorus by other hands over the span of several productions, as if Purcell died before he could put the finishing touches on the score. Other pieces perhaps added after the event are the two dances found at the end of Act II in Add. MS 31449. The first, in C major (Purcell Society Edition, XIX, 47), is thoroughly incom-

[51] This is preceded by a long Italianate symphony scored for trumpet, two oboes and strings, a transposition from D major to C major of the opening piece of *Come ye sons of art away* (z 323). As this is found in all the important manuscripts of *The Indian Queen*, the transposition was probably done by Purcell himself.

[52] For a different interpretation, see Moore, *Henry Purcell & the Restoration Theatre*, p. 163.

petent and could hardly be by either Henry or Daniel Purcell. The other, in B♭ major (xix, 48), is a corrupt version of an air from the second music of *The Fairy-Queen* (z 629/2a).

The incantation in III.ii was the model for similar episodes in *The Indian Emperour, Tyrannick Love*, and several later tragedies, notably Lee's *Sophonisba*, scenes in which music has an important role. Yet the prototype requires none. Zempoalla, racked by nightmares and pangs of unrequited love, beseeches Ismeron, whom she finds asleep in his 'dismal Cell', to 'charm the passions of a troubled heart'. She recounts a dream in which she stood before an altar holding a mighty lion by a twisted strand. A dove descended, cutting free the lion, which then attacked and killed her. Ismeron, affecting perplexity at this none-too-good omen, offers to call up the God of Dreams for an interpretation by reciting the well-known charm 'You twice ten hundred deities'.[53] Zempoalla, impatiently threatening to withhold sacrifices to the gods, urges the Conjurer on to a more extravagant incantation, at the end of which the God of Dreams rises, only to disappoint the queen by refusing to reveal the future and scolding her for even asking 'Who 'tis shall wear a Crown, and who shall bleed?' This part of the scene ends as she '*sits down sad*'.

Purcell set most of the original spoken dialogue unaltered, creating with the charm 'You twice ten hundred deities' what Burney called 'the best piece of recitative in our language' *(A General History*, ii, 392). The macabre incantation 'By the croaking of the toad' became 'a freakish air' (Moore), and the long speech of the God of Dreams was elevated to a song for boy treble and oboe obbligato, 'Seek not to know'. The rest of the Conjurer's spoken dialogue is virtually eliminated, except for 'Who's that, that with so loud and fierce a call / Disturbs my rest?', which is truncated to 'Who's that Disturbs my rest?' Is this a sign that the inexperienced Leveridge could not be trusted with dialogue?[54] The unusually meticulous Add. MS 31449 dictates precisely the order of speech and song, but fol. 33 appears to contain a redundant passage. After Zempoalla commands Ismeron to begin his conjuration, the text copyist has entered the complete charm ('You twice ten Hundred Deities . . . on her dismal Vision wait'), the recitative version of which is given on the following pages.[55] Therefore, Ismeron appears first to have spoken the charm and, when it produced no

---

[53] In the 1664 version this is printed in italic, but no stage direction indicates that it was sung. Day, in *The Songs of John Dryden*, p. 141, argues that the incantation 'was probably recited rather than sung in the original performance'.

[54] In the anonymous farce *The Female Wits* (*c.* October 1696), a satire on dramatic operas (among other things), several leading actors and singers appeared as themselves. Miss Cross, for example, had an important speaking part. In I[ii] she invited Leveridge to join her in a duet. He entered, sang, and left without speaking a word.

[55] The order of events is confused by several folios being bound in out of order. Fol. 36, which has a later exchange between Zempoalla and Ismeron (III.ii.107–18), is placed before fol. 35, the beginning of the recitative.

result, repeated it in song, a striking affirmation of the power of music, especially if Leveridge was as poor a speaker as I suspect.

Although the Conjurer refuses to reveal in words what fate awaits the queen, Purcell's G minor recitative leaves little doubt. It is a catalogue of musical symbols for death interspersed with other pitch and key associations established earlier in the play. (For the following discussion, refer to Example 21 above.) Each gloomy word ('doomed', 'discord', 'dismal') is lifted from syntactic context and draped with dissonance or chromaticism, in an eerie, melodically enhanced alliteration leaving unuttered the fateful word. Purcell imparts the meaning of the fragment 'Men are doom'd' rather than the interrogative sense of the entire line (to paraphrase, 'Tell us, earthy spirits, what is man's fate?'). Thus, in bar 8 at the word 'doom'd', an ascending line is deflected chromatically to the leading-note of the key of death. With the chilling clash between B♮ in the continuo and Ismeron's B♭ in bar 13, the voice ignores the dictates of the accompaniment; G minor will out. An especially moving moment is the setting of 'great Zempoalla' in bar 15. The recitational C has the conventional royal overtones but is also the key-note of the Indian queen's glory in the second-act masque. By resisting the harmonies implied by the bass movement from A to B♭, the voice seems to reinforce Zempoalla's stubborn pride. At the words 'what strange Fate must on her dismall Vision wait', again interpreted somewhat out of context, Purcell quotes the most potent symbol for death known to baroque musicians, the chromatic tetrachord descending in the bass from tonic to dominant. Like that of the tenor priest in Act III of *Bonduca*, Ismeron's question is made rhetorical.

The aria 'By the croaking of the toad' fully displays Ismeron's skills, both musical and histrionic. It is remarkable for the liberation of the voice from its accompaniment; the two parts have separate expositions of the main melodic idea, and their independence is doggedly maintained through the setting of the word 'pants' in a close canon. The song and recitative are abstractly connected, the links being in a sense 'corrective'. For example, the descending chromatics at the end of the invocation leave a sagging cloud of despair hanging over the scene, a feeling eased by the 'very slow' middle section of the air (Example 22), in which the climax is a rare augmented-sixth chord which depicts the key word 'unwilling'. Besides its dazzling technique, the song is also a superb vehicle for the actor. In the recitative an entranced Ismeron raises and lowers his wand to no avail. His agitation grows in the first part of the air as he tries ever more extravagant means to make the God of Dreams appear. The quick section ends almost abruptly as the boyish deity begins to rise from under the stage; the triple-metre coda is all untroubled thirds and sixths.

The scene for the God of Dreams steers the action back to the business at hand. The original speech is an elegant exercise in half-hidden mean-

Example 22. *The Indian Queen*: 'By the croaking of the toad', bars 39–49

ings. Zempoalla wants to know the future, but the spirit demurs: if man could see 'his Destiny, he wou'd not live at all, but always dye'. The challenge for the composer was to convey this formal concealment by blurring the frequent images of despair. Though Dent believes the composer 'allowed himself an undue length' (*Foundations*, p. 223), the aria is remarkably soothing; the oboe reassures the voice, anticipating or answering each new phrase. Even the opening bars are reluctant to cadence in G minor, as the leading-note is eased into from below, thereby recalling bar 8 of Ismeron's recitative. Again, Purcell isolates sections of the text while retaining the overall sense of the verse. The fragment 'where Fate is most conceal'd' carries an important cadence in an optimistic Bb major (Example 23, bars 11–13), but the music quickly slides into G major for 'too busy man', depicting by this antithesis of the threnodic key the distance between the quick and the dead. The words 'sorrows more' come to rest on a strong half-close in G minor (bar 20), but in order to conceal 'future Fortunes', the composer abandons the resolution and moves directly to D minor. The next firm cadence in G minor is at the words 'always dye'.

The music imparts an unspoken message: Zempoalla is doomed. Near the end of Act V her dream is played out. Montezuma is about to be sacri-

Example 23. *The Indian Queen*: 'Seek not to know', bars 1-24

Example 23. (Cont.)

find____ his__ sor - - rows more If fu - ture__

for - tunes__ he____ should__ know__ be - fore.

ficed on the altar when word reaches the temple that Amexia, the banished queen of Mexico, is approaching in triumph. As events close quickly, Zempoalla recalls her visit to the Conjurer:

> My fatal Dream comes to my memory;
> That Lion whom I held in bonds was he,
> *Amexia* was the Dove that broke his chains;
> What now but *Zempoalla*'s death remains?

She releases the hero and kills herself. Without adding a single word to the original scene in Ismeron's cave, Purcell transformed an innocent excursion from the plot – a fruitless conjuration – into the turning point in the tragedy.

After the brilliant songs for Ismeron and the God of Dreams in III.ii, what follows is an anticlimax – but only dramatically, since the music in the second part of the scene to divert Zempoalla's depression is perhaps the best in the play. The duet on a ground 'Ah how happy are we' and the duet and chorus 'We the spirits of the air', both in A minor, are set to anonymous verses substituted for the original song 'suppos'd sung by Aerial-Spirits'. Why did Purcell seek new words here after following the 1664 text so closely earlier in the play? Probably because the deleted lyric

('Poor Mortals that are clog'd with Earth below') continues the dreary *double entendre* of the preceding speeches. Surfeited, he sweeps away the gloom with a 'Trumpet Overture' in D major. Avoiding further comment on Zempoalla's fate, the new verses return to the original reason for her visit to the Conjurer. The spirits 'pitty tender Souls whom ye Tyrant love Controls', but are not as immune from 'human passions' as they claim. The busy, ever-shifting ground and the languorous sighs contradict the meaning of the central couplet: 'Those wild tenants of the breast / No, never can disturb our rest'. In the second piece, a *gavotte en rondeau*, the spirits explicitly answer the queen's query about Montezuma: to paraphrase, 'jealousy will tarnish your greatness; if you continue to pursue the slave (Montezuma was formerly the Inca's servant), your empire will suffer'. Ismeron has asked the aerial spirits to bring Zempoalla's soul 'back to its harmony', but they are unable to alter the prevailing mood. Reacting more like frail human creatures than inhabitants of the air, they become infected with her melancholy.

The precise location in this scene of the famous song 'I attempt from Love's sickness to fly' is uncertain. In British Library Add. MS 31449 it follows the spirits' duets, and its key, A major, implies inclusion here. Moore notes that it could 'be rendered by Zempoalla herself were she a singer; as it is, we accept the sentiments as hers' (*Henry Purcell & the Restoration Theatre*, p. 167). But the song is known to have been sung by Miss Cross, not by Mrs Knight who portrayed the queen.[56] Despite directions in two of the manuscripts (Oriel College Mus. MS Ua 36 and British Library Add. MS 31453) that it be sung immediately before the repetition of 'We the spirits of the air', 'I attempt from Love's sickness' does not fit well here. Overlooked by Purcell scholars and even by the editors of the California *Dryden* is an addition to the stage direction at the beginning of III.ii in Add. MS 31449, fol. 32v (shown in my italics): 'Ismeron asleep in the Scene. *Song here*: Enter Zempoalla'. Thus, the celebrated lyric was probably performed off stage at the beginning of the scene before the queen entered, thereby allowing her to express hidden, lyrical emotions though mute. Earlier in this chapter I proposed that had *The Indian Queen* been mounted at Drury Lane or Dorset Garden before Betterton's group left, Mrs Bracegirdle might have acted the title role, singing her own song. But she stayed at Lincoln's Inn Fields, and then the Haymarket theatre, until her retirement in February 1707, while the play remained in repertoire at Drury Lane, so she probably never had the opportunity.[57]

[56] There is a slim chance, of course, that despite Cross's being named as singer in *The Songs in the Indian Queen*, Knight may also have been capable of delivering it, since the latter sang 'O how you protest' in Thomas Scott's *The Mock-Marriage* about this time.

[57] *The London Stage*, Part 1, following p. 400, reproduces a mezzotint showing Mrs Bracegirdle as 'The Indian Queen', but the allusion is to Semernia in Behn's *The Widow Ranter*: see Highfill, *A Biographical Dictionary*, II, 281.

Similar confusion surrounds 'They tell us that you mighty powers above'. Though both *The Songs in the Indian Queen* (1695) and Add. MS 31453 place it in Act IV, naming Miss Cross as the performer, its exact position is unknown. More disturbingly, all the other early sources, including the 'Gesamtausgabe' Add. MS 31449, lack it. The lyric was surely designed for Orazia.[58] In the first scene of Act IV, she and her lover, Montezuma, are held captive by Traxalla, who offers to spare the hero if Orazia will submit. The opening couplet of the second verse could refer only to her: 'To suffer for him, gives an ease to my Pains, / There's joy in my Grief, and there's freedom in Chains'. Ideally the song should replace Orazia's touching speech (IV.i.113–22) when she is left alone to choose between her chastity and Montezuma's life. But this scene is removed from the 1695 version. Why should the most important manuscripts include not the song but an exquisite four-part instrumental arrangement, labelled variously 'fourth act tune' or 'symphony'?[59] I should guess that the piece was conceived as an act tune, the words being added later during the last-minute rush before the première or after the composer's death – or both. The practice of attaching verses to instrumental pieces was not unknown at the time, and Purcell himself seems to have condoned it.[60] The word-setting of 'They tell us' is decidedly inferior, especially toward the end of the first verse, and any comparison with 'If love's a sweet passion' from *The Fairy-Queen*, a superficially similar piece in many respects, is entirely invidious. But the instrumental version is surely by Purcell, as a glance at the inner parts suggests, especially in the second strain (shown in Example 24),

Example 24. *The Indian Queen*: song tune version of 'They tell us that you mighty powers above', bars 9–14

---

[58] Buttrey, 'The Evolution of English Opera', p. 296, posits that it concerns Zempoalla.
[59] Laurie, 'Purcell's Stage Works', p. 132, believes that it is a symphony rather than an incidental tune.
[60] See the discussion of *Rule a Wife and Have a Wife* in Chapter 4.

where suspensions resolve in one voice, only to grind against another anticipating the next chord. The act tune is genuinely pathetic, while the song is contrived, the text robbing the melody of its majesty.

Henry Purcell's final music, comprising the symphonies, recitative, and choruses at the sacrifice in Act V, is set to verses replacing the song for a single priest in the original play. The hieratic processional in F major, though grand, is wholly conventional – the least inspired of any music in the tragedy. But when the sacrifice draws near, Purcell shifts to F minor for the contrapuntal chorus 'All dismal sounds thus on these off'rings wait', which exploits the traditional dissonances of music in the 'horror key', including diminished-seventh chords and augmented triads. The effect is still formal and restrained, being the composer's usual response to group emotion, here further diluted because Montezuma, Orazia, and the Inca are spared. A concert performance of *The Indian Queen* can be unsatisfying. One listens in vain during the 'grimly dissonant' final chorus for a summation of the irony of the plot, only to hear the art lavished on transforming Zempoalla into a grandly tragic figure dissolve into pagan conventionality and contrapuntal artifice.

Daniel Purcell's hymeneal masque, which lies entirely outside the drama, requires only a little comment. To demonstrate piece by piece why he is inferior to his brother would be a pointless and depressing exercise. Yet despite the bland and spineless appearance of the music on the page, much of it would probably be very effective in the theatre. Furthermore, the tonal organization shows that Daniel tried to make his part fit into his brother's grand plan. The prologue, one will recall, is in C major/minor, with a central piece in G minor; Act II in C major/minor; Act III, G minor, then A minor/major; Act V, F major/minor; and the final masque is in C major and G major/minor. The cycle is completed by Henry's F major preliminary instrumental music, which leads to the C minor overture. So *The Indian Queen* is centred on C major, the initial bias towards the subdominant being balanced by the key of the minor dominant, G minor, and the farther removed A major of Act III. The shift to F in Act V is logically redressed by a return to the tonic in the masque. Also important is the thrice-replicated modulation from major tonic to minor dominant announced in the prologue: from the C major masque in II.ii to the G minor conjuration scene; and from the D major overture in III.ii to the A minor duets for the aerial spirits; while in the final masque the chain of pieces in C major is broken by Daniel's G minor air 'The Joys of Wedlock', which with its imitative dotted accompaniment for two recorders is a parody of Quevira's 'Why should men quarrel' in the prologue.

To condemn the Theatre Royal producers for tacking this series of lowbrow airs, dialogues, choruses, and an over-stuffed trumpet song onto the end of a serious play, thereby tarnishing Henry's magnificent music, is to ignore the fact that the operatic *Indian Queen* was moving in uncharted waters: tragic semi-opera. All the major musicals produced in the nineties had been comedies or tragicomedies; and in the tragic extravaganzas, music had not been allowed to threaten the pre-eminence of the spoken dialogue. But having added so much to *The Indian Queen*, Purcell disturbed the balance between spectacle and tragic action with music that is not simply grafted-on entertainment – even the throne-room masque in Act II is integral to the drama – but intricately embedded in the character of Zempoalla herself. Creating a true tragedy in music, he then, either through neglect or by his death, bequeathed to his younger brother the difficult task of making the play fit for the stage by providing a happy ending.

4 The Comedies

Purcell wrote music for more than twenty comedies, almost all premières. Two of them, Congreve's *The Old Batchelour* and *The Double-Dealer*, are not infrequently acted at universities and drama schools, and occasionally in the West End. Several others – three by Southerne, one or two by Durfey, and Dryden's masterpiece, *Amphitryon* – which scarcely see the light of day except in scholarly circles, ought to be prime candidates for revival. Happily, Purcell participated significantly in them. In addition to songs and dances for stock scenes such as serenades, entertainments, and the drinking of healths, music is closely associated with madness, feigned and real, the battle of the sexes, and eroticism. Unlike the serious plays and tragic extravaganzas, the comedies occasionally demand that actors perform their own songs. Some of the extraordinary parts created for singing actors are Lyonel in *A Fool's Preferment*, Cardenio and Altisidora in *1 and 3 Don Quixote*, Solon and Berenice in *The Marriage-Hater Match'd*, Fulvia and Quickwit in *The Richmond Heiress*, Friendall in *The Wives Excuse*, and Sir Symphony in *The Maid's Last Prayer*. These characters do not just sing and dance for diversion, but reveal through music facets of their personalities otherwise undeveloped.

In the comedies for which Purcell wrote music, the characters are ranked by wit and social position. The clever couples are at the top, followed by the less scintillating married ones, usually foolish city cuckolds with jilting and affected wives. At the next level in the pecking order are boorish or pompous fools, country cousins and fops, separated by a pronounced gap from plot-sparking maids, pages, footmen, and other servants; whores and ruffians, unless aristocrats, provide a rock-bottom foundation. The music is usually introduced into the plots of the second-rank dramatis personae as abortive serenades, incompetent concerts, and ridiculous love songs. Only a few of the singing characters mentioned above are of the highest order, and the clever women portrayed by Mrs Bracegirdle, for instance, were allowed to sing only when feigning madness or seized by a frisk. In general, the gay couples are above music, though songs frequently entertain or instruct leading ladies; and in Shadwell's *Epsom-Wells* Carolina, a woman of 'wit, beauty and fortune', dances a celebrated jig.

The mad song, the stock-in-trade of the most important actor–singers, is an intentionally eccentric genre also found outside the theatre in the concert rooms and the Playford song-books. There are two basic types, the first being an exuberant vehicle for a truly insane character. Other members of the cast (and the audience) listen as if on a Sunday outing to peer over the wall at Bedlam. Such voyeurism does not preclude the composer's displaying his art – in fact Purcell's mad songs are among his finest – but the singer is meant to be unbalanced, like Bess of Bedlam or Cardenio in *1 Don Quixote*, and the music does nothing subliminally to lessen his or her condition. The second type is the mad-song soliloquy. The character shares his innermost thoughts, revealing the cause of his affliction or explaining why he is feigning madness. The best examples are those for Lyonel in Durfey's *A Fool's Preferment*.

The vogue for the actor–singer and the particular popularity of Thomas Doggett led to another kind of character little noticed by drama critics: the 'accomplished fool', who, after an act or two as just another knave, shows skill in singing or dancing and is then taken more seriously by the clever people. In Durfey's *The Marriage-Hater Match'd*, for instance, Bias and his brother Solon seem as different as Tweedledum and Tweedledee. But the latter, acted by Doggett, who became known by the nickname 'Solon', attains a measure of respect in Act IV by joining the witty Berenice in a dialogue, after which she asks incredulously, 'Is this accomplish'd person a Fool?' That he possesses certain artistic talent is beyond question. But in assessing similar roles created by other actor–singers, notably the baritone John Bowman, the question of tone must be carefully considered. Does the ridiculous country squire Bowman often portrayed actually impress the clever people with his singing, or are their compliments ironical, like so many witticisms in the comedies of the period? Given Purcell's genius for capturing double meanings in the serious plays, can the music itself cut through the layers of cynicism?

Comedy in music is much harder to analyse than tragedy in music. In the serious dramas, certain devices – the descending tetrachord, the key of G minor, pungent dissonances, and others – often enhance morbid foreboding. Did Purcell also establish such a code in the music for comedies? Most of the songs and dialogues for actor–singers, excepting the remarkable mad ones for Bowman and Miss Cross, are simple, strophic, and tuneful. Naturally, their humour resides more in the verses and the manner of execution than in anything inherently funny about the music itself. There are exceptions, such as the 'broken-record' repetition in 'Man is for the woman made' in *The Mock-Marriage*. The question of musical language becomes particularly vexing when an apparently serious song is found in an entertainment that includes vulgar or patently satirical lyrics. For example, could the great duet 'No, resistance is but vain' in *The Maid's Last Prayer*, which was performed in Sir Symphony's hilarious concert shortly after some instrumental tomfoolery, have a hidden ironical message? Is it self-satirical, heard by the dullards in the audience merely as a facile display of seduction through music, and by the wits and would-be wits as overwrought passion? Surely not, for two reasons. First, the mood and tone of many scenes in plays such as *The Maid's Last Prayer* swing wildly back and forth from pathos to bawdry, from sentimentalism to slapstick. That Sir Symphony's music meeting includes both a quartet of fumbling gentleman–amateurs and a stunning duet performed by professional singers in perfectly in keeping with Southerne's kaleidoscopic approach to drama. The second reason to discount any idea that 'No, resistance is but vain' is self-mocking is purely intuitive: to set it thus would be counter to Purcell's musical personality, so movingly characterized by G. M. Hopkins as that 'forgèd feature', 'the rehearsal of own'. The composer's approach to any dramatic event or emotion, however complex, was plain and direct, thrust forward for all to hear. The best way to gauge the meaning of a puzzling scene such as that at the beginning of the last act of Crowne's farce *The Married Beau*, in which the sincerity of the adultress Mrs Lovely's apparent contrition is open to considerable question, is to listen to Purcell's music. It will speak far more distinctly across the centuries than any modern dissertation on Restoration attitudes about marriage.

Anyone who has performed or surveyed Purcell's forty or so songs for comedies and tragicomedies will surely have noticed the preponderance of pieces in A and D minor. The principal subject of nearly all the lyrics set in these keys is a man's unsuccessful pursuit of a woman's sexual favours.[1] None of the mad songs, the ill-tempered dialogues between husband and wife, the drinking songs, or those dealing merely with innocent love are in A or D minor, while those sung by characters who have recently gained sexual gratification, such as 'Celia, that I once was blest' in *Amphitryon*, are usually in G minor. The system of key associations in the music for comedies can therefore be summarized as follows: G minor, which has a threnodic function in tragedy, symbolizes *le petit mort*; since most of the songs are performed by underlings who are inept lovers, this key is fairly rare in the comic repertoire. A and D minor are linked with lust and persistent denial, with no apparent symbolic difference between them. C and F major are favoured for the mad songs and dialogues, and D major for exuberant verses with allusions to royalty. Unlike the system for tragedies in which key associations help to reveal irony and hidden meanings, the one for comedies is essentially static. Purcell simply preferred certain keys for certain kinds of lyrics, which suggests a private, perhaps even subconscious practice.

[1] There are two notable exceptions: ''Twas within a furlong of Edinboro' town', in G minor, from *The Mock-Marriage* (Jenny refuses to grant Jockey's wish), may not be by Purcell; 'There's not a swain', in E minor in one source and G minor in another, used in *Rule a Wife and Have a Wife*, was a G minor act tune to which verses about sexual denial were later added, apparently with Purcell's blessing; see discussions below.

The music for comedies does not fall into neat categories. Purcell's métier was the tragic extravaganza and the semi-opera; with a few exceptions he was usually allotted seemingly insignificant lyrics in the lighter plays, while the majority of the important songs for the actor–singers were set by other composers. And Mrs Bracegirdle, as explained above, performed only the music of John Eccles. This is not to say that Purcell was uninterested in musical comedy or, for that matter, in writing for Mrs Bracegirdle. Rather, his work on the operas and serious dramas, which carried greater prestige, left proportionally less time for the lighter forms. I will discuss the bulk of Purcell's music for comedies in groups according to playwright, since his chief collaborators – Dryden, Durfey, Southerne, and Congreve – perceived its role in their works variously. Durfey's *Don Quixote* plays are treated separately, being *sui generis* and the only comic equivalent of the tragic extravaganzas.

1. Dryden

Amphitryon

In the preface to *Albion and Albanius* (1685) Dryden offered Monsieur Grabu fulsome praise: 'When any of our Country-men excel him, I shall be glad, for the sake of old *England*, to be shown my error.' In the epistle dedicatory to *Amphitryon* (October 1690), the poet graciously ate his words. Owning that the young Englishman was as fine a composer as any on the continent, he added pompously, 'At least my Opinion of him has been such, since his happy and judicious Performances in the late *Opera*', that is, the previous season's great hit, *Dioclesian*. Purcell might have thought justifiably 'too little too late', since Dryden was mounting an already clamorous bandwagon by asking him to write act music and set three unremarkable lyrics for his new comedy. If the playwright had based his judgement of Purcell's genius only on the music for *Amphitryon* (z 572), proud though he may have been of their first joint effort, one might well wonder what all the fuss was about. It is a minor achievement compared to *Dioclesian* and even to the songs for *A Fool's Preferment*, which had been written two years earlier.

Dryden drew large parts of the comedy, one of the best plays of the period, from Molière, closely following the familiar story of Jupiter's adultery with Amphitryon's devoted wife, Alcmena. But he added two more love triangles – better called 'sex triangles' – both including the waggish Mercury, who, like his master, assumes human form for most of the play. With Jupiter in the image of Amphitryon and Mercury in that of his servant Sosia, the two deities, like Lord Rochester as mountebank, cut a wide swath through the lives of several mere mortals. In Mercury's case, the resulting misunderstandings are purely farcical. But the rapacious Jupiter's *noblesse* is entirely lacking in *oblige* when he forces a bewildered Alcmena to pick out the real Amphitryon after an eventful night with the impostor. When she chooses Jupiter (still in his human shape), her husband is nearly destroyed. Of course, Jupiter represents Charles II, and when the Thunderer appears in his true form at the end, Amphitryon feigns humility at the prospect of becoming, some months hence, the stepfather of Hercules; but Mercury, reflecting the cynical tone of the hard-nosed farce, observes that this is a fool's obeisance.

With its many magical transformations and gods in machines, *Amphitryon* would seem to offer more possibilities for music than any other comedy of the period. But Dryden, whose earlier plays include a wealth of ingenious musical scenes, eschewed such entertainments in the obvious places. And Purcell's three vocal pieces appear to have been worked into the already completed play even after it had been cast. The first comes near the end of Act III. In the preceding scenes, Jupiter, in the form of Amphitryon, steals a march on his double, who is making his way back from battle, and is warmly welcomed by Alcmena. After Jupiter leaves her bed early the next morning, her real husband arrives. Dryden takes great delight in the situation-comedy misunderstandings, and when Alcmena mentions the long night of passion, Amphitryon becomes extremely jealous and makes a stormy exit. His godly double then returns for another conjugal visit but is intercepted by Phaedra, Alcmena's money-grabbing confidante, who warns him of his 'wife's' nasty disposition. Jove bribes her to secure Alcmena's forgiveness, hoping to advance his cause by having a serenade performed beneath her window. Phaedra leads her mistress to the balcony, and Jupiter signals the musicians to begin 'Celia, that I once was blest', which is followed by a dance. The verses remind Alcmena of the night of bliss and ask her to allow her lover to return. That the song omits any reference to marriage does not lessen its relevance. In fact, it recalls Jupiter's speech to Alcmena in II.ii:

> Give to the yawning Husband your cold Vertue,
> But all your vigorous Warmth, your melting Sighs,
> Your amorous Murmurs, be your Lovers part.

The song does not soften Alcmena, who simply '*withdraws, frowning*'; Jupiter is left to regain favour with eloquently hypocritical words at the beginning of Act IV. Her mimed acknowledgement of the performance suggests that the music was an afterthought on Dryden's part. Despite being in the treble clef it was sung by the baritone Bowman, who also acted Phoebus *ex machina* in Act I, a richly humorous role which might easily have included singing. In this scene, however, he appears without explanation as an anonymous Theban musician. The piece is simple and mostly syllabic, with just a hint of the Scotch-air style detectable in the several female endings, the slurred pairs of disjunct quavers outlining third-related chords, and the lilting cadence shown in Example 1. This song (like those discussed below) was published in the 1690 play-book, complete with a six-bar ritornel for two violins and bass. Whether the symphony is supposed to serve as the dance mentioned in the stage directions is uncertain, though it seems too brief for the purpose.

Example 1. *Amphitryon*: 'Celia, that I once was blest', bars 5–8

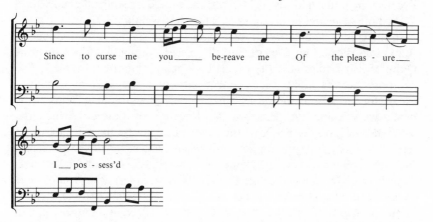

The longer musical scene near the end of the next act is the product of magic. Mercury, Sosia's double, has been pursuing the arch-tease Phaedra. To impress her, he unmasks, demonstrates his X-ray vision, and then with a stamp of the foot produces some dancers from under the stage. But first is sung 'Fair Iris I love, and hourly I dye', which Purcell altered to the more passionate 'For Iris I sigh . . .' It succinctly expresses Phaedra and Mercury's relationship: he pursues sex, not love, knowing she is as mercenary as he. The A minor setting and its brief instrumental introduction are linked by the motif of a falling third, rising minor sixth, and falling semitone, perhaps a trifle too severe and learned for Dryden's casually cynical verses. According to a stage direction, Mercury himself is supposed to sing ('Mercury's *SONG* to Phaedra'), but the music sources name Mrs Butler as performer. She also appeared in a machine in the first act – as Night. Mercury was portrayed by 'Mr. Lee', presumably the comedian Anthony Leigh rather than the singer John Lee (or Leigh). From Purcell's point of view, Bowman would have made a better Mercury than the non-singing Leigh. A surrogate singer here suggests that the songs were introduced at the last moment, leaving Dryden no time to make the alterations necessary to exploit the actor's special abilities. In all other respects, the casting was ideal, with Betterton as the overbearing Jupiter, Mrs Barry in the *tour de force*

role of Alcmena, and Mrs Mountfort and Nokes – both noted character actors – as the affected jilt Phaedra and the booby Sosia respectively.[2] Of course, Mercury (Leigh) and Sosia (Nokes) are supposed to resemble each other. So perhaps Bowman failed to get the choice part simply because he did not look enough like Nokes. Purcell's songs did not ease the casting problems. In fact, when Phaedra stamps on the ground to produce more music, the '*New Singers*' who pop up from below to perform 'Fair Iris and her swain' were none other than the recirculated Bowman and Mrs Butler. Because the latter had just performed the preceding song, she must have dashed off stage and down stairs to catch the ascending trap.

In the epistle dedicatory Dryden remarks that the pastoral dialogue in Act IV was the best received of Purcell's pieces, adding that 'the numerous Quire of Fair Ladies gave [it] so just an Applause on the third Day'. The composer set the slight verses almost entirely in the declamatory style, except for the formal and rather austere concluding rondeau 'Thus at the height we love and live'. Phaedra asks Mercury for a piece in which 'the Woman may have the better of the Man; as we always have in Love matters'. Obviously interpreting her ambiguous request in the lewder sense, the singers oblige with a skit in which a shepherdess's conventional coyness is easily shed; Iris offers to grant Thyrsis's ardent request if he promises not to 'kiss and tell'. The piece is not an especially inspired essay in the dialogue form, except for the exchange 'O kiss me longer, and longer yet, and longer' (Thyrsis) / 'Prepare to love me longer, and longer yet, and longer' (Iris), in which the depiction of the shepherd's growing frustration is too graphic to require analysis. In most of the amorous dialogues, the singers join their voices near the end to symbolize agreement or mutual gratification. But here, even though Iris says she will yield, Purcell avoids the usual anodyne of warbling thirds and sixths, never quite letting the voices come together; the cadence shown in Example 2 is especially harsh. After the music, Phaedra, hinting at some future dalliance, leaves Mercury in the lurch.

The complete score of the *Amphitryon* music, including the overture and act tunes, survives in Cambridge, Fitzwilliam Museum MS 683 (formerly MS c660); though not in Purcell's hand, it is a very early copy, perhaps dating from about the time of the première.[3] On fol. 27v a Dance for Tinkers is placed between 'For Iris I sigh' and the pastoral dialogue. This is the accompaniment for the dancers who '*come from underground: and others from the sides of the Stage*' in Act IV. That it is given only in two

[2] For a discussion of 'line casting' in comedies of the period, see Peter Holland, *The Ornament of Action* (Cambridge: Cambridge Univ. Press, 1979), Chapter 3, esp. p. 76.
[3] This is apparently the score once owned by Ralph Griffin and consulted by Barclay Squire in preparing his 'Note on the Music' for Summers's edition, *Dryden: The Dramatic Works*, VI, 539.

Example 2. *Amphitryon*: 'Fair Iris and her swain', bars 62–4

parts, treble and bass, might suggest a performance by a small stage band.[4] Why 'Tinkers'? One might as well ask why Jack-o'-Lantern and Spaniards dance in *Dido and Aeneas*. Because in grotesque or fantastic dancing, which stems from the antimasque tradition, anything was possible. In the fast section of this delightful piece with all its repeated notes (shown in Example 3), one can hear tinkers hammering away at kettles.[5]

Example 3. *Amphitryon*: Dance for Tinkers, bars 10–33

---

[4] See my article 'Restoration Stage Fiddlers and Their Music', pp. 315–22.
[5] Also found in Thomas Bray's *Country Dances*, Part 2 (1699), p. 15: 'An Entry by the late Mr. *Hen. Purcell*, the Dance, Compos'd by *Tho. Bray*'.

The Fitzwilliam Museum manuscript also reveals the order of the act tunes, which, unlike those in Settle's tragedy *Distress'd Innocence* (see Chapter 2), do not seem particularly tailored to the surrounding action. The B♭ major overture is notable for its lack of French traits, especially in the smooth rhythms of the introduction; and the concluding *adagio* should remind one that touches of the minor mode and descending chromatics do not have to sound pathetic and languorous.

Love Triumphant

Purcell wrote music for only one other new play by Dryden (excepting *King Arthur*, of course), the tragicomedy *Love Triumphant; or Nature will Prevail* (January 1694), the poet's last full-length drama. 'How happy's the husband' (z 582) is introduced at the end of the comic sub-plot, while the play's two other lyrics were set by John Eccles, with whom Purcell also collaborated later in the 1693–4 season on the first two parts of Durfey's *Don Quixote*. *Love Triumphant*, Dryden's most uncompromising split-plot play, was not a success. The serious and comic stories have a remarkable number of ingenious correspondences, but the alternating episodes are too long and discrete for coherence in either plot. Hume describes it as an intellectual achievement but an unworkable drama (*The Development*, p. 398).

Of the lyrics Eccles got the better part of a bad lot. At the beginning of Act III, 'What state of life can be so blest' (D&M No. 3664) is offered by Alphonso, Prince of Arragon, to his sister, Victoria. It expresses both mutual love and the guilt of incestuous passion (though we later learn that Alphonso was a warming-pan child and is unrelated to Victoria). Eccles does justice to the poem, but the stalking accompaniment of alternating crotchets and crotchet rests grows tedious by the third verse.

Purcell's song is performed in the first scene of Act V. Sancho and Carlos are rivals for Dalinda, but Carlos withdraws on learning that she is the mother of two illegitimate children; with mock honour, he allows Sancho, none the wiser, to marry her. When his stepchildren are sprung upon him at the wedding celebration, Sancho is furious, but the little boy and girl win him over with a dance. Carlos has composed an epithalamium that ''Twas meant a Satire; but Fortune has turn'd it to a Jest'. The verse, which seems harmless enough now, was censored by the Purcell Society, Vol. xx. It begins,

> How happy's the husband whose wife has been tried,
> Not damnd to the bed of an Ignorant bride
> Secure of what's left, he ne'er misses the rest
> But where there's enough supposes a feast.

Purcell set the two stanzas to a sprightly C major jig, first sung by Mrs Ayliff. It was followed by Eccles's 'Young I am and yet unskill'd' (D&M No. 4124), an odious piece of child pornography performed by a girl, perhaps one of Dalinda's offspring.

11. Durfey

Thomas Durfey's achievement as a playwright is difficult to assess. Best remembered today for his witty though too often coarse ballads collected in *Wit and Mirth; or, Pills to Purge Melancholy*, he was also a tireless author of numerous comedies, most of them successful, and two tragedies, the second of which, *Massaniello* (May 1699), though a failure, shows flashes of genius. Critics have not valued his stage works highly, charging that he does not explore the complexities of human relationships nearly so thoroughly as Southerne. He is also accused of choosing easy butts for satire (though the same may be said of Congreve), of preferring slapstick to witticisms (but here Shadwell far outstripped him), and, most censoriously, of allowing his characters to wallow in smut (yet at his foulest he can hardly hold a candle to Dryden). Durfey wrote with the self-assurance of success that 'I don't overload my Plays with Wit. Plot and Humour are my Province' (preface to *Love for Money*). The complaint of most concern to this study, however, is that some of the plays are mere excuses for musical shows. This may be true of *3 Don Quixote*, but in the other comedies music is nearly always used ingeniously and judiciously to extend humour, pathos, madness, and satire into realms unreachable through spoken dialogue. And Durfey alone among his contemporaries learned how to exploit the actor–singers.

Sir Barnaby Whigg

A production of the troubled King's Company, *Sir Barnaby Whigg: or, No Wit like a Woman's* (*c*. October 1681) tries to accomplish several things at once. The romantic main plot, in which the clever Gratiana wins the 'Loyal and Witty' Wilding, and the sub-plot for the foolish cuckolds, Captain Porpuss and Sir Walter Wiseacre, are purely conventional. With his hoary sea stories and nautical jargon the captain anticipates Bluffe in *The Old Batchelour* and other salty characters. The play is also a reply to Shadwell's *The Lancashire Witches*, a wild, fiercely Whiggish satire on Roman Catholicism given earlier in the season at the rival theatre. Sir Barnaby is a parody of Shadwell himself, savagely attacked in III.ii for self-professed musical accomplishments.[6] Of his skill on the lute, Sir Walter says, 'His touches are always so soft and gentle: besides, I have observ'd (Gentlemen)

---

[6] See the preface to *Psyche*; for *The Woman-Captain* (*c*. September 1679), Shadwell set his own lyrics.

that your thick squab-hand and short thumb-like fingers always become a Lute extremely.' Oblivious to the sarcasm, Sir Barnaby commands the musicians to 'Strike *F-fa-ut* sharp' and sing a song beginning:

> Farewell my Lov'd Science, my former delight,
> *Moliere* is quite rifled, then how should I write?[7]
> My fancy's grown sleepy, my quibling is done;
> And design or invention, alas! I have none.
> But still let the Town never doubt my condition;
> Though I fall a damn'd Poet, I'le Mount a Musician.

No setting of this devastating lyric survives.

Purcell's only known contribution is a song in the first act, an incidental entertainment probably meant to answer 'Now the winds roar' in Act I of *The Lancashire Witches*. Tired of effeminate pastoral airs, Captain Porpuss demands 'a Battel, a Siege, a Storm, or so', grumbling that he has not heard a decent lyric since 'Old *Broom*' died, presumably Alexander Brome (d. 1666), writer of numerous drinking songs. To set the stage, the captain begins a sea story, then gives the floor to an unspecified tenor who is later joined by a bass (but see n. 10 below). 'Blow, Boreas, blow' (z 589) recounts a violent storm at sea, during which a ship's captain swears at the mountainous waves instead of praying for deliverance.[8] Though the boisterous depiction of the tempest with wide melodic leaps and vigorous dotted rhythms resembles the recitatives of Purcell's mad songs and dialogues, the setting looks back to Locke, especially in adhering to the flamboyant declamatory style even in the triple-metre sections, such as the passage 'Then cheer my heart, and be not awed . . .' Despite these archaisms, 'Blow, Boreas, blow' is one of a handful of pre-1690 compositions to be included in the modern-minded first volume of *Orpheus Britannicus*, apparently remaining in the repertoire for many years thereafter. Burney writes that it 'was in great favour, during my youth, among the early admirers of Purcell; but this seems now more superannuated than any of his popular songs' (*A General History*, II, 393). In reliving the storm the singer claims that he and his mates scorned death; they were exhilarated when tossed up till the 'top-mast touched a star', and laughed with the sea-gods when carried 'to the deepest shades below'. But Purcell freezes a moment of terror with two bars of interpolated recitative that linger ominously over G minor (see Example 4).[9] The concluding duet in an exulting D major mocks these dangers with a dance-like display of briny lombard rhythms.[10]

[7] Shadwell's *Psyche* is based on Molière's.
[8] Compare the third verse of the storm song in *The Lancashire Witches*: 'The Saylers Swear, the high Seas rowl . . .'
[9] Source: *A Third Collection of New Songs* (1685).
[10] The solo sections would appear to be for tenor (although they are written in the treble clef); but the duet should probably be sung by soprano and bass to avoid several patches of undesirable part-crossing.

Example 4. *Sir Barnaby Whigg*: 'Blow, Boreas, blow', bars 30–5

now ___ we go Down to the deep - est shades be-low. A - las! a - las where are we now?

who,   who can tell! Sure 'tis the low – – est room ___ of   hell

A Fool's Preferment

After composing the ambitious storm song in 1681, Purcell appears to have written no theatre music for several years, except a health to James II, 'How great are the blessings' (z 494), performed between Acts II and III of Tate's 1685 adaptation of *Eastward Ho* (called *Cuckolds-Haven*), and a catch for a revival of Edward Ravenscroft's comedy *The English Lawyer* (z 594) in the same year. As suggested in Chapter 1, the long silence probably resulted from his ill-timed move from the musically orientated Dorset Garden company to the soon-defunct King's Company in Drury Lane, and from the snub of *Albion and Albanius*. Seven years separate *Sir Barnaby Whigg* and the songs for Durfey's *A Fool's Preferment, or, the Three Dukes of Dunstable* (z 571), first performed in April 1688, just a year before *Dido and Aeneas*.

The comedy is an adaptation of Fletcher's *The Noble Gentleman*. A social-climbing country wife – Aurelia Cocklebrain in Durfey, Madam Marine in Fletcher – has dragged her knavish husband to court to partake of its pleasures – gaming at basset for Aurelia and flagrant infidelity for Madam Marine. To keep her husband's money flowing, the wife pretends to be working for his preferment in the courtly circle. When the blunt squire demurs and insists on returning to his rural precincts, his wife's gentleman acquaintances, pretending to be the king's emissaries, offer to knight him. The bumpkin holds out for a dukedom, which is quickly granted. Consequently, the newly elevated Duke of Dunstable is kept in blissful ignorance of the sham until the real victim of the courtiers' ruse, the 'duchess', realizes that she is the ultimate butt of the elaborate jest.

Durfey's version differs most from its model in the character of the madman, Lyonel, Fletcher's Shattillion, whose ravings are fashioned into a warped reflection of the main plot. In the earlier play, his lunacy results from a coy denial by his betrothed, a favourite of the king. Durfey, seizing upon the suggestion of a royal liaison, fashions Lyonel into a victim of the monarch's promiscuity, an unsubtle allusion to the escapades of Charles II, for (departing from Fletcher's version) Lyonel's lover Celia has in fact been pressed into royal service. The king, having learned of the distress to the young man caused by his philandering, has released his former mistress before the play begins. The part of Lyonel was made for the actor-singer Will Mountfort, whose vocal skill had attracted attention three years before in the title-role of Crowne's popular comedy *Sir Courtly Nice* (May 1685); later, he even composed some act tunes for his own play *Greenwich-Park* (April 1691) and a song for Durfey's *The Marriage-Hater Match'd* (January 1692).[11] Colley Cibber, in making a falsely modest comparison between himself and Mountfort, praised the actor for his 'clear Counter-tenor' and 'warbling Throat', and the panache he brought to roles in which 'Singing was a necessary Part'.[12] Yet Genest thought that 'D'Urfey's worst fault is, that he has nearly spoilt the character of the madman', showing that he neither understood the playwright's reasons for having Lyonel sing nor was acquainted with Purcell's songs.[13] Fletcher reveals Shattillion's madness in his soliloquies, the one theatrical device wherein a character almost never dissembles. But Durfey gives Lyonel none; in fact he never leaves him on stage alone. His spoken dialogue seems as nonsensical and paranoid as Shattillion's, though much of it may have double meanings. Even the added lyrics do not clarify whether Lyonel's madness is real or feigned. In Fletcher's version, by contrast, Shattillion regains his wits. Durfey's stroke of genius was to allow the composer to bare the core of Lyonel's personality.

Fletcher delays the madman's entrance until the third scene of Act I, while Durfey begins the play with him. Celia gazes anxiously on the pathetic Lyonel, who is *'crown'd with Flowers, and Antickly drest'*; she admits that her unwilling affair with the king has caused his malady. His first utterance is Purcell's 'I sigh'd and I pin'd'. Although he speaks complete nonsense afterwards, the lyric has a coherent message: despite an 'abundance of brains', he lavished affection on a jilt. And the seemingly flippant second half of the song reveals an important theme: his insanity renders him as free as a child and 'as great as a King', a veiled attack on Celia's royal lover made under the protection of feigned madness. This conceit is found

[11] Mountfort also played the recorder in, for example, Dryden's *Don Sebastian* (December 1689), II.ii and III.ii.

[12] *An Apology*, ed. Fone, p. 76.

[13] *Some Account of the english Stage from . . . 1660 to 1830* (Bath: H. E. Carrington, 1832), I, 464.

in other mad songs of the period, perhaps most memorably in Purcell's 1683 masterpiece 'From silent shades and the Elizium groves' (z 370): 'And *Bess* in her Straw, whilst free from the Law, in her thoughts is as great as a King'. As will be seen shortly, this is not the only connection between *A Fool's Preferment* and Bess's little cantata. Like most of the songs for Mountfort in the play, 'I sigh'd and I pin'd' is a miniature. Tuneful and easily sung, it is clearly designed for a person of moderate vocal ability, though uncompromising in its attention to word-painting and imitative counterpoint. The opening passage, which recalls Lyonel's passion for his lost lover, is in D minor; at the mention of the king a shift is made to D major and a quick tempo. Despite Celia's protestations, Lyonel, pretending not to recognize her, proceeds bitterly to 'There's nothing so fatal as woman'. The wide vocal leaps and jagged rhythms clearly guide the performer's interpretation. Though Lyonel does not sing again until the second scene of Act III, his several babbling appearances in the interim preview events in the main plot. At the beginning of Act II a false message informs him that the king plans to hang him for treason. Shortly thereafter, Squire Cocklebrain is given the similarly fanciful news that the monarch is about to bestow offices upon him. Lyonel believes the king fears him; Cocklebrain is then told that he is being preferred because the sovereign fears his wrath if the squire is not elevated to the peerage. Though not wanting to show his true colours, the 'madman' tries to warn the witless country fellow of the elaborate scheme to trick him.

Lyonel's light-hearted mania finally turns to grief in Act III. He wanders into the house of the newly made 'duke', mumbling that Celia has married another or is dead. Two versions of this scene appear to survive. The 1688 quarto assigns him short verses beginning 'In yonder Cowslip lies my Dear' and 'I'll lay me down and dy within some hollow Tree'. These are fragments of the mad song 'From silent shades' mentioned above. Both begin and end in C major and are essentially self-contained, just two of the several perfect jewels Purcell strung together to make *Bess of Bedlam*. It has been suggested that Durfey wanted Lyonel to sing 'snatches of a well-known Purcell song just as Shakespeare's mad Ophelia sang snatches of well-known ballads'.[14] Yet published at the back of the 1688 play-book are two rather more substantial pieces to be '*Sung in the Third Act*'. The quarto was issued at least a month after the April première, and a rubric for the first piece, 'Fled is my love', states that it was sung by Mountfort, so I see no reason to think that the songs 'were replaced by the *Mad Bess* fragments'. The new pieces convey Lyonel's extreme change of mood more effectively than the rather bizarre *Bess of Bedlam* stanzas. 'Fled is my love', though concluding with a gently flowing section in triple metre, begins

[14] Olive Baldwin and Thelma Wilson, 'A Purcell Problem Solved', *The Musical Times*, 122 (1981), 445.

with a striking display of Lyonel's underlying despair. The passage shown
in Example 5 is almost too expansive for so brief a piece. The ample
melisma on 'eternal' is made to seem even longer by the departure from
and immediate return to the E major dominant chord in bars 6 and 7. The
incongruity of couching this grand emotion in such a tiny piece is carried
to extremes in the second song, ''Tis death alone'. The only hint that
Lyonel's lamentation may not be genuine is the setting of 'tomb' to a
G major chord.

Example 5. *A Fool's Preferment*: 'Fled is my love', bars 6–8

Later in the scene, the courtiers tease the 'duke' by telling him that
Lyonel has been sent by enemies to torment him. The madman then
reassumes an exuberant posture and sings 'I'll mount to you, blue coelum',
fourteen bars of C major nonsense. With its mention of playing at bowls
with the sun and moon, it anticipates the most famous of all the songs in
the play, 'I'll sail upon the dog-star', also in C major. Exactly where the
latter should be performed is uncertain. A note with the music states that
it was *'sung in the Fourth Act'*, but I can find no place for it. Is it in fact
intended for Lyonel? No performer is named, though Mountfort is mentioned as having rendered both 'Fled is my love' and 'If thou wilt give me
back my love'. Much longer and far more difficult than any other song in
the play, 'I'll sail upon the dog-star' was obviously designed for an accomplished singer. If it did replace 'I'll mount to you', it was surely the most
demanding piece Mountfort ever sang on the stage. Because the two texts
are so closely related, I suspect that Purcell over-estimated the actor-
singer's skill with 'I'll sail upon the dog-star' and was then forced to write
another for this scene, leaving an anonymous professional to render the
more difficult one between acts. One of the many attractive features of the
famous song is its strict contrapuntal structure, which reins in Durfey's
wild galactic imagery. Nearly every phrase is given a new point of imitation, often with overlapping entries. Modern editors have allowed a
garbled bar in the first book of *Orpheus Britannicus* to slip into common
currency. The best reading of the disputed passage (shown in Example 6) is
given in the earliest source, the 1688 quarto. The lyric is a mass of eccentricities but the music is wholly rational.

Example 6. *A Fool's Preferment*: 'I'll sail upon the dog-star', bars 20–1

The '*Scotch Song sung in the 4ᵗʰ Act*' is the dialogue 'Jenny, 'gin you can love', which does not apparently include Lyonel. The scene must be briefly set. Squire Cocklebrain's uncle, Justice Grub, upon learning of his nephew's preferment, has come to town to seek the same honours. The masquerading courtiers (actually gamesters) lead the old fool to believe that the path to a dukedom lies through his wife, Phillida. He therefore allows these scurrilous characters to take liberties with his only too willing spouse, even in his presence. Though *The Noble Gentleman* has a similar scene, I suspect that A. C. Sprague had Durfey's more explicit dialogue in mind when he wrote that 'the consistent and deliberate addition of filth is one of the striking things in his play' (*Beaumont and Fletcher on the Restoration Stage*, p. 240). A gamester does in fact withdraw suggestively with Phillida to a private room, but to Durfey's credit this is also the likeliest place for the performance of Purcell's dialogue, a jolly piece in G major that describes metaphorically what is taking place behind the closed door. The chorus must have given some relief to the Jeremy Colliers in the audience; Jockey and Jenny sing,

> Then since all Fortune intends,
> Our Amity shall be no dearer;
> Still let us kiss and be friends,
> And sigh we shall never come nearer.

In the last act, the duke-making plot twists itself into a final flourish of absurdity, but the play ends as it begins, with a scene for Lyonel, who seems finally to have lost all traces of reason. He enters '*in a mad posture*', interrupting the final dance of the country-folk. He thinks he has come to the underworld to find his bride: 'Great *Pluto* – know that I am *Orpheus*, and through the dismal shades of direful night, am come to seek my long lov'd *Proserpine* . . .' Lyonal pretends to confuse Euridice with Proserpine, because he would make Pluto (that is, the king) a cuckold. He continues: 'I'le charm thee God, with Musick, my soft Aires shall lull the Pow'rs of thy barb'rous Empire, and set my Love at Liberty.' Lyonel's personation of Orpheus becomes more coherent in the song that follows without pause, 'If thou wilt give me back my love': Euridice will approach 'the Queen of

Shades', Proserpine, to sue for release. In the elegantly symmetrical minuet in a placid F major, Lyonel, who has entered the Hades of fools, retrieves Celia, therewith attaining an apotheosized peace of mind. As Mountfort asked in the epilogue, are we not all a little mad?

Critics have overlooked the subtle design of *A Fool's Preferment* because they are at first appalled by the smutty language, then angered by Durfey's shiny veneer of morality. It is a brilliant play, satirical, irreverent, cynical, and, in the end, pathetic. All these qualities depend on Lyonel, and the crux of his character resides in Purcell's songs. Unfortunately, musicians have largely ignored them because, with the exception of 'I'll sail upon the dog-star', they are so deceptively simple. Yet they manifest the composer's genius for the dramatic as certainly as any of the later sophisticated airs and dialogues for the professional singers. Purcell's ability to convey different emotions through melody alone is as great a gift as all his contrapuntal ingenuity.

The Marriage-Hater Match'd

A Fool's Preferment, though unsuccessful, led to the creation of other important singing roles, most, like Lyonel, being temporarily discountenanced clever characters, or performing fools. But Purcell was a tragedian at heart, and in comedies took pains only with characters which have an aura of grandeur or pathos beneath their mad or knavish exteriors. Many comic songs for nameless singers in entertainments, such as 'How happy's the husband' in Dryden's *Love Triumphant*, possess the same polite vacuity as parts of the panegyrical welcome odes. Purcell required more than expressible words and poetic contrasts to create memorable music drama; the characters had to be sufficiently developed to merit musical intensification.

Durfey's successful play *The Marriage-Hater Match'd* (January 1692) exemplifies the division of labour among the Theatre Royal's stable of composers in the early nineties. Purcell's part is relatively minor, but close inspection of the drama helps to explain the extraordinary proliferation of songs in the later *Don Quixote* trilogy, the ultimate musical comedy of the period. The main plot is exceedingly simple. Phaebe, a witty and resilient woman who has borne Sir Philip Freewit's illegitimate child, tricks her former lover into an agreeable marriage. This thin and improbable plot was simply a means of surprising the audience by casting the chaste and aloof Mrs Bracegirdle, who nearly always portrayed characters of similar virtue and detachment in comedies, as the crafty Phaebe.[15] She appears in breeches for most of the play as Sir Philip's confidant(e), Mr Lovewell. The chief interest of the drama, however, is a thoroughly entertaining gallery of

---

[15] For an analysis of the role-playing in this work, see Holland, *The Ornament of Action*, pp. 148–51.

knaves and fools, each of which has a distinctive personality. Durfey's humane depiction of their struggle to gain each other's respect is a *tour de force*, despite the contemporary criticisms that he allowed Doggett's mugging portrayal of Solon to carry the play and that he resorted to gimcrackery, such as 'bringing a Person upon the Stage with an extravagantly broad-brimmed Hat, and a Muff of the same size . . .'[16] Charles Gildon surely comes closer the mark when he writes in Durfey's defence that 'If there be any fault in this Play, 'tis that . . . there are too many good Characters, too full of Humour . . .' (prefatory letter in the 1692 quarto).

The considerable music revolves round four characters, all but one aristocratic fools. Lord Brainless, 'A Pert, Noisy, Impertinent Boy', was acted by the formidable baritone Bowman. He pursues and eventually marries La Pupsey, a coquette who lavishes all her affection on a lap-dog. She was portrayed by Mrs Butler, who, though she did not sing in this play, was one of Purcell's favourite sopranos, winning fame a year before as Cupid in the Frost Scene of *King Arthur*. The other principal singers are the notorious Solon (Doggett) and Berenice, his intended, who, despite being one of the clever characters, is allowed to sing because she is a 'Freakish Creature', that is, devilish and light-hearted to the point of madness. The role was created by Mrs Lassells, at the beginning of a short and undistinguished career as an actress–singer.

In the first scene of Act II, in which music is the main attraction, Brainless is upstaged by the dog; but when its mistress commands the animal to sing a minuet, it can only howl as she pinches it. La Pupsey explains that 'the poor Rogue has got a desperate cold', to which Brainless quips, 'As all good Singers generally have, Madam', an obvious in-joke. After announcing that he has composed a song about the dog, he sings instead an unspecified Italian air that passes without comment. The scene continues as Berenice's suitors assemble: Captain Darewell, a brusque 'tarpaulin' reminiscent of Captain Porpuss in *Sir Barnaby Whigg*, and the cretinous brothers Bias and Solon. When the captain attempts to sing, the dog drowns him out, giving Berenice leave to take up the tune 'How vile are the sordid intrigues o'th' town', which expresses her sentiments better than his in any case. Lady Subtle, her sister, enjoys it: 'A pretty air, I like the Song too better than those I usually hear, because there's no whining Love in't.' Indeed, the lyric berates Berenice's suitors for spending more time discussing politics than marriage. The earliest source, *Comes Amoris*, IV (1693), states that both words and music are by Durfey, but in the British Library's collection of seventeenth-century single-sheet songs known as 'Joyful Cuckoldom', as well as in Add. MS 35043, fol. 6, the piece is ascribed to Purcell under the ironical title *The Disconsolate Lady's Com-*

---

[16] Rpt *The London Stage*, Part 1, p. 404.

plaint. Day dismisses the latter attribution, as does Barclay Squire;[17] but Zimmerman disagrees: 'it seems to me that both the handling of the word-rhythms and the melodic freedom show far more musical finesse than D'Urfey could ever have demonstrated' (*An Analytical Catalogue*, p. 277). However, the ascriptions in *Comes Amoris* are generally more trustworthy than those in the ephemeral broadsides collected in 'Joyful Cuckoldom', and Durfey, though not much of a composer, had a genius for adding words to the tunes of others. Even if the melody was Purcell's, the accompaniment is of humbler origins. The long, vapid bars of tonic and mediant harmonies in the first half occur at precisely the places where the tune needs a push from below.

Solon's 'Tantivee, tivee', for which no music survives, is also heard in this scene. Continuing the canine theme, it proclaims the thrill of riding to hounds. Berenice exclaims, 'Oh! *Solon* has perform'd to a Miracle, Sir', apparently a sarcastic remark. Captain Darewell, the only other auditor, does not comment on the performance. Later, in Act IV, Berenice solicits Solon's help to make Darewell jealous by inviting the fool to join her in a dialogue, 'Damon, if I should receive your Addresses', the music of which does not survive.[18] The gullible Solon forwards Berenice's plan, singing that he would do anything if she would marry him, even allow himself to be made a cuckold. After the music, she turns to the squirming Darewell and asks a double-meaning question: 'Is this accomplish'd person a Fool? When will you do as much Captain?' Impressed by his singing if not his wits, Darewell, who is not a knave, suddenly regards Solon as a serious rival and redoubles his efforts to gain Berenice's hand.

The musical high point of the play is the concert at Lady Bumfiddle's lodgings in III.ii. Before Thomas Tollet's Scotch song 'Bonny Lad, prithee lay thy Pipe down' (D&M No. 397), Lord Brainless sings the long-awaited essay on La Pupsey's lap-dog: '. . . now I will present you with my own Composition, which I lately told ye of, wherein I envy the joys of the happy Creature . . . and passionately bemoan my own Infidelity . . . I call it *Celadon*'s Complaint against Monsieur *Le Chien*.' In 'Great Jove once made Love like a Bull' (D&M No. 1201), Brainless imagines that the dog is Jupiter and he, poor mortal, is as helpless as Amphitryon. Here is the end of the fourth verse:

> I may Sing, Caper, Ogle, and Speak,
> And make a long Court, *Ausi bien*;

---

[17] *The Songs of Thomas D'Urfey* (Cambridge, Mass.: Harvard Univ. Press, 1933), pp. 144–5; Squire, 'Purcell's Dramatic Music', p. 538. Laurie ('Purcell's Stage Works', p. 186) thinks that the Purcell Society 'are right in omitting this song . . .'

[18] Just before they sing, the following speech is incorrectly assigned to La Pupsey: 'Come now, Sir, as your last Tryal, Sing the Dialogue with me, that I shew'd you in the Arbor just now – Observe Captain.' This is obviously spoken by Berenice.

And yet with one Passionate Lick,
I'm out-rivall'd by Monsieur *Le Chien*.

This was set by Will Mountfort, who acted Sir Philip Freewit, the 'marriage-hater'. Though built on a solid harmonic footing with orderly cadences in all the appropriate keys, the ungainly tune and its awkward graces show the composer to be at best an amateur; but I doubt whether Purcell could have made a funnier setting.

The last act will have a familiar ring. Berenice, who continues to torment Darewell by pretending to dote on Solon, finally agrees to marry the captain. But a plan must be hatched to keep Solon from interfering. Her maid, Pimpwell, tells the accomplished fool that the evening's masquerade will give him an opportunity to steal her lady away from his seafaring rival: 'rely upon me; I'll give ye an account of her Habit'. Naturally, Solon is misinformed about Berenice's disguise and carries off the maid instead. This resembles the fourth-act masque of Orpheus in Settle's *The Empress of Morocco*, a scene frequently lampooned or emulated in comedies of the eighties and nineties. It will be recalled from Chapter 1 that Morena, playing Euridice, is told that the villain Crimalhaz rather than her husband, Muly Labas, is to be dressed as Orpheus. In the confusion, she accidentally kills her husband. Perhaps best described as ordered chaos, the masquerade in *The Marriage-Hater Match'd* would have a marvellous effect on the stage. All the dramatis personae are disguised, but the fools and knaves are clearly identifiable by their distinctive oaths and catchphrases uttered repeatedly in the previous acts. Sir Philip ridicules Solon for being tricked into marrying Pimpwell, but the fool has the last laugh when the marriage-hater himself discovers he has wed Phaebe in what he thought was a sham ceremony.

The centrepiece of the last scene is Purcell's F major duet for soprano and bass 'As soon as the chaos was made into form' (z 602), a drinking song with pretensions to poetry. The final couplet, 'For never, my Friends, was an Age of more Vice, / Than when Knaves would seem Pious, and Fools would seem Wise', comments on the play's novel design of making even the normally clever and witty characters as addlepated and gullible as everyone else. The setting of the opening lines is noteworthy. Purcell's depiction of the scene of chaos is not harmonically disordered, as one might have expected, but constructed with carefully wrought points of imitation between soprano and bass, the first being a bar and a half apart, the second a bar, and the others at the interval of a beat, the voices finally coming together at the couplet 'They quickly did join in a knowledge divine, / That the world's chiefest blessings were women and wine'. Later, at the somewhat obscure line ''Tis a folly to think / Of a mystery out of our reaches', the music conveys Durfey's morbid meaning with a firm cadence in G minor. On the whole, the duet is disappointing and, to my mind, a missed opportunity. Having constructed an elaborate parody of Settle and Locke's masque of Orpheus, Durfey failed to take advantage of having no fewer than six actor–singers on stage – Mountfort as Sir Philip, Mrs Bracegirdle as Phaebe, Mrs Lassells as Berenice, Bowman as Lord Brainless, Mrs Butler as La Pupsey, and Doggett as Solon – to allow Purcell to create a musical climax to a very musical play.

The Richmond Heiress

The Richmond Heiress: or, a Woman Once in the Right (April 1693) is something of a sequel to *The Marriage-Hater Match'd*, in that Durfey capitalized on Doggett's triumph as Solon and created another singing fool for Bowman. Furthermore, much of the humour depends on allusions to the earlier play. But the most striking parallel is the expanded parody of Settle's masque of Orpheus. Purcell's contribution to the drama is the ambitious mad dialogue 'Behold the man that with gigantic might' (z 608) in Act II, which has all the passion and art lacking in much of his other music for comedies. Nevertheless, it is his only documented failure; at least Dryden thought it inferior to Eccles's mad song in the same scene. That the poet could have made so invidious a comparison is symptomatic of a serious imbalance between music and drama on the late seventeenth-century London stage, a condition well demonstrated in this curious play.

At the end of *The Marriage-Hater Match'd* Solon, the accomplished fool, has the last laugh. Here he is transformed into Tom Quickwit, who feigns madness and dim-wittedness, thereby making fools of everyone. Durfey wants no one to miss the connection, as this unnecessary instructional speech early in Act I shows: 'I flatter and sing to the Women, to get their Tongues on my side too: And now and then when I am desir'd by some rich Booby that's worth the managing, I can turn my Face into a Changling Grimace, and act like *Solon* in the Play; when, as I hope to be sav'd, I'm all the while bant'ring him, and thinking him the more comical *Solon* of the two, as a Man may say.' In his analysis of this 'casting for complex dramatic purposes', Peter Holland remarks, 'No one could act Solon but Dogget and the speech enforces on the audience recognition of the actor, of the role-playing' (*The Ornament of Action*, p. 158). But *The Richmond Heiress* is still a pot-boiler, the dialogue laced with allusions to Durfey's past successes.[19]

For all this, the plot is fresh and highly diverting. Quickwit offers to help his friend Frederick, the rakish protagonist, win the hand of the shrewd heiress, Fulvia, played by Mrs Bracegirdle, now returned to her stereotyped role or 'line'. To forestall an arranged marriage to the vain and dishonest Tom Romance, Quickwit suggests that the vulnerable heiress 'act a witty

---

[19] For example, in III.ii Sir Quibble says, 'You must ride upon the Dogs-star, as the mad Song says, if you would see more'; see the discussion of *A Fool's Preferment*, above.

Plate 3. Anne Bracegirdle
(engraving by J. Stow after Harding's *Biographical Mirrour*)

Plate 4. Thomas Doggett
(portrait by Thomas Murray)

Scene of Lunacy' (II.ii), which Dryden thought 'wonderfully diverting'. It is set in the house of Doctor Guiacum, a society mountebank, more amused by his patients than eager to aid their recovery. Guiacum suspects that Fulvia is already convalescing, 'because she inclines to Musick, and will often sing very sensibly'. Having been coached in her part by Quickwit, she enters *madly dress'd* and spouting nonsense with hidden satiric meaning. At one point, she imagines herself a politician and breaks into Durfey's own 'How vile are the sordid intrigues o'th' town', Berenice's song in *The Marriage-Hater Match'd*. Then, puzzlingly, the witty and swift-moving charade is interrupted by Purcell's long dialogue. Doctor Guiacum explains that to supplement the humour of Fulvia's malady he has arranged a demonstration of two of his regular patients, a soldier whose guilt at having deserted during a battle against the French has driven him insane, and a woman who 'crack'd her Brain' after her lover looked admiringly at another during a court ball. Such shameless interlarding of extraneous music is not typical of Durfey; yet Purcell's dialogue cannot avoid disturbing the flow of the scene. While Mrs Bracegirdle cooled her heels, Mrs Ayliff and the baritone Reading, who do not speak in the play, performed 'Behold the man'.[20]

The long, bizarre lyric covers much the same ground as those in Durfey's earlier musical scenes. The coward-turned-hero thinks he is engaged in vengeful combat with both Jupiter and Pluto, while the woman, obsessed with her appearance and feminine charms, imagines that she, like Alcmena and Semele, has been Jove's mistress. All the classical allusions seem to lead nowhere, yet the unrestrained imagery elicits some of Purcell's most extravagant music. The ex-soldier's delusions of grandeur are represented by the exaggerated graces in the opening recitative, while the woman's obsession is depicted more subtly. She sings,

> Who's he that talks of War,
> When charming Beauty comes:
> Within whose Face divinely fair,
> Eternal Pleasure blooms.

To make her vanity more revolting, Purcell added a word to the third line ('In whose *sweet* Face divinely fair'), which he decorates with the purposely overwrought chromaticism shown in Example 7. The singers barely acknowledge each other until the soldier, after a tremendous battle song, rolls down from the heavens 'To find my lost, my wandering sense again'. Here begins the '*Second Movement*', four stanzas set to a tune closely resembling the second part of 'From rosy bowers' in *3 Don Quixote*. Despite the infectious melody, the wit pales badly by the third or fourth

[20] At a revival sometime after 1695, the dialogue was sung by Leveridge and Mrs Lindsay; see *A Collection of the most Celebrated Songs & Dialogues* (c. 1705), pp. 13–15, and a single-sheet song in British Library G.306 (177).

Example 7. *The Richmond Heiress*: 'Behold the man', bars 43–6

verse, and the concluding duet, 'Then mad, very mad let us be', comes as a relief. Purcell, too, seems to have appreciated the imbalance between the robustious first half and the cloying regularity of the strophic second part. In the Guildhall Library autograph song-book, he omitted to write out the second, third, and fourth verses, in marked contrast with his copying out all stanzas of the other strophic songs in the manuscript. One cannot fault Durfey's basic design, however. The dialogue is supposed to demonstrate Guiacum's cure, whereby 'Frenzy will wear off by degrees'; the singers should, therefore, appear to grow more rational as the song runs its course.

Quickwit (Doggett) wanders in during the final strains of 'Behold the man' to help Fulvia (Mrs Bracegirdle) convince her suitors that she is hopelessly mad. He, too, has been behaving oddly since he was allegedly jilted by a dairy maid named Mopsee. Seeing Fulvia, he begins Eccles's 'By those pigsneyes, that Stars do seem' (D&M No. 453), while Guiacum offers a running commentary: 'She makes up to him now, the Distemper works now, they are curing one another.' Before she can respond, the mad couple are joined in a brief dance by two other lunatics. Eccles's syllabic, lightly ornamented, and resolutely diatonic setting of the opprobrious verses looks absurdly simple but, as Dryden reports, it was the play's saving grace:

Durfey has brought another farce upon the Stage: but his luck has left him: it was suffered but foure dayes; and then kickd off for ever. Yet his Second Act, was wonderfully diverting; where the scene was in Bedlam: & M[rs] Bracegirdle and Solon were both mad: the Singing was wonderfully good, And the two whom I nam'd sung better than Redding and M[rs] Ayloff, whose trade it was: at least our partiality carried it for them. The rest was woefull stuff, & concluded with Catcalls.[21]

Dryden observed a phenomenon well known in the world of music drama: the ability of a singer of modest musical skills to win bravos with 'a dramatic performance'. Doggett and Mrs Bracegirdle were comedians; Reading and Mrs Ayliff were professional singers who, unlike Bowman and Mrs Butler, were hardly ever entrusted with even a single spoken line.[22] Some

[21] Letter to William Walsh, 9 May 1693, in *The Letters of John Dryden*, ed. Ward, pp. 52–3.
[22] But after the division of the company in 1695 Mrs Ayliff acted Prue in *Love for Love* (April 1695) as a last-minute replacement for Mrs Verbruggen; she also took the role of Jocond, a boy, in *The Lover's Luck*. See Highfill, *A Biographical Dictionary*, I, 182, and Olive Baldwin and Thelma Wilson, 'Purcell's Sopranos', *The Musical Times*, 123 (1982), 603.

credit must also be given to the music, whose strengths are simplicity and a lively exchange between the singers. Near the end, the only chromatic chord of the piece allows Fulvia a delicious moment of mock pathos (see Example 8). Purcell's dialogue, admittedly hampered by a rambling and often obscure lyric, never achieves such intimacy. The ex-soldier and the vain woman speak to the gods, not to each other. If Dryden's opinion of the performance was representative, then Purcell may well have thought himself among the Philistines. But as one can see in the *Don Quixote* music, he also learned a valuable lesson from Eccles.

Example 8. *The Richmond Heiress*: John Eccles, 'By those pigsneyes', bars 71–6

The only other extant music for the first production is an anonymous song for Rice ap Shinken, a 'Welsh Beau, with a Head as barren as the Mountains in his own Country'. Somewhere in the fourth act, probably after being pummelled in a fight, he sings the famous 'Of noble Race was Shinken' (D&M No. 2579), complete with a two-bar interlude for harp.[23] Singing in dialect, Rice, who was played by Bowman, hilariously confuses personal pronouns.[24]

In the fifth act Quickwit's plan to unite Fulvia and Frederick is in shambles, as her guardian, Sir Charles Romance, has spirited her away

[23] See *Thesaurus Musicus*, I (1693).

[24] At the beginning of Act IV, stage directions require a '*Catch in three parts, in praise of Punch*'. Squire supposes this to be 'Bring the bowl and cool Nanz' (z 243) ('Purcell's Dramatick Music', p. 546). As Dryden notes, the first production was unsuccessful. But Gildon reports that 'upon a Revival and Alterations he [Durfey] has pleas'd the Town' (Langbaine, *The Lives and Characters of the English Dramatick Poets*, continued by Gildon, 1698, p. 52). Perhaps the revival included the three songs not printed in the play-book but ascribed to the play in musical sources: 'Fie Jockey' in *Thesaurus Musicus*, I (1693), p. 16; Pack's 'Maiden fresh as a rose' in *Songs Compleat* (1719); and 'Stubborn church division', sung to a ground by Solomon Eccles, in *Thesaurus Musicus*, II (1694), p. 24. None of these seems especially pertinent to the play, but the last may have replaced the ballad in V.v.

from all the suitors. But the villain, Cunnington, has a plan to abduct the heiress. During the evening's masquerade will be performed a little representation of *'Pluto, Orpheus*, and *Euridice*, of my Composing, and the Musick of Mr. *Purcels'*. Cunnington plans to take the part of Pluto, which will give him an opportunity to ravish Fulvia, who is to be dressed as Euridice. This is precisely the gambit invented by Crimalhaz in *The Empress of Morocco*. To thwart the villain's design, Quickwit has him kidnapped, so that Frederick may don the Orpheus habit. But the last-minute change of plans allows the impostors no time to rehearse, and Purcell's masque is never performed. At the climax, Frederick (Orpheus) and Quickwit (Pluto) each take one of Fulvia's hands and begin to lead her out. In a jolting departure from the play-within-the-play scenario, she looks back at Sir Charles and asks why he is allowing the abduction. Pluto and Orpheus are then unmasked and the plot backfires. She rejects Frederick because he has broken a marriage contract with her friend Sophronia. With her other suitors also now discredited, Sir Charles releases her from his guardianship. Though she appears to be leaning cynically towards Quickwit at the end of the play, Fulvia pours scorn on everyone and decides not to marry.

There is more to this scene than meets the eye. Dark clouds hung over the theatre company and over Mrs Bracegirdle in particular following the death of the actor–singer Will Mountfort a few months earlier in December 1692. He was killed in a mêlée with Captain Richard Hill and Lord Mohun after their unsuccessful attempt to abduct the actress. The scandal ended up in the House of Lords, and in the wake of the trial, questions arose about Mountfort's relationship with the celebrated virgin. The last act of *The Richmond Heiress* is a daring allegory of the sad affair, with Frederick probably representing the late lamented Mountfort. The masque not only reaffirmed Mrs Bracegirdle's chastity but gave her a chance to condemn all those who would intrigue against her. The airing of dirty linen on the public stage and under the guise of comedy may seem the epitome of bad taste, but the drama was a kind of exorcism.

Considering the numerous in-jokes and references to contemporary events, I suspect that the unfulfilled promise of Purcell's masque of Orpheus must have some hidden significance. Is this a veiled reference to the final scene of *A Fool's Preferment*, in which Mountfort as Lyonel, but pretending to be Orpheus, sings the all-too-brief song 'If thou wilt give me back my love'? Or does the broken promise of music by Purcell refer in some manner to Durfey's missed opportunity to create a masque for the actor–singers at the end of *The Marriage-Hater Match'd*? We shall probably never know, but in a very few years even the dullest poets could note the irony that the Orpheus Britannicus never set to music the legend with which he, in death, became so closely linked.

III. Southerne

By far the most underrated dramatist of the era, Thomas Southerne wrote plays that examine the darker side of human relationships. He was as capable as any of his contemporaries of weaving witty Covent Garden plots, yet each of his comedies has an underlying intellectual design that, while often producing bitter satire and sobering dialogue, is never stuffy or academic. The themes of the three plays for which Purcell wrote music seem at first glance to be only the tired clichés of Restoration society: sexual depravity in *Sir Anthony Love*; cuckoldom in *The Wives Excuse*; and gallantry in *The Maid's Last Prayer*. But without resorting to preaching, the playwright reappraises these issues and their causes, making the audience think hard about morality itself. Southerne's highly rational approach does not allow many occasions for music, besides those scenes in which the dramatis personae can participate naturally, such as the concerts in *The Wives Excuse* and *The Maid's Last Prayer*. Yet the plays include 'thematic' songs that add significantly to the drama but whose singers and/or locations are unspecified. Two of these, 'Pursuing beauty' in *Sir Anthony Love* and 'No, resistance is but vain' in *The Maid's Last Prayer*, do little to affect the course of the action or to colour the personality of any member of the speaking cast, but are among the composer's finest pieces. Purcell and Southerne must have been kindred spirits. Each possessed a faultless technique that was at its best when depicting passion.

Sir Anthony Love

As Durfey apparently designed *A Fool's Preferment* for Will Mountfort, Southerne created *Sir Anthony Love: or, The Rambling Lady* (October 1690) to exploit the talents of the actor's wife, Susannah Percival Mountfort, who played the title-role in breeches. The play was very successful, and Southerne happily gives her credit in an epistle dedicatory: critics 'never saw any part more masterly play'd: and as I made every Line for her, she has mended every Word for me . . .' This is his first comedy, and in the labyrinth of tangled plots, some of which are backwaters wisely allowed to dry up, his inexperience shows. Even the main plot is difficult to follow, perhaps on purpose. Lucia, a female rake-hell, has robbed her keeper, Sir Gentle Golding, and bolted to France, where, disguised as Sir Anthony Love, she charms the local beauties in order to confound their suitors, apparently with the aim of taking a general revenge on the male sex. The travesty casting and role-switching reach a dizzying climax when Sir Anthony, disguised as Floriante, agrees to marry Sir Gentle, who is as yet unaware that he has actually found his long-lost Lucia.

Only one of the three scenes requiring music is important to the plot. In IV.ii, while an unnamed song is performed, Sir Anthony appears for the first time *'in her Woman's Cloaths'*. She and her rakish companion Valentine have become fast friends during several adventures, though he never suspects that she is a woman. Earlier she intimates 'I am sure he [Valentine] likes me; and likes me so well in a Man, he'll love me in a Woman'. To divert his attention from his beloved Floriante, Sir Anthony arranges for Valentine to meet a young Englishwoman, who is of course herself, in a bedchamber. After the song, she uncovers her face. But he is only slightly taken aback to discover his friend is now his lover. Both are too profligate to consider marriage, and, surprisingly, their relationship changes little after the revelation. Southerne's triumph is the elimination of sex as a factor in this exploration of the fundamental qualities of male–female relationships.

Printed at the back of the 1691 quarto are three lyrics unassigned to any character. The music is preserved in Tenbury MS 785, a very reliable source dating from within a year or two of the première. Of the three, 'Pursuing beauty' (z 588/2) would be by far the most appropriate accompaniment for Sir Anthony's unmasking.[25] Purcell set only the first, second, and last of the five stanzas, cynical warnings to women to guard their innocence; the final two lines anticipate the action of the rest of the scene between Sir Anthony and Valentine.

> Pursuing Beauty, Men descry
> The distant Shore, and long to prove
> (Still richer in Variety)
> The Treasures of the Land of Love.
>
> We Women, like weak *Indians*, stand
> Inviting, from our Golden Coast,
> The wandering Rovers to our Land:
> But she, who trades with 'em, is lost.
> . . .
> Be wise, be wise, and do not try,
> How he can Court, or you be Won:
> For Love is but Discovery,
> When that is made, the Pleasure's done.

The brilliant union of bold, masculine declamation and a soft, enticing air in the first part of the song belies the myth that the recitatives and ariosos in *Dido and Aeneas* have no successors in Purcell's *oeuvre*. The opening stanza compares Valentine, gazing on the mysterious woman, to an ocean explorer, staring hungrily at a distant, unspoilt land. The next verse takes Sir Anthony's point of view. The teasing display of frail femininity is en-

---

[25] The 1691 quarto assigns it to Act II, but there is no place in that act where it could be inserted without doing more harm than good.

hanced by an imperfect cadence and sighing motifs separated by rests, moving swiftly to a vigorous staccato recitation in E minor that culminates in a powerful rise to high G and a reeling melisma (see Example 9). The sharp contrasts of this passage reflect the strong contradictions in Sir Anthony's epicene character. Purcell has grasped this ironic role reversal.

Example 9. *Sir Anthony Love*: 'Pursuing beauty', bars 11–15

Rather than a chaste woman masquerading as a wild libertine, she is a strong-willed, clever, and somewhat rapacious female rake. The final verse is set to a spry tune in which the repeat of the last strain – a long, rhythmically beguiling melisma on 'pleasure' – is written out. Interestingly, the *petite reprise* is varied in the bass only; perhaps the composer felt any further ornamentation of the vocal line would be painting the lily. This and other important details, not to mention the introductory symphony for two violins and bass, might well have been lost had the song been preserved in a printed collection instead of an early manuscript. Many songbooks omit instrumental ritornels and iron out irregularities and eccentricities in order to make all their contents conform to a simple format.

Two other scenes require songs. Southerne states in the dedication that one of these, V.iv, was cut. In this lewd episode, the hypocritical abbé, portrayed by the master comedian Leigh, makes advances to Sir Anthony, first with music and dancing, then by unbuttoning his coat and urging his 'little *Mercury*' to withdraw to an adjoining room. When Sir Anthony reveals herself to be a woman, he recoils in disgust, offering her money to avoid a scandal.[26] Leigh was not known as a singer, and no song for this scene survives.

---

[26] In the dedication, Southerne writes that he dropped the scene to avoid 'offending the Women; not that there is one indecent Expression in it; but the over-fine Folk might run it into a design I never had in my head'.

In V.ii, a tedious episode that simply reshuffles the basic elements of disguise and discovery, Sir Anthony marries Volante in a mock ceremony. While waiting for her 'husband' to come to bed, she listens to an unspecified atmospheric song. Neither of Purcell's remaining compositions is particularly apropos. The amorous dialogue 'No more, sir, no more' (z 588/3) is a forgettable piece in A minor for soprano and baritone, which the play-book assigns to Act IV. It was sung by Bowman, who was not a member of the speaking cast, and Mrs Butler, who acted Valentine's beloved, Floriante. She is not required to sing in character, which suggests that the piece was performed off stage or between acts.[27] The final lyric is the impassioned plea for free love 'In vain, Clemene' (z 588/4), by Major-General Sackville. Purcell set it strophically to a charming D minor tune. The brief interlude for oboe is found in the Tenbury manuscript but not in the other early source, *The Banquet of Musick*, IV (1692). The manuscript also includes an overture in D minor and a dance for the cast at the end of the last scene. The dance is a ground by John Eccles – not one of his better efforts – but the curtain tune is certainly Purcell's, though it is not found in *Ayres for the Theatre*;[28] the highly dissonant opening section, rhythmically obsessive canzona, and bittersweet slow conclusion are Purcell hallmarks.

The Wives Excuse

Southerne's next comedy, *The Wives Excuse: or, Cuckolds make Themselves* (December 1691), again takes a strongly feminist stance but is a much finer drama. The main characters are more believable, and the plot is immaculately coherent. Music is used much more skilfully here than in *Sir Anthony Love*, and Southerne, taking a leaf from Durfey's book, allows the several lyrics to gravitate toward Mr Friendall, whose true personality, like Lyonel's in *A Fool's Preferment*, is ultimately revealed through Purcell's songs. Friendall, too, was portrayed by Will Mountfort, that 'clear Countertenour'. The music must, however, be seen in perspective. Whereas Durfey tends to wallow in lyrics, often infusing them with an air of fantasy, Southerne introduces his realistically. And the most remarkable feature of the drama is hardly the music, but Southerne's writing himself in as Wellvile, not just a cynical observer, but a character at work on a comedy to be called 'The Wives Excuse or, Cuckolds make Themselves' (see III[ii]). He actively influences the flow of the drama, stepping in occasionally to provide plot-straightening morality. Hume notes that 'this touch aids a strong sense of the author's unhappy entrapment in a degraded society' (*The Development*, p. 387).

A sensational butt of the satire is the snobbish semi-public concert.

[27] Note that in Dryden's *Amphitryon* Mrs Butler also played a similarly confusing dual role.
[28] See Laurie, 'Purcell's Stage Works', p. 242.

Southerne was surprised that his lampoon of dilettantes who meddle in professional music-making should come in for criticism. In the caustically ironic dedication to the 1692 play-book, he writes: 'As to the Musick-Meeting I always thought it an Entertainment reasonably grown up into the liking of the Town: I introduc'd it, as a fashionable Scene of bringing good Company together, without a Design of abusing what every Body likes; being in my Temper so far from disturbing a publick Pleasure, that I would establish twenty more of 'em, if I could.' As the play opens several footmen are playing cards while waiting for their masters to leave a concert. One of them complains that, unlike the playhouse where servants are admitted to the upper gallery for the fifth act, he and his fellows must remain outside this genteel gathering. Another footman mimicks his haughty lady, who, since having travelled abroad, is too sophisticated 'to be pleas'd with the barbarous Performances of these *English*.'[29] With the ascent of the curtain the vignette fades wittily to the concert room within, where people of quality are listening to an unnamed song. Mr Friendall, professing a knowledge of music, remarks that even though he could not understand the words, they 'were *Italian*. They sung well, and that's enough for the pleasure of the Ear.' He asks his friend Courtall which he likes better, sonatas or chaconnes. Another gentleman rudely interrupts, muttering 'they may be two *Italian* Fidlers of your acquaintance, for any thing I know of 'em'. The pompous amateur rebukes him for referring to these 'masters' in such common terms. Later in the scene, the host, Mr Lovemore, asks the musicians to perform one last piece. Mrs Sightly, who was portrayed by Mrs Bracegirdle, requests an English song for a change. Wellvile seconds this chauvinistically: 'Any Song, which won't oblige a Man To tell you, he has seen an *Opera* at *Venice* to understand.' Friendall, who is emerging as a boor, suggests that one of the singers perform the lyric he gave them earlier. But the music master replies curtly, ''Tis not set, Sir'. When Friendall upbraids him for his negligence, the musician explains bluntly, as I fancy Purcell himself might have done, 'Why, really, Sir, I would serve any Gentleman to my power; But the Words are so abominably out of the way of Musick, I don't know how to humour 'em: There's no setting 'em, Or singing 'em, to please any body but himself.' Unbowed, Friendall retorts that the composer cares only about being paid.

The piece that is finally performed is not Friendall's 'unsettable' poem, but 'Ingrateful Love! thus every hour' (z 612/1).[30] One wonders what its author, Major-General Sackville, thought when he heard his verses introduced by the music master's unkind remarks about gentleman lyricists.

[29] For a further discussion, see Southerne, *The Wives Excuse*, ed. Ralph R. Thornton (Wynnewood, Pa.: Livingston, 1973), p. 29.
[30] This was almost certainly sung by a soprano and not, as Thornton suggests (*The Wives Excuse*, p. 30), by Joseph Harris, who acted the music master.

Since it alludes to Mrs Friendall's alleged infidelity, the song's message is timely, but her foolish husband, who pretends to understand the finer points of Italian arias, is oblivious to the satire. Purcell used only the first two of Sackville's four stanzas. Apparently heeding Mrs Sightly's request for an English song, he set the lyric in the 'serious' style, combining recitative in strictly measured phrases with long graces on key words such as 'triumph' and 'laugh', lacing the whole with numerous iambuses. Its key, G minor, might have been suggested by the unsung final verse: to paraphrase, 'you deny me death to ease my pain'. This is an exceedingly severe song for such humorous circumstances, suggesting that the composer intended it as a reply to the unnamed Italian one heard earlier in the scene. At all events, Southerne let it pass without sarcastic comment from the auditors.[31]

Dramatically, the most important lyric in the play is 'Say, cruel Amoret', in Act IV, which is sung by Friendall, whom Hume calls 'a truly contemptible character' (*The Development*, p. 387). Indeed, much of the business of Acts II–IV concerns his portrayal as a philandering husband ripe for cuckoldom. Near the end of the first act, Lovemore hires Ruffle, a kick-and-cuff man, to insult and attack Friendall in the street. When his wife intercedes, he appears a poltroon and later seeks vindication in an apology from Ruffle, who proves the greater coward. Friendall, though pompous and unsubtle in his infatuation with Mrs Sightly, has yet to be deemed a fool.

At the dinner party in Act IV, after displaying an imperfect knowledge of wine and tobacco, Friendall is asked to sing the song the music master refused to touch earlier. Puffed up with pride, he explains, 'Why, Faith, I was forc'd to set in my self: I don't know how you'll like it with my voice; but faith and troth, I believe the Masters of the Musick-meeting may set their own words, for any trouble I shall give 'em for the future about mine.' The song is in three stanzas, only the first of which can be sung to Purcell's music, unless part of the humour was an attempt to make the second and third verses fit the tune. The poem is a grammatical convolution but no more a sow's ear than a dozen others the composer turned into silk purses:

> Say, cruel Amoret, how long
> In billet douxs and humble song
>   Shall poor Alexis woo?
> If neither writing, sighing, dying
> Reduce you to a soft complying
>   Oh! when will you come to?

---

[31] In his interpretation of the scene, Holland goes further: 'The Music Master's despair at the prospect of having to perform Friendall's song . . . is an ironic inversion of Mountfort's fame as musician. The audience is being reminded that it is Mountfort who is acting Friendall' (*The Ornament of Action*, p. 145).

Had the music master not spoken ill of this lyric earlier, I doubt whether any modern critic would single it out as being 'so abominably out of the way of Musick'. How do the dramatis personae react to Friendall's performance?

> *Wilding*. Admirable well –
> *Mrs Wittwoud*. Sett and Sung, Sir.
> *Lovemore*. A Gentleman does these things always best.
> *Wellvile*. When he has a *Genius*.

Only Lovemore's remark is certain to be ironic, since he attempts to justify making Friendall a cuckold by exposing him as a knave. Wilding and Mrs Wittwoud, while admittedly the most depraved characters in the play, have no reason to deprecate the singer, and their concerted response is, at worst, a blandishment. Neither the lyric nor the auditors' reactions give a clear indication of how Southerne wanted the audience to perceive the performance. Only the music can settle the ambiguity of Friendall's character.

One's first reaction to 'Say, cruel Amoret' (z 612/2) is that it includes no palpable Hoffnung blunders. This is not to imply that late seventeenth-century cognoscenti would not have found it comical in ways lost to our understanding; and surely the immodest melisma shown in Example 10 is

Example 10. *The Wives Excuse*: 'Say, cruel Amoret', bars 5–10

In bil – lets - doux ___ and hum _ _ _ ble ___ song

a point of common ground for humour. With a different word – 'long', for instance – one might well admire this phrase as Purcell at his languishing best.[32] Like Beckmesser's serenade in Act II of *Die Meistersinger*, 'Say, cruel Amoret' is a theatrical representation of an incompetent song, not the work of the fool himself. Purcell both exposed Friendall's venial sins of pomposity and dilettantism *and* produced a piece of roguish charm. He thereby aided Southerne's design of holding the mirror up to nature; the Friendalls in the pit and boxes could genuinely admire the amateur's musical pretensions, while the Wellviles and the real music masters in the gallery could smile at the coxcomb.

The only other scene requiring music is the masquerade in Act V, which closely resembles the one in the last act of *The Marriage-Hater Match'd*. Before the assembled cast join in a dance, they listen to Purcell's 'Corinna, I excuse thy face' (z 612/3), a Scotch air whose limber melody ambles up and down the entire soprano range with deceptive ease. The remaining

[32] Only the melody survives, the bass part in the Purcell Society Edition, XXI, being conjectural.

song is the rondeau 'Hang this whining way of wooing' (z 612/4), which the play-book assigns to IV.i, the scene in which Friendall sings 'Say, cruel Amoret'. This is surely a misprint.[33] The song in question, performed by Mrs Butler, who does not have a speaking role in the play, would not be appropriate for that scene, and was probably heard between acts or incidentally during the masquerade. The purpose of the costume ball in Act V is to expose the despicable procuress Mrs Wittwoud. In yet another application of the *Empress of Morocco* stratagem, Friendall, having been told that Mrs Sightly will be wearing a certain kind of scarf, unknowingly leads Mrs Wittwoud out of the room. At the revolting climax, the shutters are drawn to show the adulterous couple lying on a couch. The humiliated bawd leaves after uttering a few oaths, while the Friendalls recognize this as an opportunity to part ways. Speaking quite unlike the fool he seemed earlier in the play, Friendall says to his wife, 'Madam, since 'tis impossible to make it happy between us, let us ev'n resolve to make it as easie as we can.' This brilliant drama does not end happily, and the singing coxcomb accepts disgrace with callous indifference.

The Maid's Last Prayer

In *The Maid's Last Prayer: or, Any, rather than Fail* (February 1693), Southerne continues to vent his spleen at contemporary immorality. Even more than in the works discussed above, his characters are unflinchingly real, and the satire sharp-edged. It includes more music than any of his previous plays, but only one episode need be examined in detail here – the concert represented in Act IV.

Southerne's decision to launch another full-scale attack on amateur music-making may appear puzzling, but the two episodes have different functions. In *The Wives Excuse* his target was the snobbery of 'public' concerts; the servants' personation of their masters underscores the exclusiveness of such gatherings, as does the musician's contempt for Friendall. The concert scene in *The Maid's Last Prayer*, by contrast, shows little of this bickering between the social ranks, being simply well-crafted pandemonium in which much of the humour arises from Southerne's considerable knowledge of the theory and practice of music. The concert is directed by Sir Symphony, who is only minimally involved in the main plot. Its chief purpose is diversion, even though the bullies who infiltrate and disrupt the music meeting are perhaps distorted reflections of some of the clever characters. As the scene opens, the host is preparing the instruments, musicians are arriving, and Captain Drydrubb, a foolish cuckold and the only important character who actively participates in the concert, is trying to tune a cittern borrowed from a barber because his own was broken during an evening's serenade. Amid the confusion, a bully loosens

---

[33] *Pace* Thornton, *The Wives Excuse*, pp. 30-1.

the strings of a bass viol Sir Symphony is tuning and another rubs candle wax on his bow; a third wag distracts the amateur with a technical question: 'Pray, Sir, when you lengthen a Crotchet into Quavers, and divide it by Minums, does not your Cravat-string deaden the sound of your Fiddle?' Sir Symphony ignores this delicious nonsense but rises to the bait when Sir Ruff asks, 'Can common time be consistent with a Jigg?' The host replies that he writes all his jigs in that metre.

Despite the bullies' attempt to sabotage the concert, the dilettantes finally play an unspecified instrumental piece. As Sir Symphony's running commentary is perhaps the most extensive account of the less pleasant side of late seventeenth-century 'performing practice', I quote it in full:

O Gad! there's a flat Note! There's art! How surprizingly the Key changes! O law! there's a double relish! I swear, Sir, you have the sweetest little Finger in *England*! ha! that stroak's new; I tremble every inch of me: Now Ladies look to your Hearts – Softly Gentlemen – remember the Eccho – Captain, you play the wrong Tune – O law! my Teeth! my Teeth! for God's sake, Captain, mind your Cittern – Now the Fuga, bases! agen, agen! Lord! Mr. *Humdrum*, you come in three barrs too soon.

Undeterred by the opening selection, Sir Symphony calls for a song, 'Though you make no return to my passion' (z 601/1), a hearty endorsement of adultery, stated in the play-book to have been performed by the professional soprano Mrs Hodgson.[34] Purcell set the two-verse lyric to a jig-like melody in A minor. The surrounding spoken dialogue does not suggest that it is also meant to be incompetently rendered. Its lively, popular style and lewd topical allusions continue the broad humour of the scene.

The next event is astonishing and unparalleled in any contemporary drama. Without intervening dialogue, Mrs Ayliff came forward to join Mrs Hodgson in the duet 'No, resistance is but vain' (z 601/2), one of Purcell's longest and most passionate vocal compositions. This is an internecine juxtaposition. The masterpiece could not have benefited from its placement between the gentleman amateurs' consort and Sir Symphony's bass viol solo, cut short when a bully breaks the instrument over his head. Conversely, the magnificent duet must have had a dampening effect on the raucous scene. To try to reconcile 'No, resistance is but vain' with the theme of the play is futile; the piece simply does not belong here. The lyric – by Anthony Henley, a Member of Parliament of good family – is a conventional essay on the powers of love, but its contrasting images obviously appealed to Purcell, especially these lines:

> The Fierce, with Fierceness he [Cupid] destroys:
> The Weak, with Tenderness decoys.
> He kills the Strong with Joy, the Weak with Pain.

[34] But the earliest source of the music, *Thesaurus Musicus*, 1 (1693), names Mrs Dyer as the singer. Laurie ('Purcell's Stage Works', p. 192) suggests that they were the same person.

They are set to alternating passages of bravura passagework and slow, languishing chains of chromatics, as the composer habitually treated such vivid constructions. But this merely fine music is enveloped by an extraordinary refrain. Rather than attempt to ameliorate the awkwardness of the opening couplet, 'No, no, no, no, Resistance is but vain, / And only adds new weight to Cupid's chain', in which the poet seems to have repeated the first word simply to reach a ten-syllable count, Purcell makes a virtue of this stammering by multiplying it nearly twenty-fold.

The opening section carefully balances block-like passages fixed in a single key with unstable phrases constructed of chromatic webs which, if taken together, sound all twelve notes. The first two of the tonally static units are joined without modulatory link: the opening eight bars in A minor are immediately repeated in E minor with the voice parts reversed (see Example 11). A subtler aspect of the symmetrical design is the setting of 'vain'. As if to recall the plodding rhythm of the four-fold repetition of 'no', Purcell shifts to duple metre at the last word of the line. The musical pulse is thus an inversion of the poetic:

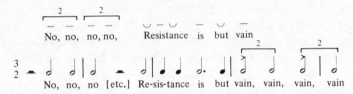

The passage comprising bars 22–33 is one of the composer's most adventurous harmonic excursions since the fantazias of 1680. Taking 'new' as a point of departure, he sounds six different keys within a mere fourteen bars, forming a chain of fifths with a third at either end. But the last cadence is only an intermediate goal, and this section concludes with a

Example 11. *The Maid's Last Prayer*: 'No, resistance is but vain', bars 1–34

Example 11 (cont.)

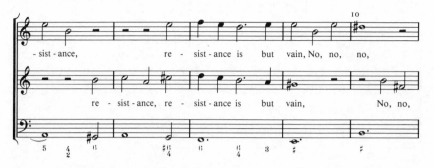

Example 11 (cont.)

rising and falling chromatic reinterpretation of the harmonically inactive opening. The recapitulation of the refrain after the contrasting middle movements (shown in Example 12) is magical, and the dovetailing, accomplished by omitting a bar of the refrain, is worthy of Mozart. The tension between the harmonically static sections and the highly volatile chromatic ones is enormous. The tonal monoliths seem to embody the 'resistance' of the poem, while the inching semitones symbolize Cupid's heavy chain and, when the sinuous lines descend, the pain of love. Yet the refrain itself includes almost no literal word-painting; Purcell did not set 'resistance', 'weight', and 'chain' in his usual graphic manner. Rather, he interpreted the power of love metaphorically as the power of music. Though it has little to do with *The Maid's Last Prayer*, the duet is one of his greatest achievements.

He provided one other song for the play, a setting of Congreve's 'Tell me no more I am deceived' (z 601/3), performed in the last act by Mrs Ayliff to the accompaniment of Sir Symphony's musicians. They are on their way to a masquerade, almost an obligatory ending for Covent Garden comedies of the early nineties. The song is remarkable only in one respect. For the second strophe Purcell changed the original melody in a few places to

Example 12. *The Maid's Last Prayer*: 'No, resistance is but vain', bars 89–97

accommodate the different word accents. I doubt that many singers would hit upon the solution given in Example 13 to the problem of trying to fit the second verse to the tune. Without this attention to detail, Congreve's cynical punch line ('I'll take her body, you her mind', a reference to Lady Malapert) would probably not be sung, and some hapless editors would conclude that Purcell had set only the first verse.

Example 13. *The Maid's Last Prayer*: 'Tell me no more I am deceived', bars 15–20 and 34–9

Example 13 (cont.)

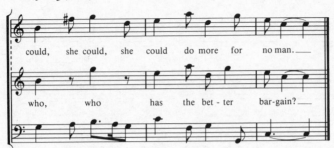

could, she could, she could do more for no man._____

who, who has the bet - ter bar-gain?_____

IV. Congreve

Purcell collaborated with William Congreve only on the early plays *The Old Batchelour* and *The Double-Dealer*. The musical scenes of both are unadventurous, though the songs and dances are rationally introduced and the lyrics allude to the surrounding action; protagonists listen respectfully to them, and a speaking character even sings in *The Double-Dealer*. Yet the songs are not quite in touch with the drama, as if Congreve were unconvinced of the wisdom of mixing the two media. These early plays give not the slightest hint that their author would, in little more than a decade, write one of the finest librettos in the English language – *Semele*. For Congreve, unlike Dryden and Durfey, operas and plays were chalk and cheese. Fools and madmen, let alone wits and rakes, do not sing art songs in his comedies. Purcell's most valuable contributions to the works discussed below are not the songs, but the two suites of incidental music. Though the overtures and act tunes are not directly related to the action of specific scenes, those for *The Double-Dealer* seem to have been strongly affected by the tone of the play.

The Old Batchelour

Despite being written to a threadbare pattern, the plot of *The Old Batchelour* (March 1693) is fresh and its stock characters are vigorous. Part of the reason for its huge success was its undoubtedly skilful type-casting, despite the last-minute changes necessitated by Mountfort's death a few months before the première. He was probably replaced by the ambitious Powell, who played Bellmour.[35] The other principals – Doggett, Mrs Bracegirdle, Mrs Mountfort, and Mrs Barry – took roles similar to those they had played many times before, while Betterton, the old bachelor, portrayed an ageing rake, thereby mocking his former speciality – the young libertine. To what extent Purcell's music contributed to the triumph is unknown.

[35] Well argued by Holland in *The Ornament of Action*, pp. 207–14.

The first song, 'Thus to a ripe consenting maid' (z 607/10), exemplifies Congreve's concern that all the music in his plays bear on the drama in some manner yet stop short of advancing the plot. In the second scene of Act II, Araminta (Mrs Bracegirdle), clever, young, and cautious in her affair with the profligate Vainlove, talks with her friend Belinda (Mrs Mountfort), an older woman whose pride and affectation invite ridicule. When Belinda and her beloved Bellmour's bantering turns suddenly bitter, Araminta intervenes to restore decorum: 'Nay, come, I find we are growing serious, and then we are in great danger of being dull – If my Musick-Master be not gone, I'll entertain you with a new Song, which comes pretty near my own Opinion of love and your Sex.' She calls for Mr Gavot to sing the above-named lyric, in which an older and wiser shepherdess, who has been wronged in love, counsels an inexperienced maid never to let a man discover too much about her, for if he does he will find that 'Every woman is the same'. However apropos, the song maintains a distance from the plot. Araminta is certainly the wiser and warier of the two women, but Belinda is the decayed beauty, the 'old repenting Delia'. The lyric does not, therefore, express the exact feelings of either character. The actor who portrayed Mr Gavot is not named in the dramatis personae, yet the song is for a tenor, though in the treble clef.[36] In the Guildhall Library song-book, Purcell wrote out the second verse to show that it should be sung despite some awkward word underlay.

The second and more important lyric, 'As Amoret and Thyrsis lay' (z 607/11), is heard in III.iv as the main attraction of a musical entertainment arranged by Heartwell, the old bachelor. A complex character, vain and foolish in his outward disdain for marriage, and the butt of the stratagems and much of the humour of the clever people, he secretly loves Silvia. When he discovers that their wedding in Act V is a hoax, the attempt to hide his bitter disappointment by bravely restating the advantages of bachelorhood is deeply moving. But Congreve's belated compassion is not mooted in Act III; before we can weep for Heartwell, we must first laugh at him.[37] Believing the way to Silvia's mercenary heart lies through music, he hires singers and dancers to entertain her. She indulges him only to regain Vainlove's affection. The three-verse lyric 'As Amoret and Thyrsis lay' should have caused Heartwell acute embarrassment, since it is the most gauche song of courtship imaginable. The first stanza describes sexual passion in the usual pastoral manner, but the second oversteps the boundary of good taste:

[36] Laurie ('Purcell's Stage Works', p. 193) suggests Bowman, but the tessitura would appear to lie too high for him.

[37] Holland stresses the importance of casting: '. . . while Betterton the rake is mocked, Betterton the great tragedian is also necessary for the understanding of Heartwell's self-dramatising posturing, the libertine's pose rendered ridiculous' (*The Ornament of Action*, p. 209).

The fearful Nymph reply'd – Forbear,
I cannot, dare not, must not hear:
Dearest *Thyrsis*, do not move me,
Do not – do not – if you Love me.
O let me – still the Shepherd said;
But while she fond Resistance made,
The hasty Joy, in struggling fled.

This requires no exegesis; I shudder to think what choreography might
have been devised for the 'Dance of Anticks' immediately following. Given
his skill in expressing the 'energy of English words', it is disappointing that
Purcell set only the first verse. Like the second, it is a narration of an exchange between a shepherd and shepherdess rather than a dramatic dialogue. Accordingly, Purcell cast it as a true duet, avoiding the alternating
phrases characteristic of the pastoral dialogue. In the second book of
Orpheus Britannicus (1702), the earliest source, the voice parts are written
in treble and bass clefs, though the upper part lies at least a third higher
than Purcell's usual soprano range and is therefore probably intended for
a tenor. A male duo would cast further indignity on Heartwell's futile
courtship, since the singers could represent the serious contenders for
Silvia's favours – Vainlove, who has seduced and abandoned her, and Sir
Joseph Wittol, whom she finally marries. The oily parallel thirds and
sixths between the voices add to the lecherous quality of the lyric; and at
the 'dénouement' the jarring dissonances in the bass contribute to the dire
lack of resolution (Example 14). Purcell thus conveys the message of the

Example 14. *The Old Batchelour*: 'As Amoret and Thyrsis lay', bars 64–9

second and third verses without having to set them, since this metaphorical death is clearly not a satisfactory one.

The music for the 'Antic Dance' may have been the first act tune of *The
Fairy-Queen*, a jig in G minor (z 629/6). In British Library Add. MS
35043, fol. 7, this dance follows 'Thus to a ripe consenting maid' and is
labelled 'Another song in the Old Batchelour'. The performance order of

the superb and highly varied act tunes is unfortunately unknown, and the imposing, at times sombre A minor overture would seem an incongruous prelude to the vaguely light-hearted mood of the first scene.[38]

The Double-Dealer

Of all the plays for which Purcell wrote music, the reader is most likely to be familiar with *The Double-Dealer* (November 1693), Congreve's second comedy and his first masterpiece. Yet this frequently revived drama is rarely reunited with its original music. The reasons are understandable if still unforgivable. The song in Act II, 'Cynthia frowns whene'er I woo her' (z 592/10), is long and fairly difficult, requiring a professional singer to do it justice. Cost-conscious producers may cut it and then be reassured to discover that it is not badly missed. The omission of the incidental music may be as easily justified, and its replacement – by odd movements of Brandenburg Concertos in a recent London revival – defended on the ground that it is simply that: incidental, supposedly composed only to mark time between acts and to entertain the audience before the curtain goes up. A well-informed director might even note that Purcell himself was commissioned to supply new music for old plays and occasionally borrowed an air or an overture from his own suites to use in a new drama. But *The Double-Dealer*, perhaps more than any other play mentioned in this chapter, is much the poorer without its original act music.

The 'comedy' is an anatomy of treachery. Lady Touchwood is a passionate adulteress, ruthless in her design to ruin Mellefont and prevent his marrying Cynthia. Her sometime collaborator, Maskwell, is worse, his villainy lacking all wit and honour, as he attempts to deceive everyone by telling selective truths – that is, by 'double-dealing'. The secondary characters, Sir Paul and Lady Plyant, Lord and Lady Froth, Lord Touchwood and Brisk, founder in a sea of infidelity. Only Mellefont and Cynthia are virtuous, but the preservation of their happiness and the ultimate reward of marriage are Pyrrhic victories on a battlefield of immorality.

The act music includes the usual sorts of pieces Purcell wrote for other plays in the early nineties: a large, warm French overture in F major (z 592/1), more appropriate to the lighter drama of *The Old Batchelour* than to the serious business of this one, though it does end in F minor; stylish minuets, forthright hornpipes; and contrapuntal airs of widely different moods. The two pieces in A minor stand out not only for their exceptional beauty but in their bold treatment of cross-relations, which is extreme even for Purcell. Thus far I have not speculated on the dramatic

---

[38] Three of the act tunes were published in *Apollo's Banquet* (1691), and the whole set is ascribed to Durfey's *Bussy D'Ambois* (March 1691) in Royal College of Music MS 1144. The incidental music may, therefore, have been originally written for the earlier play and re-used in *The Old Batchelour*, though the ascriptions in MS 1144 are not very trustworthy.

significance of these and other quirks of part-writing in the instrumental music, because they appear so frequently. While noting their affinity with certain keys and admitting that a composer of Purcell's resourcefulness might make special use of dissonance, I have taken Westrup's warning to heart:

It is one of the poses of pretentious scholarship to chortle with glee whenever these clashes occur. This is extravagant. It is right to insist that a modern reprint should make no attempt to whitewash the original. But it is ridiculous to pretend that all passages of this kind have a divine loveliness. The 'false relation' was merely a technical device of the period, in which the logical progress of independent parts was considered more important than euphony (*Purcell*, pp. 250–1).

Despite the admonition, I still regard the A minor air (z 592/4) in *The Double-Dealer* as peculiar.[39] It begins with some routinely rich suspensions on the strong beats of bars 2 and 3 of Example 15, but the careful listener would be jerked to attention when in bar 4 the viola's delayed sounding of E grinds against the bass part, which is making an early departure from the dominant. This teeth-rattling dissonance seems to

Example 15. *The Double-Dealer*: Air, bars 1–8

[39] Laurie ('Purcell's Stage Works', p. 264) suggests that this piece and the hornpipe discussed below comprised the first music. But since the song in Act II is also in A minor, one of the dances may have been an act tune.

open the floodgates in bars 5 and 7. Far from being 'the logical progress of independent parts', the double cross-relations F♮/F♯ and G♮/G♯ are downright perverse.[40] In the second strain (Example 16), the simultaneous sounding of G♮ and G♯ is less severe, because it alone of such passages in the piece seems a genuine exigency of part-writing.

Example 16. *The Double-Dealer*: Air, bars 21–2

Voice-leading 'irregularities' are even more acute in the A minor hornpipe (z 592/5), given complete in Example 17. The clash between E and F in the violins in the first bar recalls bar 4 of the air; the change from an E major to a C major chord at the beginning of the second half again places a strain on G♯ and G♮. The most daring stroke is saved for the penultimate bar, in which the contending notes finally collide to create a shimmering, out-of-focus dominant chord. Westrup concludes his diatribe against swooning over cross-relations by remarking that they 'can be striking if

Example 17. *The Double-Dealer*: Hornpipe

---

[40] The Purcell Society editor was bewildered by these passages (XVI, 200). In bar 5 he changes the viola's F♮ to F♯ on beat 3 in order to avoid a cross-relation, but the equally pungent ones in bar 7 are allowed to stand.

Example 17 (cont.)

there is contrast between the two opposing strands – between a soprano and tenor, or a violin and voice; but if the clash occurs in the same octave between voices or instruments of the same timbre, the result can be hideous; and no amount of reverence for the past should deter us from saying so' (*Purcell*, p. 251). I should hesitate to call any of those in the A minor air and hornpipe hideous. Most are well hidden in inner voices and at a quick tempo would be unnoticed by all but listeners with the keenest ears. Yet the dissonance is always present just beneath the surface, adding a bittersweet flavour to the melodies, much the way Maskwell's subterfuge poisons the straightforward plots of the other characters. This is only a metaphysical connection, but a less fanciful one can be found between the instrumental pieces and the song in Act II.

The romantic couple, Mellefont and Cynthia, upon surveying the marital discord everywhere around them, are cynical about their prospects. Marriage is like a card game, says Cynthia, 'and Consequently one of us must be a Loser'. 'Not at all,' responds Mellefont; 'only a Friendly Tryal of Skill, and the Winnings to be Shared between us.' The witty repartee ends abruptly when some musicians cross the stage. Mellefont asks them to rehearse the song they are going to sing for a gathering at Lord Touchwood's house. As if by coincidence, the lyric continues the simile between marriage and gaming, telling of a 'Cynthia' (Purcell changed this to the less blatant 'Celia' in the Guildhall Library manuscript) who wants it both ways – to be courted but not undone: 'Thus, in doubting, she refuses; / And not Winning, thus she loses'. The gather-ye-rosebuds second verse warns her not to be overtaken by 'Age and Wrinckles'. Mellefont simply thanks the musicians, and neither he nor his friend remarks on the cutting appropriateness of the song. Though Purcell's setting, sung by Mrs Ayliff, may suggest how the lovers should react, I can detect no overt signs of passion, submission, or even humour in this long, intricate piece. The two verses are given different music, and the second part is oblivious to the poetry. The repetition of single words and short phrases is extreme, and the passage shown in Example 18 seems to have been conceived separately from the text, which is highly unusual for Purcell. Cynthia's ambivalence toward the pleasures and pains of love is

Example 18. *The Double-Dealer*: 'Cynthia frowns', bars 45–52 (bass omitted)

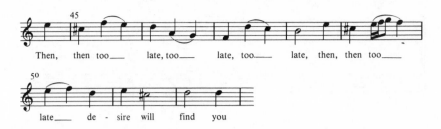

reflected by the tonal scheme. The opening phrase (Example 19) moves resolutely to a firm imperfect cadence on E major which is followed immediately by a passage in C major.[41] This sudden change of direction produces a cross-relation between the G♯ in the harmony and the G♮ in the voice, as pronounced as any of the clashes in the air and hornpipe. And

Example 19. *The Double-Dealer*: 'Cynthia frowns', bars 1–6

near the end, shown in Example 20, the chromatically altered imitation in the bass, which is demanded by the harmonic progression, helps release the tension created by the earlier oblique dissonances. That this happens at the word 'past' is doubly satisfying. Here Cynthia's reservations about Mellefont seem to dissolve. In Peter Wood's 1978–9 production of *The Double-Dealer* at the National Theatre, the lyric was reset by Harrison Birtwistle as a duet for a man and a young boy, who after singing presented Mellefont with the music. Obviously displeased, he thanked them in a sarcastic tone and tore the paper in two, a not unreasonable response

---

[41] Source: Guildhall Library autograph.

Example 20. *The Double-Dealer*: 'Cynthia frowns', bars 81–5

to the new setting. Purcell's version could never elicit such a definitive re-action, perhaps for good reason. The couple's complete lack of acknowl-edgement of the song is similar to Congreve's handling of another moment of great dramatic intensity. When Maskwell is exposed in Act V, we crave to hear his cries of agony, but they are suppressed; he 'hangs down his head' and speaks no more. Perhaps the silence after the song implies a victory as well.

Purcell did not set the other lyric required by the play. In Act III during an episode that provides some welcome levity, several characters are gos-siping about their friends. Cynthia says, aside, 'I find there are no Fools so inconsiderable in themselves, but they can render other People contemp-tible in exposing their Infirmities.' Lady Froth twaddles on about an elderly lady who paints her face 'so exorbitantly'. She recalls that Brisk has made a song upon her. Apologizing that 'I don't know what to call it, but it's Satyr', she asks Lord Froth to sing it, even though nothing has been said about the latter's ability in music. But Froth was acted by Bowman, who needed no introduction as a singer.[42] The silly lyric was even set by the actor himself (D&M No. 166). The label 'Satyr' surely applies to the music as well as the poem. I should guess that the song, given complete as Example 21, was intended as a dig at Purcell. The studied melismas and overdone repetition of 'now' are only slight exaggerations of his character-istic vocal style (compare 'no' in 'No, resistance is but vain' in *The Maid's Last Prayer*). The actor and the composer had a long and fruitful asso-ciation extending back to *Theodosius* in 1680, and this was probably a friendly ribbing.[43] But one should note that only a few months had passed since Purcell's mad dialogue in *The Richmond Heiress* had failed to please; perhaps there is more to this send-up than meets the ear.

---

[42] Holland notes that 'Bowman, placed in the company of Powell and Mrs Mountfort as Brisk and Lady Froth, provides an important clue to the play's design' (*The Ornament of Action*, p. 215), but does not discuss this scene.

[43] Bowman may have begun his professional career as a singer in the King's Music in the seventies. In 1685 he was appointed to the private music of James II and retained a court position until the early years of the reign of William and Mary; see Highfill, *A Biographi-cal Dictionary*, II, 198–201. His and Purcell's paths must have crossed many times.

Example 21. *The Double-Dealer*: John Bowman, 'Ancient Phillis has young Graces'

An - cient Phil - lis has____ young_ Gra - ces, young Gra -

- - - ces; 'tis a strange thing, a

strange but a true one; Shall I tell you, tell you, tell you? Shall I tell you how

she her - self shall make____ her own Fa - ces; And each Morning, Morning,

Morn - ing still wears a new one; where's the Won - der now, now, now,

now? where's the Won - der now, now, now now? The Won -

- - der, now, now, now, now, now, now, now, now?

v. Other Comedies of the Early Nineties

In addition to the songs in the works of the major playwrights, Purcell set
lyrics in four new comedies by the lesser lights Thomas Wright, John
Crowne, Edward Ravenscroft, and Thomas Scott. Only one of these plays,
Crowne's *The Married Beau*, was much of a success, but each includes
scenes in which music plays an important role. Whereas Southerne and
Congreve appear to have admitted songs reluctantly into their plots, letting the lyrics embellish rather than steer the action, the minor authors,
especially Wright and Crowne, gave music much freer rein. Purcell continued to share the honours in these plays with his Theatre Royal colleagues, providing the more difficult and sophisticated songs for the professionals, with Eccles writing most of the simpler but more dramatic ones
for the actor–singers. An unexpected benefit of the peculiar arrangement
is that Purcell was able to compose many duets, being unhampered by the
limitations of the singing actors, who rarely performed *en ensemble*. For a
speaking character suddenly to break into song put burden enough on
dramatic verisimilitude; for two voices to express something designed for

one would have been intolerably artificial, except in special circumstances such as the final choruses of pastoral dialogues.

The following plays have little in common except Purcell's music. *The Female Vertuoso's* is an adaptation from Molière; *The Married Beau* is an up-to-date sex farce; *The Canterbury Guests* is a lewd intrigue comedy that could have been written twenty years earlier; and *The Mock-Marriage* is a wobbly bell-wether of the new morality creeping into the plays of the mid- and late nineties. They are discussed in this, their chronological order.

The Female Vertuoso's

A month after composing the Birthday Ode for Queen Mary, *Celebrate this festival* (z 321), performed on 30 April 1693, in which the theatre singers Bowman and Mrs Ayliff took part, Purcell was back at Drury Lane to write a duet for a far less auspicious occasion, the première of *The Female Vertuoso's*. Its author, Thomas Wright, a stage machinist for the United Company, had fashioned an adaptation (it has been called a 'hash') of Molière's masterpiece *Les Femmes savantes*. He took much from his model: the rival sisters, a weak husband and his domineering wife, a foolish poetaster, and the various stratagems employed to gain a mother's consent to the marriage her daughter desires. Yet he strips Molière's plot of its satire on philosophy, injecting in its place those staples of late seventeenth-century English comedy – bullies, a sham shotgun wedding, and a Cambridge-educated fop. Haters of Restoration drama will view Clerimont's victory over Lady Meanwell in Act V as the final straw, since in *Les Femmes savantes* Philaminte (Lady Meanwell) remains stubbornly true to her philosophy. In Wright's version, her convictions crumble and both she and her idealistic daughter Lovewitt are discredited. The last vestiges of satire are nearly destroyed by this ham-handed transformation, but by allowing the ladies' change of heart to be achieved largely through a performance of Purcell's duet 'Love, thou art best' (z 596), Wright pushes the adapter's licence to the limit.[44]

The climax is prepared by an improbable chain of events too tedious to recount here. In brief, to gain Mariana's hand Clerimont must prove to his future mother-in-law, Lady Meanwell, that he does not hate poetry. This is a trite and ignominious means of cutting off Molière's ingenious intrigues. The haughty matriarch will never allow 'into my Family a Despiser of Wit, one who knows well enough I'm an Author, and never had the manners to ask me to read any of my Works to him'. Clerimont replies with mock indignation, 'I am not, Madam, such an Enemy to Wit as your Ladyship makes me, I love it but as a Gentleman, without either Pride or Affectation; I could Entertain the Company with a small Essay of my Poetry, a SONG I

---

[44] Puzzlingly, the lyric was also set by Ralph Courteville and is preserved in a single-sheet engraving in, for example, British Library G.304(96), headed 'The Prerogatives of Love'.

made yesterday, if you could promise your selves patience enough to hear
it.' Lady Meanwell agrees to this test of his worthiness. The lyric, 'Love,
thou art best' – which, ironically, was penned by a woman, Anne, Countess
of Winchelsea – does in fact establish Clerimont as a poet but at the same
time offends Lady Meanwell: '. . . to affront Philosophy to my face, is a
Crime never to be atoned for . . . to make an Example of this Unmannerly
[a pun?] Composer of Songs, I'll inflict upon him the Curse of a silly Por-
tionless Wife'. Her chagrin is a *non sequitur*, since she, unlike Molière's
Philaminte, has not shown the slightest interest in philosophy; this is the
wrong place for Wright to have turned to his model for guidance. The lyric
reads harmlessly: to summarize, God raised man above the beasts by
giving him the capacity to love; whatever the philosophers say, only love
can improve man's soul. Purcell's G minor duet for sopranos is a lovely
piece that avoids extravagant treatment of lines such as 'Music without
thee [Love] is but noise'. In the excerpt given in Example 22, the matter-of-

Example 22. *The Female Vertuoso's*: 'Love, thou art best', bars 42–59

fact narrative in D minor with its rather bleak harmonies warms up immediately to F major when Heaven speaks.[45] The passage apparently
meant to offend Lady Meanwell is the setting of 'philosophers' to a derisive, laughing figure shown in Example 23. This is humorous but exqui-
sitely tasteful. Purcell seems genuinely committed to realizing Wright's

[45] Source: *Comes Amoris*, v (1694).

Example 23. *The Female Vertuoso's*: 'Love, thou art best', bars 76–80

feeble wish that the song bring credit to Clerimont while discountenancing Lady Meanwell. The achievement is therefore far greater than could ever be revealed by a concert performance.[46]

The Married Beau

Crowne's successful comedy *The Married Beau: or, the Curious Impertinent* (April 1694) deserves to be better known. It has a simple but effective blend of sex and sentiment, and the part of Mrs Lovely would be a dream for an actress able to convey its extreme subtlety. The plot is straightforward for the first three acts, but twists itself into an almost incomprehensible snarl in the final scenes. The newly married Mr Lovely asks his friend Polidor to try to seduce his wife to test her fidelity, and she fails with flying colours. After news of the adultery leaks out, her husband views the destruction of her reputation as a perverse victory. But Mrs Lovely's public display of remorse in Act V, the keystone of the play's supposed moral foundation, needs to be carefully examined.

Like most of his fellow comic dramatists, Crowne draws a distinct line between the clever people and fools. The play is unusual in that the knaves are in the minority, an imbalance that helps to tone down the bedroom-farce scenes. The character upon which these episodes centre, Squire Thomas Thorneback, is an accomplished fool, a role created by Doggett, the celebrated Solon of *The Marriage-Hater Match'd*. In the first act he seems as coxcombical as his companion and rival, Sir John Shittlecock. But in Act II he is elevated to the ranks of the clever after demonstrating skill at singing and dancing. The main vehicle of this transformation is Eccles's passionate yet wistful song 'O fye, what mean I'.[47] It makes Sir John green with envy and even impresses Mrs Lovely, since later in the play she attempts to blame Thorneback for her adultery. When this ploy back-

---

[46] The play requires one other song. In Act III Sir Maggot Jingle, played by Bowman, sings 'Should King Lewis, with all his might' (a translation of Molière's 'Si le roi m'avait donné'), no setting of which survives.

[47] For a brief discussion, see my article 'Restoration Stage Fiddlers and Their Music', pp. 318–19. A modern edition of the song is in *Eight Songs by John Eccles*, ed. M. Pilkington, pp. 18–19.

fires, she calls him an 'odious Fool', but he deals the *coup de grâce* by exposing her greatest failing – vanity: 'You believe all the World's in love with you. I never valued you, forsooth' (Act V). Like Maskwell in *The Double-Dealer*, her humiliation is followed by a speechless exit from the stage.

Purcell's only song for the play, 'See where repenting Celia lies' (z 603/10), was sung by Mrs Ayliff, who was not a member of the speaking cast. Yet, surprisingly, it plays a far more important role in the drama than Thorneback's. At the beginning of Act V, Mrs Lovely is discovered alone, apprehensive that her husband has learned of her affair with Polidor. Borrowing from tragedy the convention wherein music entertains an ill-fated and melancholy protagonist just before the catastrophe, she asks her maid for a reassuring song. The 'catastrophe' that follows is the final assignation with her erstwhile lover. Whether genuinely contrite or cleverly sensing that Polidor intends to betray her waywardness, she loudly praises her husband and storms out indignantly. How did Purcell interpret this important scene? Is his song a clear signal of repentance, or a parody of tragic remorse, as the *double entendre* in the first line strongly implies?

> See! where repenting Celia lyes,
> With Blushing Cheeks, and down-cast eyes,
>   Bemoaning, in a mournful shade,
>   The ruins in her heart and fame,
>   Which sinful love has made.
> Oh! let thy Tears, fair Celia, flow,
>   For that Coelestial, wondrous dew,
> More Graces on thee will bestow,
>   Than all thy Dresses, and thy Arts cou'd do.[48]

Because Mrs Lovely neither weeps at her sins nor confesses them to her husband, Purcell's pathetic, even tragic, setting comes as a great surprise. The opening, given in Example 24, is stark, the singer alone, like Mrs Lovely, exposed to the world. Seizing prematurely on the image of cleansing tears, Purcell altered 'down-cast eyes' in the second line to the more liquid 'melting eyes' over which he draped a long melisma. 'Oh! let thy Tears, fair Celia, flow' is a passionate lament that draws the singer to the depths of despair – and to G minor – from which she arises renewed, her tears having granted absolution. Importantly, the exaltation of the final phrase (Example 25) is achieved by the music alone, since the satirical meaning of the text is delayed and thus obscured by repeating the insignificant words 'than all'. The song may not erase all doubts about this complex character, but it suggests that her declaration of marital obedience be taken seriously. However one may view Mrs Lovely's progress in Act V, the singer has died of shame and been reborn through repentance.

Sometime after the summer of 1695, Eccles composed a song to replace

---

[48] Purcell did not set the second verse.

Example 24. *The Married Beau*: 'See where repenting Celia lies', bars 1–8

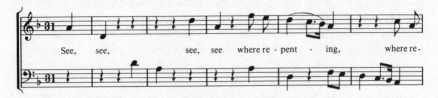

Example 25. *The Married Beau*: 'See where repenting Celia lies', bars 55–62

Purcell's, called 'Beyond the desart Mountains'.[49] Its message is similar, but more heavy-handed. Celia sings,

> Farewell ye Thoughts of sinfull Love
> Whose Tempting Joys our ruin prove
> Fleeting pleasure in Moment past
> But oh! ye pains of guilt for Ever last.

Cast in F minor with a lush four-part string accompaniment, it is a beautiful piece but offensively sentimental in its dramatic context. That Eccles was asked to write this substitute song shows that *The Married Beau* was probably revived at Lincoln's Inn Fields after the 1695 split, though no

---

[49] In British Library Add. MS 29378, fols. 179–81.

record of its performance survives. This also implies that the Drury Lane company retained the original music, except of course Eccles's song for Thorneback in Act II.

For the première Purcell also provided an overture and act tunes, a suite that finds him at the height of his powers as a composer for instruments.[50] The performance order of the pieces is unknown, and their possible dramatic functions are a matter for speculation. But one of them, the C major Hornpipe on a Ground (z 603/9), deserves special comment. Purcell's compositions on repeating basses are celebrated for ingeniously obscuring the harmonic periods of the ground by overlapping phrases in the upper voices. This brilliant work, however, is absolutely regular in its four-bar phrases, though a mass of contradictions in other respects. It is a hornpipe in rhythm, a chaconne in style, but a rondeau in form; the opening tune returns twice in the top part and twice hidden in the second violin. The most extraordinary aspect of the piece is its obstinate figuration (see Example 26). The mechanical patterns in the first violin persist despite the

Example 26. *The Married Beau*: Hornpipe on a Ground, bars 20–4

changing harmonies below, while the second violin's obsession with the repeated melodic third E to G must have had comic overtones.[51] Is this mindless call of the cuckoo a wry allusion to Mr Lovely, the mindless cuckold of the play? If the interpretation seems far-fetched, the reader should know that Godfrey Finger did precisely this in his incidental music

[50] The 'Slow Air' in D minor (z 603/2) was perhaps written earlier, since it is a transposition from G minor of the Magicians' Dance in Act I of *Circe*.

[51] The hornpipe is not as modern-sounding as the version given in the Purcell Society Edition, xx, 101–3, where it has been wrongly transcribed. For a correct rendering, see Laurie, 'Purcell's Stage Works', II, 27–30.

for *The Husband His own Cuckold* (February 1696) by John Dryden, Jun., calling one of the act tunes 'Cuckoe'.[52]

The Canterbury Guests

The last play for which Purcell wrote music before the United Company ceased acting at the end of 1694 was Edward Ravenscroft's farce *The Canterbury Guests; or, a Bargain Broken* (c. October 1694), the only new work mounted at Drury Lane during that bitter autumn. The casting shows that the battle lines between Betterton's disgruntled majority and the rest of the troupe had already been drawn. None of the secessionist cabal (Betterton, Mrs Barry, Mrs Bracegirdle, and the others) appeared in the play. The leads, Powell (Careless) and Doggett (Dashwell), were to remain at Drury Lane, as were the inexperienced and second-rank actors who also appeared in the play. Even the music suggests that the theatre's principal composer of comic songs had by this time declared his intention to leave. The dialogue in Act III seems tailored for Eccles, but it was assigned to his erstwhile collaborator.

The Canterbury Guests, knocked together from some of Ravenscroft's other works, is a laboured variation of the old story in which a clever heiress, mismatched with a fool, tricks her guardian/parent into letting her marry a gay blade. The playwright tries to ease the ennui with graphic displays of gluttony, a proverb-spouting country knight, and a frantic episode of bedroom farce as obscene as any devised during the period. To prepare the way for this last, the barriers of good taste are broken down in Act III when Careless, Captain Durzo, and two whores are entertained by a dialogue between feuding housewives, entitled 'Good neighbour, why do you look awry?' (z 591). For this piece Purcell removed his peruke and painted the crudity of the verses with an abandon that rivals Eccles's coarser essays in the genre. The two women merrily exchange insults in 6/4 time until one accuses the other of trying to seduce her husband. A change to duple metre and furious dotted rhythms underscore the rude reply. The argument becomes ever more heated until the wives sing different words at the same time. The Purcell Society Edition, Vol. XVI, accidentally omitted a bar of the climactic passage, given correctly in Example 27.[53] When the second wife threatens violence, the husbands intervene in a homophonic duet to stress their peace-making role. This rebarbative piece has none of the graceful humour of the composer's better-known dialogues, such as 'Now the maids and the men' from *The Fairy-Queen*, but it perfectly complements the debauchery.

[52] In British Library Add. MS 35043, fol. 81v, Bodleian Library Mus. Sch. MS c.72, p. 3, Royal College of Music MS 1144, fol. 28v, and Los Angeles, Clark Library, Finney partbooks, p. 58.

[53] Source: *Thesaurus Musicus*, III (1695).

Example 27. *The Canterbury Guests*: 'Good neighbour, why do you look awry?', bars 73–8

The Mock-Marriage

After the secession of Betterton's faction in early 1695, the Theatre Royal was left with few actors of standing and almost no singers. Nothing is known of the pressure that may have been put on Purcell to leave the Patent Company or what induced him to remain. But the surviving calendar of stage performances strongly suggests that Drury Lane owed what success it had during the extremely difficult 1695–6 season to his music. Rich, the manager of the company, must have given the composer a free hand; no longer having to share the limelight with Eccles in supplying music for the glut of comedies mounted in the seasons before the rebellion, Purcell came into his own as he turned almost exclusively to tragedies and old heroic plays. In fact, during the final burst of creativity, which included *The Indian Queen*, *Timon of Athens*, *Bonduca*, and *The Libertine*, he wrote songs for only two new comedies.

Thomas Scott's *The Mock-Marriage* was first performed in the summer or early autumn of 1695.[54] The inexperienced playwright followed a for-

---

[54] In a letter of 26 October 1695, Dennis writes, 'There has just been a Play Acted call'd *The Mock Marriage*' (*Letters upon Several Occasions*, p. 125). But Laurie ('Purcell's Stage Works', p. 218) notes that Gildon reports that the play was well received considering 'the Season of the Year', which suggests a summer production (*The Lives and Characters of the English Dramatic Poets*, p. 121).

mula for success: a Covent Garden plot with clever women extricating themselves from arranged marriages; yet another parody of the masque in *The Empress of Morocco*, very similar to the one in *The Richmond Heiress*, but without music; and the type-casting of Powell and Mrs Verbruggen (formerly Mrs Mountfort) as Willmot, a philanderer ripe for reform, and Clarinda, his crafty tamer, who wears breeches. But the rest of the principals are hollow: Lady Barter is a poor imitation of a Mrs Barry-type adulteress; Marina, a witty virgin, cries out for Mrs Bracegirdle; and Sir Arthur, a shameless composite of Lord Froth (*The Double-Dealer*), Sir Symphony (*The Maid's Last Prayer*), and Friendall (*The Wives Excuse*), suffers badly from the lack of Bowman, the obvious man for the part. As it happened, the first Sir Arthur, Michael Lee, had to have the important song 'Man is for the woman made' sung for him. The loss of the veteran comedians was not, however, a complete disaster. The play 'met with pretty good success' (Gildon, *English Dramatic Poets*, p. 121), and Mrs Knight's portrayal of Lady Barter permitted this character to perform her own song in II.ii (Mrs Barry, for all her versatility, did not sing).

Willmot hopes to rekindle his illicit affair with Lady Barter, but she is hypocritically displeased at his infatuation with Clarinda. She forestalls his advance into her bedchamber by making him listen to 'Oh! how you protest' (D&M No. 2479), a light-hearted teasing lyric in which she flatly refuses to grant his wish. Such pixyishness is rarely encountered in a Barry-type adulteress, and it is somewhat out of character for Lady Barter here. Since Mrs Knight, unlike Anne Bracegirdle at the rival theatre, did not go on to a singing career, one may suppose that her performance was unremarkable. Though most authorities ascribe 'Oh! how you protest' to Purcell, the earliest source, *Deliciae Musicae*, III (1696), does not name the composer.[55] The strophic setting is well crafted and engaging; the accompaniment, though simple, has a few brief points of imitation against the tune. But stylistic criteria are not very reliable in determining the authorship of folk-like pieces such as this, and to assign it to Purcell on these grounds alone presupposes incorrectly that his contemporaries were incapable of producing the occasional hit. His colleagues at Drury Lane after Eccles left – Courteville, Ackeroyde, and Leveridge – should not be ruled out, though I think Leveridge the least likely candidate. Since Morgan supplied the act music for *The Mock-Marriage*, perhaps he wrote the song as well.[56]

Doubts about authorship also surround the far more famous song in Act III, ''Twas within a furlong of Edinboro' town' (Z 605/2), the verse by Durfey. In this scene, Willmot hires musicians to serenade Lady Barter. He asks them to play 'some brisk wanton Air or other, to quicken her Imagi-

[55] The song is first attributed to Purcell in *Wit and Mirth*, IV (1706).
[56] See my *Music in the Restoration Theatre*, pp. 201-2.

nation; and then the Song I gave you'. The lyric is not exactly appropriate, but it does reflect the strongly moral tone of the play: Jenny refuses to be tempted by the roguish Jockey. One of the finest of all Scotch songs, it enjoyed a wide circulation in many different arrangements. The earliest source, again Book III of *Deliciae Musicae*, does not name a composer. An undated single-sheet engraving probably issued before 1700 ascribes it to Purcell and adds the valuable information that it was sung by 'the Girl', presumably Letitia Cross (British Library G.312[51]). But in British Library Add. MS 22099, dating from about 1705, a keyboard version (fol. 9) is attributed to 'Mr Cla—', probably Jeremiah Clarke, though this may mean simply that he arranged it. Were it not for these bibliographical problems, few authorities would doubt that the song is Purcell's.[57] All the clichés of the Scotch-air style – lombard rhythms, an ambling chain-of-thirds melody, a III$_6$–I cadence and other modal progressions – are fashioned into a wonderful evocation of rustic courtship in 'the rosy time of year'. The bass line of the *Deliciae Musicae* version is inelegant, but perhaps purposely rough and folk-like. If not by Purcell, ''Twas within a furlong' is Clarke's best song.

'Man is for the woman made' (z 605/3) in Act IV is unquestionably by Purcell.[58] Sir Arthur, the Bowman-line fop, boasts that he is a composer. To demonstrate his genius, he has arranged a private concert for friends. As the scene opens, he instructs the musicians to 'keep your Countenances. You Fidlers generally make worse Faces than *Sir Martin*;[59] if your care in the performance, does but equal mine in the composure, I'me sure 'twill be very agreeable.' But rather than be hoist by his own petard, Sir Arthur asks a 'pretty *Miss*' to sing the song, presumably Letitia Cross. Motteux's lyric, called a 'Roundelau' because of its A-B-A form, is a catalogue of tasteless metaphors. Purcell exposes the fool with great style. Enclosed by a flamboyant burden is a thrice-repeated triad that bears Sir Arthur's pattering *faux pas* (see Example 28). When one can no longer stand the broken record, the refrain returns abruptly. The stroke of genius allowing one to tolerate all three verses is the reharmonizing of the first bar of the chorus

Example 28. *The Mock-Marriage*: 'Man is for the woman made', first verse only

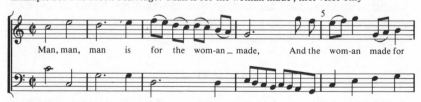

Man, man, man   is   for the wom-an _ made,   And the wom-an made for

---

[57] See, for example, Westrup, *Purcell*, p. 156.
[58] See *Deliciae Musicae*, III (1696).
[59] A reference to the celebrated musical scene in Act V of Dryden's Sr *Martin Mar-all* (August 1667).

Example 28 (cont.)

(bar 15) to break the inane alternation of tonic and dominant chords. 'Man is for the woman made' is one of Purcell's funniest songs, hinting at an appealing facet of his musical personality. In the midst of composing the highly sophisticated and deeply moving scores for *Bonduca* and *The Indian Queen*, the great tragedian found time to write a deceptively simple song for an entirely forgettable comedy.

VI. Revivals

In contrast to the volumes of music he wrote for revivals of serious dramas, Purcell composed only a handful of pieces for new productions of old comedies. In 1685 he reset the abusive lyric 'My wife has a tongue' (z 594) as a catch for the fiddlers in the tavern scene in Act III of Ravenscroft's *The English Lawyer* (*c*. December 1677).[60] He also produced a catch, 'At the close of the evening' (z 599), for an unrecorded revival of Beaumont and Fletcher's *The Knight of Malta*.[61] *The Gentleman's Journal* for April 1694 includes one of the instrumental tunes from *The Fairy-Queen* (z 629/1b) with a text by N. Henley, 'There's not a swain on the plain', of which Purcell apparently approved, since he copied it into the Guildhall Library song-book, transposed from G minor to E minor. 'Joyful Cuckoldom' (No. 26) states that this was sung by Mrs Hudson in a revival of Fletcher's *Rule a Wife and Have a Wife*, perhaps at the beginning of Act III. The date of the production is unknown.

Purcell also wrote a duet, 'Leave these useless arts in loving' (z 579), for a 1693 revival of Shadwell's popular sex farce *Epsom-Wells*, first acted in December 1672. Most of the music for the original production survives (except the act tunes), including Robert Smith's excellent setting of 'Oh how I abhor the tumult and smoak of the Town' (D&M No. 2475), a satire on country life sung by a London fiddler in Act III. This is one of the longest lyrics in any comedy before *Don Quixote*, and it rambles badly. But Smith produced a clearly articulated structure built round a constellation of secondary key centres. The other important verse, 'How pleasant is mutual Love' (D&M No. 1448) in Act II, was set wretchedly by Staggins. His cross-relations *are* hideous, more by accident than design, and the final cadence is preceded by an inexcusable set of consecutive fifths. Even if Purcell's 'Leave these useless arts in loving' did not have a similar text, one might guess that it replaced Staggins's song. Why the master chose to set the later lyric for soprano and bass is not immediately apparent. In II.i Carolina asks her maid to 'Sing that Song Mr. *Woodly* taught you'. For Woodly himself to join in would make little sense. It is not one of Purcell's memorable efforts, but he did arrange it as a soprano solo in the Guildhall Library song-book.

The Tempest

Although no performance record survives, Davenant and Dryden's version of *The Tempest* was probably revived in the summer or autumn of 1695. First acted in 1667 and published in 1670, it had been converted into an ingenious musical in 1674.[62] One of the very few works to occupy the

---

[60] Zimmerman, *An Analytical Catalogue*, p. 270, follows Squire's incorrect statement that the play has no place where the piece could be introduced.

[61] The piece is first linked to the play by *Apollo's Banquet*, II (1691), No. 73.

[62] For a summary of the controversy over the extent of Dryden's participation in the 1670 version, see George Robert Guffey, *After The Tempest* (Los Angeles: Augustan Reprint Society, 1969), pp. iv-xiii, and Mongi Raddadi, *Davenant's Adaptations of Shakespeare*, Studia Anglistica Upsaliensia, 36 (Uppsala, 1979), pp. 14-15, 119-49. The changes made for the 1674 version are usually attributed to Shadwell, who is known to have written the verse for 'Arise, ye subterranean winds'. Guffey, however, concludes that the work was probably 'the creation of a number of hands' (p. ix), though offering no evidence to support this statement.

rocky ground between true opera and play, the Restoration *Tempest* had behind it the great Elizabethan and Jacobean traditions of the masque and lyrical spoken drama. Taking Ariel's songs as a point of departure, the adapters allowed the new musical scenes to grow naturally from the plot, which was modified specifically for this purpose. For example, the masque of devils in II.iii is meant to nettle Alonzo and Antonio for their usurpation; it is a graphic representation of their guilty consciences. And in an episode joining the spoken and musical worlds of the drama, Ferdinand expresses his sorrow in song, while Ariel sings the echoes. In its 1674 guise, *The Tempest* was revived several times during the nineties and the first decade of the next century. Even the music stubbornly attributed to Purcell mostly replaces that of Locke, Hart, Reggio, Humfrey, and Banister, though the text of the masque in Act V has been considerably altered for the later setting.[63]

Yet the British Orpheus did compose one song for a revival, 'Dear pretty youth' (z 631/10), the lyric of which is not found in any of the late seventeenth-century quartos of the play. That it is included in the earliest manuscript of the otherwise anonymous version, British Library Add. MS 37027, largely accounts for the persistent misattribution of the entire score. With its many stage directions, cues and cuts showing it to have been used in a stage performance, Add. MS 37027 is an important document, and the handwriting, which at first glance appears to be turn-of-the-century, would seem to torpedo Laurie's theory that Weldon composed the bulk of the score after 1710. On closer inspection, however, one finds many post-1700 features: consistently applied natural signs, full key signatures, and so forth.[64] The manuscript shows no trace of primacy, only vigorous alteration and assimilation. A marginal note even states that Purcell's song, for soprano in A major, should be sung by tenor down a tone. There is, however, little doubt when and why 'Dear pretty youth' was added to the play. At its first appearance in *Deliciae Musicae*, III (published about November 1695), the rubric tells a great deal: 'A New Song in the *Tempest*, Sung by Mis *Cross* to her Lover, who is supposed Dead'. From this one knows that the play in question is the 1670 or 1674 adaptation and not Shakespeare's, because in IV.iii of the former, Ferdinand wounds his rival Hippolito (a role added by Davenant), and the would-be rake seems to die. The victim's beloved Dorinda (Miranda's sister, another new character) playfully urges him to awake, having had no experience with death. Clearly, this is the part taken by the adolescent Letitia Cross, who joined the reorganized Drury Lane company in the spring of 1695, be-

---

[63] See Laurie, 'Did Purcell Set *The Tempest*?', *passim*.

[64] Laurie thinks Add. MS 37027 'unlikely to date from before 1715' ('Purcell's Stage Works', p. 139), a suspicion all but confirmed by the watermark, an eighteenth-century 'Pro Patria' with countermark 'I V', a combination which Heawood (*Watermarks* [Hilversum: Paper Publications Society, 1950], No. 3696) dates *c*. 1724.

coming Purcell's main soprano. Therefore, the revival almost certainly occurred between that time and the composer's death in November, a period when Miss Cross is known to have sung other pathetic songs in plays, 'O lead me to some peaceful gloom' in *Bonduca* being a good example.

'Dear pretty youth' is innocently cheerful. The singer, having recently discovered the power of her sexuality, asks how Hippolito can sleep in her irresistible presence. But when she touches him ('Alas! my dear, you're cold as stone'), Purcell interjects a moment of panicky, chromatic recitative, after which Dorinda continues the revivification. Though the song would appear to pander to the then current vogue for maudlin effects, especially involving children, the composer found in her naïveté a pure vein of pathos.

Placing 'Dear pretty youth' in its proper context does not, however, solve the problems surrounding the 1695 revival of *The Tempest*. What music was used for the rest of the opera? Accepting for the purposes of argument Laurie's strong case that it could not possibly have been the mock-Purcell score, one must also rule out Purcell's having written another version of which 'Dear pretty youth' is the only surviving fragment. He is extremely unlikely to have taken on yet another lengthy project in his last months. Spring productions of new semi-operas had become a tradition. *Dioclesian*, *King Arthur*, and *The Fairy-Queen* all had April–June premières; the lack of a new opera in 1693 was probably owing to the crippling expense of the last of the major works. And in 1694 the first two parts of *Don Quixote* amounted to a spring opera, while *The Indian Queen* was clearly to have been the major production for 1695, delayed until the autumn because of the division of the company. A new production of *The Tempest* during the composer's last season is out of the question, and I should guess that 'Dear pretty youth' was merely added to a revival of the 1674 version.

VII. The Comic Extravaganza: *Don Quixote*

Purcell's career with the Theatre Royal can be described as hourglass-shaped. In three successive seasons at the beginning of the nineties he composed the semi-operas, each a triumph but very costly. During the 1692–3 and 1693–4 seasons his output for the stage dwindled to a trickle; no new dramatic operas were produced and the company turned more to comedies. Eccles emerged as an important figure in the theatre during the lean years. Then after the Lincoln's Inn Fields playhouse was re-established in mid-1695 with Eccles as resident composer, Purcell poured forth a huge amount of music for the revivals of serious dramas. In the absence of primary evidence, one might attribute the dry spell of 1693–4 to

the Theatre Royal's penury and perhaps even to Purcell's chagrin at having
to share the stage with an inferior composer. But this notion is dashed by
the first two parts of Durfey's audacious dramatization of *Don Quixote* in
May 1694. These highly successful productions – the last hurrahs of the
United Company – were collaborations, the lyrics being divided almost
equally between Purcell and Eccles. The venture drew the best from each
composer. Eccles's portion is completely worthy, and for Part 2 he even
created what was in its day the most famous of all mad songs, 'I burn, I
burn, my brain consumes to ashes'. Purcell ended two seasons of apparent
frustration by producing some of his most passionate music, including the
great baritone monologue 'Let the dreadful engines'. There is no evidence
that he resented sharing the honours with Eccles, and it would be entirely
wrong to omit the lesser man's music from any performance or analysis of
Don Quixote.

As noted earlier in this chapter, Durfey's theatre works have generally
been met with critical contempt. For *The Comical History of Don Quixote*
(Parts 1 and 2, May 1694; Part 3, November 1695), the response is bewil-
derment. While those familiar with Cervantes's novel will feel at first completely comfortable with the characterization of the Don and Sancho
Panza, they will soon realize this is a Restoration comedy that ate halluci-
natory mushrooms. The knaves are grown fantastic, reducing the romantic
characters to cardboard cut-outs. Slapstick is debased into assault with
deadly weapons; magic is deflated into bad practical jokes. Pathos is replaced by sickly-sweet sentimentalism; metaphorical death is transformed
into real death. Cuckolds are twisted into madmen, marriage into legal-
ized prostitution, and patriots become jingoes. The trilogy is a Fellinian
crazy-quilt that comes completely unstitched in Part 3. If tone was a problem in Durfey's earlier comedies, it is a nightmare here, and critics are inclined to dismiss the plays, bending to Nicoll's opinion that Cervantes's
novel is impossible to dramatize (*A History of English Drama*, 1, 277). Yet
one knows from *A Fool's Preferment* and *The Richmond Heiress* that
Durfey, though pompous, was no fool. Is *Don Quixote* therefore an elaborate lampoon of the conventions of Restoration comedy? Essentially
not. The queer tone is best explained by viewing the plays as a revolving
show-case for the composers.

The late seventeenth-century London theatre was, despite occasional
flights of fancy, an extremely rational institution in which actors expressing anything in song that might better be spoken were regarded as absurd,
except when lyrical outbursts were enveloped by magic or madness. Contemporary tragedy was well equipped to incorporate such scenes, hence
Purcell's predilection for the genre. On the other hand, comedy's much
stronger sense of dramatic verisimilitude placed severe restrictions on the
introduction of genuinely integral music. The most serious violation of

this principle occurs, ironically, in the superbly naturalistic concert scene in Southerne's *The Maid's Last Prayer*, in which Purcell's duet 'No, resistance is but vain' completely undermines the realism by introducing emotions far more believable than any expressed by the speaking characters. Durfey's clever solution to the problem of emotional imbalance between music and spoken dialogue in comedy was to cloak *Don Quixote* with an air of wildly irrational fantasy. The achievement of these plays is the liberation of music from the inhibiting verism of the genre. I am convinced that in the songs and masques discussed below satire does not lurk beneath the surface display of pathos, madness, and bawdry, except in one episode. The most striking aspect of both Purcell's and Eccles's music is that it takes itself absolutely seriously.

1 *Don Quixote*

In the first two parts of *Don Quixote*, the division of labour between the composers did not strictly follow the pattern of the previous comedies, in which Eccles wrote most of the humorous songs and dialogues for the actor–singers and Purcell the reflective, more serious airs and duets for the unnamed professionals. In fact this protocol was turned on its head in Part I of the trilogy, with stunning results. The first musical episode, the Don's sham knighting in II.i, was entrusted to Purcell. The centrepiece of the tawdry ceremony, which includes a dance of knights errant slaying a dragon (no music survives), is the sprawling duet for countertenor and baritone, 'Sing all ye muses' (z 578/1). It is both a grandiloquent invocation and a graphic battle song that follows a soldier in pursuit of the enemy, his disregard of superficial wounds, a siege, and the winning of a fair maiden's hand through valour. While Durfey may have tongue in cheek, the music is pure of heart. The abrupt changes in the narrative are exaggerated by dynamic markings, tempo indications, and frequent shifts of metre, as illustrated in Example 29. As the soldier narrowly escapes death, the cadence in G minor is deflected by an E♭ in the countertenor, and the main key, C major, immediately returns. Remarkable passages abound in

Example 29. *1 Don Quixote*: 'Sing all ye muses', bars 91–100

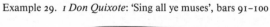

Example 29 (cont.)

the rest of the piece, as in the simple but effective rests at the phrase 'Till Fate claps her wings'. Later, more extravagant musical language reflects the key words of the lines 'No luxury in peace, / Nor pleasure in excess / Can *parallel* the *joys* the martial hero crown' with exactly parallel major thirds as seen in Example 30. Notice also the shift to the parallel minor, the key in which the piece ends. The major-minor tonic relationship is not at all unusual for Purcell, but here it may foreshadow gathering clouds. After the music, the 'Knight of the Ill-favour'd Face' is more drubbed than dubbed, when Vincent, the innkeeper, cuts open his head with the instrument of confirmation. Swathed in plaster, Don Quixote is ready to sally forth.

Example 30. *1 Don Quixote*: 'Sing all ye muses', bars 155–8

Durfey plunges straight into the gloomiest of the adventures, as the scene changes to '*A Deep Grove*' for the funeral of Chrysostome, a young Englishman who has died of a broken heart. Ambrosio delivers a bitter eulogy in which he attacks his late friend's 'murderer', the perfidious Marcella, with heroic-play vehemence. When the 'cruel Tygress' later defends herself, Durfey elevates the dialogue to rhymed couplets. In stark contrast to the surrounding farce, the scene seems to parody the serious genre. But Eccles's music does not support this idea. The bier is carried in while a shepherdess sings languidly in D minor 'Young Chrysostome had Virtue' (D&M No. 4120), followed by the astonishingly mournful dirge 'Sleep, poor Youth, sleep in Peace' (D&M No. 2997), as the body is lowered into the grave. Scored for soprano, bass, three recorders and continuo, the long composition reveals a threnodic gift hardly detectable in Eccles's earlier music. The excerpt given in Example 31 is sombre and hypnotic. Purcell had no monopoly on ingenious ground basses with tragic symbolism, nor was he the only composer whose music could produce a lump in the

Example 31. *1 Don Quixote*: John Eccles, 'Sleep, poor youth, sleep in peace', bars 44–60

Example 31 (cont.)

be se - vere

throat. Eccles's setting of 'Sleep and indulge thy self with rest; / Nor Dream thou e'er shall rise again' would move the hardest heart with its sweeping modulations.[65] The main purpose of the funeral scene is to portray the unrepentant Marcella so unfavourably that Don Quixote's later chivalrous defence of her against unarmed shepherds will appear wholly preposterous. But to appreciate the black humour, the audience must first be made to feel grief at the death of a person who has had no role in the drama: Chrysostome. The dirge is thus tragic in the absence of tragedy; its irony will be apparent only in Part 2, when Marcella, a victim of vengeful perfidy, goes mad, her ravings expressed in Eccles's song 'I burn, I burn'.

This scene acquires another dimension when one considers that Marcella was portrayed by Mrs Bracegirdle, still at the centre of the scandal surrounding Mountfort, the actor who died in the aftermath of her attempted abduction. Ambrosio, shocked that Marcella would dare show her face at the funeral of the man she rejected, asks if she feels pity for his dead friend, whose accomplishments (as Durfey is at pains to disclose) included philosophy and music. She replies, 'Pity's the Child of Love; and I ne'er yet Lov'd any of your Sex, I might have some Compassion for his Death; but still the Occasion of it moves my Mirth.' Ambrosio cries in disbelief, 'Have you no Remorse?' She mercilessly insists, 'I rather look on him as a good Actor; that Practising the Art of deep deceit, as Whining, Swearing, Dying at your Feet, Crack'd some Lite Artery with an overstrain, And dy'd of some Male Mischief in the Brain.' Her impassioned disavowal of any responsibility for Chrysostome's death now takes on another meaning, and the allusion to Mountfort is as unmistakable as it is double-edged. Once more Durfey provided Mrs Bracegirdle with a public forum from which to reply to rumours and accusations.[66] Her defender to the death, like Chrysostome, was an actor, singer, composer, and (in an important departure from Cervantes) an Englishman, but emphatically *not* her lover. She feels 'some Compassion', but his death was a misadventure and not the result of her neglect; so minimal is her guilt that she can even laugh at the absurdity of his demise. The much lamented 'good Actor' should finally be laid to rest. The truly tragic tone of Eccles's dirge may well have been inspired by Mountfort, and is not simply a foil for the antics

[65] This passage is printed with my essay 'Music as Drama', p. 230.
[66] See the discussion of *The Richmond Heiress* above.

of Don Quixote. Perhaps Purcell felt no urge to write the music for this scene because he had already honoured the actor by supplying the anthem sung at his interment in St Clement Danes on 13 December 1692.[67]

The most serious problem Durfey faced in dramatizing a work as episodic as *Don Quixote* is that he had little time to develop secondary characters. Eccles's dirge speaks volumes about Ambrosio and Marcella, but the sub-plot is now abandoned and not taken up again until Part 2. Instead, the playwright tackles a completely different romantic triangle in Act III. Cardenio has gone mad because he believes his beloved Luscinda deserted him for his best friend, the devious Fernando.[68] But Cardenio does not appear until Act IV, so Durfey set Purcell the difficult task of quickly developing his personality through music. In 'Let the dreadful engines' (z 578/3), his first utterance in the play, one learns that Cardenio, like King Lear, is tormented by the realization of his own insanity.

The forty-line lyric is one of the longest Purcell set. He reacted to the violent changes of mood and unbridled imagery with a series of reflex-like responses: wild, thrashing *secco* recitatives; a truly pathetic and lyrical air; jocular, earthy ballads; and highly ornamented declamations. Yet the diverse elements somehow fit together coherently. The most obvious order imposed on the poetic chaos is a symmetrical tonal scheme (each letter below represents a discrete section; upper-case shows major keys, lower-case minor ones):

Part I	F	f	F
	(graced recit.)	(graced recit.)	(ballad)
Part II	C	c	
	(*secco* recit.)	(pathetic air)	
Part III	F	f	F
	(*secco* recit. and arietta)	(graced recit.)	(ballad)

The grand design – major/minor tonic followed by major/minor dominant – reinforces the underlying drama. F major represents Cardenio's brash exterior, manifested at the beginning by cosmic delusions of grandeur and at the end by a devil-may-care dismissal of all women as scolding, money-grabbing witches. His inner despair is depicted in the F minor sections; C major is reserved for brief moments of towering rage; and C minor is the key of the pathetic aria placed at the emotional core of the song when Cardenio recalls his lost youth. This is the longest section and thus explains the apparent imbalance of the second part in the diagram.

[67] Luttrell, *A Brief Historical Relation of State Affairs* (Oxford: Oxford Univ. Press, 1857), II, 641.

[68] In a scene cut from the first production, the rakish Fernando is tamed. As penance for having deceived Cardenio, he spends most of the rest of the play devising a way to bring the madman down from the mountains for medical treatment.

Purcell made two versions, the first (A) published in *The Songs to the New Play of Don Quixote* (1694) and the second (B) an arrangement for soprano in the Guildhall Library song-book. Most of the variants in the manuscript are simplified graces, inserted rests, and the odd shake.[69] But one change in the opening recitative (in Example 32) makes the connec-

Example 32. *1 Don Quixote*: 'Let the dreadful engines', bars 9–12 (bass omitted)

tions between key and affect more explicit.[70] The Eb in bar 10 of the second version appears like a crack in Cardenio's brave façade, paving the way for the baring of his soul in the C minor air. Another integrative device (present in both versions) is the pairing of Db or a Db major chord with the words 'cold' and 'cool'. Yet the profounder sentiments of the song are expressed far more subtly. In Example 33, an excerpt from the central air, Cardenio's persistent return to the high G depicts his clinging to a vision of 'flow'ry groves'. When the phrase is repeated in the dominant minor, the vision has slipped far away. The hollow repetition renders the ensuing cadence in Eb major, a voluptuous conjuration of the sleeping Luscinda, an even greater phantasm.

'Let the dreadful engines' is the most difficult song Purcell wrote for Bowman. Its lofty tessitura confirms that the actor–singer was not a bass but a true baritone, with complete control of high G. Interestingly, this note is saved for moments of dramatic tension, as in Example 33, rather than used merely as a graphic representation of height. For instance, at the phrase 'That mounting reach the skies', the line rises only to F. The singer is also required to act. Cardenio enters 'in Ragged Cloaths, and in a Wild

---

[69] Purcell wrote out only a few bars of the continuo part in the manuscript.
[70] In version B Purcell changed the first two notes of bar 10 from semiquavers to quavers.

Example 33. *I Don Quixote*: 'Let the dreadful engines', bars 83–96

where, where are now, where are now, where are now those flow - 'ry__

groves, Where Zeph-yr's fra-grant winds did play? Ah! where are

now, where are now, where are now those flow - 'ry__ groves

Posture'. His shifts of mood are extremely violent, yet he must also appear to know exactly what he is doing. Later in Act IV, when Don Quixote asks why the madman has chosen the eremitic life, Cardenio, seemingly in control of his emotions, begins the story of his parting from Luscinda. But the tale grows gradually slyer as he recalls their heated argument about 'a modern Madman call'd *Don Quixote*, a strange whimsical Monster, in which I affirm'd, That the Bright, Renowned, and Peerless *Dulcinea*, fam'd Mistress of that foolish frantick Ideot, had once a Bastard by her Apothecary'. Don Quixote's indignation provokes a mad fit, during which Cardenio beats the knight and his squire. The complete change of character, always played with a twinkle in the eye, should be anticipated in the song.

'Let the dreadful engines' is the musical high point of *I Don Quixote*, but not the only song in the final three acts. In III.ii the knight does battle with a singing barber whom he mistakes for a noble adversary.[71] Later in

---

[71] The barber's song, 'With my Strings of small Wire' (D&M No. 4000), suggests that he accompanied himself on the cittern. The complete text of the ditty, not given in the 1694 quarto, appeared later in *Wit and Mirth*, III (1707). Thus it may not have been heard in its entirety at the first performance, since it does not appear in *The Songs to the New Play of Don Quixote* (1694).

the same scene, Sancho and his master free the treacherous Gines de Pas-samonte and his fellow galley-slaves, believing them to be political pris-oners. One of them thanks the Don by singing Purcell's air 'When the world first knew creation' (z 578/2), a rollicking paean to the criminal life. And at the end of the fourth act, Sancho, who was portrayed by Doggett, sings and dances Eccles's smutty ballad ''Twas early one Morning' (D&M No. 3493), a detailed account of the squire's wedding night.

All the music discussed above grows naturally from the drama. And even the final entertainment in Act V is provided with a flimsy rationale. The characters from the romantic sub-plots have banded together to frighten Don Quixote into giving up knight-errantry by convincing him that the inn is enchanted. One could ignore such foolishness except for Purcell's splendid masque (z 578/4), a lengthy composition that knits the play's seemingly incongruous and trivial themes of low humour, pathos, and wanton brutality into a satisfying dénouement. The principal figure in the entertainment is Cardenio, who regains his sanity in the first scene of Act V after a reconciliation with his rival, Fernando. He claims not to remember the encounter with the Don in the mountains, yet the spark of the masque is the suspicion that Cardenio may not be fully cured. Pre-siding as the enchanter Montesmo, he is aided by two players from the *carnaval*, Melissa and Urganda. They propose various nasty ways to dis-pose of Don Quixote, who is put in a cage with Sancho near the end of the masque to be roasted alive. Purcell chose G minor, a fitting key for an exe-cution, and interpreted the stage direction of 'Dreadful sounds of Musick' at the beginning as a four-bar symphony built on the lament bass. Car-denio's opening recitative, 'With this sacred charming wand', is sweeping and prolix, but more controlled than the spectacularly erratic passages of 'Let the dreadful engines'. He sings to the sombre accompaniment of violins, like the Sorceress in Act II of *Dido and Aeneas*. Purcell endows Durfey's pasteboard 'Inchanteresses' with distinctive personalities. Ur-ganda is made the 'heavy' with a rather ponderous recitative in which she claims to be able to conjure storms, and maintains a dour demeanour in the later air 'Nature restore', its ground bass perhaps reflecting her im-placably serious character. Melissa, by contrast, is almost mischievous. She can make nature smile and 'Love's dear momentary rapture long'. But when Montesmo ridicules Don Quixote for feelings of self-importance, Melissa is the first to offer her services in his destruction with a brisk G minor air, 'I've a little spirit yonder', which recalls the final section of 'Let the dreadful engines' and looks ahead to the lighter moments of 'From rosy bowers' in Part 3. She is pulling the Don's leg, of course, but the key remains G minor. Urganda and Montesmo protest that the death proposed by their enchanting colleague is too easy, and the baritone prescribes fire and damnation in a distasteful concluding verse not printed in the 1694 play-book.

Plate 5. Thomas Durfey
(anonymous engraving)

Plate 6. Letitia Cross
(engraving by J. Smith after T. Hill)

Appear ye fat fiends that in limbo do groan
That were, when in flesh, the same souls as his own;
You that always in Lucifer's kitchen reside
'Mongst sea-coal and kettles and grease newly fried
That pampered each day with a garbage of souls
Broil rashers of fools for a breakfast on coals
This mortal from hence to convey try your skill,
Thus fate's and our magical orders fulfil.

At these lines Purcell shifts to the ballad style and G major in a dance-like finale.

2 Don Quixote

With this good-humoured masque *The Comical History of Don Quixote* begins a decline. Most of the musical scenes in Part 2 are indolently incidental, and the knight's adventures are even more ridiculous than those in the first part. To save the sinking ship, Durfey tried to pump some life into the sub-plot neglected since the second act of Part 1. Diego, a villain new to the saga, abducts the proud Marcella intending to ravish her. Ambrosio, the friend of the late lamented Chrysostome, comes to her rescue. Mistaking his valour for an olive branch, she develops a soft spot for her former adversary, though he is secretly determined to avenge his friend's death. Marcella was once again played by Mrs Bracegirdle. Durfey, if not obsessed with Captain Hill's attempted kidnapping of the actress, at least enjoyed sailing close to the wind with thinly veiled enactments of the event in his plays. In the preface to Part 2, he justifies Marcella's abduction and its consequences with the claim that she must be punished for her callous reaction to Chrysostome's death, but everything points to the exploitation not only of Mrs Bracegirdle's special talents but of her sensational private life as well. True to form, Durfey adds a twist.

Ambrosio is unable to forgive Marcella for her role in the death of his friend, and cruelly rejects her entreaties. Like Cardenio, she is driven mad by unrequited love, a condition expressed in Act V by the famous song 'I burn, I burn' (D&M No. 1497), set by Eccles. Durfey acknowledges her performance as a key to the play's success. The song was 'so incomparably well sung, and acted by Mrs. *Bracegirdle*, that the most envious do allow, as well as the most ingenious affirm, that 'tis the best of that kind ever done before'. The 'most envious' might well have included Bowman and the 'most ingenious' Purcell, but the composer was not apparently offended by this slight of 'Let the dreadful engines', since a year later he composed a song upon 'Mrs Bracegirdle Singing (I Burn &c) in ye play of Don Quixote'.[72] The success of Eccles's mad song may have been sealed by a memorable performance, but one must also acknowledge its inherent

[72] Guildhall Library MS Safe 3, fol. 67v. See the discussion of *The Spanish Fryar* in Chapter 2.

strengths. In E minor, a key that Purcell rarely used in his theatre music, it is made up of several contrasting miniatures typical of the genre. The opening decorated recitative is harmonically static and bombastic. The contrapuntal rage aria 'Blow, blow, the Winds great Ruler blow' relents only at a steamy passage shown in Example 34. The trippingly jolly ballad

Example 34. *2 Don Quixote*: John Eccles, 'I burn, I burn', bars 25–7

bring the Po and the Gan-ges hith-er, 'tis Sul-try, sul-try, sul-try Weather

''Twas Pride, hot as Hell, / That first made me Rebell' is tinged with irony at least as acid as that of the final section of 'Let the dreadful engines'. The concluding frenzied air 'Off ye vain fantastick Toys' is preceded by a pathetic recitative in the tonic major (see Example 35). It is easy to patronize Eccles's song for a heavy reliance on meretricious effects, but it

Example 35. *2 Don Quixote*: John Eccles, 'I burn, I burn', bars 44–8

A-dieu, a-dieu_trans-port-ing Joys a-dieu,___ a-dieu trans-

-port-ing_ joys; off

deserves to be famous. Judging by the previous pieces for the actress, 'I burn, I burn' pushed Mrs Bracegirdle to her limits with a raw theatricality often lacking in Purcell's stage music, especially that for the singing actors. No one would deny pre-eminence to 'Let the dreadful engines', but how much of its lavish figuration and intricate tonal design can have got beyond the footlights? Eccles, I believe, understood the actor–singers better than his colleague: he knew how to exploit their histrionics and how to cover their vocal shortcomings. As is explained below, Purcell's setting of 'From rosy bowers' in Part 3 owes much to this mad song of Marcella's.

The rest of the music in Part 2 has considerably less bearing on the drama. In I.ii, a pair of anonymous songs (D&M Nos. 1720 and 4089) are heard amid the confusion of the duke's banquet. Near the end of the second act, Mrs Ayliff, dressed as a milkmaid, sang Eccles's 'Ye Nymphs and Sylvan Gods' (D&M No. 4049) in a tangential episode aptly described by Cardenio (who does not sing in this part) as a 'strange Entertainment'. During the first scene of Act III, in which Marcella all but declares her ill-fated love for Ambrosio, Captain Pack's 'Damon let a Friend advise ye' (D&M No. 790) was sung as fruitless encouragement for him to reciprocate. Sancho Panza and his family are diverted by Purcell's uninspired dialogue 'Since times are so bad' (z 578/6), rendered by 'a Clown and his Wife' at the end of Act IV. The clown is actually a farmer who, like Sancho, wants to leave the countryside and seek his fortune in towns and foreign lands. It takes his patient wife eleven pages of music (in the Purcell Society Edition, Vol. XVI) to persuade her husband to stay on the farm. In one of these entertainments was probably also heard Purcell's Scotch air 'Lads and lasses, blithe and gay' (z 578/8), sung by Mrs Hodgson. The brief C major tune captures the lilt of the northern dialect with astonishing simplicity. The bouncing octave at the beginning propels the melody in its graceful descent, the bass joining in near-lockstep at the half-bar.

Purcell's main contribution to Part 2 is the famous trumpet song 'Genius of England' (z 578/7). In the 1694 quarto this piece is incorrectly inserted into Marcella's mad scene near the beginning of V.ii. Instead, it should be heard in the duke's entertainment later in the act. Like the final masque in *King Arthur*, the play loses all track of time and place, and the show is a disgraceful debate between the emblematic heroes of England and France. First, St Dennis sings a pair of hilarious verses in a French accent, beginning,

> De Foolish *English* Nation,
> Dat Former Conquest brag on;
> Make strang a Discourse
> Of St. *George* and his Horse,
> And de Murd'ring of de Dragon . . .

The limp-wristed anonymous setting is blasted by Purcell's pompous trumpet tune and the vanquishing appearance of St George himself, who calls forth the Genius of England, sung by Mrs Cibber, the daughter of the trumpeter Matthew Shore, who probably played the brave responses. The piece would stir the throng at the Last Night of the Proms, but in its original context it is an overblown and misguided display of patriotism. Durfey's dramatization, which until this point is like reading the original novel during a thunderstorm – brilliant in flashes – has degenerated past the point of redemption.

3 Don Quixote

Despite their flaws, the first two instalments of the trilogy were well received, but the third, acted by the inexperienced Theatre Royal troupe in November 1695 after the company had divided, was a conspicuous failure. In the preface Durfey blames everyone but himself: because the comedy was rushed into production, the first performance was marred by 'some unlucky accidents'; the songs, 'which I used to succeed so well in', were badly executed; the dancers were not up to the job; and the puppet show in IV.ii was too far up stage to be heard by the audience. Without actually saying so, Durfey places the onus on the young actors, perhaps unfairly, since other plays of theirs were well received during this first difficult season after Betterton's departure. But the recasting of the principal roles in the sequel probably contributed to the defeat.[73] The part of Don Quixote, created by Bowen, was given to the upstart Powell, more at home playing rakes than a foolish and – in this part – tragic knight errant. Sancho Panza, portrayed first by Doggett and then by Underhill, both celebrated character actors, was taken by the nonentity Mr Newth. The most stimulating of the secondary characters in the earlier plays, Cardenio and Marcella, do not reappear, perhaps because they were too closely identified with Bowman and Mrs Bracegirdle, now at Lincoln's Inn Fields. But none of these difficulties and compromises would necessarily have sunk the play. Its failure was primarily a musical one. Almost all the actors and professional singers who took roles in Parts 1 and 2 had left the company with Eccles. And Purcell, preoccupied with *Bonduca* and *The Indian Queen*, not to mention his fatal illness, wrote only one song for the third part. Yet Durfey, despite the hopeless odds, was determined to make this the most musical of the three *Don Quixote* plays. The other composers known to have been involved in the project are Courteville, Morgan, and Ackeroyde.[74] The chief singers were Leveridge, Edwards, and, most notably, Miss Cross, upon whose young shoulders fell a great burden.

All these performance problems might seem trite when one considers the play itself, in which flashes of brilliance are rare indeed. Following the trend of Part 2, the action is largely shifted away from Don Quixote; if the plot has any focus, it is the marriage of Sancho's daughter, Mary the Buxom. The rest is a frayed string of musical entertainments. This is not to say that the music itself is unworthy. Courteville's songs for the pastoral

[73] For a further assessment of the effects of the changes, see Holland, *The Ornament of Action*, p. 69.
[74] Several pieces in *New Songs in the Third Part of the Comical History of Don Quixote* (1696) are anonymous. None, I think, is by Purcell.

wedding in Act II are of high quality, especially the booming bass aria 'Cease Hymen, cease thy brow' (D&M No. 492), presumably a vehicle for Leveridge.

The only important singing character is Altisidora, a skittish girl (played by Miss Cross) who is appointed to try to lure Don Quixote away from the nonpareil Dulcinea. In III.ii she sings the enticing lyric 'Damon Feast your Eyes on me' (D&M No. 793), set by Morgan, who altered the first line to 'Damon turn your Eyes to me', apparently in order to exploit a triplet figure reminiscent of the one in Purcell's duet 'Turn then thine eyes' in *The Fairy-Queen*. The Don, however, is unmoved by this 'most Melancholy miserable' madrigal. Her next song demands much more attention. In Act V, she is encouraged to make an even more extravagant and cruel effort to seduce the old knight: 'I intend to teize him now with a whimsical variety, as if I were possess'd with several degrees of Passion – sometimes I'll be fond, and sometimes, freakish; sometimes merry, and sometimes melancholy, – sometimes treat him with Singing and Dancing, and sometimes scold and rail as if I were ready to tear his eyes out.' As her friends watch from behind the scenes, she acts out her little charade, the climax of which is Purcell's 'From rosy bowers' (z 578/9).

'The last SONG the Author Sett, it being in his Sickness', is also his greatest theatre piece.[75] It is far less sophisticated than 'Let the dreadful engines' and lacks the tragic grandeur of Dido's Lament; it cannot ravish the body and soul as does 'Two daughters of this aged stream' in *King Arthur*, nor does it raise the hackles as effectively as the Frost Scene. But Purcell's swan song strikes closer to the heart of the human condition than any of these, with the pure and unguarded expression of an artist who had no time left for artifice. This piece transcends the drama, as if the composer, perhaps working from his deathbed, had no idea of its role in the play.

In the 1696 quarto, the lyric is arranged into five 'movements', with the labels 'Love', 'Gaily', 'Melancholy', 'Passion', and 'Frenzy', respectively. Whether or not the composer took any notice of these impertinent instructions is unknown, but it would be silly to suppose that the various passages represent *just* these coarse emotions. And one will notice a greater number of variants than normal between the poem and the text printed with the music. Many words are changed, particularly in the second verse:

1696 quarto	*New Songs in . . . [3] Don Quixote*
Or if more influencing,	Or if more Influencing
Be doing something airy,	is to be brisk & airy
With a Hop and a Bound,	with a Step & a bound
And a Frisk from the round,	& a frisk from ye Ground
I'le trip, trip like a Fairy.	I will trip like any Fairy

[75] The rubric appears in *Orpheus Britannicus*, 1 (1698).

and in the last movement one line is completely different:

1696 quarto	New Songs in . . . [3] Don Quixote
Wild thro' the Woods I'll fly,	wild thro' the Wood's Ile fly
And dare some savage Boor . . .	Robes, Locks shall this be tore . . .

The latter emendation is a notable improvement, which not only avoids an infelicitous *double entendre* but sharpens the image of the singer plunging madly through the wilderness of 'a thousand Deaths'. Purcell probably made the alteration, but the sources of the music do not permit us to know for certain.

This is a long lyric, only three or four lines shorter than the mammoth 'Let the dreadful engines', but much more tightly constructed. Its six sections are made up of three units, a recitative and air each. Of the declamatory parts, all but the last are decorated, though the graces are much less elaborate and more concentrated than those of the earlier mad songs and dialogues, perhaps an indication that Purcell had finally learnt the virtue of simplicity in composing for the actor–singers. The key is C minor with some breathtaking interpolations in the parallel major, much in the manner of Eccles's 'I burn, I burn' in Part 2. Another possible influence of the earlier piece is the setting of 'No, no, I'le straight run mad . . .', which rattles up and down the tonic major triad in typical Eccles fashion. This is a far more effective depiction of raving lunacy than the complex *volate* of 'Let the dreadful engines', though one must remember that Altisidora, unlike Cardenio and Marcella, is only feigning madness.

There is little doubt why Purcell earned the sobriquet 'Orpheus Britannicus'. Like several of his best songs, 'From rosy bowers' concerns the power of music to move the gods. In the first verse, crudely described as 'Love', the singer asks Cupid to tune her voice to win Strephon's heart. After the warm and yearning invocation, the second movement, marked 'Gaily', is simpering in its jollity. It closely resembles the middle part of the mad dialogue in *The Richmond Heiress* ('By this disjointed matter'), the coda of Cardenio's song in *1 Don Quixote* ('When a woman love pretends'), and Melissa's teasing air in *1 Don Quixote* ('I've a little spirit yonder'). But the prancing tune is ennobled when thrown into relief by the recitative that follows. Until this point, one could imagine that the sentiments are only Altisidora's, but in the passage given as Example 36 Purcell

Example 36. *3 Don Quixote*: 'From rosy bowers', bars 44–51

Example 36 (cont.)

- spair___ must end the fa-tal___ pain,   Cold___   de - spair, cold, cold___   de - spair

completely loses sight of the practical joke on Don Quixote. This is a cry
of real despair. The setting of 'Death' is bone-chilling. Purcell had used the
rising diminished octave E♮–E♭ a month or two earlier in the tenor recitative in III.ii of *Bonduca* ('And Dye with Roman Blood the Field') ironically
to foreshadow the slaughter of the Britons.[76] Here it distorts the leaping
E♭ octave heard several times throughout the piece as a unifying motif.
This passage is so sobering that the ensuing madrigalisms, which might
seem absurdly naïve in another context, leave the listener awe-struck.
'Falls' is set to descending pairs of adjacent notes, 'tempests blow' to
stormy roulades; and most memorable are the halting offbeat hesitations
in the line 'My pulse beats a dead march', in which 'beats' is ornamented
with written-out trills (called 'beats' in Purcell's time). The next section,
'Or say ye Powers' (which Durfey calls 'Passion'), dissipates much of the
morbid tension of the recitative with the detached formality of a pristine
da capo aria, in which the return to the beginning is skilfully interlocked
with the end of the *B* section.

The final verse, 'Frenzy', is fast and furious indeed, but also includes the
most rigorous imitative counterpoint of the entire piece. Altisidora's complete lack of control is thus expressed by the most rational music. But the
bravura coda does not return us to the frivolous mood of the spoken
drama. 'Ah! 'tis all in vain, / Death and Despair must end the fatal Pain'
still rings in one's ears. How foolish the actor portraying Don Quixote
must have felt to follow the song with 'This I confess, another Heart might
charm, but mine is Constant as the Northern Star – and *Dulcinea* only
must Enjoy it'.

Altisidora and the rest of the tormentors have finally gone too far. The
next scene discovers a broken Don Quixote on his deathbed making a will,
a fine dramatization of the closing pages of the novel. The playwright's

[76] See Chapter 3, Example 18. The diminished octave in Example 36 does not appear in the
version in *Orpheus Britannicus*, in which the E♮ on 'vain' rises by a diminished fourth
directly to A♭. The reading given here is from *New Songs in the Third Part of the Comical
History of Don Quixote* (1696), the earliest source. Though this version is generally more
corrupt than *Orpheus Britannicus*, especially in the bass part, I see no reason not to attribute the diminished octave to the composer. Note also that the E♭–A♭ falling fifth on
'Death' anticipates the one two bars later, B♭–E♭, on 'Cold'.

only indulgence is Basilius's superfluous acknowledgement of the Don as 'A *Solon* – A *Solon* – I say still', a reference to Durfey's own creation in *The Marriage-Hater Match'd*. Reducing the immortal Don Quixote to 'a fool who knows he is one' is a monstrous simplification, but for the playwright it was a necessary *apologia*.

I should like to believe that Purcell designed Altisidora's song as a harbinger of Don Quixote's death and that during its performance the protagonist was so stricken by its power that he could only play out the rest of the scene in the shattered whisper of one who has seen a vision of his own demise. But, alas, such a reading cannot be wrung from the spoken dialogue. What finally breaks Don Quixote is a fight with Sancho over Dulcinea. In a strict analysis, the song is just another entertainment, much like Ackeroyde's dialogue about incest, 'Ah my Dearest Celide' (D&M No. 67), sung by Altisidora and her brother at the end of the play. But anyone who appreciates how faithfully Purcell tried in other circumstances to serve poets far less sensitive to music than Durfey will realize at once that 'From rosy bowers' was composed *in extremis*.

Part II
THE OPERAS

Plate 7. Thomas Betterton
(portrait from the studio of Kneller)

5 *Dido and Aeneas*

Purcell's only all-sung opera, *Dido and Aeneas*, first performed in the spring of 1689 at a girls' boarding-school in Chelsea, is by far his best-known theatre work, the only one with a secure place in the modern reper-toire. More has been written about it than all the semi-operas and plays with music combined. Why has this diminutive drama, privately per-formed before the composer had established himself in the professional theatre, achieved such fame? Is it musically superior to *King Arthur* and *The Fairy-Queen*? Is it more dramatic than *The Indian Queen*? Are its principal characters more skilfully etched in song than Cardenio and Alti-sidora in *Don Quixote*? Purcell would surely be amused to see us survey his entire output for the stage – the balefully ironic songs for *Theodosius*, the elegant incantation in *Circe*, the Frost Scene and fourth-act Passacaglia in *King Arthur*, the immolation of Don John in *The Libertine*, the sacrifice in *Bonduca*, the Conjurer's aria in *The Indian Queen*, and the mad song in *3 Don Quixote* – and slight it all for a school masque that was not publicly staged during the composer's lifetime. *Dido* certainly includes some fine music and is understandably appealing to modern audiences because it seems to conform to the nineteenth-century idea of tragedy in music, but we must keep it in the perspective of Purcell's *oeuvre* and the late seven-teenth-century London theatre world. That it is a true opera should not blind us to its flaws.

Virtually all that is known about the première is recorded on the first page of the libretto, probably printed for distribution to the audience.[1] It is by Nahum Tate, a minor playwright and tireless adapter of Shakespeare, who was to succeed Shadwell as poet laureate in 1692. The opera was given at a school run by Josias Priest, a choreographer at the Theatre Royal and, since the sixties, an important dancer in the London playhouses. The only firm indication of the year of the première is Durfey's spoken epilogue, published in his *New Poems* in the late autumn of 1689. The libretto states simply that the opera was performed 'By Young Gentlewomen'; it sheds no light on who may have sung the part of Aeneas – if indeed it was intended for a man – not to mention the bass, tenor, and countertenor parts in the choruses. *Dido* was not the first such entertainment given at a school for girls in Chelsea. In 1676, Thomas Duffett and John Banister's *Beauties Triumph*, a half-spoken, half-sung dramatization of the Judgement of

---

[1] The only copy is in the Royal College of Music. A facsimile is found in the Purcell Society Edition, III (rev. M. Laurie), xiii-xx.

225

Paris, was acted at a 'New Boarding-School for Young Ladies and Gentle-women' in the same house later occupied by Priest. The school masque may not have been an annual event at Chelsea, but both in and out of London spring musicals were probably commoner than records suggest.[2]

Backgrounds

The most conspicuous precursor is Tate's tragedy *Brutus of Alba: or, The Enchanted Lovers* (summer 1678), a thinly disguised retelling of the fourth book of *The Aeneid*. In the preface to the quarto the author claims that he originally called the play 'Dido and Aeneas', but on the advice of friends altered it to avoid his characters' being invidiously compared to Virgil's. Instead, he exhumed Geoffrey of Monmouth's tale in *Historia Regum Britanniae* that Brutus was Aeneas's great-grandson. The play finds the hero en route to conquer Albion, diverting to Syracuse to enact with its queen his great-grandfather's ill-fated affair with the queen of Carthage.[3] While the two works have essentially the same plot, the in-fluence of *Brutus of Alba* on *Dido and Aeneas* has been exaggerated. *Brutus* is a full-blooded heroic play, a complex and fantastical fabrication centred on the classical conflict of love and honour, whereas *Dido* is pure opera, with simple but intense characters from which all verbal fat has been boiled away. The main persons represented in the two works do bear superficial resemblances:

Brutus	Aeneas
Queen of Syracuse	Dido, Queen of Carthage
Amarante, her confidante	Belinda
Ragusa, a sorceress	Sorceress

but to bolster an analysis of Purcell's characters with those of the play can lead to erroneous interpretations. First of all, the reasons for the cata-strophe – Aeneas's abandonment of Dido and her subsequent death – are different. In *Brutus* the royal pair consummate their love under the in-fluence of a philtre administered by the sorceress. The queen's guilt at this sin is nonetheless acute and contributes to her fatal derangement. In *Dido* the consummation is ambiguous, and on the surface neither guilt nor madness is a major factor in the queen's death. As many writers have pointed out, the problem with the opera is Aeneas, little more than a glori-fied pawn in an evil game of magic. He deserts Dido because the Sor-ceress, motivated by an ill-defined hatred for the queen, tricks him into

[2] See Neal Zaslaw, 'An English "Orpheus and Euridice" of 1697', *The Musical Times*, 118 (1977), 805-8.
[3] For a discussion of the links between the two legends, see John Buttrey, 'Dating Purcell's Dido and Aeneas', *Proceedings of the Royal Musical Association*, 94 (1967-8), 54-8, and Robert R. Craven, 'Nahum Tate's Third *Dido and Aeneas*: The Sources of the Libretto to Purcell's Opera', *The World of Opera*, 1 (1979), 65-78.

believing that Jove has commanded him to waste no more time 'In Loves delights'. In the play, however, Brutus's exit is agonizing and protracted. Asaracus, his boyhood friend and fellow warrior, is so sickened by the hero's dalliance with the Queen of Syracuse that he kills himself. Finally brought to his senses by this ultimate sacrifice, Brutus honours Asaracus's dying wish and sails away to Albion. Though Aeneas is the mere shadow of Brutus, both he and Dido are far more human than their counterparts in the play.

Little attention has been paid to the original music in *Brutus of Alba*, which requires the modest amount of song and dance typical of most of the new tragedies mounted in the years of financial retrenchment between *Circe* in 1677 and *Theodosius* in 1680. In the second scene of Act II, set in the tomb of the late King of Syracuse, priestesses sing some stanzas beginning 'Sleep ye great Manes of the Dead' (no music survives). And after the hunt in Act III, a dance is performed round Diana's fountain as the storm gathers. The most important music is reserved for the final scene, after Brutus has sailed. As in Virgil, the nearly mad queen pathetically asks her confidante to follow the hero and bid him return, in strong contrast to the operatic Dido's stubborn resolve and more mysterious love-death. But it is too late, and all Amarante can do is try to calm the queen's ravings with 'Soft Musick, and complaining Songs'. Inserted here, immediately before the queen's death, is Thomas Farmer's G minor setting of 'Bid the sad forsaken Grove' (D&M No. 370), sung by an attendant who personates Venus mourning the death of Adonis (verse by Thomas Wright):

> . . .
>   Ah hapless Deity,
> And still more wretched 'cause she may not Die.
> Can there be further joy in the Celestial store,
> Now my best Heav'n *Adonis* is no more . . .
> . . .
> The Skies too find a thousand Eyes to weep.
>   Ah you deceitfull Skies,
> When my *Adonis* fell where were those Eyes?

That the myths providing the librettos for Blow's *Venus and Adonis* and Purcell's *Dido and Aeneas* should be fused in music in the final scene of *Brutus of Alba*, a play steeped in the legendary origins of the British monarchy, is of seminal importance.

Venus and Adonis, upon which *Dido* is closely modelled, was performed about 1682 as a private entertainment for Charles II. Like Purcell's opera, it seems to have made little impression, though it is hardly less a masterpiece. No part of the score was printed at the time, nor did it gain the composer a reputation in the theatre, if indeed the retiring Blow desired this kind of fame. Yet the selection in 1684 of Grabu as composer for

Dryden's *Albion and Albanius* must have been felt as a slap in the face by all native theatre composers, including Blow, to judge by the laureate's touchy and defensive preface to the libretto. A romantic notion persists that in *Dido and Aeneas* Purcell was showing Dryden and the theatrical establishment a better way to write an English opera. But the two works are hardly comparable, nor would any of their contemporaries have thought them to be of the same genre. Yet *Albion and Albanius* inevitably affected *Dido*, the latter's basic dramatic unit of recitative–air–chorus–dance stemming as much from Grabu's opera as from any genuine *tragédie lyrique* that may have been performed in London in the late eighties. And the prologue to *Dido*, in which Phoebus, Venus, Spring, nymphs, shepherds, tritons, and nereids sing, is clearly reminiscent of *Albion and Albanius*, all the more so because both works were allegories designed to compliment the British monarchy.

Dido is not then, as some critics claim, the only example of a rare species, a single sprig of green in an opera-barren theatrical tradition. But why did it languish in total obscurity until 1698, when the protagonist's opening aria, 'Ah! Belinda, I am press'd', appeared in the first book of *Orpheus Britannicus*, the only part of the score published before 1700? A school performance would not necessarily have meant oblivion: both the libretto and some of the songs of Duffett and Banister's *Beauties Triumph* of 1676 were published after its suburban première, as was some of Richard Goodson and John Weldon's music for an *Orpheus and Euridice* given at a school near Oxford in 1697. Nor was the English audience's failure to show an interest in autonomous, all-sung music drama entirely responsible for the lack of a revival at the Theatre Royal during Purcell's lifetime. The work could have been presented as an afterpiece or entertainment in a play, as indeed it was in 1700 and 1704. The selection of 'Ah! Belinda' for *Orpheus Britannicus* is hardly surprising, because it is the one substantial air in the opera without a built-in chorus. Even so, the concluding ritornel is omitted from the anthology, as are many such symphonies of other theatre songs.

Did the composer himself suppress the opera? Surely he could have made the adjustments necessary for the publication of excerpts, as he or his agents did to *Dioclesian* and parts of *The Fairy-Queen* shortly after their premières. As suggested in Chapter 1, the year 1690 is a watershed for Purcell. The editors of *Orpheus Britannicus*, who obviously had access to most of the composer's vocal music, decided to print very few songs known to have been written before 1690. Even after *Dido* made its professional début in 1700, critics did not count it among the composer's great works. In 1710 Charles Gildon wrote: 'Let any Master compare *Twice ten hundred Deities*, the Music in the *Frost Scene*, several Parts of the *Indian Queen*, and twenty more Pieces of *Henry Purcel*, with all the *Arrieto's*,

Dacapo's, Recitativo's of *Camilla, Pyrrhus, Clotilda, &c*
which excels.'[4] Eight years later, the same author, wh[o]
below, intimately acquainted with *Dido*, repeated th[e]
Frost Scene is a great achievement.[5] The absence of any [i]
opera in the writings of North, Addison, and other early [e]
century critics does not necessarily imply that *Dido* was regarded a[s]
worthy, only that other works, particularly parts of *King Arthur* and *The*
Indian Queen, were considered far more impressive.

The Allegory

In his 1967 doctoral thesis 'The Evolution of English Opera between 1656
and 1695', John Buttrey argues that nearly all the major operatic works of
the period were designed to compliment the monarchy if not the monarch.
The clearest example is, of course, *Albion and Albanius*, in every sense a
royal opera. Buttrey maintains that *Dido*, too, had an allegorical purpose
that emerges when the work is viewed against the background of the first
year of the reign of William and Mary.[6] In the prologue, Phoebus's glorious passage over the sea refers to William's expedition to England in 1688.
And the descent of Venus, whose lustre, Phoebus admits, 'does Out-Shine
/ Your Fainter Beams, and half Eclipses mine', obviously alludes to Mary
II. These lines neatly express the unique division of the monarchy into
king and queen regnant, whereby William administered the government in
both their names. And the opera proper includes more than one reference
to sharing the throne, as in the first-act chorus 'When Monarchs unite how
happy their State, / They Triumph at once o'er their Foes and their Fate'.
But a closer interpretation of the opera as allegory engenders a major
problem. The story of a prince who seduces and abandons a neurotic queen
would seem a tactless way to honour the new monarchs. Buttrey accounts
for the apparent *faux pas* by viewing the opera as a cautionary tale; Tate
dramatizes 'the possible fate of the British nation should Dutch William
fail in his responsibilities to his English queen . . . [the] choice of subject
was apparently intended to reflect the political turbulence that must have
been uppermost in many minds in 1689'.[7] But even this charitable reading
leads to unflattering parallels. Aeneas, legendary great-grandfather of
Brutus the founder of Albion, leaves his beloved queen and sails across the
sea to liberate a foreign land and establish a new kingdom. A cynic might
therefore have seen in the Trojan prince William of Orange, the dour and
reluctant hero, preparing to leave Holland for his destiny in England. But
then Dido would symbolize Mary, a linkage that Tate surely wanted to
avoid, cautionary tale or no.

[4] *The Life of Mr. Thomas Betterton* (1710), p. 167.
[5] *The Complete Art of Poetry* (1718), p. 103.
[6] 'Dating Purcell's Dido and Aeneas', pp. 51–62.
[7] 'Dating Purcell's Dido and Aeneas', p. 60.

The Aeneid Book IV was not only inapt for William and Mary in 1689 but had been unlucky reading for other seventeenth-century monarchs as well. Tate was probably unaware of the pall that the story had supposedly cast over the final years of Queen Mary's grandfather, Charles I. James Welwood reports that during the king's residence at Oxford during the Civil Wars he was invited to take the *Sortes Virgilianae*, then a fashionable way of divining one's future by opening the works of Virgil and selecting a passage at random. Charles hit upon *The Aeneid*, IV.606–37, in which Dido curses Aeneas, swearing he will die violently before enjoying his kingdom in days of happiness.[8] Later Charles II was goaded to war with the cry that Holland was a Carthage to Britain's new Rome.[9] And during the Exclusion Crisis an anonymous satirical pamphlet, *The Conspiracy of Aeneas and Antenor* (1682), issued in reply to *Absalom and Achitophel*, disguises James, Duke of York, as Aeneas. The crude couplets of the final page are not kind to the Trojan hero:

> And to revenge the Walls he favour'd most,
> Shipwrack't the *Traytor* on the *Lybyan* Coast:
> 'Twas from this Land he got his Love mishap,
> But after sleeping in fair *Dido*'s Lap,
> Who coud have Dreamt of such an After-Clap?
> From hence to *Rome* the Miscreant Exile flys,
> Depending most upon his Enemies;
> His promis'd Empire he demands of Fate,
> Neither regarding Subjects Love nor Hate . . .

Given its potentially unpleasant connotations, Tate was forced to adapt the Classical tale, already deeply entwined with the supposed origins of the British monarchy, to the political climate of the Bloodless Revolution and, above all, to disengage Queen Mary from a symbolic link with Queen Dido. This required major changes of plot, motivation, and characterization. I believe that the gaping ambiguities of the libretto – the reason for Dido's grief in Act I, the uncertain consummation of the couple's love in Act II, the enchantresses' unmotivated hatred of the queen, and even the manner of Dido's death – are owing directly to the potentially sensitive nature of the allegory. Had Tate followed Virgil as closely as in *Brutus of Alba*, faithfully depicting the queen's obsessive love for Aeneas, their winter of debauchery, her paralysing guilt, extreme bitterness, and blazing anger at his departure, eyebrows would have been raised from Chelsea to Whitehall.

A radical alteration of the basic structure of Virgil's account of the Queen of Carthage is the introduction of the Sorceress and her witches –

---

[8] *Memoirs of the most Material Transactions in England* (1700), p. 100.
[9] Consider, for example, Shaftesbury's famous *Delenda est Carthago* speech of 1672, in which he urged Parliament to support the second Dutch war; discussed in K. H. D. Haley, *The First Earl of Shaftesbury* (Oxford: Clarendon, 1968), p. 317.

or, to be precise, her enchantresses, since Tate never calls them witches in the 1689 libretto. They provide the catalyst for the tragedy; but their hatred of Dido is not explained. A desire to 'share in the Fame, / Of a Mischief' is their only motivation. The witches have long troubled critics. Robert Moore cites them as 'the sole example in the opera of a Restoration cliché from which we have become alienated'; they disturb modern audiences, 'who demand at least some approximation to psychological realism' (*Henry Purcell & the Restoration Theatre*, pp. 52–3). Dent believed they lack human emotions, noting that the Sorceress 'is a type, not an individual' (*Foundations*, pp. 189–90). The witches are of course 'symbols of the malevolence of destiny', as Westrup remarks (*Purcell*, p. 116). The Sorceress herself makes this clear: 'The *Trojan* Prince you know is bound / By Fate to seek *Italian* Ground' (II.i). She is simply hastening Aeneas's inevitable departure from Carthage, while vowing the queen's destruction. Ragusa, the sorceress in *Brutus of Alba*, plays a tangential role in the queen's death, being only a soothsayer and plotter against the government. But her counterpart in *Dido* is a powerful antagonist, 'almost as impressive a figure as Dido herself' (Moore, p. 52), whose malignity is highly developed. Indeed, one could argue that the villainess represents not 'the gods of destiny' but the dark side of the queen. Roger Savage even proposes that the scenes for the witches are a 'black parody', from which the 'sentiments and rituals of the court can be grotesquely guyed by the spirits . . .'[10]

Though Dent viewed the introduction of the witches as highly implausible, he acquitted Tate of the charge that their appearance should have been better justified: 'one might imagine that Restoration audiences could not conceive of an opera without them' (*Foundations*, p. 185). He is of course alluding to Davenant's 1663–4 version of *Macbeth*, whose scenes for Heccate and the witches, expanded from Shakespeare and set to music by Locke, Eccles, and Leveridge at various times during the period, are widely acknowledged as a major source for Tate's enchantresses.[11] The members of both covens are called 'weyward sisters', and they express their 'motiveless malignity' in similar terms, as shown in the following examples:

Davenant	*Tate*
To us fair weather's foul, and foul is fair (I.i)	Destruction's our delight, delight our greatest Sorrow (III)
We shou'd rejoyce when good Kings bleed (II.v)	From the ruin of others our pleasures we borrow,

[10] 'Producing *Dido and Aeneas*', *Early Music*, 4 (1976), 399.

[11] See *Five Restoration Adaptations of Shakespeare*, ed. Christopher Spencer (Urbana: Univ. of Illinois Press, 1965), pp. 14–16. Dent exaggerates the role of witches in the drama of the time, as does Moore, *Henry Purcell & the Restoration Theatre*, p. 52. Cauldron-stirring hags of the sort depicted by Middleton, Shakespeare, and Davenant are rare in both plays and semi-operas.

Have I not reason *Beldams*? (III.viii)
But whilst she moves through the foggy Air,
Let's to the Cave and our dire Charms prepare (III.viii)

Elisa bleeds to Night . . . (III)
Say *Beldam* what's thy will? (II.i)
In our deep Vaulted Cell the Charm wee'l prepare,
Too dreadful a Practice for this open Air (II.i)

But these are only superficial resemblances. In Davenant, the witches' chief functions are to prophesy the bloody succession from Duncan to Macbeth and to add scenic and musical spectacle. Ludicrously overdrawn to symbolize the protagonists' malevolent ambition, they are, paradoxically, crucial to the action and dramatically redundant. The enchantresses in *Dido* play quite a different role. They both prophesy and cause catastrophic events.

An equally important source for the witches of the opera are the earthy crones in Shadwell's strange and very popular play *The Lancashire Witches* (*c.* September 1681), whose three main elements the playwright tries only half-heartedly to integrate. First, the play is a romantic comedy in which the clever women, Isabella and Theodosia, resolve never to marry the fools betrothed to them by their boorish fathers. Loosely attached to this routine plot is a savage satire on Roman Catholicism, embodied in the vile Irish priest Tegue O Divelly and the meddling chaplain Smerk. In the years following the Popish Plot when the succession of the Catholic Duke of York became increasingly likely, attacks on religion carried strong political implications, and several scenes of the sub-plot were duly cut or drastically shortened by the Master of the Revels. The third and most noteworthy ingredient is the witches, unabashedly introduced to exploit the musical and mechanical advantages of the Dorset Garden theatre. Downes even describes the play as 'a kind of Opera, having several *Machines* of Flyings for the Witches . . .' (*Roscius Anglicanus*, p. 38). Shadwell acknowledges a debt to Shakespeare (actually Davenant) but stresses that unlike the witches in *Macbeth*, which he incorrectly believed to have been created entirely from the bard's imagination, his wayward sisters are based 'from Authority' on real people. In notes appended to the end of each act, he documents their ritualistic cant and weird behaviour with voluminous references to various writings on witchcraft. The leader, Mother Demdike, is a model for the Sorceress in *Dido*, especially in her unmotivated evildoing. Tate seems to have taken the idea for the storm that ruins Dido and Aeneas's hunting party from Shadwell. Mother Demdike spoils Tom Shacklehead's hare-coursing in Act I with mischievous magic, then conjures up a spectacular tempest. Tate's enchantresses even speak like Shadwell's witches. For example, in II.ii of the opera the bogus Mercury sings 'To Night thou must forsake this Land, / The Angry God will brook no longer stay', an echo of Mother Demdike's 'Come, Sisters, come why do you stay? / Our business will not brook delay' (I.i). But Tate's greatest debt to Shadwell is the Sorceress's air of not-quite-human glee at her misdeeds.

Tracing the sources of the enchantresses in *Dido* does not, however, explain their important role. In *Macbeth*, the witches are the postilions of an inevitable train of events. In *Brutus of Alba*, their malevolence is spectacular though of little effect. And in *The Lancashire Witches*, they themselves become the tragic victims of superstition, prejudice, and a kangaroo court. Shadwell's play nevertheless holds the key to the virulent role of the Sorceress in *Dido*. Though the playwright's announced purpose for including the witches was 'to make as good an entertainment as I could, without tying my self up to the strict rules of a Comedy' (from the preface), he also wanted their mystical and altogether distasteful ceremonies to satirize Catholic ritual. By the fourth act, there is little difference between the inquisitor Tegue and the victim, Mother Demdike. Of the priest, the cynical Lady Shacklehead remarks, 'I do not know what to think of his Popish way, his Words, his Charms, and Holy water, and Relicks, methinks he is guilty of Witchcraft too, and you should send him to Gaol for it.' Thus averting the censor's heavy hand, Shadwell makes the witches represent the Catholic clergy.

An allegorical purpose of the enchantresses in *Dido* can now be postulated. The greatest threat to the stability of the English monarchy in 1689 was the restoration of James II and the attendant resurgence of popery. In the opera the destruction of love between Dido and Aeneas and therewith any hope of a joint reign is accomplished by cheap magic. Considering the close connection between the wayward sisters and Roman Catholicism in Shadwell's *The Lancashire Witches* and the strong influence of Mother Demdike on the Sorceress, one must conclude that the witches in *Dido* symbolize a new popish plot, as mindless as the original one of 1678 but still with potentially fatal consequences.[12] This interpretation, however repugnant, best explains why Tate replaced Virgil's 'cruel fate' and his own love-and-honour conflict in *Brutus of Alba* with the Sorceress's ritualistic evil as the engine of tragedy.

Although Tate is faithful to his source in depicting Dido as a woman wronged in love, he eliminates virtually any trace of *The Aeneid*'s preoccupation with her sexual indulgence and subsequent guilt. To attribute the omissions, simplifications, and obfuscations of Virgil's detailed account of her psychopathy solely to the epigrammatic brevity of the libretto and the tender age of the performers is a naïve interpretation. Having chosen a story with potential application to Queen Mary, Tate is forced to suppress Dido's faults in favour of a noble, almost austere righteousness. This compromise is felt most acutely in Act I. The queen refuses to reveal the

---

[12] The hypothesis is closely paralleled in Mary Chan, 'The Witch of Endor and Seventeenth-Century Propaganda', *Musica Disciplina*, 34 (1980), 205–14.

cause of her melancholy ('I am prest, / With Torment not to be Confest'). Nearly all writers on the opera have assumed that she, like Virgil's Dido, is suffering 'the anguish of love'. Moore, for example, describes her as 'lovesick', 'perplexed', and reluctant 'to yield to love' (*Henry Purcell & the Restoration Theatre*, p. 41). Tate makes no reference to the cause of her anxiety: Virgil's queen is in mourning for her late husband, Sychaeus, in whose memory she has taken a pledge of chastity; but she has also developed an overpowering attraction for Aeneas. Perhaps Tate omitted to mention this conflict in order to avoid showing how easily Dido forgets her solemn vow to the dead king. At all events, her affliction seems more a neurosis than an heroic dilemma, as if the librettist were still tied to the necromantic Queen of Syracuse in *Brutus of Alba*, who remains physically married to her dead husband (called Argaces), spending each night in his tomb, sometimes in the company of his ghost. Her existence is a living death, certainly an allusion to be kept out of the minds of the 1689 audience. Of course, Dido should not be burdened with baggage from the earlier play, but mere widowhood does not adequately explain her stubborn resistance to Aeneas's courtship and then her silent submission. As is shown below, Tate's attempt to rid his protagonist of the flaws so vividly described by Virgil caused more problems than it solved.

Measure for Measure

After Purcell's death in November 1695, all his semi-operas and tragic extravaganzas apparently remained the property of the Theatre Royal.[13] During the next eleven years of intense competition between the old company and Betterton's new theatre in Lincoln's Inn Fields (a rivalry that ended with a sweeping reorganization of the London playhouses in 1706), the Theatre Royal repeatedly revived all Purcell's major stage works except *The Fairy-Queen*, the score of which was lost shortly after the composer's death (see Chapter 8). But while the company was milking the music of 'the late Mr. Purcell' for all it was worth, *Dido and Aeneas* was nowhere to be seen, a sign that the theatre did not possess a copy. Early in 1700 the opera finally made its professional début as a series of masques in Charles Gildon's adaptation of *Measure for Measure*, given not at Drury Lane but at Lincoln's Inn Fields.[14] *Dido* is, then, Purcell's only major stage work for which Betterton was able to obtain the rights. The 1700 production is of utmost importance in understanding how the composer's near contemporaries interpreted the opera and why the surviving score is a fragment of the original.

[13] Though no document allocating repertoire to the two companies exists, such a separation of musical works composed before spring 1695 can be deduced from a survey of performance records.

[14] The attribution is found in an advertisement appended to *Love's Victim* (1701): 'Measure for Measure a Comedy alter'd from *Beaumont* and *Fletcher* [*sic*] by Mr. Gilden'.

In the essay 'New Light on "Dido and Aeneas"', Eric Walter White offers an excellent analysis of how the opera was altered when conjoined with the play, noting also that *Dido* was not merely 'given as an interlude', as Alfred Loewenberg had maintained, but that *Measure for Measure* was itself considerably changed to accommodate the music.[15] But why was Shakespeare chosen as midwife? The inspiration was, I think, *A New Opera; called, Brutus of Alba: or, Augusta's Triumph* (October 1696), a bilious musical extravaganza typical of the post-Purcell era.[16] *A New Opera* and *Measure for Measure* are remarkably similar in more than one respect: in both an absent ruler appoints a deputy whom he suspects of hypocrisy and corruption in order to expose him. Asaracus in *A New Opera* and Angelo in *Measure for Measure* preach sexual morality while trying to ravish honourable women. Angelo threatens to execute Isabella's brother unless she satisfies his lust; Asaracus compromises Amarante by making her appear unvirtuous. And in both works, masques are offered as parables to reform the villains. Furthermore, *A New Opera* is an important link in the chain of royal or would-be royal operas that includes *Dido*. Dent erroneously describes the 1696 semi-opera as a cut-down version of Tate's 1678 tragedy *Brutus of Alba*, an assertion repeated by several later authorities.[17] Set in Britain after Brutus's conquest, *A New Opera* is a completely different story; for much of the play the king and his son Locrinus are away fighting a war in Gaul.[18] This is of course allegorical. Brutus, also called Albion, represents William III, who was abroad fighting the French in 1696. The protagonist's triumphant arrival at the Cliffs of Dover in the second scene of Act IV is thus a metaphor of the Bloodless Revolution, and the elaborate masque in Act V is a premature celebration of the Peace of Rijswijk in September 1697. Many other events and characters are also symbolic. For example, Asaracus, who mismanages the kingdom during Brutus's absence, is banished but not executed, an obvious reflection of James II.[19] The full importance of *A New Opera* is reflected by the stage directions for machines, some of which are taken with little modification from Dryden and Grabu's *Albion and Albanius*.[20] Dent thought the later

[15] 'New Light on "Dido and Aeneas"', in *Henry Purcell, 1659–1695*, ed. Imogen Holst (London: Oxford Univ. Press, 1959), pp. 14–34.

[16] The actors Powell and Verbruggen signed the dedication, but do not claim to have written the libretto.

[17] *Foundations*, p. 178; and see, for example, *The Works of John Dryden*, xv, 330.

[18] The re-use of the names of characters in Tate's *Brutus of Alba* undoubtedly led Dent and others to assume that the two works are related. In addition to those mentioned above, *A New Opera* also includes Ragusa (Amarante's confidante) and Sozimon (Amarante's supposed paramour, who does not, however, appear).

[19] Asaracus may also be a parody of a less exalted person. In Act II, the faulty editing of the 1696 quarto is apparent when the speech prefix '*Asaracus*' becomes '*Rich*' in a few places, a blunder that suggests this character may also represent the very unpopular manager of the Theatre Royal, Christopher Rich.

[20] Holland (*The Ornament of Action*, p. 45) shows that other sets were adapted from several earlier semi-operas.

semi-opera even incorporated excerpts from *Albion and Albanius* (*Foundations*, p. 178); in fact, many of the lyrics are crudely paraphrased from Dryden's libretto, and even its most famous song did not escape:

Albion and Albanius (II.ii)	*A New Opera* (IV.ii)
Old Father *Ocean* calls my Tyde:	Hark, I am call'd; old Father Ocean
Come Away, come away;	Calls my Tide;
The Barks upon the Billows ride,	Come away.
The Master will not stay;	On the Mounting Billows dancing,
The merry Boson from his side,	See the Royal Bark advancing;
His Whistle takes to check and chide	The Waves, the Wind and Sea,
The lingring Lads delay,	Are all at *Albion*'s dear Devotion.
And all the Crew alowd has Cry'd,	
Come away, come away.	

Throughout *A New Opera* are sprinkled many such lyrics originally designed to entertain Charles II and James II, now refashioned for William III.[21] This was an ironical compliment – the virtual re-use of a Caroline drama to honour the Dutch king. The recycling of an allegorical masque as a moral fable is a notion carried over directly to the 1700 adaptation of *Measure for Measure*.

Gildon drew on Davenant's version of *Measure for Measure* – called *The Law Against Lovers* (February 1662) – as well as on Shakespeare; but the 1700 reworking is closer to the original, because the part of Mariana is restored and the scenes Davenant had borrowed from *Much Ado About Nothing* are eliminated. Like most late seventeenth-century redactions of Elizabethan and Jacobean plays, it is marred by the imposition of contemporary morality; for example, Claudio and Julietta have been secretly married before she becomes pregnant. But such proprieties do little to blunt Gildon's main objective, which is to let the action revolve entirely round Angelo and Isabella. *Dido and Aeneas* plays an important role in this design.

The stated purpose of the 'play'-within-the-play is to sweeten Angelo's 'Sour Temper'. In the absence of the duke, he has priggishly resurrected an old statute against fornication. First to be condemned for infringing it is the worthy Claudio. Escalus, the deputy's chief minister, who believes in tempering justice with mercy, has arranged a performance of the little opera as an apologue to show Angelo the possible consequences of enforcing too zealously a law against nature. Aeneas is thus meant to represent Claudio, and Dido the violated Julietta. The allegory implies an interpretation of the central ambiguity of *Dido and Aeneas* in direct opposition to almost all modern criticism: in the new context, the lovers have

---

[21] Daniel Purcell supplied the music, but none of his surviving songs is a setting of the paraphrased lyrics. See *The Single Songs, With the Dialogue, Sung in the New Opera, Call'd Brutus of Alba* (1696).

committed a sin punished by the havoc wrought when the Sorceress tricks Aeneas into abandoning the queen. Angelo acknowledges the design, but instead of being morally instructed or even moved by the tragedy, he sees *himself* as Aeneas, an anti-heroic perversion of Virgil's protagonist.

In I.i Lucio explains that the opera will be heard in four separate parts in order not to tire Angelo with too much music at once. Shortly before the first entertainment, which is placed near the end of Act I, Claudio's sister, the virtuous Isabella, appeals to Angelo to pardon her brother for his crime. The deputy says he will consider her suit when 'the Opera is over'. As in Shakespeare, he is smitten by her beauty, but Gildon abridges the memorable soliloquy through which Angelo's hypocrisy begins to surface (Shakespeare, II.ii.162–86) and supplies a transition to the first act of *Dido*:

> I'll think no more on't, but with Musick chase
> Away the Guilty Image.
> Musick they say can Calm the ruffled Soul,
> I'm sure a mighty Tempest ruffles mine.

Instead of quelling his lust, the masque fans the flames. After the first act, he says:

> This Musick is no Cure for my Distemper;
> For, every Note, to my Enchanted Ears,
> Seem'd to Sing only *Isabella*'s Beauty,
> Her Youth, her Beauty, and her Tender Pity
> Combine to ruin me! Ha! Dost thou then
> Desire her foully?

The next act of the opera is presented after the second interview (II.ii), in which Angelo tells Isabella that her brother will be spared if she will submit to his desire. While mulling over her refusal to acquiesce, he listens to the scenes in which the Sorceress plots Dido's destruction, a storm spoils the hunting party, and the spirit '*in likeness of* Mercury' commands Aeneas to leave the queen and sail on to his destiny. Angelo twists the masque into a grotesque metaphor of his designs on Isabella:

> All will not do: All won't devert my Pain,
> The Wound enlarges by these Medicines,
> 'Tis She alone can yield the Healing Balm.
> This Scene just hits my case; her Brothers danger,
> Is here the storm must furnish Blest Occasion;
> And when, my Dido, I've Possess'd thy Charms,
> I then will throw thee from my glutted Arms,
> And think no more on all they soothing Harms.

Note that he reads far more into the second act of the opera than the elliptic plot suggests, comparing Claudio's death sentence for fornication, and the leverage it gives him with Isabella, to the tempest that offers Dido the 'Blest Occasion' for satisfying her lust. But according to Tate's 1689 libretto, Aeneas has already 'enjoy'd' one night *before* the storm scatters the hunting party. By hammering home this allegory, Gildon exploits the very aspect of *The Aeneid* that Tate attempted to obscure. When one strips Book IV of the interference of the gods, the cause of the human tragedy is that Dido regards her submission in the cave during the storm as tantamount to marriage, whereas Aeneas does not. In the memorable words of Dryden's verse translation,

> The queen, whom sense of honour could not move,
> No longer made a secret of her love,
> But called it marriage; by that specious name
> To veil the crime, and sanctify the shame.

But Aeneas later tells her that he never 'pretended to the lawful claim / Of sacred nuptials, or a husband's name', which applies directly to Angelo's seduction and abandonment of Mariana before the play began. The opera thus emphasizes the monstrousness of his hypocrisy in condemning Claudio for violating the sacred vow of marriage.

The third act of the opera is placed in III[ii]. Escalus tells Angelo that the final entertainment will 'compose your Thoughts for pleasing Slumbers'. But the villain is distracted throughout the performance, because he expects Isabella, who has promised to meet him at this hour, to appear. Delaying her entrance until just before the end of the opera is a *coup de théâtre*: as Dido dies of shame (at least in Angelo's mind), Isabella seems ready to offer up her virginity. Unmoved by the great musical tragedy just acted before him, he mutters malevolently, 'I see my Ev'ning Star of Love appear'.[22] Purists may view the joining of opera and play as a misguided conflation that saps the lifeblood from each, but I think the union provides a valuable, if indirect, insight into how the composer's near contemporaries may have interpreted the troublesome ambiguities surrounding Aeneas. When the allegorical links to William III are severed, the Trojan prince emerges as the hypocritical opportunist of Dido's dying accusations. Gildon's adaptation removes Purcell's opera from its pedestal of royal panegyric, transforming it into a story of intense human passions. Dido's love for Aeneas is a *carpe diem*, not in the literal sense, but in the Freudian: an immoral sexual liaison for which she must ultimately pay. As is explained in the following section, *Measure for Measure* also left an indelible mark on the sources of the music.

---

[22] Isabella was portrayed by Mrs Bracegirdle, who was by this time the leading soprano at Lincoln's Inn Fields. Although the 1700 quarto of *Measure for Measure* does not give the singers' names, it is conceivable that she may also have taken the part of Dido.

The Librettos and the Tenbury Score

The state of the surviving sources of *Dido and Aeneas* is the most deplorable of any of Purcell's major stage works. The earliest score, Tenbury MS 1266 (now in the Bodleian Library), dates from no earlier than 1750 and disagrees with Tate's 1689 libretto in two significant ways: it lacks the French-style allegorical prologue and the chorus 'Then since our Charmes have Sped' at the end of Act II. The differences between the manuscript and the libretto have long dogged scholars. If Purcell originally set the prologue and verse at the end of Act II, why are they not preserved in Tenbury? Does the score in fact bear any resemblance to the one used for the Chelsea première, or is it thoroughly corrupt both in detail and general dramatic outline, like many mid-eighteenth-century manuscripts of Purcell's other stage works? To answer these questions one must begin with the librettos.

Though the libretto printed in the 1700 version of *Measure for Measure* corrects many misprints and freely alters the stage directions of Tate's original, the two are closely related. For example, the play-book compositor repeated a blunder found in the 1689 text near the beginning of Act III: '*Elisas* ruin'd; ho, ho, ho, next Motion. . .' The Tenbury score divides the speech and inserts the accidentally omitted 'our':

> *1st & 2nd witches*. Eliza's ruin'd, ho, ho, ho.
> *Sorceress*. Our next motion. . .

In addition to minor variants, the order of the scenes is different in the two librettos:

1689 libretto	*1700 libretto*
Prologue	Act I, the Palace
i Phoebus, Venus, et al.	Act II.ii, the Grove (expanded)
ii Spring	II.i, Sorceress's Cave
iii Shepherds	
Act I, the Palace	Act III, the Ships
Act II.i, Sorceress's Cave	Prologue
II.ii, the Grove	i Phoebus, Venus, et al. (Spring omitted)
Act III, the Ships	ii Shepherds
	iii Mars, Peace (new scene)

The prologue is placed at the end of the play to serve as a celebration of the duke's Solomonic wisdom in preserving Isabella's chastity and Claudio's life. As an introduction, this scene, which is entirely separate from the opera itself, would have obscured the allegory. As a final entertainment, it had to be provided with a vacuous new ending – a debate between Mars and Peace – which displaced the entry of Spring and advanced the original dialogue for a shepherd and shepherdess into second position.

The reversal of the order of scenes in Act II is illogical, because in the 1700 version the Sorceress's declaration that her 'elf' shall appear to Aeneas in the form of Mercury is made after the event. White's explanation of the transposition is as good as any: rearranging the scenes allowed the second part of the opera to end with the only spectacular machine effects in the play.[23] After the Echo Dance, six furies sink below the stage and four others fly up. The furies seem to have been Gildon's invention, because Tate's libretto, which requires no machine effects in this scene, calls for a dance of '*Inchanteresses and Fairees*'. But exigencies of staging would not appear to account wholly for the radical change in the order of events in the opera, especially considering how carefully Gildon exploits the allegorical connections between the two works. As noted above, Angelo misreads events depicted in the opera when he likens the storm to the death sentence imposed on Isabella's brother. The transposition of scenes in Act II may therefore be a clumsy attempt to relate the opera more closely to the play, by allowing Angelo to reason that he and Isabella, like Dido and Aeneas, have not yet had the 'Blest Occasion'. This sequence would also mirror Tate's *Brutus of Alba*, in which the episode at Diana's fountain (the Grove scene in the opera) occurs *before* the consummation.

I may be giving Gildon more credit than he deserves, but the other major alteration to Act II clearly underscores the parallel between opera and play. After the bogus Mercury delivers the fateful message to Aeneas, Gildon inserted a twenty-four-line dialogue for two friends of the hero, who debate what course he should take.[24] One counsels him to follow the dictates of his heart and remain with Dido, while the other reminds him of the greater rewards of fame and glory. Aeneas has already resolved to leave ('Yours be the blame, ye Gods, for I / Obey your will – but with more Ease cou'd dye'), but after hearing his friends' conflicting advice he wavers: 'Ye Sacred Powers instruct me how to choose, / When Love or Empire I must loose'. This is a blatant reference to Angelo's crisis of conscience. No music survives for these added verses, but, as Laurie suggests, they were probably set by Eccles, Lincoln's Inn Fields's chief composer, and not, as White believes, by Daniel Purcell, who worked exclusively for Drury Lane.[25] Eccles's involvement in the production is confirmed by the recent discovery of the violin parts of his act music for *Measure for Measure* in a

23 'New Light on "Dido and Aeneas"', pp. 23–4.
24 Reproduced in part in White, 'New Light on "Dido and Aeneas"', facing p. 24. The dialogue may have been suggested by Aeneas's conference with the shipfitters Mnestheus, Sergestus, and Serestus, *The Aeneid*, IV.288–91. Craven, in 'Nahum Tate's Third *Dido and Aeneas*', p. 72, argues that the added lines, because of their supposed links to *Brutus of Alba*, were cut from the 1689 performance, but his evidence is inconclusive.
25 Laurie, 'Purcell's Stage Works', p. 55; White, 'New Light on "Dido and Aeneas"', p. 31.

Newberry Library manuscript (Case vM 3.1 p985, fols. 4–5v).[26] All are in G major and have no obvious connection with Purcell's opera.

The Tenbury manuscript restores the scenes in Act II to their original sequence, while omitting Gildon's debate between Aeneas's friends, and is therefore closer to the original libretto than to the one printed in the *Measure for Measure* quarto. Placing great faith in a score copied more than sixty years after the event and ignoring the contrary evidence provided by the librettos, Dent maintained that Purcell did not set the prologue, and if he did, 'it is no great loss' (*Foundations*, p. 180). He also thought the composer cut the chorus at the end of the Grove scene, 'feeling that the despair of Aeneas made a more dramatic end to the act' (p. 182). And recently an argument has been advanced that Tenbury, 'except perhaps for the missing Prologue, reflects Purcell's original intentions'.[27] Most musicians who have performed and studied *Dido* conclude, however, that the chorus and dance at the end of Act II are indeed lost. The gap is clearly shown by the overall tonal plan, which is characteristically balanced:

Acts	Principal key centres			
I	c	C	(e)	C
II.i	f	F	(d)	F
II.ii	d	D	(a)	–
III	B♭	g	(c)	g

The first two scenes begin in minor keys and end in the parallel major. The third act opens in the major and concludes in the relative minor. Each main section includes at least one important piece in a key that temporarily disrupts the scheme: in Act I the E minor chorus 'Cupid only throws the dart'; in II.i the D minor duet 'But ere we this perform'; in Act III the recitative 'Thy hand, Belinda', which begins in C minor and modulates back to G minor. The second scene of Act II begins like the preceding ones in a minor key and then shifts to the parallel major, but ends with an A minor recitative that leaves the act dangling in a different key from the one in which it began. Furthermore, the formal chain of air (or duet), chorus, and dance that terminates all the other scenes is broken here. Many editors and directors have felt the need to insert music in D minor or D major to complete the act.[28]

---

[26] See Richard Charteris, 'Some Manuscript Discoveries of Henry Purcell and His Contemporaries in the Newberry Library, Chicago', *Notes*, 37 (1980), 8–9.

[27] Ellen T. Harris, *Handel and the Pastoral Tradition* (London: Oxford Univ. Press, 1979), p. 139.

[28] Dart and Laurie supply a chorus and dance in D minor (the chorus a *contrafactum* of 'To celebrate his so much wished return', z 344/7c – transposed from E minor – and the dance a hornpipe from *The Married Beau*, z 603/3). Michael Tilmouth also opts for D minor in his new-composed finale for II.ii appended to Savage's 'Producing *Dido and Aeneas*', 405–6. In Benjamin Britten and Imogen Holst's reconstruction (London: Boosey &

How was this music lost? Let us hypothesize that Purcell set Tate's 1689 libretto virtually as it stands, changing a word here and there, dividing a few choruses into solos and ensembles, giving some of the Sorceress's couplets to the enchantresses, and strengthening Belinda's part by transferring a line or two from Dido – the kinds of alterations that opera composers from Monteverdi on made to their librettos as a matter of course. After its première, the score was put away and forgotten until Purcell's widow made his papers available to the editors of *Orpheus Britannicus*, who extracted only one aria from the opera. A year or two later, Betterton acquired the manuscript and probably paid Eccles to adapt it for *Measure for Measure*. The composer set the additional verses sandwiched between Aeneas's soliloquy and the witches' chorus in Act II and wrote a grand finale for the prologue. *Dido* proved successful enough to be revived in January 1704, when it was attached to Ravenscroft's three-act farce *The Anatomist*, a popular play that incorporated Motteux's masque *The Loves of Mars and Venus* (first produced in November 1696 with music by Eccles and Finger). *Dido* was also added to a revival of *The Man of Mode* later in 1704. Even if Etherege's masterpiece was presented in a moderately abridged form, the inclusion of the expanded version of *Dido* must have made for a very long evening. The opera was probably stripped of the prologue for one of these performances. Furthermore, I suspect that the editor for the 1704 revivals, knowing that in 1700 new music had been added after Aeneas's monody in the second act, lopped off the end of the scene at that point, unaware that he was also removing Purcell's original setting of the witches' chorus that followed the interpolated dialogue. Therefore, a well-intentioned attempt to purge the opera of music it had acquired when joined to *Measure for Measure* may explain the apparent gap at the end of Act II. The Tenbury score was, then, almost certainly based on a manuscript at least three stages removed from Purcell's original.

But Tenbury shows many signs of having been copied from an early manuscript, one used for a theatrical rather than a concert performance.[29] Fortunately, the copyist made practically no attempt to modernize its antiquated notation: the viola part is in the mezzo-soprano clef; the key signatures of C minor and F minor mostly omit the flats on the sixth degree of the scale; except in two instances discussed below, sharps and

Hawkes, 1961), the first half of the chorus is, again, in D minor (a reworking and transposition from C minor of 'What flatt'ring noise is this' from *The Indian Queen*), then shifts to D major for 'A dance that shall make the spheres to wonder . . .' (based on 'To Urania and Caesar' from the 1687 Birthday Song for James II, z 335/9, originally in C major), returning to D minor for the Groves dance (the canzona from the overture for *Sir Anthony Love*).

[29] For a discussion of the various 'concert versions' post-dating Tenbury, see the Purcell Society Edition, III (rev. Laurie), ix-xii.

flats rather than natural signs are used to cancel accidentals;[30] and accidentals are not necessarily cancelled by the bar-line. Perhaps the best clue to the date of Tenbury's source is the minimal bass figuring, which is limited to essentials. Continuo figuring was undergoing significant change about the time Purcell died. Compare, for instance, the profusion of symbols added to pieces in the first book of *Orpheus Britannicus* (1698) with the sparse figures in the pre-1695 prints from which many of the songs were copied. Purcell's own figuring in the few extant autographs of theatre music is also very simple, often petering out altogether after a line or two. In view of the many archaic features of the notation, I should guess that Tenbury was copied from a manuscript dating from about 1700.

Given his literal-mindedness, the scribe may have signalled some of his own tiny changes in the first act. The only natural signs of the entire score are those shown in Example 1, from the arietta for the 'second woman'. By

Example 1. *Dido and Aeneas*: 'The greatest blessing fate can give', bars 1–9 as in Tenbury MS

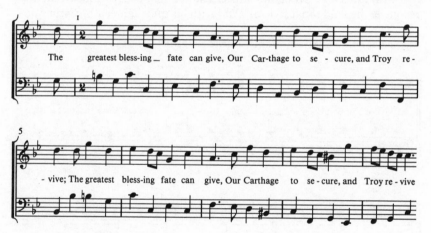

using the new-fangled device here, the scribe may have wanted to show that the accidentals in the bass at bars 1 and 5 were not in his source and are thus editorial (note the 'B♯' in bars 7 and 8). All modern editions include them because they make a strong progression. But one must remember that *Dido* is an early work and such harmonic 'irregularities' are not uncommon in Purcell's pre-1690 music.

The key of C minor, in which the opera begins, causes problems for editors of late seventeenth-century music, because the signature normally has only two flats. A careful copyist, such as Purcell, overcame potential ambiguity by indicating the A♭s individually. But other scribes, in fact the large majority, relied on the performer to supply the appropriate sixth

---

[30] The natural sign came into common use in England after 1710.

degree and even the sharp on the seventh according to the melodic direction and harmonic context. An editor must proceed warily; adding accidentals creates a more tonal, minor-key idiom that might be anachronistic.
The Tenbury scribe was aware of this danger. He starts the score boldly
with a two-flat signature for the C minor overture and Belinda's first air,
writing in the A♭s while leaving the A♮s unsigned. But at the first chorus,
'Banish sorrow, banish care', he mixes the modern three-flat signature with
the old seventeenth-century notation. Dido's aria 'Ah! Belinda' and the
following recitative, both in C minor, return to two flats. The next chorus,
'When monarchs unite', appears to have been written out initially in the
old style, but an A♭ was later added to the key signature, perhaps in a different hand. Should the chords marked with asterisks in Example 2 have A♭ or
A♮? Of course, we are used to hearing this piece with every A flatted, but
the only unequivocal A♭ of the chorus is in bar 7. To sing all the others as
A♮ produces (especially in bar 11) a distinctly modal sound not inconsistent with Purcell's early choral music. The Tenbury copyist endeavoured to
reconcile the fluid tonal style of *Dido* with his mid-eighteenth-century no-

Example 2. *Dido and Aeneas*: 'When monarchs unite'

tation, happily accomplishing this without eradicating the archaisms of his source. He must have been an antiquary of rare musical sensitivity.

Such attention to detail does not suggest the sort of person who would have omitted sections from his source. Although he worked from an early manuscript, it was probably mutilated, already lacking the prologue and chorus at the end of Act II. Furthermore, the scenes are grouped differently from the 1689 libretto and in a manner inconsistent with the *Measure for Measure* play-book:

	1689 libretto	*Tenbury score*
Palace	I	I.i
Cave	II.i	I.ii
Grove	II.ii	II
Ships	III	III

The manuscript thus has a long first act and a rather short second one, an imbalance exaggerated by the missing witches' chorus. The editor of the new Purcell Society score elected to retain the 'more logical' format of Tate's libretto.

Besides the librettos, the only evidence that Purcell did in fact set the prologue is the 'Overture in M^r P Opera' in Royal College of Music MS 1172, fol. 38. Notwithstanding the C minor overture at the beginning of Act I, the opening scene for Phoebus and Venus would also have needed an instrumental introduction.[31] On stylistic grounds the ascription to Purcell is hardly in doubt, though the copyist wrote, then cancelled, 'M^r J Clarke' between the viola and bass parts at the end of the canzona.[32] But is the opera mentioned in the rubric *Dido and Aeneas*? As Laurie notes, all Purcell's major stage works are well supplied with overtures, except *Circe*.[33] The piece in question is in G minor, a key that would complete the tonal cycle of *Dido*. But it also accords well with the existing music for Davenant's tragedy, whose principal keys are (in order) C major, C minor, C major, G minor, and C major. The question must therefore remain open.

Music and Drama

The correspondences between Blow's court masque *Venus and Adonis* and the similarly proportioned *Dido and Aeneas* are too numerous to be co-incidental. Each is an all-sung three-act miniature tragedy with French-

---

[31] Compare, for example, the music in Ravenscroft's three-act tragedy *The Italian Husband* (November 1697), which included the masque *Ixion*. Eccles's overture in B♭ preceded the play proper, while the masque began with a different piece scored for strings, oboes, trumpets, and kettledrums; see my *Music in the Restoration Theatre*, pp. 185–6.

[32] The only other source, Cambridge, Magdalene College MS F.4.35(1–5), is without ascription.

[33] 'Did Purcell Set *The Tempest*?', p. 45, n. 8.

style prologue, in which an imperious woman loses her lover. And the works share a number of musical and structural features, including a carefully balanced tonal plan centring on G minor, pervasive descending chromatics to depict both grief and impending doom, moments of comic and pastoral relief, and a final reflective chorus. The main dramatic difference between the operas is, of course, that Adonis's death is accidental, whereas Dido's is the result of human frailty and conflict. Like all great tragedians, Purcell avoids sentimentalism by accentuating the irony of the fatal catastrophe. But this too he may have learnt from Blow. The anonymous libretto for *Venus and Adonis* compensates for a lack of impellent conflict by exaggerating the hackneyed irony of the familiar story: Adonis wants to die metaphorically upon Venus's breast, is diverted by the hunt and wounded by a boar, then dies in earnest in the final scene. This is not unlike the main human action of the fourth book of *The Aeneid*, though without the moralistic retribution. Virgil achieves a fusion of sex and death by having Dido stab herself with Aeneas's sword, then die on the bed in which they consummated their love. While Tate purged his libretto of such explicit imagery, he did allude to the parallel theme of *Venus and Adonis*. In the scene in the grove after Dido has succumbed to desire, Aeneas boasts of his hunting prowess by displaying on the end of his spear a 'Monster's Head', presumably that of the elusive wild boar mentioned in *The Aeneid*, IV.159. A phallic symbol if ever there was, this refers both to Dido's 'specious marriage' and to Adonis's fatal hunt. Aeneas even mentions his mother at this point, remarking that the boar's tusks are larger than 'Those did Venus' Huntsman tear', a linkage that foreshadows the disastrous result of the royal pair's illicit union. Dido's response, 'The Skies are Clouded', a panicky *non sequitur*, is as much a reaction to the sudden reminder of her sin as it is to the gathering clouds conjured by the Sorceress. It is remarkable how often *Dido and Aeneas* relies on *Venus and Adonis*, both literally and figuratively, at important moments such as this.

Whereas Blow's masque may have provided Purcell and Tate with the basic ingredients of musical tragedy and allowed them to express metaphorically what they dared not say openly, it did not furnish them with a model for the most compelling feature of their opera: Dido is consumed from within rather than destroyed by circumstances imposed by fate or perfidy. Hers is not a fall from grace, but a progress from anguish, through guilt and rage, to morbid resignation. The entire opera is a relentless descent to the grave, in which the Lament is the inevitable goal of a grand musical scheme. Almost everything is directed to the final aria; even the seemingly salubrious music at the end of the first act and the sailors' quayside jollity at the beginning of Act III are charged with forebodings of tragedy.

The tonal scheme, a constellation of keys clustering round G minor, is an archetype of the principal associations of key and affect found in Purcell's later theatre music. The plan, outlined above in reference to the missing music at the end of Act II, is a paragon of simplicity, its chief function being to propel the story swiftly and to emphasize almost to the point of excruciation the underlying irony. The first two scenes have the same design: they open gloomily in a minor key and end exuberantly in the parallel major. In the first, Dido's C minor anguish is followed by her courtiers' celebration in C major of the amorous alliance with Aeneas; in the second scene, the Sorceress's solemn incantation in F minor is succeeded by the enchantresses' hand-rubbing glee in the parallel major over their forthcoming mischief. Presumably, the second scene of Act II, which begins in D minor, would replicate this plan if its missing finale were recovered. The pattern is reversed in the third act, when the sailors unknowingly join the witches in a swaggering Bb major prelude to the impending G minor tableau.

The French overture plunges directly into the gloom hanging over Dido's court. The first section writhes with a chromatic tension that seems to lead nowhere; the tortuous descent of the bass after a three-bar tonic pedal graphically points the drama on its way, and the incessant quavers of the canzona are obsessive. The representational function of the main key centres in this act is transparent. Belinda, Dido's confidante, and the courtiers try to lift the queen from her severe C minor into the regal parallel major. The opening arietta and chorus, though firmly in the tonic, are resolutely cheery and move easily into the softer mediant and submediant. Dido's air 'Ah! Belinda' is a miniature *da capo* aria, complete with an opening declamatory passage. The first couplet, 'Ah! Belinda, I am press'd / With torment not to be confess'd', is haltingly irregular, its rhythm ragged and fractured. The aria proper, 'Peace and I are strangers grown', begins at the tenth statement of the bass pattern with a melody whose head motif is the same as the ground's. Of the many masterstrokes, perhaps the most noteworthy is the recapitulation of the principal melody in bar 48 after the modulation to G minor; the bass has unobtrusively returned to C minor a full eleven bars earlier. Despite such intellectual feats, the music remains expressive, as when Dido touches on the royal key, then shuns it with a melancholy downward slide (Example 3). Purcell's characterization of the anguished queen is also conveyed by the low range of this aria.[34] This perhaps accounts for the *Orpheus Britannicus* editor's decision to transpose it up a tone to D minor.

The recitatives and ariosos, about which much has been written, seem to me no more 'heaven-sent' than the declamatory sections of many of the

---

[34] In general, Dido's range in the rest of the opera is almost exactly that of the later Mrs Ayliff-type soprano, that is, roughly equivalent to a modern mezzo but with a high tessitura.

Example 3. *Dido and Aeneas*: 'Ah! Belinda', bars 40–4

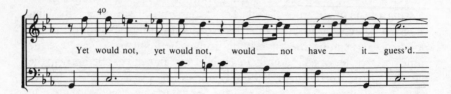

songs and dialogues discussed in Part I of this study. They are celebrated because, for once, the singers are protagonists rather than decorative nymphs and shepherds. The recitatives in the first act are especially interesting, being the battleground for Dido's struggle of conscience. The exchange shown in Example 4 is the most important, revealing a decided

Example 4. *Dido and Aeneas*: 'Whence could so much virtue spring?', bars 1–12

shift in the queen's dolour as the music clarifies the most obscure couplets of the libretto. Dido's questions are rhetorical, since presumably she has already been entertained by Aeneas's recounting his heroic exploits (*The Aeneid*, Books II and III). Dardan Anchises is of course his father, Venus his mother. Belinda's woeful tale is therefore the trail of tears the prince has followed since the sack of Troy. The recitative begins with C major bombast appropriate to storms and battles. To depict Aeneas's inherited virtues, Dido sings alternately in the keys of war and love, thus being lifted into the major tonic by her own reverie. Belinda's response, which, like the queen's preceding air on a ground, begins in C minor and modulates to G minor, gently chides Dido for her extravagant display of grief; the upward slide on the word 'woe' is especially mocking. Confirmation that the queen has finally succumbed to her courtiers' exhortations comes in the closing lines of the recitative. Though the passage shown in Example 5 is as chro-

Example 5. *Dido and Aeneas*: 'Whence could so much virtue spring?', bars 19–25

matic as any thus far, its ascending semitones signal rising passion, and the modulation to the parallel major is now firmly secured.[35] These two pages of music cover much emotional ground, and the dizzying speed of the drama has troubled some authorities, particularly Westrup: 'It is impossible not to feel in *Dido* that the episodes and individual movements sometimes succeed each other too rapidly' (*Purcell*, p. 124). But in this scene, the balletic duet and chorus that follow, 'Fear no danger to ensue' (frequently cited as the most Frenchified numbers in the opera), give the audience ample time to absorb Dido's change of heart.[36]

---

[35] Compare the similar lines in Dryden's *Albion and Albanius*, III.i.15–16: 'Unhelpt I am, who pity'd the distress'd, / And none oppressing, am by all oppress'd'.

[36] Both Spink (*English Song Dowland to Purcell*, p. 223) and Moore (*Henry Purcell & the Restoration Theatre*, p. 51) mention the French flavour.

Aeneas's entrance is an anticlimax, his recitative lacking a distinctive character. But the exchange with Dido is important to the greater musical structure. His question to the queen ('When . . . shall I be bless'd?') is in a bold G major; her response ('Fate forbids what you pursue') and his protest ('Aeneas has no fate but you') send the music coldly through A minor to E minor, an association of key and affect that is reaffirmed in Act II when the elf disguised as Mercury appears to Aeneas to remind him of his destiny. The modulation to E minor, though handled smoothly, disrupts the monolithic tonal scheme, heralding the intrusion of desire, which makes a symbolic appearance in the following contrapuntal chorus, 'Cupid only throws the dart'; appropriately, this piece contains a high concentration of pungent dissonances, especially at the words 'dart' and 'wounds'. Hitherto the chorus has simply echoed business already concluded by Belinda and the 'second woman', but here the courtiers do far more than comment on the action; they represent an abstract force.

Although Dido utters not another word in this act after the frosty 'Fate forbids what you pursue', jubilance prevails in Belinda's air 'Pursue thy conquest', the chorus 'To the hills and the vales', and the Triumphing Dance. The queen's silence results not merely from the compressed dimensions of Tate's libretto but from her shame at having buried her grief so quickly. Yet the courtiers' exaltation is genuine if not entirely unrestrained. The most beguiling moment of the first-act finale is the passage shown in Example 6. Superficially, this 'English' cadence is only a touch of

Example 6. *Dido and Aeneas*: 'To the hills and the vales', bars 5–8 (strings omitted)

word-painting, but the intrusion of G minor, the key in which Dido will die, into a chorus celebrating her amorous triumph is a cruel irony. This interpretation can be taken a step further. In *Brutus of Alba*, the lovers drink the philtre that leads to their 'adultery' at Diana's 'cool shady fountains'. The composer has thus already begun the fusion of sexual passion and death that has its finest expression in the Lament.

The Triumphing Dance, which is built on a four-bar ground, is one of Purcell's happiest inspirations. The melodic periods are locked to the bass until the fourth variation, in which the violins double the length of the previous phrases. The majestic sweep of dotted rhythms is supported harmonically by transposing the bass to G major for one statement, clearly a case of the tail wagging the dog. Of the four grounds in the opera, only the last is immutable.

By positing the witches as symbols of religious zeal, I have tried to acquit them of the charge that they do not behave rationally. But what is most unsettling about the first scene of the second act is the juxtaposition of the Sorceress's impressively sombre recitative and the freakish glee of her enchantresses' choruses. Savage's idea that the scene is a black parody of the first act is surely the best explanation for its more bizarre effects.[37] The two episodes have the same dramatic design, but with twisted ironies. The Sorceress, like Dido, is also consumed – not with grief, but with hate. She relieves her anxiety by plotting to destroy the queen. The tonal plan, which is much less rigid than that of Act I, reflects the parallel resolutions of inner conflict. The chorus, who sing in the major mode, coax the Sorceress from her F minor recitative, whose accompanying strings are like bitter treacle. But she returns gravely to the minor in order to reaffirm the modulation to the parallel major, then overshoots to C major at the line 'Depriv'd of fame, of life and love'. The ensuing chorus 'Ho, ho, ho', which is in the new and unexpected key, is thus a taunting reminder of 'Fear no danger', the first piece in Act I to be unequivocally in C major. The parodistic function of the witches' scene is at its clearest here, as the Sorceress, despite the efforts of her weird courtiers, controls the action and the highly representational tonal scheme, precisely as Dido did earlier.

Intertwined with the warped references to the first act are frequent hints of later action. The Sorceress's instructions to the elf who will personate Mercury are fraught with anticipation. In Example 7, mention of Aeneas's

Example 7. *Dido and Aeneas*: 'Ruin'd ere the set of sun?', bars 4–7

destiny draws the music to G minor, and the word 'fate' is underscored by a diminished-seventh chord – rare in the opera – over a tonic pedal. The distant sounds of the hunt, represented by the violins flourishing a D major chord, will be transformed into the tempest in the following scene.

---

[37] 'Producing *Dido and Aeneas*', p. 399.

The witches' ceremony ends with the chorus-and-dance formula of the first act. 'In our deep vaulted cell', justly famous for its echoes, was probably inspired by Locke's far more elaborate but less successful 'Great Psyche shall find no such pleasure' in Act I of *Psyche*. Each of Purcell's

Example 8. *Dido and Aeneas*: 'In our deep vaulted cell', bars 15–19 (strings omitted)

echoes is either three or six beats long, with a stress on the second or fifth beat; the shift of accent to the third beat at the hemiola cadence shown in Example 8 coincides felicitously with eerie cross-relations. The Echo Dance of Furies is a further grotesquerie. Dent's analysis is penetrating:

The amusing thing about the echoes is that they never reproduce the exact harmony of the original phrases; this ingenious device gives them a delightfully fantastic character, as if the human witches on the stage were answered by spirit dancers who strangely distort their movements (*Foundations*, p. 193).

The piece can easily sound over-elaborate, especially in a laboured performance. One should recall that the 1689 libretto specifies a dance of '*Inchanteresses and Fairees*'; the 'furies' seem to have originated with the 1700 production of *Measure for Measure*.

The swift pace of the action is all but arrested in the next scene, the leafy grove. Dido's courtiers entertain Aeneas after the 'hunt', a poetic euphemism for their love-making. The song on a ground, 'Oft she visits this lone mountain', performed by the 'second woman', recounts the story of Actaeon, who was killed by his own hounds. It thus joins the hunting metaphor to the idea of Dido's being destroyed from within by shame. The air is like the queen's ground in Act I in that the plastic vocal phrases seldom coincide with the bass periods. As noted in the discussions of 'Ah! Belinda' and the Triumphing Dance, Purcell's approach to ostinatos was never pedantic; he frequently extends or transposes them to other keys for contrast or to support melodic fancies that exceed the harmonic limits of the given bass. In 'Oft she visits' the ground strays briefly at one point (shown in Example 9) for what would appear to be textual rather than purely musical reasons. The modulation to A major, no more than an harmonic legerdemain, is meant to draw attention to 'mortal wounds'. The ground is also broken once in the attached dance, with an equally brief excursion to F major.

Example 9. *Dido and Aeneas*: 'Oft she visits this lone mountain', bars 17–25

The hypnotic pieces in D minor make the outburst of the storm in D major all the more electrifying, as Dido reacts excitedly to the atmospheric fireworks depicted by the shimmering chord in the strings. Belinda starts the stampede back to Carthage with 'Haste, haste, to town'. But Aeneas, whose recent travels have apparently inured him to foul weather, remains to hear the enunciation from '*The Spirit of the Sorceress . . . in likeness of Mercury*'. Her recitative, 'Stay, Prince, and hear', is unremarkable, conveying none of the enchantresses' sinister motivation in either words or music. Aeneas's response is another matter. Unquestioningly, almost enthusiastically, he accepts the command to set sail, then recalls his promise to the queen: 'Let Dido Smile, and I'll defy / The feeble stroke of Destiny'. With a two-and-a-half-bar aspirated melisma on the repeated words 'But Ah', Purcell transforms Tate's cardboard Trojan into Virgil's procrastinating ingrate, a hero among belligerent men but a coward to a spurned woman. The music is suspended on the dominant, E major – unresolved until the final cadence and painfully decorated by adjacent semitones – while Aeneas wails an elaborate exclamation that Dido will recall with utter humility during the Lament. One may feel some momentary sympathy for Aeneas, but his agony is purposely exaggerated. Critics have over-estimated the significance of the recitative by accepting its exposed position at the end of Act II in the Tenbury manuscript as a feature of Purcell's original design, ignoring the fact that in both the 1689 and 1700 librettos the scene ends with the reappearance of the witches. The irony of Aeneas's instant decision to leave Dido, which he regrets only after the fact, is spoilt without an immediate reminder of the Sorceress's role. The act originally ended with the Groves Dance, performed *for* the witches 'By the Nymphs of Carthage'; Dido's courtiers now unknowingly entertain a new queen.

The jaunty music for the sailors at the beginning of Act III has an underlying vein of cynicism. After the first couplet, 'Come away, fellow sailors . . .', the soloist sings

> Take a boozy short leave of your nymphs on the shore,
>> And silence their mourning
>> With vows of returning,
> But never intending to visit them more.

This is a crude quayside version of Aeneas's heroic crocodile tears to be shed later during the confrontation with Dido. In both air and chorus, the inner couplet is set to a chromatically descending tetrachord. Though beginning on the note C, it nevertheless leads to a strong cadence in G minor, a distinctly unsubtle foreshadowing of the ground in Dido's Lament. The sailors' insensitivity to the prince's dilemma is almost an act of disloyalty. Have they missed the irony, or have they become the puppets of the Sorceress, like the courtiers at the end of the preceding act? In the 1689 libretto 'Come away, fellow sailors' has the speech prefix '*Cho*', which Purcell divided into air and chorus. Tate's stage direction is important: '*Scene the Ships.* Enter *the Saylors. The Sorceress and her Inchanteress*'; this implies that the witches are to observe the entertainment from the side of the stage. In the *Measure for Measure* play-book 'Come away, fellow sailors' is assigned to the Sorceress, a considerable licence in light of the lyric's salty character. In the Tenbury score the air is given to a treble sailor, and the manuscript even delays the entrance of the witches until after the ensuing dance. A single-page engraving of 'The Saylors Song' published about 1700 states, however, that the air was sung by the tenor Mr Wiltshire. One interpretation of this conflicting evidence is that Purcell intended 'Come away, fellow sailors' for the disguised Sorceress as a pied-piper enticement to the men to board the ships; but the 1700 adapter, aware of the need for another male soloist, reassigned the song to a tenor. This possibility casts doubt on the usual portrayal of the Sorceress by a singer with a dark mezzo-soprano or contralto voice, often tinged with a sinister nasality. Most women who undertake the role try to maintain the menacing aura of the opening recitative of Act II in all the subsequent solos. But the Sorceress, like Mother Demdike in *The Lancashire Witches* and Ragusa in

Brutus of Alba, is a freakish hag capable of assuming any shape or persona in an instant. Apparently overlooked by modern music directors in their casting decisions is the fact that her vocal range is the same as Dido's – an octave and a fifth from middle C to high G. And her tessitura, like the queen's, begins rather low and gradually ascends. The Sorceress's final song, 'Our next motion', a sprightly piece indeed, lies quite high, and has therefore caused many a hapless contralto, especially those who favour the nasal approach, some discomfort.

Further evidence of the Sorceress's possible role in hastening the sailors on their way is the witches' exit music, a skittish dance tantalizingly described in the 1689 libretto: 'Jack *of the* Lanthorn *leads the* Spaniards *out of their way among the Inchanteresses*'.[38] This obviously reflects the exotic choreography devised by Priest, for whose pupils the opera was written. Some authorities have assumed that 'Spaniards' is a synonym for 'sailors';[39] the sense of the stage direction may be, therefore, that Will-o'-the-wisp leads the sailors out from among the witches, who are perhaps disguised as the 'Nymphs of the Shore'. Of course, so-called Spanish dances had enjoyed a vogue in the public theatres during the sixties and seventies, an inheritance from the Stuart masque, but the fad had all but passed by 1690. A precedent for the incongruous appearance of an Iberian in a school masque was set by Duffett's *Beauties Triumph* performed in Chelsea in 1676, in which a 'Spaniard' sang and danced a sarabande in honour of Juno. But Purcell's dance is as unlike a sarabande as possible, the abrupt changes of metre and character obviously tailored to the grotesque movements of the dancers. The inclusion of Jack-o'-lantern is equally whimsical. Probably referring more to a special effect than to Will-o'-the-wisp, it may have been inspired by the machine effects at the end of the first act of *The Lancashire Witches*. Clod, like Diogenes, is groping his way through a storm, when 'One of the Witches flies away with [his] Candle and Lanthorn, Mother *Demdike* sets him upon the top of a Tree, and they all fly away Laughing.'

The third act is the emotional inverse of the first. After the B♭ major bustling of the sailors' and witches' somewhat disorganized celebration, the orderly G minor threnody begins with Dido and Aeneas's bitter parting. The dialogue of this scene relies more heavily on *Brutus of Alba* than does any other in the opera, as the following excerpts show:

Brutus. Hold, hold! by all that's good . . .	*Aeneas*. By all that's good,
	Dido. By all that's good, no more . . .
. . .	. . .

[38] In the 1700 quarto this is simply called 'A Dance of Wizards and Witches'.
[39] See, for example, Laurie's Purcell Society Edition, III, 85, and Moore, *Henry Purcell & the Restoration Theatre*, p. 57.

Brutus. 'Twere Woman's Fraud t'have
    ruin'd with your Smiles,
But to betray with Tears, the
    Crocodile's.

Dido. Thus on the fatal banks of Nile,
    weeps the deceitful crocodile.

Tate chose to model the principal confrontation of the opera not on Brutus's final leave-taking but on the episode in Act IV in which the queen wretchedly confesses her sin of 'adultery' to the confidante Amarante. Thus the scene begins as if in mid-conversation, and a listener unfamiliar with the earlier play would assume that Belinda has just reassured the queen that the prince still loves her. But Tate's Dido, like Virgil's, already knows why Aeneas has come; it is an intuition born of guilt. She sings 'Earth and Heav'n conspire my fall'; though fondly believing that Aeneas will 'offend the gods, and Love obey', she realizes that her undoing is of baser origins. His timorous announcement of departure is set to a rising chromatic line that creeps from C minor to G minor, a cowardly retrograde of Dido's noble descent in the recitative preceding the Lament (Example 10). In the queen's scornful reply to his decision, Purcell reduces the lofty dialogue to its human essentials. Dido's first reaction to Aeneas's 'By all that's good' is a derisive parroting of his pompous indignation, but the next repetition (shown in Example 11), with the cross-relation between B♭ in the voice and B♮ in the bass, is stabbingly cynical. After this stunning moment, the dialogue resumes a stiff formality. In the closing duet Aeneas hollowly assures Dido that he will stay, an echo of the deceitful vows the sailors made to their shore nymphs at the beginning of the act. Though the former lovers sing resolutely and at the same time, they no longer sing together.

Example 10. *Dido and Aeneas*: 'Your counsel all is urg'd in vain', bars 18–23

Example 11. *Dido and Aeneas*: 'Your counsel all is urg'd in vain', bars 29-34

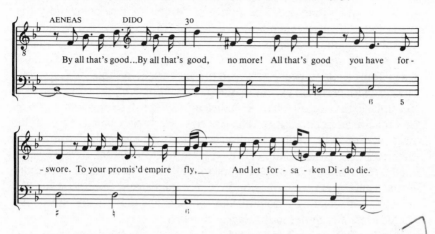

Separating the bitter farewell and Dido's Lament is the chorus 'Great minds against themselves conspire', which, despite its brevity, gives a feeling of the passage of considerable time.[40] It bridges the gulf between emotional extremes and is structurally reflective, beginning in B♭ major and ending in G minor, thereby restating in an orderly, formal manner the abrupt shift of tonal centre that occurred earlier between the Witches' Dance and Dido's recitative 'Your counsel all is urg'd in vain'. Thus, as in the first two acts, an important modulation is in effect accomplished twice. The second half of the chorus stresses a poignant melodic figure shown in Example 12. The diminished fourth flanked by adjacent semitones is a

Example 12. *Dido and Aeneas*: 'Great minds against themselves conspire', bars 7-10 (strings omitted)

[40] See Joseph Kerman, *Opera as Drama* (New York: Vintage, 1956), pp. 57-8.

motif that in various rhythmic guises permeates the opera, appearing prominently in more than a dozen numbers. Of course it helps to unify the work, but one must recognize it as a regular feature of Purcell's grammar for music in minor keys; in the theatre works it is commonly associated with grief or weeping. *Bonduca*, for instance, is laced with rising diminished fourths. It appears in two more elaborate variants in *Dido and Aeneas*: with ascending semitones and descending diminished fourth (for example, in the overture, bars 5–6; the chorus 'Banish sorrow', bars 11–12; and the Sorceress's recitative 'The Queen of Carthage', bars 6–7), and the rarer version with falling semitones and rising diminished fourth (in Belinda's 'Shake the cloud', bars 4–5; Dido's 'Ah! Belinda', bars 3–5; and the Witches' Dance in Act III, bars 19–21). As if to underscore the immense concentration of emotion in 'Great minds' and to prepare for the torrent of descending chromatics in the Lament, only in the chorus do both forms of the grief motif appear together.

The Lament is Tate's farthest departure from the fourth book of *The Aeneid*, since the operatic Dido, probably in acknowledgement of the allegorical resemblance to Queen Mary, dies in a manner as unlike Virgil's queen as could be imagined. Instead of cursing her former lover, 'Exoriare aliquis ex nostris ossibus altor' (May there arise from our bones some avenger), she leaves the pathetic injunction 'Remember me, but ah! forget my fate'. In fact, the only hint of Virgil's Dido is found in the line just before the Lament, 'Death is now a welcome guest'; the word 'guest' is important, as it recalls the queen's plea in IV.323–4:

> Oh, I am dying! To what, my guest, are you leaving me!
> 'Guest' – that is all I may call you now, who have called you husband.[41]

Purcell reinstates much of the irony Tate tried to suppress.

The recitative before the Lament, far from simply foreshadowing once more the inexorable descent to the grave, seems to summarize the entire drama. Dido turns again to her confidante and to C minor ('Thy hand, Belinda'), descends into the Sorceress's black key of F minor ('darkness shades me'), and then, before retreating to G minor for the last time, grasps for her C major glory only to have it slip away ('More I would, but Death invades me').[42] Westrup has ably described the paradox of 'When I am laid in earth': though casting the climactic air in the utterly conventional mould of the Italian operatic lament, 'Purcell rises within narrow limits to monumental grandeur' (*Purcell*, p. 123). It also derives much splendour from its sheer inevitability. Throughout the opera, most of Dido's music sags under the weight of descending chromatics; her first air, also sung to a repeating bass, modulates to G minor. The grounds themselves are a

---

[41] *The Aeneid of Virgil*, trans. C. Day Lewis (London: Hogarth, 1952), p. 81.
[42] Compare Example 3, above.

deceptively naïve symbol for earth and the grave. The accompanying strings, which could have easily produced a maudlin effect, are an ironic reminder of the Sorceress's recitatives. The violins gradually rise to enfold the voice with weeping appoggiaturas, thereby overriding the unpleasant association with the witches and supplying the pathos Dido's melody assiduously avoids. As several writers have noted, the setting of 'ah!' (shown in Example 13) is astonishingly beautiful. Each of the previous melodic

Example 13. *Dido and Aeneas*: 'When I am laid in earth', bars 35–8

phrases has marked the arrival at the note D in the third bar of the ground with a dominant chord. Dido's simple, non-dominant decoration of the fifth scale degree recalls Aeneas's laboured and artificial exclamation in his second-act recitative: 'But ah! what language can I try'. Here, however, as appoggiaturas collide in the violins, the voice slides away into oblivion, releasing Dido from the chromatic chain that pulled her relentlessly to the Lament.

Purcell faced a dilemma from which only a handful of composers of musical tragedy have been able to escape: how to write a dénouement that neither disturbs the delicate balance between pathos and irony with unnecessary moralizing nor simply spins out the climactic masterpiece for sustained and therefore diminished effect. The final chorus, 'With drooping wings', avoids both traps and is therefore perhaps an even greater achievement than the Lament, as it transports the drama to another plane. The chorus echoes the pervasive descent of Dido's air, but the chromatics have abated. About mid-way through, in the passage given as Example 14, the second, less common form of the grief motif returns. The emotional crest is reached with the heart-stopping rests shown in Example 15. There in the alto part is the last statement of the familiar motif, now magically softened with an F♮ which a composer of more pedantic mind might well have left sharp for consistency's sake. With a single stroke, Purcell removes the sting of death.

Example 14. *Dido and Aeneas*: 'With drooping wings', bars 14–17 (strings omitted)

Example 15. *Dido and Aeneas*: 'With drooping wings', bars 26–30 (strings omitted)

Here the Tenbury manuscript ends, but the final item in the 1689 libretto is a *'Cupids Dance'*, in keeping with the sequence of air, chorus, and dance that closes the previous scenes. 'With drooping wings' seems an inappropriate accompaniment for dancers, unlike 'Fear no danger' in Act I, which is followed by the stage direction *'Dance this Cho. The Baske'*. Tate's libretto requires three other dances not found in the Tenbury score: in Act I, a *'Gittars Chacony'*, and in Act II, a *pas de deux* for *'Drunken Saylors'* as well as another *'Gittar Ground'*. None of these stage directions is found in the 1700 quarto of *Measure for Measure*, nor does that text mention the Cupids' Dance. But the Tenbury manuscript provides a tiny clue that the opera may have originally ended with a dance. 'With drooping wings' lacks a final double bar-line; all parts finish as does the first violin shown in Example 16. In manuscripts of the period, the ends of pieces or large sec-

Example 16. *Dido and Aeneas*: 'With drooping wings', bars 29–30, first violin

tions thereof are nearly always marked with a terminal flourish, an embroidered double or treble bar-line finished off with several tight turns.[43] Such a device is found in the Tenbury score at the end of Act II, scene i. Working on the assumption that the scribe attempted to make a diplomatic transcription of his source, one might conclude that the final folio or two – that is, the Cupids' Dance – had already been removed. As he marked the added accidentals in Belinda's arietta in Act I with natural signs (see Example 1), so the copyist may have signalled the incomplete state of the final act by leaving the chorus without a terminal flourish or even a closing bar-line.[44]

How does Dido die? The final ambiguity would seem to matter little in light of the tragic power of the music. Tate's decision to replace Virgil's bitter and violent end to Book IV with pathetic resignation would seem to rule out a spectacular suicide with Aeneas's sword, though earlier in the third act the Sorceress prophesies that Dido 'bleeds to Night, and *Carthage* Flames tomorrow'. Yet none of the main sources of the opera – the 1689 libretto, the 1700 play-book, or the Tenbury manuscript – includes a stage direction for her death. In *Brutus of Alba*, the Queen of Syracuse succumbs after a fit of insanity, recovering just long enough to realize that 'My malady at last has prov'd my Cure, / My Griefs at last have swell'd to that degree / To break my o're-charged Heart and give no Ease'. The final scene of the play is set in '*the Cell*', presumably the dead king's tomb discovered first in Act II. This evokes the disturbing image of the queen dying on Sychaeus's catafalque in Rubens's *Death of Dido*. A burial vault also figures prominently in the opera. As Dido begins her final recitative, '*Cupids* appear in the Clouds o're her Tomb'. The 1700 libretto does not include this important stage direction and also omits a line from the penultimate couplet. The final chorus is given thus:

> With drooping Wings you Cupids come,
> Soft and Gentle as her Heart,
> Keep here our Watch and never part.

'To scatter Roses on her Tomb' is deleted, implying that bars 11–14 were cut, thereby leaving the music two beats out but preserving the overall har-

---

[43] The double ending of the chorus would not appear to account for the anomaly, because even the second ending of the canzona in the overture is closed with a single bar-line.

[44] The word 'Finis' is written at the bottom of the last chorus, but in a much larger, perhaps different, hand.

monic sense. Gildon's removal of the funereal trappings leads to a startling conclusion: that Dido does not die. Absurd as this may seem, the absence of any reference to the tomb reinforces the allegorical links to the main plot of *Measure for Measure*, since Dido represents Isabella, who survives Angelo's lustful advances with her chastity intact.

If, as Buttrey argues, *Dido and Aeneas* was intended as a cautionary tale to remind King William of his responsibilities to his wife and his new kingdom, then for Queen Mary's counterpart to die at the end of the theatrical paean would have been the epitome of bad taste, even if portrayed by a schoolgirl 'unscarr'd by turning times' and isolated from the cynicism of court and theatre. If, on the other hand, the operatic queen were left to linger on the point of death during her lover's 'absence', the parallel would have been slightly less embarrassing. But as the nineties wore on and the king's absences became more frequent and protracted, a public performance of *Dido and Aeneas* would have become increasingly awkward politically, and after Mary's death in December 1694 it would have been unthinkable, since the tragic ending would have implied that William's neglect was in some way responsible for his wife's passing. For the heroine to survive in defiance of Virgil would disturb a modern audience more than a Restoration one, accustomed to such curiosities as *Romeo and Juliet* and *King Lear* with happy endings. Yet remove the fatal catastrophe, and *Dido* collapses into a harmless masque. While cold and rational history tells us that unadulterated, apotheosis-less tragic opera was unknown to seventeenth-century England, we cannot ignore our response to Purcell's miniature. It is tragic because Dido, wronged in love and crossed by fate, sings her own threnody. The composer approached the drama forthrightly with characteristic simplicity and a thorough understanding of Book IV of *The Aeneid*. Despite the laundered and starched libretto, the music restores Dido's obsessions, neuroses, even the sexual desire that Tate prudishly removed or clumsily transformed into heroic virtue. And most important of all, she dies through the music. Purcell must therefore bear the ultimate blame for the initial obscurity that greeted his masterpiece. Leaving aside the questions of the English attitude towards all-sung opera, the Chelsea schoolgirl performers, changing musical tastes, and theatre politics, the most obvious reason why *Dido and Aeneas* was not publicly performed during the composer's lifetime is that it was an affront rather than a compliment to the new monarchs.

6 Dioclesian

In early 1690 when the Theatre Royal managers decided to mount the first large musical work of the reign of William and Mary – indeed, the first new semi-opera since *Circe* of 1677 – they turned to a play written sixty-eight years earlier, Massinger and Fletcher's *The Prophetess*. A clear indication that *Dido and Aeneas* had caught the attention of the theatrical establishment at its otherwise inauspicious première in Chelsea the year before was their selection of Purcell as the sole composer for this ambitious operatic undertaking. *The Prophetess*, or *Dioclesian* as it is known in musical circles, is his first great achievement for the public theatre, and its success left him the indisputable master of the genre. In addition to Dryden's pompous vote of confidence proffered in the dedication to *Amphitryon* (see Chapter 4), the managers of the Theatre Royal rewarded the composer by commissioning two more semi-operas for the following seasons, *King Arthur* and *The Fairy-Queen*.

Dioclesian was a direct response to *Albion and Albanius*, but because England's first full-length opera was – to fair Albion's everlasting consternation – composed by a would-be Frenchman, a certain amount of jingoism has coloured scholars' regard for the two works. *Dioclesian* has been viewed as a salvo in a war of tastes, Purcell's attempt to blast Grabu and the French influence from the London stage in the hope of gaining Dryden's respect and collaborative pen. The operas should be compared, however, on less partisan grounds. Grabu's magnificent full score of 1687, handsomely printed and carefully corrected by hand, is followed four years later by the slimmer but also painstakingly produced and hand-corrected volume entitled *The Vocal and Instrumental Musick of the Prophetess, or The History of Dioclesian*.[1] That these are the only folio *partiture* printed in England in the seventeenth century is surely no coincidence. Purcell's reply also extends to details. The gigantic C major chaconne which ends the second act of *Albion and Albanius* is answered by Purcell's fifth-act ground in the same key. The foreigner's stylish choruses are matched by the Englishman's grand and uncharacteristically diatonic ones, complete with a French bassoon, the first ever in an English score. But did Purcell regard *Dioclesian* as an instrument of vindication, an extended lesson for Dryden on the true path to an English national opera? And was the late king's penchant for Frenchified opera still a bone

---

[1] For the locations of corrected copies, see the Purcell Society Edition, ix (rev. M. Laurie), xiii.

of contention in the anti-Gallic atmosphere of Williamite England? The document that sheds the most light on these questions is Purcell's dedication to the score itself.

The epistle, addressed to Charles Seymour, the Duke of Somerset, is a model of informed supplication.[2] After noting that poetry and painting have achieved a degree of perfection in England, Purcell attempts to reconcile the French and Italian forces reshaping his native musical style:

Musick is yet but in its Nonage, a forward Child, which gives hope of what it may be hereafter in *England*, when the Masters of it shall find more encouragement. 'Tis now learning *Italian*, which is its best Master, and studying a little of the *French* Air, to give it somewhat more of Gayety and Fashion. Thus being farther from the Sun, we are of later Growth than our Neighbour Countries, and must be content to shake off our Barbarity by degrees. The present Age seems already dispos'd to be refin'd, and to distinguish betwixt wild Fancy, and a just, numerous Composition.

This does not sound like a man who bore a grudge against the establishment for passing him over as composer for *Albion and Albanius*. And the veiled acknowledgement of the superiority of the art encouraged by Louis XIV ('Thus being farther from the Sun . . .') and the gracious plea for *les goûts réunis* do not strike me as ironic. Seen in the context of an age in which paying obeisance to French culture was no longer a public necessity, the preface is all the more extraordinary – but then it may not have been written by Purcell, since a manuscript copy in Dryden's hand survives.[3] Roswell G. Ham made a strong case for Dryden as ghost writer in an article published in 1935, and the *Dioclesian* preface has been duly added to the poet's canon by the editors of the new *Works*.[4] Although the published epistle has an unmistakably Drydenesque ring, and the rough draft may well be 'printer's copy, unique in its kind' (Ham, p. 1069), I believe Purcell had a role in its composition. Dryden's manuscript varies considerably from the printed version, chiefly in the deletion of two long passages, neither of which seems particularly well written. The first is a long-winded diatribe against painting, which would appear unworthy of Dryden if only for its serious internal inconsistencies; it contradicts the premise that visual art is one of the glories of the Restoration, remarking that painting 'is a dumb Lady, whose charmes are onely to the eye'. After suggesting that Dryden removed this passage for later expansion and

[2] Though he succeeded Halifax as Speaker of the Lords in 1690, Somerset was coolly received by William III because of his cordial relations with Princess Anne. The choice of dedicatee was not, therefore, merely a political expedient.
[3] British Library Stowe MS 755, fols. 34–35v.
[4] Ham, 'Dryden's Dedication for *The Music of the Prophetesse*, 1691', *Publications of the Modern Language Association*, 50 (1935), 1065–75; and *The Works of John Dryden*, XVII, 324–6, 482–4; Ham's argument that Dryden, not Betterton, was also responsible for the alterations of the play has not been generally accepted. See, for example, Laurie, 'Purcell's Stage Works', pp. 77–8.

refinement, Ham then has to admit that it does not accord well with the ideas expressed in the *Parallel betwixt Poetry and Painting* of 1695 ('Dryden's Dedication for *The Music of the Prophetesse*', p. 1072). The second cancelled passage, a particularly scathing and tasteless attack on inferior poets who have no ear for verse or music, was surely cut because of its churlishness. This is certainly one of Dryden's favourite hobby-horses, but not one so original or provocative that a composer such as Purcell could not also have ridden it.

The version of the dedication published in *The Works of John Dryden*, Vol. xvii, omits two brief passages that are of interest to musicians. The opening sentence of the quotation given above originally read, 'Musick is yet but in its Nonage: a prattling foreign child which rather gives hope of what it may be hereafter in England, than what it has hetherto produc'd . . .' This would have insulted both the older English composers like John Blow, who was still active, and the many continentals employed in London at the time. The writer's particular distaste for outlandish musicians bursts through at the words 'a prattling foreign child'. The other deletion (shown in my italics) is even more scurrilous: 'Thus being farther from the sun, we are of later growth, than our Neighbour Countryes; and must be content to shake off our barbarity by drgrees; *and leave the hedge notes of our homely Ancestours*.'[5] He wants it both ways: on the one hand, English music is 'studying a little of the French air', while on the other, it is a 'prattling foreign child'. The writer was a bitter man, struggling to keep his contempt for his 'homely Ancestours' beneath the surface. These internal inconsistencies suggest a collaboration. Dryden may have set down Purcell's ideas or worked the composer's notes into acceptable panegyric, then edited out the rough spots. Alternatively, Purcell, who was behind schedule in producing the printed score and worried that his subscribers would be chagrined by pirated editions, invited Dryden to write a dedication.[6] But upon reading the draft, he asked the poet to soften the passages that seemed to condemn the entire English musical tradition. In the light of Dryden's generally low opinion of English composers, the second alternative is the likelier, though literary critics might find it hard to explain the muddled state of the original draft. Its caustic tone would seem to fit the post-1688 Dryden better, but only because so little is known of Purcell's character.

Albion and Albanius

While he may have felt no prejudice against foreigners, Purcell surely had equivocal feelings about Louis Grabu. In 1668, the Catalan's appointment

---

[5] 'Hedge' is somewhat obscure here, but the *OED* preserves the writer's probable meaning: 'Done, performed, produced, worked under a hedge, in by-ways or clandestinely, as . . . hedge-notes'.

[6] For an account of the publication difficulties, see the Purcell Society Edition, ix (rev. Laurie), x.

as Master of the King's Violins had caused resentment among some English musicians.[7] And his dominance of native theatre music during the exciting seventies seems to have been thwarted only by Locke's rude gifts for the stage and outspoken contempt for continental music. Years later, in 1683, when Grabu was recalled from Paris to collaborate with Dryden on *Albion and Albanius* (see Chapter 7), Purcell may well have seethed, though he must have known the decision was essentially political and was made at the highest level. Was Grabu a force and a talent to be reckoned with? Most modern critics have summarily dismissed him as 'a pallid Frenchman', a 'caricature' of Lully (Dent, *Foundations*, p. 166), 'an inept composer', and the object of Dryden's 'egregiously misplaced judgment' (Moore, *Henry Purcell & the Restoration Theatre*, p. 71). For this largely unfair assessment one has mostly to thank the cocky Pelham Humfrey, who, as Pepys reports, had become more French than the French and thus thought himself superior to everyone, especially to Grabu, who 'understands nothing, nor can play on any instrument, and so cannot compose' (*Diary*, 15 November 1667). Grabu's reputation was further pummelled by an anonymous doggerel rhymer of 1685, who found his surname inherently funny. Here is a verse of a famous ballad called 'The Raree-show':

> *Bayes*, thou wouldst have thy skill thought universal,
>> Tho' thy dull ear be to musick untrue;
> Then whilst we strive to confute the Rehearsal,
>> Prithee learn thrashing of Monsieur *Grabu*.[8]

What the detractors of the French composer have failed to point out is that the limping poem is supposed to be from the actors who had been temporarily put out of work by a 'play' set entirely to music and therefore not requiring their services. Its purpose is made clear by the second verse:

> Each actor on the stage his luck bewailing,
>> Finds that his loss is infallibly true;
> *Smith*, *Nokes*, and *Leigh* in a Feaver with railing,
>> Curse poet, painter, and Monsieur *Grabu*.

Twentieth-century critics have preferred to repeat these colourful and sensational attacks on Grabu rather than look closely at the score of *Albion and Albanius* itself, whose admittedly daunting use of French clef-groupings should not have prevented their judging the quality of the 320 pages of music contained therein.

The editors of Vol. xv of the new Dryden edition are the first modern commentators to point out that there is not the slightest hint in contemporary documents that the failure of *Albion and Albanius* was its com-

[7] See *The Works of John Dryden*, xv, ed. Earl Miner et al., 336–7.
[8] Bayes is of course Dryden. The complete ballad was reprinted by Hawkins in *A General History*, II, 707; see also Highfill, *A Biographical Dictionary*, s.v. Grabu.

poser's fault (*The Works,* xv, 343–61). But Grabu will never have many champions. His misfortune was to have created the only kind of opera he could, a *tragédie lyrique.* Dent's hatred of the work is tinged with glee, while at the other extreme Zimmerman's recent reassessment is a model of musicological diplomacy that clears Grabu of all charges of ineptitude but falls short of a vindication, concluding that 'As performable opera, the work is probably irretrievable.'[9]

Albion and Albanius is of course an allegory, 'a Tory history of the Restoration period' (Hume, *Development,* p. 363). Albion is Charles II and Albanius the Duke of York, later James II. In the preface to the 1687 score, Grabu writes that the plot 'was too thin a Veil for the Moral not to shine through the Fable'. This is a sizeable understatement, because after Act I Dryden, the master of political satire and ingenious weaver of subtle allusions to contemporary events in his plays, practically dispenses with the tedious metaphor. For example, in the second act Zelota tells Pluto that

> Y'have all forgot
> To forge a Plot
> In seeming Care of *Albion*'s Life;
> Inspire the Crowd
> With Clamours loud
> T'involve his Brother and his Wife (II.i.84–9).

This is simply twaddle about the Duke of York, Catherine of Braganza, and the Popish Plot. And in Act III, when Asebia explains that Tyranny and the other villains have 'brib'd the Lawyers tongue, / And then destroy'd the Law's', any remaining shreds of the 'thin Veil' are finally blown away. Dryden originally planned the first act of the opera as a French-style prologue to the semi-opera *King Arthur*, which helps explain the extreme transparentness of the allegory. But for reasons explored below in Chapter 7, the main piece had to be deferred for six years. To fill out the allegorical part of the entertainment, Dryden added two more acts in the same vein, creating, as if by chance, a full-length all-sung opera. This change of plan is reflected by the marked difference between the first act, a set of undramatic tableaux which depict events leading to and including the Restoration, and the following scenes, persuasive enactments of Charles's political tribulations. Guided by Hermes, the king stumbles through several crises, which are treated more as external irritations than as tests of character. Albion's behaviour is exemplary rather than heroic, and unfortunately for the composer, the story lacks internal conflict, the lifeblood of good opera.

To locate the best music, one need only look to the most dramatic scene, II.ii. Here Albion must decide whether to send his brother into exile. The

[9] *The Works of John Dryden*, xv, ed. Zimmerman et al., 355.

king's grand three-verse soliloquy shows restrained frustration. Hermes descends into the gloom, faced with the difficult task of consoling Albion and at the same time counselling Albanius's banishment. Grabu delivers the bitter pill with a shift from plain recitative to lush *accompagnato*. When the messenger warns the king of dire consequences should his brother remain (shown in Example 1), the music conveys an agitation worthy of Purcell. The jarring clash in bar 13, an extravagance that Grabu rarely allowed himself, punctuates Hermes's cutting message. This passage, indeed the whole scene, is remarkable because the music responds instantly to the changing moods of the verse, while retaining an elegant homogeneity. Though the word-setting is seldom this good, the opera is not as execrable as Dent and Moore would have us believe. And Purcell must have viewed it with more envy than contempt. If nothing else, *Albion and Albanius* spurred his dramatic muse. While perhaps scorning the blandness and obsessive correctness of Grabu's instrumental part-writing, he must also, as a consummate contrapuntalist, have marvelled at the complete control in the five-part symphonies, whose inner voices show a suavity rivalling the finest continental music of the day. Purcell surely realized that Grabu did not attempt to interpret Dryden's rich verse with

Example 1. *Albion and Albanius*: Louis Grabu, passage in II.ii (pp. 150–2)

Example 1 (cont.)

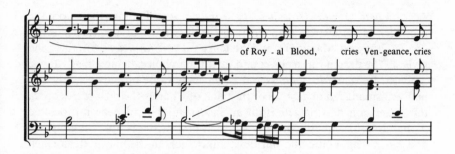

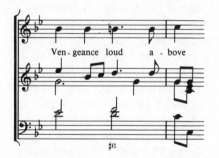

elaborate melismas and complex rhythms, because the foreigner's experience was limited mostly to setting a language which has no tonic accent.

The opera may be irretrievable, but it was sunk by political circumstances, not artistic incompetence. The laureate's folly in writing *Albion
and Albanius* was that, considering the turmoil England had endured
from the Exclusion Crisis to the Rye House Plot, any political allegory was
bound to misfire. The Duke of Monmouth's rebelliousness was no secret,
and the absence from the opera of his direct counterpart was dictated as
much by the unpredictability of current affairs as by deference to the king.

Would Charles reinstate his illegitimate son? Would the succession pass smoothly to the Duke of York? The sketchiness of the plot and its simple and direct reflections of the royal brothers permitted Dryden a great deal of latitude, retrospective as well as prophetic. And Charles's untimely death in the midst of final rehearsals required only 'the addition of twenty or thirty lines, in the Apotheosis of *Albion*', to make the opera 'entirely of a Piece'.[10] Lully's *tragédies lyriques* are also allegorical, but Quinault had leisure to work within a much more stable theatre of events. *Albion and Albanius* was doomed, whether sooner by Monmouth's Rebellion, which came to a head during the week of the opera's première, or later by the Glorious Revolution.

The Prophetess

According to Downes (*Roscius Anglicanus*, p. 42), Thomas Betterton, the producer of Dryden's failed opera as well as most of the earlier semi-operas, adapted Massinger and Fletcher's *The Prophetess* for the 1690 revival. The drama was a clever and fortuitous choice, being a ready-made reply to *Albion and Albanius* and an uncanny satire on the decadent and badly mismanaged final years of the reign of Charles II. In Dryden's opera the succession had passed from an incorruptible and heaven-protected monarch to his equally virtuous brother, despite the people's ingratitude and much democratic and puritanical mischief. In the play, a debauched emperor and two aspiring ones try to reconcile problems in the succession with the help of a blowzy prophetess. Here is the plot in a nutshell. The soldier Diocles avenges the murder of the old emperor, Numerianus, and for his trouble is awarded half the empire by the new emperor, Charinus. But Diocles, convinced that glory must be tempered with humility, abdicates in favour of his nephew, Maximinian. None of these characters, noble or otherwise, acquits himself very well. Delphia is only a second-rate prophetess, who makes prognostications under the influence of alcohol and indigestion. Diocles is a fop and a fool, whose humility is forced upon him by stratagem. He cushions his return to rural life by purchasing a great farm in Lombardy and equipping it 'like an Emperor'. Charinus seems barely aware of the political manoeuvring swirling round him, and Maximinian, driven by jealousy and ambition, tries to assassinate Diocles to prevent the possibility of his reclaiming the throne.

As shown in Figure 2, Charinus, a cowardly and procrastinating king, reflects the tired and bewildered Charles II, who watched with feigned detachment as James and Monmouth vied for accession. Diocles and Maximinian, also in avuncular relationship, contend for half the empire. The lawful heir, Diocles, can thus represent James II, whose reign was

[10] Postscript to the preface to *Albion*.

Fig. 2

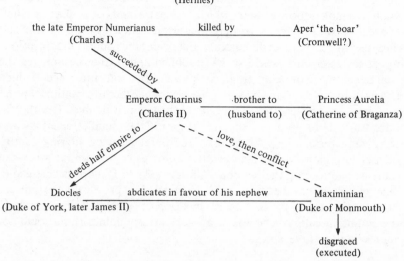

Delphia, the prophetess
(Hermes)

the late Emperor Numerianus ————— killed by ————— Aper 'the boar'
(Charles I)   (Cromwell?)

succeeded by

Emperor Charinus   ·brother to   Princess Aurelia
(Charles II)   (husband to)   (Catherine of Braganza)

deeds half empire to   *love, then conflict*

Diocles   abdicates in favour of his nephew   Maximinian
(Duke of York, later James II)   (Duke of Monmouth)

disgraced
(executed)

hardly secure, while the ambitious Maximinian, his tenuous claim to the throne forfeit because of treachery, is Monmouth. This happy coincidence also applies to other characters. Hermes, in the opera Albion's protector and always in the thick of things, is satirized by Delphia, the central personage who controls the action. The satire extends to events as well. In Act V, Maximinian's speech ridiculing Charinus for his weak response to the murder of the old emperor, who might represent Charles I, could easily have been heard as a reminder of royalist inactivity during the Commonwealth. In the same scene, Aurelia quells Maximinian's fear of being deposed with the suggestion that her brother Charinus be assassinated, a sharp reminder of Catherine of Braganza's alleged role in the Popish Plot. This gallery of flawed characters is a welcome antidote to Dryden's nauseously patriotic *Albion and Albanius*, and though the parallels are wholly coincidental, Betterton intensified the send-up of the royal opera by careful editing.

In his study of Beaumont and Fletcher, Arthur C. Sprague expresses surprise that, except for the insertions of the inaugural songs in Act II and the masque in Act V, Betterton's alterations are almost entirely limited to fastidious verbal emendations, wherein the general replaces the specific, the vague the vivid, the figurative the literal, and so forth.[11] The lightness of revision has been overlooked by other modern commentators, who follow Montague Summers's erroneous remark that the play required a

[11] *Beaumont and Fletcher on the Restoration Stage*, pp. 154–7.

'drastic curtailment of the dialogue to admit of a number of songs and dances'.[12] *The Prophetess* has not been radically cut, and as Sprague remarks, 'The very fact that so much of the original dialogue was retained unaltered makes those changes which do occur stand out in sharper relief' (*Beaumont and Fletcher*, p. 157). Betterton edited with an ear for late seventeenth-century sentimentality, but even the tiniest modifications reveal a greater purpose. First, he simplified and further besmirched the character of Maximinian (that is, Monmouth) and attempted to hide Diocles's humble origins by surgically removing the information that he is 'a man most miserable, / Of no rank' (I.ii), 'a private man' (II.iii), who once 'Liv'd both poor and obscure' (IV.vi). Other smaller deletions and word-substitutions help to intensify the parallelism by altering contradictory terminology. For example, the ironic aside in I.iii that 'wise men must be had to prop the Republick', a reference to Diocles, is changed to read 'wise men must be had to prop the State'. And practically the only cut in the entire second act is Diocles's mention of 'The fruitfull Vineyard of the commonwealth'. If he was meant to represent James II, he could not very well utter these words.[13]

The Music

Despite the ready-made satire, *The Prophetess* would seem an undesirable choice for operatic treatment. The plot does not lend itself well to inserted masques, either of the integral sort found in *The Indian Queen* or the embellishing and awe-inspiring ones of *King Arthur*. The hand that deftly sharpened the implicit parody wielded an axe when opening up Fletcher's story to receive Purcell's music. Diocles's execution of the regicide Aper thus afforded an occasion for a solemn, though nevertheless tasteless, celebration (II[iii]). The hero's battlefield victory, engineered by Delphia's shoddy magic, also provided an opportunity for distinctly heroic music (IV[iv]). This shameless interlarding bothered the author of *A Comparison Between the Two Stages*:

How ridiculous is it in that Scene in the *Prophetess*, where the great Action of the *Drama* stops, and the chief Officers of the Army stand still with their Swords drawn to hear a Fellow Sing – *Let the Soldiers rejoice* – 'faith in my mind 'tis as unreasonable as if a Man shou'd call for a Pipe of Tobacco just when the Priest and his Bride are waiting for him at the Altar.[14]

---

[12] *The Restoration Theatre* (London: Kegan Paul, 1934), p. 234.

[13] Buttrey gives *Dioclesian* a different political interpretation (see 'The Evolution of English Opera between 1656 and 1695', esp. p. 243), noticing a connection between Diocles's accession by defeating Aper and William's deposition of James II. But even in the operatic version, Diocles is so offensive that to represent William without affront his character would have had to be extensively reconstructed.

[14] *A Comparison Between the Two Stages* (1702), ed. Staring B. Wells (Princeton: Princeton Univ. Press, 1942), p. 30.

He should have known that such lapses of verisimilitude are endemic to almost all operatic works. But the adaptation did present one insoluble problem that accounts for the major weakness of the score. *Dioclesian*, unlike the composer's other semi-operas and nearly all the tragic extravaganzas, has no sympathetic character upon which Purcell could focus expressive music. For example, in Act III the celebrated song 'What shall I do to show how much I love her?' charms the mean and vindictive Aurelia, but, as explained below, this was a miscalculation: unlike Zempoalla or Bonduca, Aurelia is an antagonist beyond redemption, not a tragic heroine. The score is of high if uneven quality and Purcell was certainly justified in publishing it, but the music makes us feel nothing for any of the speaking characters.

The most unsettling of the masques, in Act II, is called 'highly criminal' for being a 'business independent of' the drama (*A Comparison Between the Two Stages*, p. 30). In the original, this scene is the climax of the first half of the play and the point from which the dialogue assumes a decidedly cynical tone. For nearly two acts, Diocles, with unacknowledged help from his nephew Maximinian, has been crisscrossing the countryside killing every swine he can lay his hands on, an unthinking response to Delphia's prophecy that he will become emperor after slaying a mighty boar ('Imperator eris Romae, cum Aprum grandem interfeceris'). The befuddled hog-butcherer finally solves the riddle when he receives word that Charinus has offered a reward for the head of Volutius Aper, captain of the guard, who is suspected of murdering the late king. In the second scene of Act II, which relies on a stage property for its effect (as do all the best scenes of the play), Aper enters with the royal litter, claiming to bear the 'sick' emperor. Diocles throws open the curtains to reveal the body; guided by Delphia, who hovers overhead in a chariot, he slays Aper. This stunning action needs to be followed quickly by Diocles's pompous exultation and his too-hasty acceptance of the senate's offer of half the empire. But following a cue in the 1622 text for 'Musick', Betterton tips in Purcell's lengthy succession of instrumental prelude, bass solo, chorus, soprano solo, trumpet symphony, duet, chorus, countertenor solo, chorus, trumpet ritornel, trio for men, chorus, ritornel again, and another countertenor solo, ending with a miniature verse anthem.

Should the music celebrate the death of Aper or underscore his vilification? Should it solemnize Diocles's coronation or rejoice in it? Or should it lament the death of Numerianus instead? Perhaps Purcell and the librettist, presumably Betterton, could have reconciled these conflicting emotions had they been able to stimulate our memories of an honourable or tragic victim. But the music must salute the unsavoury Diocles without much conviction and perfunctorily mourn Numerianus, who died before the play began. The masque is a lament without object. The words of the opening air and chorus reflect an unfocussed point of view. Diocles is hailed for ridding the land of Aper, an act that fills the singer's heart with joy; but at the same time the villain is denounced and the emperor's funeral commanded, all in eight lines of text set to a mere twenty-four bars of music. After a solemn prelude in G major, the bass line strides majestically downward to depict 'great' Diocles's 'courageous' act. Here Purcell recalled Locke's favourite way of expressing violent sentiments – a chain of descending thirds (compared in Example 2a–c). After a choral paean to the

Example 2a. *Dioclesian*: 'Great Diocles the boar has kill'd', bars 24–8 (strings omitted)

Command? Down, down, down, down the blood-y vil-lain falls

Example 2b. *Cupid and Death*: Matthew Locke, from the first entry

If a warm fit thus pull him down

Example 2c. *The Empress of Morocco*: Matthew Locke, 'Masque of Orpheus'

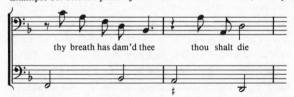

thy breath has dam'd thee thou shalt die

gods ('Sing Iô's') which replies irrelevantly to a call for funeral rites, a shift is made to G minor for the soprano air 'Charon the peaceful shade invites'. Moore assumes that this dirge is addressed to Aper and thus shows 'sympathy for the slain tyrant, an indication that characterization is irrelevant' (*Henry Purcell & the Restoration Theatre*, p. 138). But it is obviously offered to Numerianus. The song includes most of Purcell's G minor clichés – a tetrachord bass, a sighing vocal line, and grinding clashes involving the leading-note. The opening passage, shown in Example 3, is a study in the avoidance of perfect cadences in the tonic, and the progression from bars 3 to 4 (ii6–i) is one of the oddest in all Purcell – as if the obligatory modulation to the relative major has happened before the piece begins. Purcell hints that the shades enveloping the slain emperor are not as restful as the lyric would have us believe: 'peaceful' is uttered immediately after the abrupt abandonment of the dominant in bars 10 and 11 and then repeated two bars later with the simultaneous sounding of both forms of the sixth scale degree (see Example 3).

Example 3. *Dioclesian*: 'Charon the peaceful shade invites', bars 1–15

The following trumpet symphony is brilliantly Italianate, but the tempo marking '*Very slow*' for the first five bars puts me in mind of the aching arms of the extras who portrayed the 'chief Officers of the Army', lining the sides of the stage 'with their Swords drawn'. In the succeeding series of C major choruses and heroic arias, Purcell drew heavily on *Albion and Albanius*. This is among the grandest, cleanest, most 'correct' music he ever wrote. Fully staged with a large chorus, Roman armour and weapons glinting in brilliant lighting, trumpets well in tune, and a countertenor able to bring a *Heldentenor* quality to 'Let the soldiers rejoice', the effect would be awe-inspiring. But in a concert performance, one might conclude that Lully handled ceremonies such as this with more style and restraint.

With these hollowly heroic lines behind him, Purcell was able to return to a more characteristic tone, one that Dent's French acquaintance described as 'toujours romantique et sentimental, toujours en mode mineur' (*Foundations*, p. 203 n.). The countertenor aria 'With dances and songs', a low-key, sombre celebration of Diocles's enthronement, is preceded by an intricate accompanied recitative, the like of which was not heard again until the fifth act of Durfey's *1 Don Quixote* (1694). The aria itself, composed on a ground (the first of four ostinato pieces in *Dioclesian*), is hypnotic yet, except in the closing symphony for recorders, somewhat laboured. Admittedly, my view of the song is coloured by the questionable part-writing of the passage shown in Example 4. Not wishing to play Burney's game of tracking down crudities, I should point out that the rules of composition were sometimes loosened for pieces on grounds.

The final chorus of the scene, 'Let the priests and processions the hero attend', is Purcell at his best, and with different words it might be an excerpt from an anthem. The richly dissonant counterpoint, so lacking in the earlier choruses, is here abundant. And the Handelian 'ascent to

Example 4. *Dioclesian*: 'Since the toils and the hazards of war's at an end', bars 66–8

Let the hus-bands and true lov - ers greet 'em

heaven', with rising scales and unexpected arrival in E♭ major, is the first masterstroke of the score (see Example 5).

After the interminable interruption, the soldiers can sheathe their swords and the drama continue. Diocles, praised for honour and courage in the masque and having renamed himself Dioclesianus, accepts Charinus's offer of the princess Aurelia, while conveniently discarding Delphia's ugly niece Drusilla. In some 'business' added by Betterton, the prophetess shows displeasure by sending forth 'a dreadful monster', which disintegrates like a Chinese dragon into a Dance of Furies. The music required

Example 5. *Dioclesian*: 'Let the priests with processions the hero attend', bars 124–9
(strings omitted)

Purcell's printer to apply an impressive amount of ink to the page, most of it for the demisemiquavers of the sweeping roulades. The elaborate notation might be seen as a French and particularly Lullian influence, but, as in an antimasque dance, the radically different sections were probably carefully tailored to fit Priest's grotesque choreography. (Not dissimilar are the Echo Dance of Furies and Witches' Dance in *Dido and Aeneas*.) The 'Soft Musick that's plaid just before the Dance of Furies' is noteworthy because it was closely tied to the stage action. The prelude begins innocently, almost gropingly in a sweet C major, but as the monster creeps from the shadows and is seen to be horrid, the music becomes more chromatic and tortuous, mixing flats and sharps in equal numbers. Here Purcell drew for inspiration not on Grabu, but on the 'hedge notes' of his 'homely Ancestours'. The beginning of Locke's extraordinary overture to the 1674 *Tempest* probably served as model: the one continues with a depiction of a violent storm, while the other leads to a furious dance.

The second act of Fletcher's play ends with a dead march as Numerianus's body is carried off, but Purcell replaced the march with an instrumental version of 'Let the soldiers rejoice'. The next item in the 1691 full score is the magnificent canon on a ground for two recorders and basso continuo, played 'in the third Act', though precisely where is difficult to say. Perhaps it underscored Maximinian's soliloquy which opens the first scene, but the canon drips with pathos while the speech burns with envy for Diocles.

Act III is largely devoted to a counter-plot in which uncle and nephew become rivals for Aurelia.[15] The centrepiece is the well-known song 'What shall I do to show how much I love her?' The fatuous lyric, supposedly Maximinian's, is designed to lure the vindictive princess away from his uncle and forms part of Delphia's plan to persuade the wayward Diocles to return to Drusilla. Since the prophetess has already prepared Aurelia for Maximinian's advances, the musical philtre is redundant. Purcell seems to have badly misjudged the dramatic context; the music is far too good for its purpose, namely, to allow the puppet Maximinian to stand 'gazing on the Princess all the time of the Song', while Aurelia is ready to run to his arms anyway. The comic hyperbole of the lyric seems to have been overlooked or ignored: 'What shall I do to show how much I love her? / How many millions of sighs can suffice?' Enhanced by the crystalline melody and languishing symphony for oboes, Aurelia's artificially induced passion suddenly acquires an heroic-play unreality. Purcell probably replaced the inappropriate song for a revival with 'When first I saw the bright Aurelia's eyes', published three years later in the second book of *Thesaurus*

---

[15] This act also includes the Chair Dance, thrown in as a whimsical display of Delphia's magical powers; it is mentioned in the prologue to *The Fairy-Queen*. See Dent, *Foundations*, pp. 198–9.

Musicus.[16] In A major, an acceptable key for the tonal scheme, this fine song has an entirely different character, being a virtuoso display piece for the singer Mrs Ayliff, its sentiments of 'piercing joy' and 'pleasing pain' being only skin deep. One could sit back and admire the singer's skill and even tolerate the would-be lovers' sexual attraction for each other. But the original song, simple and strophic, draws us unwillingly into their illicit love, penetrating the heart but not the understanding. Caught between a desire to express an intense, one-dimensional passion and a subtle, complex, and above all irresolute plot, Purcell removed one of his greatest inspirations.

The first three acts of *The Prophetess* are almost completely free of the heroic bombast certain to induce rigor mortis in modern audiences. But even the best of the Beaumont–Massinger–Fletcher plays seem an act too long. Here it is the fourth, in which the tedious sub-plot is summarized in dumb show and by a chorus. Betterton recast these time-saving devices as straight dialogue, a piece of hack work that would make the 1690 version largely unacceptable to a discriminating modern audience. The following scene includes another elaborate discovery and more music. In the opera, Charinus, Maximinian and Aurelia have been captured by an invading army, with Delphia controlling the battle in order to humiliate Diocles, who is thus seen by his soldiers to be more effective in combat with pigs than with Persians. The semi-emperor finally submits to the termagant and repents of his perfidy. Had he not done so, the prophetess assures him, she would have driven Aurelia to suicide, underscoring the threat by revealing the tomb intended for the princess, complete with her likeness. The image sends Diocles once again into forbidden rapture; as he approaches her monument, the same 'Soft Musick' that preceded the Dance of Furies in Act II is played. Purcell even asked the printer to reproduce the piece note for note in the 1691 score.[17] The repeat of the sinister prelude again provokes apprehension, but in a proto-Hitchcock *coup de théâtre* the tomb explodes with a puff into a Dance of Butterflies. If the treble and bass parts were played by themselves, the dance would be a perfect specimen of harmonic and contrapuntal regularity. But the inner parts provide delightfully incorrigible suspensions, appoggiaturas, added sixths, and other seasonings, as if Purcell spilt the entire contents of the pepper-pot into this one piece. The butterflies, like the monster in Act II, are not quite what they seem.

Chastened, Diocles is allowed a routine victory over the Persians, which

---

[16] 'A New Song in the *Prophetess*, or the History of *Dioclesian*, Sung in the Third Act', the fourth scene of which is the only possible location for vocal music. The song was also printed in *The Gentleman's Journal* for December 1693.

[17] The extravagant redundancy may be a gibe at Grabu's score of *Albion and Albanius*, in which paper-saving rubrics indicate multiple uses for some instrumental pieces – for example, 'The AYRE for the Gods of the *Floods* is to be played betwixt the Act[s], Page 167'.

is celebrated with a brave trumpet song and chorus. The coronation music of the second act was muted by the presence of a dead king awaiting a much-needed burial, but the fourth-act paean is untainted. Purcell elevates the key to D major, and the acclamations of 'Great Diocleslan' are not ironic. The countertenor air 'Sound Fame, thy brazen trumpet' cannot vie with its cousin in *The Fairy-Queen*, 'Thus the gloomy world', but to obscure its surprising delicateness with a performance of too much bravura would be a mistake; 'Let all rehearse', the chorus to which the air leads, has enough of this sort of thing. The closest Diocles comes to being ennobled by music is at the setting of the lines given in Example 6, for which Purcell interrupts the heroic triple-metre chorus with a shift to D minor for nine bars of unexpected solemnity. The exotic and mysterious word 'embalm' is depicted by third-related major chords, in a manner reminiscent of the phrase 'And the voice of the turtle' in the anthem *My beloved spake* (z 28). This passage is no mere formality, but foreshadows Diocles's soon-to-be-acquired vulnerability.

Example 6. *Dioclesian*: 'Let all rehearse', bars 110–17 (strings omitted)

As if nudged by Purcell's exalted music, the action leaves its earthy foundations and takes flight into the realms of heroic drama. With sickly magnanimity, Diocles abdicates in favour of his nephew Maximinian, who is immediately racked by fears that he may be deposed as easily as he was enthroned, a conflict left unresolved even at the end of the play. The second scene of Act V is set in Lombardy, where peasants, prompted by Delphia, offer Diocles and Drusilla an entertainment upon their arrival at the rural retreat. Purcell's Country Dance, replacing the song for a spirit who sings from a well in the original version, is an especially felicitous piece. The simple bass, rocking from tonic to subdominant in imitation of rustic music, supports a graceful, lilting melody, joined in thirds and sixths by the second violins. The tranquillity is disturbed only by the viola's insistence on a turning figure with a gamy F♮, shown in Example 7, bars 2 and

Example 7. *Dioclesian*: Country Dance, bars 1–8

6. The dance needs to be considered in context. Delphia, who becomes increasingly agitated during the performance, stops the music about midway. When Diocles protests, the prophetess replies, 'I am only careful of your safety. Be not disturb'd my Son, sit down again. [To the country folk] And now, finish your Dance.' Unseen by Diocles, Maximinian and Aurelia have entered at a distance, determined to assassinate the former emperor. One of the best strokes of the play is the vitiation of the idyllic dénouement by the only real threat to Diocles's life. On the surface all appears peaceful, but the viola signals trouble brewing within. The dance captures the irony far more effectively than spoken dialogue could hope to do.

The Masque

The plot draws to a close with heroic-play predictability, Diocles trying to reason with his would-be assassins, whose hands are stayed only after a flaming vision in the heavens frightens them into begging forgiveness. Unquestioningly, he accepts their apology and asks Delphia to serve up an entertainment fit for an emperor. The famous pastoral masque follows, forty-five minutes of continuous music and dance, in the early eighteenth century one of Purcell's most popular stage works. Except for an occasional thrust at politicians in general and a wry reference to Diocles's dutiful and unenthusiastic courting of Drusilla, it has little connection with the play itself; and Purcell's refined and delicate music must have been all but overwhelmed by the scenic flummery. The setting is 'a delightful valley', the conceit is Love's taming of an ill-tempered Jove, and the principal event is the latter's appearance early in the masque when a huge machine descends, filling practically the whole stage 'from the Frontispiece . . . to the further end of the House'. The machine itself comprised four separate stages, stair-stepped toward the back where was depicted 'the Pallace of the Sun . . . terminated with a glowing Cloud, on which is a Chair of State, all of Gold, the Sun breaking through the Cloud, and making a Glory about it'. The five main entries took place, first, on the stage proper, then successively on each higher level of the machine. Instead of accumulating singers and dancers during the masque for a grand finale, the progressively smaller platforms allowed for fewer and fewer performers. Thus, the concluding chaconne 'Triumph victorious Love', which a modern stage director might use as an excuse to build to a climax involving the entire cast, was sung by a countertenor, tenor, and bass, placed high in the clouds near the back of the stage. The effect was more lofty than overpowering.

As the masque opens, the assembled speaking cast sits attentively at either side of the forestage, while Cupid calls to sylvan supernumeraries who respond chorally from behind the scene. In a gently swinging air in C major, 'Let the Graces and Pleasures repair', the soloist announces that the celebration is designed for the 'blest pair', presumably Maximinian and Aurelia, news that should have cast a pall over the whole affair. But a bacchanal and a sylvan, both basses, begin the revels with a rollicking duet. The mood and mode change abruptly from the jollity of C major to a sombre prelude for strings and oboes in C minor, during which the mighty machine descended leisurely to the stage, bearing Jove, here in his true heliacal form. In the following chorus, 'Behold O mighty'st of gods', Purcell painted with broad strokes, avoiding the chiselled minuscules characteristic of the music intended for individuals. Even at the setting of

> The gay, the sad,
> The grave, the glad,
> The youthful, and the old,
> All meet as at the day of doom,

the opposites blur into one grand sweep, only 'gay' being slightly decorated in the soprano part. This passage seems to disprove the theory of key associations, since 'gay' is set to a B♭ major chord, 'sad' to F major, 'grave' to C minor, 'glad' to G minor, 'youthful' to E♭ major, and 'doom' coincides with an important cadence in G major. Purcell was, however, neither pedantic nor unsubtle, and, as explained below, the tonal scheme of *Dioclesian* conforms to his usual procedure.

Two trumpets then join the strings for the C major Paspe, which provided music for the first entry dance, executed on the stage in front of the machine by an unspecified number of Heroes. Much of the masque and indeed the whole opera is in C major, so the shift to A minor for the soprano duet 'Oh the sweet delights of love' is a significant event. One of Purcell's most seductive pieces, it ranks with 'Two daughters of this aged stream' in *King Arthur* in sheer wickedness. Suddenly the one-dimensional characters of the pasteboard Arcadia spring to life. In the 1690 play-book the lyric begins '*Ah* the sweet Delights . . .' Purcell's preference for 'Oh' is important, since he typically set the exclamations in different ways. 'Ah' is often a more potent utterance, associated with death, resignation, or *le petit mort*, and is usually sung to a quick rising figure, as later in the dialogue 'Tell me why'. 'Oh', by contrast, is in the dramatic music more overtly sexual and expresses intense desire rather than the consummation of passion. This is often depicted with longer descending melismas, or elaborate treatment is avoided, allowing the singer to convey the baser emotion without cumbersome artifice. Through this tiny emendation the composer was better able to achieve the panting effect of the opening phrase, which forms the refrain of the rondeau.

The next entry is performed on the first stage of the machine, the key shifting from A minor to D major for the bacchanals, who sing the duet 'Make room', a boisterous announcement of the entrance of their leader.[18] Purcell probably wanted something other than a hearty, drunken welcome for the god of wine, since the oboes are asked to 'play soft' when he appears. Perhaps Bacchus should begin tentatively, as if nursing a hangover, gradually falling into the raucous spirit of the scene. Near the end of the entry the chorus observe impertinently that Jove should fully approve of their behaviour, since he himself 'gain'd Heav'n by love and good drinking'.

After the bacchanal, one of Cupid's followers sings the strophic air in D

---

[18] According to the 1690 quarto, the entry should begin with a dance for two couples. In the score, however, the duet and chorus open the entry and are followed by the Dance for Bacchanals. Laurie ('Purcell's Stage Works', p. 79) suggests that Purcell himself may have penned the additional lines of text for Bacchus not found in the play-book.

minor 'Still I'm wishing', which reflects Diocles's supposed desire for Drusilla. The song is rather stodgy, and the momentum of the masque is temporarily lost. Like 'What shall I do' in Act III, it was probably replaced in a revival by a piece published in *The Gentleman's Journal* (December 1693), 'Since from my dear Astrea's sight', also in D minor and described in another source as being 'Sung in the last Act'.[19] The replacement is simpler and in a more direct, intimate style. Though the text expresses essentially the same sentiments as 'Still I'm wishing', it mentions no member of the cast, the poet substituting the all-purpose 'Astrea' for Drusilla. The new lyric is laden with purple images, and Purcell set them to the usual clichés; but in the second part of the air in particular these stock gestures are arrayed for splendid effect. The melody leaps up tortuously at the line 'with weeping eyes, / And bleeding heart I lie', much in the manner of similarly emotive passages in later pieces.[20] The song literally dies away to nothing with drooping, off-beat repetitions of the final word. When copying this piece into the Guildhall Library song-book, the composer was apparently seized by a brilliant afterthought. The bass, replacing a long, harmonically straightforward descent at the end, rings the changes at the first mention of 'die' (see Example 8). The quaver scales create a daring jangle of cross-rhythms against the melody. This is highly refined music for the chamber, and I wonder if it might not have been overwhelmed by the paint and glitter of its original surroundings.

The third entry begins with the D major Canaries danced by four women on the next higher level of the machine. Nothing has happened in

Example 8. *Dioclesian*: 'Since from my dear Astrea's sight', bars 51–60

[19] *Thesaurus Musicus*, II (1694). Another setting of 'Since from my dear', by Samuel Ackeroyde, was published in the same issue of *The Gentleman's Journal*.
[20] Cf. 'Divine Andate!' in *Bonduca* and 'From rosy bowers' in *3 Don Quixote*.

either the masque or the play itself to prepare for the intensity of the ensuing dialogue between the shepherds Corinna and Mirtillo. No coy flirtation and eventual rejection, the stuff of nearly all the pastoral dialogues of the period, this is a graphic depiction of amorous pursuit, submission, and consummation – the latter through music alone, however. From the beginning one can hear that 'Tell me why' was designed for professionals capable of executing difficult rhythms and passage-work. For the first few pages the text is deceptively routine, as Mirtillo asks Corinna why she denies him, the shepherdess replying 'You're above me, / I respect but dare not love ye'. He promises not to deceive her, making the double meaning crystal-clear: 'I love her, therefore cannot be above her'. Punctuated by frequent rests, his jagged, chromatic line rises to a fever pitch. In the response to this outburst, Purcell allows the shepherdess to die metaphorically through the traditional tragic associations for G minor (see Example 9). The descending bass line and the irregular resolution of the first-inversion dominant chord in bars 120–1 are powerful symbols for death. The setting of 'Ah!' is also noteworthy, especially in bar 129, where the abandonment of the dominant at the rising figure in the voice part is reminiscent of the removal of the sting of death in Dido's Lament. At the end, when Mirtillo joins Corinna in the chorus, Purcell avoids the conventionally static and unresolved titillation with which most pastoral dia-

Example 9. *Dioclesian*: 'Tell me why', bars 118–34

logues end, as once again the singers' passions are raised and quelled – now together. This should have been a fragment of an Italianate opera, not a bit of musical fluff for an overblown masque.

For the following entry the action moves up to the next level of the machine as 'two Youths' dance. The key shifts to G major for an air sung by one of the Pleasures, a contrapuntal chorus, and a soprano air omitted from the 1691 full score but easily found in the contemporary song-books.[21] Unfortunately, this worthy music is an anticlimax after the masterful dialogue 'Tell me why'.

The fifth and final entry begins with a dance performed 'on the farthest Stage by Two Children', whose size aided the theatrical perspective: had the performers been adults, Jove's throne would have looked like a piece of doll's furniture. The fine G major dance moves directly into the C major trio on a ground, 'Triumph victorious Love', which can be viewed as a vanquishing reply to Grabu's chaconne in *Albion and Albanius*. Although they share the same key and metre, the pieces are actually poles apart. Purcell's bass is unchanging, except for one division discussed below, while Grabu's undergoes continuous variation; the former is the familiar chaconne pattern, the latter the descending tetrachord. And despite the grandeur of the English piece, it is tightly constructed with not a variation too many, while the French behemoth could be saved in performance only by splendid dancing. Purcell's male trio is relieved in the interludes by three separate groups of instruments, the trumpets, oboes, and strings, which toss several bellicose motifs back and forth. The most striking section is the setting of 'Thou [Love] hast tam'd almighty Jove' (see Example 10). Here Purcell shifts to C minor, a key that previously marked

Example 10. *Dioclesian*: 'Triumph, victorious Love', bars 78–86

[21] The soprano air, 'Let us dance', is in *The Gentleman's Journal* (October 1692) and *Comes Amoris*, IV (1693).

Example 10 (cont.)

Jove's appearance. But the god has now been tamed by Love, and though the music reflects a disposition still sour, his surrender is symbolized by the obstinate E♮s of the bass. The modulation is thus never quite accomplished. Purcell used this pungent major–minor mixture in other theatrical chaconnes, the first music for *King Arthur* and the Chinese dance in the last act of *The Fairy-Queen*, but in *Dioclesian* it plays a climactic role.

Immediately after the ground, the masque concludes with a paean to Love scored for full chorus and orchestra. All the singers and dancers re-appear on '*the several divisions of the Machine*' and perform '*a Grand Dance to the time of the* Chorus'. But because this is an English opera, the actors sitting on the sides of the forestage must rouse themselves before the curtain falls. Drums are heard at a distance as Charinus, finally learning of Diocles's distress, comes to the rescue. Delphia urges the former emperor to greet the Johnny-come-lately, but 'great Dioclesian' replies, 'Oh Mother! I have the will, but not the pow'r to do it', an ironic summary of his relationship with the prophetess.

Massinger and Fletcher's play did not accept Purcell's music gracefully. The interpolation in Act II temporarily chokes off the swiftly moving plot. The song for Aurelia in the third act is at odds with the drama, and the grand celebration of Diocles's battlefield heroics in Act IV is an embarrassing over-reaction to a victory gained by underhanded tactics. The masque, however, is inserted near the end where it can do the least damage, being self-contained and not having to rely on the play for survival. Despite the disjointedness of the musical episodes, the score is much of a piece, the connection between the dances in Acts II and IV an obvious cohesive device, as is the tonal scheme. The opera is centred in C major, Purcell's favourite key for scenes of celebration, especially when royalty are present. C minor, on the other hand, is associated with sadness or subdued awe. The relationships, very plain in *Dido and Aeneas*, are also exploited in the second act of *Dioclesian*, in which the main events are the discovery of Numerianus's body, the killing of Aper, and the installation of the new emperor: hence the muted celebration in C minor mingled with rather pompous music in the major mode. The perfunctory lament for the dead emperor, 'Charon the peaceful shade', is, not surprisingly, in G minor. The misguided love song in Act III, 'What shall I do', is in D minor, one of the two tonalities Purcell associated with eroticism in the music for comedies. The grand celebration of Act IV is in D major, the other trumpet key, and contrasts with the equivocal C major–minor music of the second act. The masque has essentially the same key organization, except that G minor now symbolizes metaphorical death.

Dioclesian does not fulfill the expectations raised by *Dido and Aeneas*, even though the two works belong to entirely different genres. Despite an occasional masterstroke, it is the weakest of the major stage works. Purcell was of course severely handicapped by the adaptation, which lacks the essential ingredient of the other successful semi-operas from the 1674 *Tempest* to Motteux's *Island Princess*: either a character to bridge the gap between the spoken and songish parts – an Ismeron, Zempoalla, Grimbald, or Ariel – or masques that reflect and amplify the play itself. The entertainments and spoken dialogue in *Dioclesian* are on different planes, without being mutually beneficial. But the problem is also musical; many of the numbers lack the boldness, the 'forgèd feature' of the other semi-operas. How much of this blandness is owing to the influence of *Albion and Albanius* is impossible to know, but the satirical design of Betterton's reworking was not conducive to Purcell's obvious desire to compose a grand and heroic score. When the gilt and paint are washed away, the pure gold that remains is in the dances. As the fantazias attest to his genius for the old contrapuntal style, so these pieces establish him as the sole English master of a new counterpoint. The tunes sing with a French airyness, but the inner parts spin out the acerbity, wit or passion demanded by the choreography. Purcell's instrumental melodies were alamode, but he never lost a love of the irregular part-writing of his 'homely Ancestours'.

7 *King Arthur*

The events leading to Dryden and Purcell's momentous collaboration on *King Arthur* (May or June 1691) are well known. According to a letter from Lord Preston to the Duke of York dated 22 September 1683, the king sent Betterton to Paris 'to endeavour to carry over the Opera'. Finding that impracticable, the actor had to settle on returning with Louis Grabu, the former master of the King's Violins, who was well acquainted with Lully's *tragédies lyriques* and therefore, so Preston believed, capable of composing 'something at least like an Opera in England for his Majesty's diversion'.[1] The poet laureate takes up the story in the preface to *Albion and Albanius*. Despite the king's desire to see a French-style drama, Dryden wrote instead an English opera similar to the 1674 *Tempest*, that is, a play 'Written in blank Verse, adorn'd with Scenes, Machines, Songs and Dances'. As yet unnamed, the new work was to be augmented by an all-sung prologue representing the restoration of Charles II in a series of emblematic tableaux. In a letter to Tonson written in August 1684, Dryden reports that he had already split the project into two parts. He expected 'the singing opera', presumably *Albion and Albanius*, 'to be playd immediately after Michaelmasse' (29 September), while he still had one act 'of the opera' (*King Arthur*?) to write and was in no hurry to finish it.[2] At this point Dryden's account becomes vague. Because of 'some intervening accidents', the main piece was set aside and the prologue expanded into the three-act opera *Albion and Albanius*. What prompted the change of plans is unknown; one would guess that the king's Francophile tastes prevailed over Dryden's chauvinism. Yet, as explained below, the reasons for shelving the musical play are far more complex.

---

[1] *Historical Manuscripts Commission Seventh Report*, Part I (London, 1879), Appendix, pp. 288a, 290a; see also *The Works of John Dryden*, xv, 341.

[2] *The Letters of John Dryden*, ed. Ward, p. 23. Ward suggests that 'the singing opera' is *The Tempest*. Dryden would not, however, have used this term for a semi-opera, which in any case is not known to have been revived in 1684. Edward L. Saslow, in 'Dryden in 1684', *Modern Philology*, 72 (1975), 250–2, proposes that *Albion and Albanius* was first performed on 29 May 1684, more than a year before its well-established 3 June 1685 première. Hume exposes Saslow's error in 'Studies in English Drama 1660–1800', *Philological Quarterly*, 55 (1976), 463. Saslow also suggests that *King Arthur* was to have been mounted on 23 April 1684, citing as evidence a reference to Saint George's Day (23 April) in the opening dialogue. But this speculation ignores Dryden's admission that 'the opera' was not yet finished in August and overlooks the probability that the version published in 1691 is considerably different from the first draft.

Allegorical Designs

Dryden states that *King Arthur* is the last thing he wrote for Charles II: 'though he liv'd not to see the Performance of it, on the Stage; yet the PROLOGUE to it . . . was often practis'd before Him at *Whitehal*' (preface to *King Arthur*). Why was the semi-opera withdrawn before the king's death on 6 February 1685, while *Albion and Albanius* was duly performed with a hastily appended apotheosis in June of the same year? This was still a sensitive subject in 1691, as Dryden writes in the preface to *King Arthur* that he was forced 'to alter the first Design' in order 'not to offend the present Times, nor a Government which has hitherto protected me', a tantalizing admission that raises several important questions. To what extent does the published play-book resemble the original, which does not survive? What was the political design of the 1684–5 version? What were the 'intervening accidents' that prevented a performance in 1685? Does the revision also have a political component? Avoiding these questions altogether, one of Dryden's biographers believes that *King Arthur* was adapted to the times 'by omitting the politics'.[3] Roberta Florence Brinkley is even more categorical, suggesting that 'all the real substance of the story had been removed, and what remained was only a fantastic account of Arthur's battle with the Saxons'.[4] But the poet's having 'To alter the first Design' does not necessarily mean that the opera as finally published is devoid of political overtones. The years from the Rye House Plot, through the Glorious Revolution, to the beginning of the reign of William and Mary are so crowded with intrigue and shifts of fortune that almost any play can be interpreted allegorically if only the critic delves deeply enough into historical detail. Yet *King Arthur* was almost certainly designed originally to compliment Charles II; therefore the plot and dramatis personae probably reflected major events and leading figures of the time. We know that the 1684–5 entertainment – let us call it 'Arthur of Britian' – was to begin with an all-sung prologue, which later became the first act of *Albion and Albanius*. As Dryden writes in the preface to the earlier opera, the principal singers, Mercury, Thamesis, Democracy, Zelota, and so forth, were to sing in the play, while the actors miming Albion and Albanius (neither sings in the first act of Grabu's opera) would be joined by their fellow players to portray Arthur, Oswald, Emmeline, Merlin, and the other speaking characters. Whereas the prologue is a thinly veiled enactment of the restoration of Charles II, I should guess that 'Arthur of Britain' was to

---

[3] L[eslie] S[tephen], *Dictionary of National Biography*, s.v. Dryden, John.

[4] *Arthurian Legend in the Seventeenth Century*, Johns Hopkins Monographs in Literary History, III (Baltimore: Johns Hopkins Press, 1932), p. 144. Joanne Altieri, in a recent study ('Baroque Hieroglyphics: Dryden's *King Arthur*', *Philological Quarterly*, 61 [1982], 450), holds out little hope for finding political allusions in the opera ('such attempts seem doomed to failure').

be a complex allegory of more recent events, something like a dramatized sequel to *Absalom and Achitophel*.

This conjectural reconstruction is not without foundation. The greatest threat to the stability of the reign of Charles during its final years was the Exclusion Crisis, an intricate series of political manoeuvres intended to block the accession of the Roman Catholic Duke of York and to have the king's eldest son, the protestant Duke of Monmouth, declared legitimate. The leading exclusionist was Anthony Ashley Cooper, the first Earl of Shaftesbury, a recent president of the privy council. The Bill of Exclusion was defeated by Parliament in the autumn of 1680 thanks largely to the debating skill of George Savile, Marquis of Halifax. Dryden's famous poem *Absalom and Achitophel* is a satire of this affair from the royalist point of view, in which Absalom is Monmouth, Achitophel is Shaftesbury, David is Charles II, and Jotham is Halifax. The Exclusion Crisis is also treated obliquely in *Albion and Albanius*, and Shaftesbury was tastelessly depicted on a painted scene in the third act. Reference to Monmouth is assiduously avoided, yet until Charles's death many influential people, including Halifax and Dryden, hoped that he would be restored to favour, because they believed Monmouth less dangerous within the royal fold than without. Near the end of the preface to *Absalom*, admittedly a lamb to the lion that follows, the poet writes: 'Were I the Inventour, who am only the Historian, I should certainly conclude the Piece, with the Reconcilement of *Absalom* to *David*. And, who knows but this may come to pass?' Dryden was, of course, inventor (that is, playwright) as well as historian, and *King Arthur*, even in its 1691 form, is a salubrious allegory of the desired conclusion.

Despite the poet's claim to have altered the work to suit the times, echoes of the struggles of Monmouth and York are still clearly audible in the published version. The theme of *King Arthur* is the reconciliation of princes, and like *Absalom and Achitophel* it is as much concerned with the advisers who guided the affairs of state from behind the scenes as with the public actions of the protagonists themselves. This is apparent from Dryden's choice of dedicatee for the semi-opera, the Marquis of Halifax, whose 'piercing wit and pregnant thought' (to quote from *Absalom*) helped steer the nation through an incipient civil war, two wrenching changes of government, and numerous stratagems. Like Charles II, Halifax was a 'trimmer' – that is, one who is willing to modify his convictions for the sake of expediency. Dryden admired this trait, since he believed that rigid opinions and unswerving loyalty in times of political instability could only lead to bloodshed. *King Arthur* is thus a celebration of compromise and reconciliation, and above all of the role played by sagacious and flexible advisers who, through tactful manipulation, prevented their masters from blundering heroically from one disaster to another.

Although Dryden was well acquainted with Geoffrey of Monmouth's *Historia Regum Britanniae* and other sources of Arthurian legend, the plot of the opera is essentially his own creation, except for the fourth-act scene in the Enchanted Grove which is based on Canto XVIII of Tasso's *Gerusalemme liberata*.[5] Ostensibly the argument is Arthur's quest for a unified Britain. But most of the action centres on Emmeline, the blind daughter of Conon, Duke of Cornwall. Though betrothed to Arthur, she has formerly been courted by Oswald, the Saxon King of Kent, who would settle the dispute honourably on the battlefield. But after defeat by the Britons, he abducts Emmeline, and Arthur's attempts to free her occupy the rest of the plot. Dryden provides the warring kings with balanced ranks of advisers. On the Britons' side is Conon, an avuncular figure who offers more sympathy than advice; his Saxon counterpart is Guillamar. The two kings' chief counsellors are the magicians Merlin and Osmond, who are in turn assisted by the spirits Grimbald and Philidel. The latter, an airy epicene, has formerly served the Saxons' heathen gods, but after witnessing the carnage of the battle in Act I he becomes a Christian sympathizer and defects to Merlin. One of Dryden's happiest characters, Philidel is a trimmer whose shift of allegiance is prompted by 'a sense of Human Woes'. The allegorical correspondences of 'Arthur of Britain', undoubtedly disturbed by the death of Charles II, are summarized as follows:

Britons (Royalists)	*Saxons* (Whigs)
Arthur (Charles, then James) —— Emmeline —— Oswald (Monmouth)	
Conon (?)	Guillamar (Essex?)
Merlin ⎱ (Halifax)	Osmond ⎱ (Shaftesbury)
Philidel ⎰	Grimbald ⎰

Standing between the opposed forces is Emmeline, the blind hostage, who was, I believe, meant to personify the national conscience. Early in the play she is innocently vain and infatuated with Arthur, her dialogue peppered with bawdy *double entendres*. Her abduction by the Saxons is thus an apologue of Shaftesbury and Monmouth's seduction of the country by dangling before it the prospect of a protestant succession. When Philidel restores Emmeline's sight in the second scene of Act III, she loses her clumsy naïveté and is then able to feel genuine love for Arthur and to see the ugliness of her gaoler, Osmond. During this episode, Oswald, affected by a sleeping-draught administered by the evil wizard, has kept his promise not to ravish the fair captive. By disassociating the Saxon king from the foul designs of the counsellor, Dryden alludes to Shaftesbury's using Monmouth as a pawn in his attempt to block the succession of the Duke of

---

[5] See *Dryden: The Dramatic Works*, ed. M. Summers, VI, 233-4. David Charlton, in '*King Arthur*: Dramatick Opera', *Music & Letters*, 64 (1983), 183-92, places the opera more generally in the *Orlando Furioso* tradition.

York. This reinforces the central theme, but the reconcilement is on terms clearly favourable to Arthur, who magnanimously allows the vanquished Oswald to retain a modicum of honour. Despite the playwright's implication that he had suppressed the political overtones of the original version, the 1691 semi-opera is strewn with shards of the allegory of the vying dukes, the lauding of Halifax, and the damning of Shaftesbury. The threat of Monmouth's Rebellion pushed 'Arthur of Britain' further into the wings, and the duke's execution in mid-July 1685 rendered a public performance impossible.[6]

Six years later when Dryden dusted off the manuscript of the ill-fated dramatic opera with an eye towards collaboration with Purcell, he found it to be unacceptable in the current political climate. One should note first that theatrical censorship in the reign of William and Mary was far less common than during the turbulent years of the Popish Plot, the Exclusion Crisis, and the Rye House assassination attempt (1678–82). Nevertheless, plays and their prologues were still occasionally prohibited. Dryden's *Cleomenes*, which treats an exiled king sympathetically, was temporarily banned on 9 April 1692. And Shadwell was responsible for having Dryden's prologue to *Dioclesian* suppressed because of its alleged criticism of William's Irish campaign.[7] But an even greater political embarrassment accompanied the revival of *The Spanish Fryar* on 28 May 1689. Obviously not having read Dryden's tragicomedy but apparently assuming that a work forbidden by the previous government should be given an airing in her reign, Queen Mary asked to see it in May 1689. When she heard Pedro recite the first-act speech, 'Very good: She usurps the Throne; keeps the old King in Prison; and, at the same time, is praying for a Blessing: Oh Religion and Roguery, how they go together!', the queen called for a hood to conceal her discountenance as the pit buzzed and clucked upon 'any application of what was said'.[8] There is no evidence that when finally produced in 1691 *King Arthur* had a similarly offensive odour, but it must surely have elicited knowing glances from both Whigs and Jacobites, despite Dryden's attempt to scramble the original allegory. Arthur was now clearly William III and Oswald the deposed James II. Their single combat in Act V, in which Arthur would emulate his 'Fam'd Ancestor' Aeneas when he 'Fought for a Crown, and bright *Lavinia*'s Bed', not only reaffirms the royal blood line from the Trojan prince to Brutus of

---

[6] Buttrey interprets the conflict between the Saxons and Britons as an allegory of the disputes between Catholic and protestant factions. The restoration of Emmeline's vision symbolizes 'the English people's first sight of their king [Charles II] in his true colours', that is, as a Roman Catholic. Although his analysis is centred more on general religious issues than mine, we agree that Oswald and Osmond reflect Monmouth and Shaftesbury; see 'The Evolution of English Opera', pp. 248–60.

[7] See R. P. McCutcheon, 'Dryden's Prologue to *The Prophetess*', *Modern Language Notes*, 39 (1924), 123–4.

[8] Quoted in *The London Stage*, Part 1, p. 371.

Alba, but also enacts the Battle of the Boyne, fought between William and James in late June 1690, almost exactly a year before the première of *King Arthur*. This meaning is further evinced when in the same scene Oswald accuses Arthur of stealing his 'Crown and Mistress', to which the bold Briton replies that the Saxon had earlier avoided a fight, an unsubtle allusion to James's ignominious flight as the Prince of Orange approached London in late 1688. The allegory is finely honed in other scenes as well. For example, at the parley in Act II, Arthur reminds Oswald that they were formerly allied, probably a hint at William's frequent pledges of loyalty to James II both before and after his accession in 1685. Throughout the opera, Dryden rarely misses an opportunity to stress Oswald's heroic character. And in the sacrifice scene in Act I, in particular, his invocation to the Teutonic deities, 'Hear and revenge my Father *Hengist*'s death', is easily read as James II recalling his father's execution.

The Arthur-as-William interpretation is weakened by two anomalies. Oswald, an invader from the continent who is 'Revengeful, rugged, violently brave', is a clearer reflection of William III than of James II. And Dryden's own continuing loyalty to the exiled king brings sharply into question the widely accepted patriotic purpose of the opera, epitomized by the fifth-act masque in celebration of Arthur's victory.[9] On the surface, the 1691 *King Arthur* seems to advocate a reconciliation of William and James for the greater good of the kingdom, but it is startlingly easy to argue that the protagonist represents James II and Oswald, William III. This possible reversal of roles is important in assessing the tone of the elaborate religious ceremony in Act I. Under the Arthur-as-William scenario, the pagan ritual becomes a parody of the Roman rite, an unsettling hypothesis in the light of Dryden's conversion to Catholicism in 1686. Purcell's music, which has a strong Anglican flavour, may therefore suggest an Arthur-as-James interpretation, thus making the 'heathen' sacrifice a satire of protestantism. But more on this subject later. If indeed Dryden intended such an arcane design, then it was well enough hidden to evade the censor's attention. And Queen Mary herself 'was not displeas'd to find in this Poem the Praises of Her Native Country; and the Heroick Actions of so famous a Predecessor in the Government of *Great Britain*, as King *Arthur*' (dedication). But even this reported approbation smacks of a double meaning; her famous predecessor could well be James II.

Most susceptible to a waggish application of the 1691 allegory is Emmeline. While in 'Arthur of Britain' she was probably meant to embody

---

[9] Moore (*Henry Purcell & the Restoration Theatre*, p. 73) is the most enthusiastic advocate of the patriotic theme. Only one authority has expressed any doubt about the sincerity of the chauvinism of the masque: Michael W. Alssid, 'The Impossible Form of Art: Dryden, Purcell and *King Arthur*', p. 142. Altieri, 'Baroque Hieroglyphics: Dryden's *King Arthur*', pp. 445–6, takes a novel view of the masque in Act V as a transformation of 'court masque into city pageant', a celebration of 'Lord Mayor's day, with all its bourgeois connections'.

the national conscience, in *King Arthur* she must also have been seen as Mary II. Dryden naturally had to eschew the traditional consort, Guinevere, in view of her adultery with the usurper Mordred. Yet the playwright sailed very close to the wind by placing Emmeline between the Saxons and the Britons, thus paralleling Queen Mary's monumentally awkward position vis-à-vis her husband and her recently deposed father. To make the heroine the daughter of Conon, Duke of Cornwall, may have been a way to cloud the picture, but it hardly helped matters; according to Geoffrey of Monmouth, Utherpendragon begot Arthur on the Duchess of Cornwall after being transformed into the likeness of her husband, Gorlois.

The only character whose allegorical identity would be unchanged from the conjectural 1685 version to the published revision is Merlin, who represents Halifax, advisor to Charles II, James II, and William III – the work's dedicatee. The wizard is portrayed as ageless, almost god-like, the only mortal in the opera to descend in a machine (at the beginning of Act II). Despite his necromantic skills, he is not omnipotent, but acts only as a guide and counsellor. When Arthur faces his severest challenge in the enchanted grove, Merlin warns the king of the perils but cannot accompany him during the ordeal. The magician's withdrawal from the action in Act IV and reappearance just before the dénouement probably allude to Halifax's retirement from public life a few months before the première. Dryden's much-admired trimmer, having helped avert several potential catastrophes, now stepped aside to allow the monarchs to fend for themselves.

The Case for an English Opera

A comparision of Dryden's description of the abortive semi-opera of 1684–5 with the play-book published in 1691 reveals some discrepancies which suggest that, in addition to suppressing its original political overtones, the poet also altered the dramatic structure. While the original work was to have been 'a Tragedy mix'd with *Opera*', *King Arthur* is closer to comedy than to any other genre. Dryden also states that in its first manifestation the fable was to have been 'all spoken and acted by the best of the Comedians; the other part of the entertainment to be perform'd by the same Singers and Dancers who are introduc'd in' the prologue. But a noteworthy feature of the semi-opera is the lack of segregation of the singing and speaking casts, unlike *Dioclesian* and other similar works of the nineties. In fact two important characters, the spirits Grimbald and Philidel, both sing and speak; and the protagonist, while not expressing himself in song, is nevertheless drawn deeply into the musical episodes. Described on the title-page as a 'Dramatick Opera', *King Arthur* is the only one of Purcell's major works for the professional stage not adapted from an earlier play. It was of course influenced by Dryden and Davenant's redaction of

The Tempest: the principal musical scenes of both plays are the products of magic; Merlin, Emmeline, Philidel, and Grimbald are modelled on Prospero, Miranda (and Dorinda), Ariel, and Caliban, respectively. But the work to which it owes a far greater debt is *Psyche*, the archetypal dramatic opera.

Despite its well-springs in the *tragédie-ballet* of Molière and its affinity with the operatic *Tempest*, Shadwell and Locke's *Psyche* (February 1675) was an immensely innovative and daring work.[10] The first English musical extravaganza without a tap-root in the Stuart masque or the early Restoration play with music, it comes closer to true *dramma per musica* than any of Purcell's theatre works except *Dido and Aeneas*. Locke realized the significance of the achievement and published the vocal music in a handsome quarto with the proud and defiant title *The English Opera*.[11] The preface, written in his inimical style, is a vigorous defence of the practice of mixing music and spoken dialogue on the stage. But much more important, the epistle makes a cogent case for a national opera, of which *Psyche* is unveiled as prototype. While admitting the necessity of punctuating his music with such 'interlocutions' as are 'proper to our *Genius*', he claims to have captured the essence of Italian opera by employing a variety of musical types and styles, including 'Counterpoint, Recitative, Fuge, Canon, and Chromatick Musick'. To make these ingredients truly theatrical and capable of moving the passions, he occasionally resorts to 'extravagancies in some parts of the Composition', including the violation of the rules of consonance and dissonance. And the composer now assumes a dominant role.

Shadwell, who was as vain as Locke was obstreperous, demurred. In the preface to the play-book, he acknowledges that some of the verses were made with an ear to music, 'in which I cannot but have some little knowledge, having been bred for many years of my Youth to some performance in it'.[12] Except for one song in Act V, he claims to have instructed the composer what should be cast as solo, duet, chorus, and so forth, as well as dictating 'what manner of Humour I would have in all the Vocal Musick'. *Psyche* may not be a true opera, but it caused a classic conflict between librettist and composer. Purcell and Dryden apparently waged a similar battle over the lyrics in *King Arthur*, a dispute that the composer seems to have won handily. In the preface to the latter, the poet reports by way of a sly apology that he was 'oblig'd to cramp my Verses' in order to make them 'harmonious to the Hearer . . . because these sorts of Entertainment are

---

[10] Analysed by Dent, *Foundations*, pp. 108–24.

[11] G. B. Draghi's act music and dances were omitted 'by consent of their Author'. The volume also includes Locke's instrumental music for *The Tempest*.

[12] For this and similar boasts, Shadwell was smartly satirized in Durfey's *Sir Barnaby Whigg*; see Chapter 4.

principally design'd for the Ear and Eye'. Furthermore, he generously owns that in dramatic operas his art 'ought to be subservient to' the composer's. One should appreciate, however, that this concession applies only to the musical episodes. Since more than half of *King Arthur* is spoken, Purcell had won the battle but not the war.

Despite the skirmish in the prefaces, the synthesis of music and drama in *Psyche* is remarkably good, certainly unmatched in any later semi-opera, even *King Arthur*. This was accomplished by ameliorating what was later recognized as the chief liability of the genre: the awkwardness of 'passing from a Song to plain and ordinary Speaking', the unavoidable consequence of maintaining a separation between spoken dialogue and music, as Addison observes in *The Spectator* (3 April 1711). But in *Psyche* one can detect little difference between the verse which is sung and that which is spoken, the shift from one to the other being less abrupt than in those later works in which poets exaggerate the difference between lyrics and dialogue. Also aiding cohesiveness is the antagonist, Venus, who expresses herself entirely in song in Acts I and III, while only speaking in Acts IV and V. *Psyche* is not, of course, flawless. Whatever the quality of Locke's music, perhaps the most serious weakness is the grossly different rates at which the story is told alternatingly in music and spoken dialogue, an imbalance felt most sorely in the first two scenes of the fifth act. With a great deal of the plot yet to be played out, Shadwell temporarily curtails the music to regain dramatic momentum. The high point is reached when Cupid finally persuades his mother to restore Psyche to life, accomplishing this neither with exalted poetry nor with plaintive music, but by flying up to Venus's departing chariot and forcing her to return. Nearly all the musical spectaculars of the era have *deus ex machina* effects, but this is one of the few works in which the machinist was called on to provide the climax; though it contains no music, this scene epitomizes the genre. Dryden does not publicly acknowledge the fact, but *King Arthur* borrows many of the techniques evolved by Shadwell and Locke in this, the first 'English opera'.

The Music

The sources for *King Arthur* are a confused assortment of more than sixty manuscripts and miscellaneous publications, none of which includes the complete music. Only one score dates from before 1695, and it is a fragment. Margaret Laurie has carefully collated and evaluated this mass of material in the revision of the Purcell Society Edition Vol. xxvi, though a substantial amount of music in the first production has not been recovered and several of the main manuscripts are unreliable in parts, as her thirty-odd pages of critical commentary suggest. This disorder implies that Purcell's drafts of the various masques were never copied into one volume which then served as exemplar. The music for Acts I and II is well preserved, as is that for the Frost Scene. But no settings of the lyrics sung at the restoration of Emmeline's sight in Act III survive, and all the sources for the Temptation Scene in Act IV and the final masque are in disarray. Tenbury MS 785 (now at the Bodleian Library), dating from shortly after the première and by far the earliest and most trustworthy source, includes only the music for Act I; yet no other manuscript was copied from it, and the brilliant trumpet and oboe symphony embedded in the midst of 'Come if you dare' is found nowhere else. One wonders if the other main sources, mostly copied after 1700, miss out similar details in the rest of the score.

The absence of a discernible stemma among the most important scores suggests a far more complicated early stage history than for Purcell's other major works. *King Arthur* was revived at least twice during the composer's lifetime and was frequently performed in the winter of 1691-2. I suspect the two overtures assigned to the opera were intended for different performances. The one in D major for trumpet and five-part strings is taken from the 1690 Ode for Queen Mary's Birthday, *Arise, my muse* (z 320/1), and may have been pressed into service in the last-minute rush before the première, while the one in D minor for strings was perhaps composed for a revival, despite the marginal notation in the Royal College of Music copy of *Ayres for the Theatre* stating that it is a part of the second music. [13] The opera remained in repertory at Drury Lane in the late nineties, and parts of it made cameo appearances in other works in the early eighteenth century. Frequent revival meant frequent change. The decidedly un-Purcellian setting of the first verse of the final lyric in Act V, 'St. George, the Patron of our Isle', was probably added to a production after his death, perhaps the one in early 1698 attended several times by Lady Morley. [14] The tailoring of the masques for the Theatre Royal's Purcell medleys of 1704 and the gala concerts of his dramatic music given in the Stationers' Hall in 1711 may account for most of the missing music. [15]

Considering Purcell's accomplishments in the realm of serious drama in the last year of his life, one might wonder why *King Arthur* proved to be his most successful stage work. It provides few incidents on which he could exercise his gift for tragedy, and the only scene with a potential for pathos – the slaughter of the battle in Act I – is rendered whimsical by the Saxons' eagerness to suffer a glorious death after finding their courage in bowls of wine. Among the singing characters, the most intense passion is expressed by the Cold Genius, whose aria far exceeds the simple portrayal of climatic discomfort, striking instead an awesome note of fear. This grossly inflated emotion is immediately punctured by Cupid, who chides

[13] See the Purcell Society Edition, xxvi (rev. M. Laurie), 173-4.
[14] See *The London Stage*, Part 1, pp. 491-3.
[15] See Michael Tilmouth, 'A Calendar of References to Music in Newspapers Published in London and the Provinces (1660-1719)', *R.M.A. Research Chronicle*, No. 1 (1961), 53-81.

the Genius for his pomposity. The Frost Scene crystallizes the dramatic plan of the opera, which is in fact an extension of the political design: heroism, passion, even patriotism are ridiculed by humorous juxtaposition. The solemn sacrifice becomes a bacchanal. The Arcadian vision of guiltless pleasures is blurred by a reminder of the possible consequences of pre-marital sex. And in the wryest twist of all, Arthur's subjects, after defeating the Saxon foe, are obliged to step out of character and pay homage to their present king, a Dutchman. Purcell's music must be interpreted in the light of these ironies.

The sacrifice in Act I is problematic. Dryden depicts Oswald and the Saxons not as heathen villains but as worthy, even honourable adversaries. Grimbald, on the other hand, who is charged with recruiting the victims for the sacrifice, is exceedingly cynical about the religiosity of the ceremony, and describes the volunteers as 'Fools, so prodigal of Life and Soul, / That, for their Country, they devote their Lives'. Dryden's intentions as to whether the Saxons were to represent Jacobites or Williamites, or whether in fact the pagan sacrifice should mesh with the 1691 allegory at all, are unclear.[16] It was an awkward way for Purcell to have to begin. The music is entirely coherent, though Westrup senses 'a contrapuntal stodginess' (*Purcell*, p. 133), while Dent notices that 'it is too severe and noble for the character of the savage Saxons', explaining its dramatic incongruity as the composer's not yet having learnt how to suggest 'local colour' (*Foundations*, pp. 209–10). Though far more intricate and varied than the closely related 'We must assemble by a sacrifice' in *Circe*, the first masque in *King Arthur* lacks the note of grand foreboding heard in that stately conjuration of Pluto, even though many Saxons soon die on the battlefield. Once again, Purcell turned to the symphony-anthem style, with male soloists and short choral responses in the opening section. Thomas Gray, upon hearing the 1735–6 revival, was able to tell Walpole that in this scene 'the Songs are all Church-musick'.[17] Purcell's favourite baritone, John Bowman, listed in the 1691 play-book as Grimbald, also sang the elegant and moderately decorated tenor part in the sacrifice, in stark contrast to the spoken blasphemy quoted above. While the vocal writing is generally unremarkable, the instrumental introduction and interludes are piquant reminders of an earlier contrapuntal style that is anything but stodgy; the symphonies give welcome relief to the rather pale choruses (see Example 1, bars 114–16).

A much-admired passage in the music of the first act is the sombre F minor setting of the line 'Dye, and reap the fruit of Glory', but it too is

---

[16] The sacrificial victims are '6 Saxons in White'. Cf. the fantastic dance of the '*Boys in White*' in III.i of *Albion and Albanius*. The latter represented the 'innocent' followers of the Duke of Monmouth; see *The Works of John Dryden*, xv, 376–7.

[17] *The Correspondence of Gray, Walpole, West and Ashton*, ed. Paget Toynbee (Oxford: Clarendon, 1915), I, 57.

emotionally restrained. A more dramatic passage, shown in Example 1, precedes it. Purcell prepares to cadence in G minor, but despising death, resolves to the parallel major instead. Rather than return (as Dryden directed) to the first line of the chorus, 'Brave Souls to be renown'd in Story', Purcell launches directly into the drinking-song 'I call ye all to Woden's hall' after the F minor section. The spirited *Ite missa est* avoids the rollicking abandon of the bacchanals in *Dioclesian*, but is nevertheless a peculiar finale. Michael Alssid, believing that the masque 'must have been an amusing, enlightening exercise for Purcell', detects 'an intentional contrast between the lugubrious rhythms and simple repetitions of "*We have sacrificed*" and certain contemporary anthems which a Restoration audience would have instantly recognized' ('The Impossible Form of Art', pp. 133-4). This may be, but a dichotomy of tone pervades the sacrifice scene, and the music leaves a modern audience puzzled by the difference between what they see and what they hear.

Example 1. *King Arthur*: 'Brave souls, to be renown'd in story', bars 114-22

Example 1 (cont.)

The essential business of the first act – the battle – occurs off stage in heroic-play fashion. After considerable commotion behind the scenes, the victorious Britons enter to a symphony for trumpets and oboes and then sing 'Come if you dare', as rousing a piece in C major as ever Purcell wrote.[18] Yet both this and the preceding sacrifice are only tableaux, as neither composer nor playwright breaks new ground in the first act. But for the exquisite writing for orchestra, this could well be an episode from an ordinary tragicomedy.

Act II moves in a new dramatic mode. Merlin descends in a chariot drawn by dragons and recruits Philidel, a deserter from Osmond's evil band, to steer the Britons, pursued by Oswald and the Saxon stragglers, away from quaking bogs. Grimbald, last heard singing the mellifluous tenor part in the sacrifice, enters disguised as a shepherd. In rustic dialect

---

[18] This is perhaps the scene parodied in Act I of *The Female Wits* (see below). During the rehearsal of her semi-opera, the playwright Marsilia asks the audience to imagine a battle between the scenes: 'And from the Castle let the Trumpets and Violins join in a Tune of Victory. So, there's a Battle well over.'

301

he directs Arthur on the path to disaster, while Philidel, making no attempt to camouflage his elfish nature, sings the warning 'Hither this way, this way bend'. The song and chorus are so beguiling that the shift from tragicomedy to true opera may have gone unnoticed. The main plot is borne, if only briefly, by music, as Philidel unmasks Grimbald as a 'Malicious Fiend' and leads the Britons to safety. The only other episode in Purcell's major stage works that approaches this degree of integration of music and spoken dialogue is the Conjurer's Scene in III.ii of *The Indian Queen*, though it lacks the important ingredient of 'Hither this way': the metamorphosis of stage action into musical gesture. Purcell's means are deceptively simple. Philidel sings a D minor air, answered by a chorus of spirits lent to him by Merlin. But Grimbald's followers occasionally break in with exact echoes that give Arthur no clue which group to trust. After the chorus, Conon begins to suspect the 'shepherd' is not what he appears, and the Britons prepare to follow the airy spirits. Grimbald realizes that he too will have to resort to music. Apologizing in an aside for a voice made hoarse by 'Sulph'rous Steams', he sings the swinging A major air 'Let not a moonborn elf mislead ye', which, though written in the bass clef, lies higher than Bowman's tenor part in the sacrifice scene. With this lofty compass and bright key, Grimbald tries to sound as unlike his gruff self as possible. Arthur is nearly fooled by the charade, but Philidel's choir again strikes up 'Hither this way' to bring the Britons to their senses. Before he sinks with a telltale flash, Grimbald mutters, 'Curse on her [*sic*] Voice, I must my Prey forego'. The crisis averted, Philidel and the airy spirits conduct Arthur and his soldiers to solid ground with 'Come follow me', a long, intricate piece with a great deal of text repetition. The action thus slows to a halt as Purcell fully exerts a composer's prerogative. One now believes Dryden's concession in the dedication that 'my Art, on this occasion, ought to be subservient to his'.

The next scene finds Emmeline and her attendant Matilda in a pavilion awaiting Arthur's return. Their mildly salacious banter is interrupted by a group of country folk offering an entertainment. Being 'Kentish Lads and Lasses', they are in fact Oswald's subjects; by paying their respects to Emmeline, they hint at a desire for a united Britain. Purcell's setting of 'How blest are shepherds', a superb statement of pastoral repose, masks a *double entendre* that J. A. Fuller Maitland thought acceptable in Victorian London but too lewd to be sung uncensored at the 1897 Birmingham Festival.[19] The shepherds' earnest *carpe diem* is answered by a rather more explicit duet for women, 'Shepherd, shepherd, leave decoying'. The sullying of the men's innocent inclinations is emphasized by a shift from G major to the parallel minor. The symphony for oboes and recorders, an

---

[19] 'Purcell's "King Arthur"', in *Studies in Music by Various Authors*, ed. Robin Grey (London: Simpkin, Marshall, Hamilton, Kent, 1901), p. 195.

exact anticipation of the duet, is a teasing reply to the shepherds' gesture of good will: '*Here the Men offer their Flutes to the Women, which they refuse*'. This bit of vintage Dryden merely continues the veiled crudities of Emmeline's earlier dialogue. The men quickly sign marriage contracts, and the scene ends with a skipping G major chorus, 'Come, shepherds, lead up a lively measure'.

As mentioned earlier, an inherent problem of semi-opera is the contrast between the rates at which the plot is propelled by music and by spoken dialogue. Dryden attempts to alleviate the sluggishness with which the music-laden story has progressed in the first two acts with a burst of incident. Oswald and Guillamar stray into the Britons' camp and abduct Emmeline. Arthur, his confidence shaken by the kidnapping, agrees to hold a summit conference with Oswald, but the Saxon refuses to negotiate the release of his prize and instructs Osmond to throw up a magical defence round his stronghold. Even Merlin cannot break the spell but at least consents to honour an outstanding promise to cure Emmeline's blindness. All this, including some horseplay between Philidel and Grimbald, happens in a mere five or six pages of spoken dialogue. The pantomime-like segment – improbable, contrived, and so compressed as to be confusing – is perhaps the remnant of an allegory of the stormy relationship between Shaftesbury and Halifax, since it leads to the mystical restoration of the heroine's vision, obviously a symbolic moment. The music of Philidel's lyrics accompanying this action, as well as that for the thirty-line masque of airy spirits who congratulate Emmeline, is lost. Fuller Maitland suggests that Purcell never set the verses 'because the introduction of music at a point of such dramatic importance was felt to be a little out of place' ('Purcell's "King Arthur"', p. 188), but this opinion ignores the fragmentary state of even the largest manuscripts.[20]

The next scene in Act III is the '*Prospect of Winter in Frozen Countries*', which includes the most memorable music of the opera. The masque, which the eighteenth century deemed one of Purcell's greatest works, was occasionally mounted as a separate entertainment. Its dramatic rationale is unashamedly flimsy. Emmeline, seeing Osmond's lechery in his grizzled visage, is frozen with fear. Rather than force himself upon her, the magician attempts to thaw her affections with an instructive masque in which Cupid warms the passions of the inhabitants of a country 'cak'd with Ice'. The skit is of course emblematic. Alssid interprets it as expressing 'the themes of rebirth occurring on various levels – in restored vision, in Philidel's return to heaven, in the renewal of the Arthur–Oswald friendship, in Britain's birth' ('The Impossible Form of Art', pp. 138–9). But a more obvious conceit is the awakening of desire in Emmeline, who was formerly able to feel only adolescent infatuation. The Frost Scene begins

[20] See the Purcell Society Edition, xxvi (rev. Laurie), viii.

when Cupid, descending in a machine to the accompaniment of a brisk C major symphony with French flourishes, sings the recitative 'What ho! thou genius of this isle'.[21] Roger North vividly describes the original performance by Charlotte Butler, who also portrayed Philidel: '. . . when Mrs Butler, in the Person of Cupid, was to call up Genius, she had the liberty to turne her face to the scean, and her back to the theater. She was in no concerne for her face, but sang a *recitativo* of calling towards the place where Genius was to rise, and performed it admirably, even beyond any thing I ever heard upon the English stage' (*Roger North on Music*, p. 217). Since North recounts the story to illustrate his notion that women singers who produce a strained sound when trying not to distort their faces should wear masks, his judgement cannot be taken as the last word on her voice. But Cibber, too, admired her musicianship; though principally an actress, she 'was allow'd, in those Days, to sing and dance to great Perfection'.[22]

As Dent notes, the greatness of the Cold Genius's aria 'What power thou art' lies 'in the musical idea itself' (*Foundations*, p. 213), a remarkable achievement in view of the heavy emphasis on scenic spectacle. Westrup, always anxious to deflate earlier writers who gushed about the Englishness of Purcell's inspiration, points out that the Frost music was probably suggested by a similar scene in Lully's *Isis* of 1677 (*Purcell*, p. 134).[23] But the suave 'shivering chorus' from the fourth act of the *tragédie lyrique* has little in common with the Cold Genius's first aria, except the application of wavy lines whose exact meaning is unknown. Whether it is executed *tremolando*, *vibrato*, *ondeggiando*, or even *sul ponticello*, as various enthusiasts have recommended, makes little difference; the effect is the same. The quavering strings begin with a conventional chain of harmonies, but in the fifth bar (see Example 2) the tonal centre is momentarily obscured by chromatically descending first-inversion chords, a progression that would have been regarded as daring even a hundred years later. The Genius's journey from beneath the stage is depicted by ascending semitones in the vocal part harmonized with an astonishing variety of sophisticated chords, all lying securely within the orbit of C minor. In the second section, 'See'st thou not how stiff, and wondrous old', Purcell spices the lush harmonies with more pungent dissonances – augmented triads, tone clusters, cross-relations – to bring the word 'bitter' into sharp focus. Until now the aria has been merely dazzling, but the final phrase sobs with

[21] The 1691 quarto reads 'What ho, thou Genius of the Clime'.

[22] *An Apology*, ed. Fone, p. 94: 'In the Dramatick Opera's of *Dioclesian*, and that of *King Arthur*, she was a capital, and admired Performer. In speaking too, she had a sweet-ton'd Voice, which, with her naturally genteel Air, and sensible Pronunciation, render'd her wholly Mistress of the Amiable, in Many serious Characters.'

[23] If the Frost Scene was included in the first version of the opera, then one might interpret it topically as a glance back at the extraordinarily cold winter of 1683–4, when, as Evelyn reports in his diary on 9 January 1684, shops and booths sprang up on the frozen Thames.

Example 2. *King Arthur*: Prelude while the Cold Genius rises, bars 1–8

passion; Purcell summons all his craft to capture the literal meaning of the stammering line 'Let me, let me, freeze again to death'. After a cadence in the tonic and a crotchet rest (see Example 3), the Genius re-enters on high Eb, the biting ninth of an augmented secondary dominant and the first of a chain of powerful appoggiaturas. The word 'freeze' in bar 58 occurs with the only Db in the voice, thus making the part fully chromatic.[24] The desire to keep the singer's part completely independent of the bass line during the final chromatic descent yields a pair of adjacent minor seconds, Bb–A and Ab–G, against the viola part in bar 60 (Example 3). These sound almost tame after the previous dissonances.

The aria is a *tour de force*. Its purposely antiquated chromatic style, reminiscent of Locke's and Blow's bizarreries, helps to paint a picture of the hoary Genius. Yet the carefully calculated, occasionally abstract harmonies are profoundly moving, as they twist a feeling of awe into a vision of agonizing death. Only a consummate dramatist could follow this desperately serious piece with Cupid's air 'Thou doting fool, forbear', in which the god mercilessly derides the Genius for exaggerating his condition. The simple, teasing rondeau in C major is the antithesis of the foregoing aria. The Cold Genius immediately acknowledges his extravagance in 'Great Love, I know thee', in which the voice, now locked to the bass line, moves in large vacuous gestures, apologies for the tortured lines of the C minor aria, while the diatonic quavers of the accompanying violins are almost simpering. We, not Purcell, have taken ourselves too seriously. The music manipulates our emotions, drawing us in by its sheer technical mastery, then ridiculing our pretension to sophistication. The Frost Scene

---

[24] Compare the similar excursions into remote flat keys to depict the same word in later songs, such as 'Sweeter than roses'.

Example 3. *King Arthur*: 'What power art thou', bars 57–63

invites reflection on two of the previous musical episodes. Do not the sacrifice and the pastoral follow the same pattern? Are we not also gulled by
them? Despite the Saxon hocus-pocus, we accept 'Woden, first to thee' as a
facsimile of a symphony anthem, until the rug is pulled out from under
our piety by a drinking-song. 'How blest are shepherds' makes wistful
Arcadians of even the dourest souls, until the shepherdesses remind us of

the biological consequences of innocent pleasure. If Purcell and Dryden ventured to satirize religion, morality, and passion, will patriotism, the oft-cited theme of *King Arthur*, escape similar treatment?

The rest of the Frost Scene avoids the mock gravity of the opening aria. Having warmed the Genius, Cupid repeats the process with the other inhabitants of the frozen landscape. Another C major recitative, 'No part of my dominion', leads to a rather mechanical grosteque dance, which procedes the chorus 'See, see, we assemble'. Despite its return to C minor and its indulgence in an occasional augmented chord, the latter avoids the chromatic writhing of the earlier aria. As in the confrontation between Philidel and Grimbald in Act II ('Hither this way'), the drama of the Frost Scene is packed into the first few pages, while the bulk of the music, though of high quality, is merely an entertaining spinning-out of the victory. The stylized quaking of the Cold People is supplanted by a series of rhythmically vigorous pieces, the final song of the third act being 'Sound a parley', which Dryden designed as a solo for Cupid but which Purcell realized as a rondeau for soprano and bass, presumably the Cold Genius. It is a reconciliation unencumbered by any hint of the earlier chromatic passion, except for a flatted seventh degree in the bass of the refrain, given as Example 4. The intrusion of G minor into a song of triumph will be recalled later in a similar context.

With two acts remaining, the plot has painted itself into a corner. Emmeline is still Osmond's prisoner, and Arthur must attempt another rescue. The action of the fourth act is therefore *déjà vu*, but its music is

Example 4. *King Arthur*: 'Sound a parley', bars 318–24

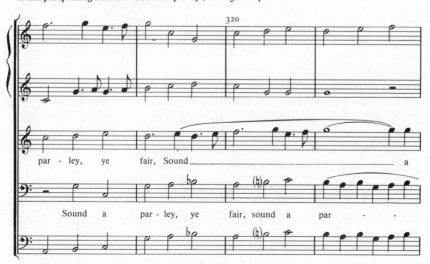

Example 4 (cont.)

par - ley,___ ye ___ fair,___ and   sur - ren - der.

- ley,   ye   fair,___ and ___ sur - ren - der.

closely linked to the protagonist. Before the hero ventures once again into the enchanted grove, Merlin warns that all he will encounter is illusion, and thus begins the dreamlike Temptation Scene. The first test of Arthur's powers of discrimination is provided by two Spenserian sirens who arise from a stream and show themselves naked to the waist. No music survives for the opening lyric, 'O pass not on', but its message is largely repeated in the duet 'Two daughters of this aged stream are we'. In this magnificent demonstration of imitative counterpoint, Purcell accomplishes the seemingly impossible task of enticing the hero with almost irresistible sensuality yet at the same time warning him to keep away. This is illustrated in Example 5, an excerpt from the middle section. The invitation to bathe, sung first in the all-too-revealing key of death, is repeated in the less sinister subdominant. But the sirens answer their own question ('What danger from a naked foe?') as they rise to ever more piercing dissonances. The choice of key underscores the dramatic irony. Though it often symbolizes metaphorical death, as earlier in 'Shepherd, shepherd, leave decoying', here G minor masks the threat of actual death with explicit eroticism, a conceit fully expressed in the next piece.

Arthur is barely able to resist the 'Fair Illusions'. As he sets off again in search of Emmeline, nymphs and sylvans appear from behind the trees. In the 1691 quarto, Dryden wanted the two-verse lyric 'How happy the lover' set as a minuet to serve as the accompaniment for a dance. Purcell produced instead a grand G minor passacaglia, the longest single piece of the score. With ritornels for alternating strings and oboes, built-in solos,

Example 5. *King Arthur*: 'Two daughters of this aged stream', bars 17–30

duts, trios, and choruses, and a continually varied four-bar bass, it resembles Grabu's mighty 'Chacon' in the second act of *Albion and Albanius*. The emphasis is clearly on dance, and the progressively more intricate instrumental variations suggest a constantly changing choreography.
As a concert piece, the passacaglia is, for all its ingenuity, merely hypnotic.
Not until the thirty-third variation (of fifty-nine all told) are two state-
ments of the ground elided by avoiding a perfect cadence (bar 130). The
increasingly complex, rather cerebral interplay between the two choirs of
instruments reaches a climax about midway through; then the ritornels

Example 6. *King Arthur*: 'For love ev'ry creature', bars 147–67

cease. Otherwise, there is little accumulation of the tension felt in Purcell's other theatrical grounds, and only two passages eschew artifice in favour of a more direct means of expression. In the duet for soprano and bass 'For love ev'ry creature', the voice parts, carried away with Monteverdian abandon, seem at times oblivious to the dictates of the bass (see Example 6, especially bars 153 and 164–7). The enraptured singers even wrest the bass from its steady course to cadence for the first time outside the tonic key (bar 159).

The final part of the passacaglia is not well preserved in the sources, and Laurie supplies an editorial bass part to the variation for three sopranos, 'In vain are our graces', because it 'seems necessary to complete the harmony' (Purcell Society Edition, XXVI, 195). The trio is a striking departure from the previous variations. The singers themselves are probably meant to symbolize the three Graces, a play on the words of the verse. Their siren song recalls the naked river nymphs, while the lyric is also a cynical reminder of the coy shepherdesses in Act II. One line of the printed text is slightly expanded from 'When Age furrows Faces, / 'Tis time to be wise', into ''Tis *too late* to be wise' (my italics). The music confirms that this, one

Example 7. *King Arthur*: 'In vain are our graces', bars 206–13

of numerous minor emendations to Dryden's text, was actually made by the composer and not by a careless copyist (see Example 7). The sudden appearance of the A major dominant chord, the paradoxical climax of the entire ground, is a final alarm to rouse King Arthur from his dangerous G minor reverie. In the three main sources of the opera – Royal Academy of Music MS XXIV.B, British Library Add. MS 31447, and Oxford, Oriel College MS Ua 35 – this section is separated from the passacaglia and placed with the music for Act V. I think the blunder suggests that Purcell did omit the basso continuo for this variation; the copyists, unaware that the trio is simply the second verse of the lyric, interpreted the radical change of texture and the temporary cessation of the harmonic ostinato as the beginning of a new piece.

A liability of most semi-operas is that after the splendours of the fourth-act entertainment the culmination of the spoken plot seems insipid by comparison. Dryden overcomes this problem in *King Arthur* in much the way Shadwell does in *Psyche*: by allowing stagecraft – rather than dialogue alone – to lift the story through the climax. Arthur finds the 'goodly Tree' which controls the enchantment of the grove, and begins to hack away. Blood spurts from its trunk and Emmeline's plaintive voice is heard within. But the king, by now a veteran of illusion, completes the gory task to break the spell. The principal dramatic event of the last act is the single combat between Arthur and Oswald; described in detail in the stage directions, it is almost a ballet, or in Sir Walter Scott's eyes 'a hiero-glyphic'.[25] In the flanking dialogue Dryden lays bare the allegory. Oswald pledges that if he should fail, he will forfeit the crown and Emmeline. Arthur retorts, 'That's two Crowns', a reference to James's vacant throne being filled by both his daughter and his son-in-law. A few lines later Dryden rubs in the irony with Arthur's victory speech: 'I wou'd Restore thee fruitful *Kent* . . . But that my *Britains* brook no Foreign Power, / To Lord it in a Land, Sacred to Freedom'.

The final masque, conjured by Merlin as a vision of the future 'Glories of our Isle', is a motley assortment of chauvinistic, pastoral and humorous lyrics that Purcell set in a wide range of styles. Alssid proposes several schemes to make these lions and lambs lie down together; but none is satis-factory, and he concludes with an air of desperation that the 'variegated verbal–musical approaches suggest that the nation's greatness depends on variety' ('The Impossible Form of Art', p. 142). No single key can unlock the thematic complexities of the masque.[26] Operating on several levels, it is a litmus test of cynicism, offending as well as delighting both rabid jingo and disillusioned patriot. The masque opens with a transformation scene,

[25] *The Works of John Dryden*, ed. Scott (London: W. Miller, 1808), VIII, 170, n.
[26] Charlton ('*King Arthur*: Dramatick Opera') views the 'proto-Mozartian' sequence of keys in the masque as its main unifying device.

as Merlin waves his wand to reveal a stormy sea. Aeolus descends from the clouds singing the famous baritone song 'Ye blust'ring brethren of the skies', a graphic depiction of the abatement of wind and waves. Thrashing semiquavers in the strings give way to quavers, and crotchets to minims. At first the singer is all but engulfed by the tumult, but as it subsides he arches upward to an exultant high G.[27] These grandly simplistic effects are underpinned by the part-writing, which, after the fugal opening, approaches chaos as the headstrong inner voices grind ferociously against treble and bass. When the rhythmic values increase, the harmony becomes uncluttered and pure. The song is in two sections, the first in C major and the second, 'Serene and calm', in which recorders replace the strings, in the parallel minor. The latter part uses only two of the eleven remaining lines of text. But the aria is well balanced as it stands, there being no reason to assume that it lacks a final section, since the major–minor tonal design is one of Purcell's favourites.

The scene continues as an island bearing the seated figure of Britannia rises *'to a soft Tune'*. This is the first and only spectacular machine effect in the entire opera, and Purcell glorifies it with a splendid symphony in which the contrasting rhythmic forces of the preceding air are reconciled. The bass resumes the stately progress of the quiet part of the C major section, while the violins dash off Italianate arpeggios in semi- and demisemiquavers.[28] These dissimilar figures seem at first to resist synchronization, as in bars 4 and 7 the harmonies outlined in the treble parts change before the drowsy bass, the one-beat delay seeming an eternity. The symphony includes one other harmonic surprise. Near the end, just after the main melodic motif is inverted, the cadential formula shown in Example 8 is troubled by a familiar bugbear (compare Example 4, above). Whether one interprets it as a recollection of Arthur's brush with death in Act IV, a reminder of the cost of Britain's glory, or simply the minor dominant of a prolonged English cadence, the G minor chord in bar 24 cuts through the symphony like an arctic wind.

The duet and chorus for Pan, a nereid, and their followers, 'Round thy coast', is a paean to a land of plenty. The setting is reserved, wisely avoiding explicit representation of the catalogue of the island's natural resources. A noteworthy passage is the approach to the E major cadence at the end of the first half ('On thy green to graze below'). The harmony in the bar before the cadence is obscure in the skeletal duet version, but when the alto and tenor parts are added in the chorus, the goose is turned a swan.

The most perplexing piece in the masque is 'For folded flocks', a male-voice trio. The lyric, a tribute to the strength of the national economy,

[27] The vocal range suggests Bowman as the singer.
[28] While the three treble parts are labelled 'violins' in Royal Academy of Music MS xxiv.b, Laurie notes that the uppermost is playable on a natural trumpet (Purcell Society Edition, xxvi, 196).

Example 8. *King Arthur*: Symphony in Act V, bars 23–5

would seem to offer a composer little to work with, despite a heavy dose of Classical allusions. The music is pure anthem, subdued, richly contra-puntal, yet all the words are audible, as if Purcell were setting his favourite psalm. I suspect, however, that beneath all the suavity he was having fun. The passage given as Example 9 is almost a parody of an English cadence. Perhaps he is simply painting the text with a touch of musical alchemy, but it would be difficult to imagine a more outrageous concentration of cross-relations.

That this holy composition is followed by the jolly, blasphemous folk-song 'Your hay it is mow'd' should come as no surprise, as the sequence is merely an exaggeration of the coupling of the sacred and the profane heard at the sacrifice in Act I. But I doubt whether many in Purcell's audience would have appreciated the connection at such long range. In fact the inclusion of a vignette of peasant life in a patriotic masque was ridiculed in a contemporary farce as a vulgar pandering to popular taste. The anonymous burlesque *The Female Wits* (autumn 1696) satirizes, among other targets, Dryden and semi-opera in the spirit of *The Rehear-sal*. In Act I Letitia Cross, who appeared as herself, says that the opera-within-the-play she and her fellow actors are practising is to have fancy costumes, and she recalls sarcastically that the exotic habits worn in Dryden's *Don Sebastian* 'enliven'd the Play as much as the Pudding and Dumpling Song did *Merlin*'. This is a reference to the third verse of 'Your hay it is mow'd' in *King Arthur*:

> For Prating so long like a Book-learn'd Sot,
> Till Pudding and Dumplin burn to Pot;
> Burn to Pot,
> Burn to Pot. . .

Example 9. *King Arthur*: 'For folded flocks', bars 28–31

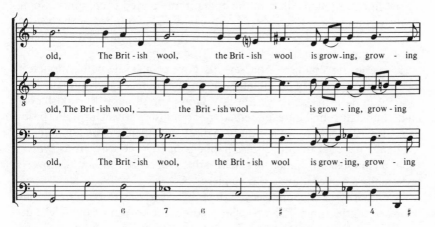

Most of the satire of *The Female Wits* is well aimed, but not all references to Purcell are so unkind. In the same scene Marsilia, who represents Mrs Manley, announces that in her play she places language and plot above music, unlike her fellow operá librettists, who 'take care of the Songish part, as I may call it, after a great Man', that is, Purcell.[29]

The song for Venus, 'Fairest isle', hailed by many as Purcell's finest, needs little exegesis. The tune is matched perfectly to the lyric; even the agitated, searching harmonies usually found near the beginning of the second strains of Purcell's binary pieces – incipient development sections, if you will – coincide here with the sanguine lines 'Cupid from his Fav'rite Nation, / Care and Envy will Remove'. The instrumental arrangement of

---

[29] Note the dig at Dryden's term 'songish part', which he coined 'for want of a proper *English* Word' in the preface to *Albion and Albanius*, *The Works of John Dryden*, xv, 4.

the song published in *Ayres for the Theatre* is, I think, an equally stunning achievement, though where in the opera it was played is unknown. Some of its harmonies are different from those required or implied by the bass of the song, and who, knowing only the vocal version, could have predicted the IV$_6$ chord on the strong beat of the second bar?

The amorous dialogue 'You say, 'tis Love creates the pain', though it opens with a beautiful declamatory air in G minor, is conventionally passionate, and the five-verse lyric by 'Mr. Howe', presumably the rakish poet and politician John Howe, presented the composer with an insoluble problem. Because each stanza is a discrete discourse, there can be no dramatic exchange between the singers, as happens in 'Tell me why' from *Dioclesian*, a composition similar in several other respects. 'You say, 'tis Love' is essentially a chain of five separate pieces.[30]

The final lyric is comprised of three brassy verses to be sung by one representing Honour. The first, 'St. George, the patron of our isle', survives as a mindless ground for soprano, two trumpets, and continuo, relegated to the appendix of the Purcell Society Edition Vol. xxvi because it is unworthy. The other two stanzas are found in all the major manuscripts as a march-like 'Grand Chorus', certainly by Purcell, which pays obeisance to King William III:

> Our Natives not alone appear
>   To Court this Martiall Prize;[31]
> But Foreign Kings, Adopted here,
>   Their Crowns at Home despise.
>
> Our Soveraign High in Aweful State,
>   His Honours shall bestow;
> And see his Scepter'd Subjects wait
>   On his Commands below.

Amid the ruffles and flourishes there is a curious oxymoron: 'Scepter'd Subjects'. How can a monarch's subjects be endowed with the symbol of royal authority? This may be a reference to Queen Mary, left to manage state affairs during her husband's frequent absences, or – to give it a cynical interpretation – perhaps Dryden is alluding to her father, James, the deposed sovereign. Purcell's mostly homophonic setting strides with tonic–dominant pomp and glitter, the staggered entries of the second strain obscuring only the penultimate line of the verses quoted above. But near the end of the forthright chorus is a truly awkward progression (shown in Example 10) that apparently cannot be explained away by faulty manuscripts or Purcell's love of quirky harmonies. The first beat of bar 19

---

[30] Charlton, in contrast ('*King Arthur*: Dramatick Opera'), considers the dialogue the climactic piece in the masque, 'as potent and apposite to growth as Dido's lament is to dissolution'.

[31] That is, the Order of the Garter.

Example 10. *King Arthur*: 'Our natives not alone appear', bars 15–23 (instruments omitted)

seems to demand a dominant chord, with G in the bass and B in the tenor; the E and C in the lower voices simply sound wrong. Is this a perverse musical pun? While the sopranos point the way firmly to a cadence in the dominant, the lower voices return prematurely to the tonic in defiance of the melody. In this somewhat puffed-up chorus of public supplication to the 'Soveraign High', his 'Scepter'd Subjects' discreetly reveal a stubborn independence. While it would be rash indeed to interpret this brief passage as evidence of the composer's Jacobite leanings, Dryden, had he had an understanding of the rudiments of music theory, would have been pleased with his collaborator's small act of disobedience. Theirs was an age of disguise and cynicism. If poets relished hiding treason in the plots of plays, should one be surprised to find composers attempting analogous gestures in the music for those plays?

Although *King Arthur* was Purcell's greatest popular success, it was by no means the most lavish of the semi-operas. Downes reports that it was 'Excellently Adorn'd with Scenes and Machines' (*Roscius Anglicanus*, p. 42), but the play-book has practically no description of the stage effects so richly detailed in *Albion and Albanius*, *Dioclesian*, *The Fairy-Queen*, and most of the new operas produced after Purcell's death. Except in the fifth-act masque, the Dorset Garden stage machinery seems to have been used for little more than routine ascents and descents. Of the greatly admired Frost Scene we have no detailed account until Gray's description of the 1735–6 revival (*Correspondence*, pp. 58–9):

the first Scene of it is only a Cascade, that seems frozen; with the Genius of Winter asleep & wrapt in furs, who upon the approach of Cupid, after much quivering, & shaking sings the finest song in the Play: just after, the Scene opens, & shows a view of arched rocks coverd with Ice & Snow to ye end of ye Stage; between the arches are upon pedestals of Snow eight Images of old men & women, that seem frozen into Statues, with Icicles hanging about them & almost hid in frost, & from ye end come Singers . . . & Dancers all rubbing their hands & chattering with cold with fur gowns & worsted gloves in abundance.

Gray was impressed by more than scenery, and earlier in the same letter he succinctly describes the special aura that any competent production of the opera should create: 'the inchanted part of the play, is not Machinery, but actual magick' (p. 57). What distinguishes *King Arthur* from the rest of Purcell's major stage works, indeed from all other examples of the genre, is that the music achieves a pre-eminence not by overwhelming the listener with constantly blaring sound, but by insinuating quiet charm through sophistication (the Cold Genius's aria) and rustic simplicity ('Your hay it is mow'd'). Paradoxically, this intimacy of expression is accomplished by a greater mingling of the orchestra, chorus, and vocal ensembles than in any other Purcell stage work. And underlying all the grand effects is an attention to detail which belies the common belief that the Restoration dramatic opera is an unplanned conglomerate of gaudy excesses. Despite the length of the musical scenes, *King Arthur* is still essentially a tragicomedy in which the songish part does not seriously disrupt the unities.

Even without its music, *King Arthur* is a perplexing work. Hume is certainly justified in calling it patchy reading and a 'potpourri' (*The Development*, p. 405). This perceived unevenness is, I think, the result of Dryden's having transformed what was originally a heartfelt parable of royal reconciliation into a backhanded compliment to a king for whom he did not much care. The Theatre Royal was not the Académie Royale de Musique, and I cannot fully accept Buttrey's thesis that virtually every operatic work mounted in London in the late seventeenth century was perforce a paean to the monarchy. *King Arthur* may well be, as Moore claims, the first English national opera, but it is not a royal one. Westrup detects 'a patriotism of the spirit . . . beneath the conceits and conventions that form the crust of Dryden's text', an almost Rupert Brookeian 'holiness' embodied in such pieces as 'Fairest isle' and 'Your hay it is mow'd' (*Purcell*, p. 136). But in transferring Victorian sentimentality to the dramatic opera, one must necessarily paper over huge cracks in the panegyrical façade. Only the politically naïve could have heard it as a celebration of the British monarchy. *King Arthur* is an audacious study in irony.

8 The Fairy-Queen

The Fairy-Queen (first version, May 1692; second version, February 1693) was the last and costliest of the Dorset Garden extravaganzas mounted before the dissolution of the United Company in early 1695. Despite the splendid music, it is the most controversial of the semi-operas, largely because it is an adaptation of *A Midsummer Night's Dream*. The rewriting of Shakespeare during the Restoration is a touchy subject, often regarded by authorities and laymen alike as one of the blackest marks against the age. The old-guard scholars – H. H. Furness, Hazelton Spencer, Allardyce Nicoll, and others – preferred to ridicule the adaptations than to study them seriously. More recent writers – notably Christopher Spencer, Roger Savage, and George R. Guffey – have treated them more as theatre pieces than as butchered literary masterworks. The debate is between purists, whose fundamental objection to any tampering with Shakespeare's texts is of course irrefutable, and those critics who view the process of adaptation as a function of production. Before advocating the latter position, I must restate two important considerations often overlooked by both sides. First, Sir William Davenant, the most strongly condemned of the early Restoration adapters, may well have been legally obliged by the terms of the patent granted him in 1660 to 'reform' (that is, to alter and modernize) the plays before mounting them, though whether this required more than simply expunging 'all prophanenesse and scurrility' has recently been debated.[1] But the trend was set. Some plays that acquired significant amounts of song, dance, and spectacle, such as *Macbeth* and *The Tempest*, bore their added burden more or less gracefully, and became perennial favourites in their new clothes, in some cases holding the stage throughout the eighteenth century. Secondly, several different kinds of Shakespearean alterations were made during the period, ranging from irredeemable redactions such as Tate's heavily cut *King Richard the Second*, sufficiently disfigured to make plot and characters mere shadows of their former selves, to worthier plays, such as *All for Love*, for which *Antony and Cleopatra* is the source of an essentially new work.

---

[1] See John Freehafer, 'The Formation of the London Patent Companies in 1660', *Theatre Notebook*, 20 (1966), 27. For an opposing view, see Mongi Raddadi, *Davenant's Adaptations of Shakespeare*, p. 21, and Gunnar Sorelius, 'The Early History of the Restoration Theatre: Some Problems Reconsidered', *Theatre Notebook*, 33 (1979), 52–61.

The Adaptation of Shakespeare's Play

The Fairy-Queen falls between these extremes. Not unexpectedly, scholarly opinion is divided. Among music historians, Dent is the most censorious, calling the opera 'a barbarously mutilated version' of the original play (*Foundations*, p. 216), a sentiment shared by the modern drama historian Hume, who views it as 'mangled' (*Development*, p. 209). Furness, often cited as the first to pour vitriol on the Shakespearean alterations, is in fact far less condemnatory of *The Fairy-Queen* than any writer before Gunnar Sorelius. While ridiculing the infantile poetry of the interpolated masques, he pays the adapter a near-compliment: 'there are omissions, it is true, but there is no attempt at "improvement"'.[2] But, as explained below, Furness had not actually read the 1692 play-book, an oversight that might account for the uncharacteristically tepid judgement. Hazelton Spencer is in two minds about *The Fairy-Queen*. While sneering that such musical and scenic embellishments of Shakespeare 'do not call for serious criticism' (a surprising admission considering that he devoted a book to the subject), he notes elsewhere that the adapter's 'treatment of the text, while ruthless in excision, is commendable in its lack of verbal improvements'.[3] This opinion is echoed by Sorelius, who is surprised that in 'this rigmarole of spectacle, music and dance' Shakespeare escaped 'comparatively unchanged in tone and essence'.[4] We need to discover what the 1692 reviser hoped to accomplish and to test Westrup's statement that the opera 'is simply a succession of masques, which have so little connection with the play that no one who merely heard the music would have the remotest suspicion that it was an adaptation of Shakespeare's *Midsummer Night's Dream*' (*Purcell*, p. 137).

The identity of the adapter is unknown. W. Carew Hazlitt suggested Dryden, apparently because the poet's works are advertised at the foot of the title-page of the first edition.[5] Many bibliographies and library catalogues follow F. C. Brown's attribution to Settle, proposed in his 1910 biography of the playwright.[6] But this claim is also fanciful. Brown states that in the unsigned preface to the 1692 quarto 'the author calls the piece his first opera, a statement which might have been made by Settle' but not Dryden. The epistle includes no such remark; Brown has merely confused an excerpt from the prologue to Davenant's *The Siege of Rhodes* with the

---

[2] *A New Variorum Edition of Shakespeare, A Midsommer Nights Dreame*, 8th edn (Philadelphia: Lippincott, 1923), p. 340.

[3] *Shakespeare Improved*, pp. 322–4.

[4] *'The Giant Race before the Flood': Pre-Restoration Drama on the Stage and in the Criticism of the Restoration*, Studia Anglistica Upsaliensia, 4 (Uppsala, 1966), p. 165.

[5] *Bibliographical Collections and Notes on Early English Literature*, 2nd ser. (London: B. Quaritch, 1882), p. 185.

[6] *Elkanah Settle: His Life and Works* (Chicago: Univ. of Chicago Press, 1910), p. 96.

preface itself.[7] Although no contemporary account of the semi-opera sheds any light on who prepared it for the stage, Betterton is a reasonable guess. He was involved in all the previous Dorset Garden operas, almost certainly reworked *The Prophetess* in 1690, and was paid to prepare *The Indian Queen* for Purcell, though he apparently backed out of the latter project with the onset of the 1694–5 actors' rebellion (see Chapter 3).

A Midsummer Night's Dream was not popular during the Restoration, and except for a revival that left Pepys cold (*Diary*, 29 September 1662), no other performance is recorded before the première of *The Fairy-Queen*. Yet it was a natural choice for conversion into a semi-opera. Besides turning the play into an entertainment at least half of whose running time is devoted to music, dance, and scenic transformations, the adapter's chief aim seems to have been to retain as much of the *Dream* as his brief would allow. The original text includes five important musical scenes, all giving composer and choreographer considerable latitude. In II.ii the fairies sing Titania to sleep with the air and chorus 'You spotted snakes'; and in III.i she is awakened by Bottom's bestial lyrics 'The ousel cock' and 'The finch, the sparrow, and the lark'. The queen's recovery in IV.i is accompanied by instrumental music, after which the fairy monarchs celebrate their renewed marital concord with a dance. In Act V the mechanicals' Bergomask is an open-ended invitation for songish drollery. And music is vital to Oberon and Titania's final appearance, though whether one or both is meant to sing and whether a lyric is missing after V.i.382 are subjects of a debate begun by Dr Johnson's 'series of the Scene' analysis.[8]

With such a rich palette of operatic possibilities, one may wonder why Purcell and his collaborators decided to divide the cast exclusively into actors and singers, dispensing with most of Shakespeare's lyrics, ignoring the characters who do sing, and concentrating the new music into four masques (adding a fifth for the 1693 revival). The restructuring does not seem to have been dictated by practical considerations. If the composer had wanted Oberon and Titania to sing in Act V, then Bowman and Mrs Butler were well equipped to take the parts. And if Bottom had been expanded into a singing role, Doggett could have managed moderately difficult comic songs. I detect Purcell's involvement in this deliberate separation of forces, because *The Fairy-Queen* reflects a trend seen in other less lavish theatre works produced between 1692 and 1694, in which he preferred to set incidental songs for the non-speaking professional singers, leaving Eccles to write for Mrs Bracegirdle and the other singing actors (see Chapter 4). But the key to the plan behind the adaptation is the treatment of the artisans' play-within-the-play, the only major structural alteration

---

[7] See Milhous and Hume, 'Attribution Problems in English Drama, 1660–1700', p. 15.
[8] See *A Midsummer Night's Dream*, ed. Harold F. Brooks, The Arden Shakespeare (London: Methuen, 1979), p. cxxiii, n. 3.

of the *Dream*. For the composer, it occupies the most important position in the play – the centrepiece of the spacious, almost leisurely dénouement, the logical place to insert a long, incidental entertainment. But the Lamentable Comedy was removed from Act V and combined with the rehearsal in the wood in Act III, probably because 'Pyramus and Thisbe' set as a comic finale would detract from the musical theme of both original and gently reworked operatic version.

In the *Dream* music serves two distinct functions: for the fairies it induces sleep and conjures fantastic visions, while the mortals' songs and symphonies are intended to awaken or dispel illusion. Accordingly, the dream begins with the queen's lullaby in Act II, while Bottom's raucous ditties wake her after the application of the love-juice. The pairs of mortal lovers sleep peacefully during the fairy rulers' dance, but are then roused by the sound of Theseus's hunting-horns. And to bring the action full circle, we, the external audience, are lulled to sleep by Oberon and Titania's final music. Most of Purcell's interpolations, at least in the 1692 version, pertain to the world of dreams and fairies, disregarding the mortals. This bias required some minor reworking of the spoken dialogue leading to the masques and the discarding or amplification of Shakespeare's lyrics, but the change of focus does only a little harm to the play itself, as the following synopsis shows.

Act I. The 1692 play-book (hereinafter called Q1692) closely follows Shakespeare's opening scene, but some of the dialogue is compressed, cut, or rewritten in order to remove Hippolyta and Philostrate, to suppress the locale (Athens and a nearby wood), and to reduce the ambiguous time of action in the original from two or three nights to a single night and day. Also deleted is Theseus's invocation of the death penalty against Hermia should she disobey her father's command to marry Demetrius. The absence of Philostrate, the master of the revels, whose chief function in the *Dream* is to present Theseus with a choice of entertainments in Act V, results from the replacement of 'Pyramus and Thisbe' by Purcell's fantastical masque, imposed upon the dumbfounded mortal audience by Oberon as a demonstration of his supernatural powers. The lifting of the death threat hanging over Hermia appears to be a squeamish emendation, though other unpleasantnesses remain in Q1692. The poetry most consistently modernized here and throughout the play is the dialogue of the pairs of lovers, in which scarcely a line has not been touched up. But these changes are nearly all fastidious rather than substantive. The most heavily rewritten speeches are the soliloquies, and Helena's in I.i.226–51 ('How happy some o'er other can be! / Through Athens I am thought as fair as she') is no exception.[9] Perhaps not coincidentally, these are the passages to which modern editors are wont to append the greatest number of explana-

---

[9] References to act, scene, and line are in all cases to the Arden edition.

tory notes; by 1692 a veil of obscurity had already begun to descend over Shakespeare's imagery.[10]

The second scene of Act I, in which the artisans devise a play to celebrate the anticipated nuptials, corresponds closely to the *Dream*, except that Quince casts himself as Thisbe, ordering Flute to play another role. The distribution of the parts continues until I.ii.85, at which point the rehearsal in the forest in the third act of the original is inserted. The truncation, necessary to accommodate the far more disruptive removal of the performance of the Lamentable Comedy from Act V, may explain the vagueness of the locale, since in Shakespeare the mechanicals make their plans in Athens, then retire to the wood for their rehearsal in order not to be 'dogged with company, and our devices known' (I.ii.96–7). In Q1692 the two scenes are combined in a single setting – unspecified, but presumably the 'Palace' in which the act begins. The rearrangement produces only one awkward moment: Bottom questions Quince about the way Pyramus dies before having time to study his part.

Act II. The fairy protasis is faithful to Shakespeare, and the adapter makes no attempt to gloss over Oberon and Titania's marital strife, though its causes receive a different emphasis. The queen's doting on the Indian boy is made the main bone of contention between them, but the story of how Titania assumed guardianship after his mother's death is removed. All mention of the fairy monarchs' recent adultery with mortals, including Oberon's dalliance with Hippolyta, is also excised, prudery that may explain the absence of Theseus's Amazon. I detect no attempt to manufacture the kind of political allegory hypothesized for *Dioclesian* and *King Arthur*, and indeed these changes may have been made to avoid unflattering parallels between the fairy rulers and William and Mary.

The most surprising omission from this scene is Titania's famous foul-weather speech (II.i.81ff), a topical allusion to the dislocation of the seasons experienced in 1594 (see the Arden edition, pp. xxxvi–xxxvii). This is a major loss, but it may have been considered redundant when weighed against Purcell's masque of the seasons added to Act IV.[11] As in the first act, the heated dialogue between Demetrius and Helena is tinkered with, presumably to make it more comprehensible to a late seventeenth-century audience. But the adapter, who understood the Shakespeare extremely

---

[10] One curious omission from the first scene that does not fit the pattern outlined above is the cutting of I.i.171–4, in which Hermia promises to meet Lysander in the wood, swearing to do so 'by that fire which burn'd the Carthage queen / When the false Trojan under sail was seen'. See Chapter 5 for a discussion of the possibly unpleasant implications of this metaphor during the reign of William and Mary.

[11] Cf. Roger Savage, 'The Shakespeare–Purcell *Fairy Queen*', *Early Music*, 1 (1973), 213: 'Cutting this may seem criminal until we discover that, though it is taken away with one hand, it is given back with the other in the form of the emblematically apt and musically superb Masque of the Seasons late in Act IV . . . at the point when Oberon and Titania are reconciled . . .' But see below for a different interpretation of the symbolism of the masque.

well, carefully preserves the original meaning, and is even influenced by the usage he attempts to modernize. Consider the two versions of Helena's speech, II.i.232–4:

Shakespeare	*Q1692*
The dove pursues the griffin, the mild hind	The Dove chases the Vulture; the mild Hind
Makes speed to catch the tiger – bootless speed,	Makes haste to catch the Tyger; prepostrous Chace,
When cowardice pursues and valour flies!	When Cowardice pursues, and Valour flies.

Note that Q1692 borrows the archaic literal meaning of 'preposterous' (that is, backside foremost) from Shakespeare's III.ii.121, Puck's perverse observation that 'those things do best please me / That befall prepost'rously'.

Most of Shakespeare's second scene, the singing to sleep of Titania, is replaced by the first masque, an insertion preceded by twenty lines of new dialogue cobbled together from various passages of the original. At the end of the masque, the act continues with an abridged version of Lysander and Hermia's elopement, in which the latter's defence of her virtue is underscored by the stage direction *'They lye down at a distance'*, that is, away from each other. The scene ends at II.ii.82 of the original, after Puck administers the love-juice to the wrong youth, a confusion facilitated by Q1692's dressing both Lysander and Demetrius in 'Embroider'd Garments'.

Act III. The masque of sleep so enlarges the second act in Q1692 that the conclusion of Shakespeare's II.ii – Lysander's awakening and falling in love with Helena – must be transferred to the beginning of Act III, the second scene of which is devoted to the play-within-the-play. Except for the removal of two-thirds of the prologue (V.i.126–50), 'Pyramus and Thisbe' is acted much as in the original, though now a rehearsal attended only by Puck rather than a performance heckled by Theseus, Hippolyta, and the two Athenean youths. Much of the humour arising from the aristocratic ridicule is lost, and even the mispunctuation of the prologue is corrected, since no auditor clever enough to appreciate the hilarious blunders is present. Curiously, Q1692 gives Puck some of Theseus's biting rejoinders (V.i.180–1, for example), to which Bottom, in the role of Pyramus, replies as if conversing with his fellows. On the surface, their dialogue is perplexing, because Puck is still supposed to be invisible, awaiting the right moment to frighten away the mechanicals and clap on the ass-head. The scene could be made to work by careful blocking, but it is an awkward sequence. Viewed sympathetically, Bottom's unwitting conversation with Robin Goodfellow foreshadows the weaver's impending assification and entry into fairyland, and even helps prepare the much more startling departure from Shakespeare's text at the end of Act V, when the mortals encounter the fairies without the benefit of dreams, an enchanted forest, or love potions.

In view of Leveridge's and Lampe's successful musical versions of the Lamentable Comedy, one may wonder why Purcell did not seize the opportunity to create a miniature comic opera.[12] He too was a skilled satirist, as is ably demonstrated in the scene for the drunken poet added to *The Fairy-Queen* in 1693. But one must remember that 'Pyramus and Thisbe' is a burlesque of amateur acting, while the later masques send up Italian *opera seria*. In 1692 Purcell had no operatic tradition to lampoon, and a musical rendition of the play-within-the-play could do no more than capture the spirit of the original. Before condemning the semi-opera for altering the sequence of events in the *Dream*, critics should appreciate that the removal of the artisans' comedy from the fifth to the third act was the only way to preserve it.

At the end of the play-within-the-play, but before the excised Bergo-mask, Act III resumes its original sequence. Shakespeare's lyrics for the newly translated Bottom appear in Q1692, but Purcell is not known to have set them. The sexual aspect of Titania's infatuation with the monster is one of the celebrated ambiguities of the *Dream*, and Harold Brooks represents a consensus of scholarly opinion when he notes that 'even a controlled suggestion of carnal bestiality is surely impossible: jealous Oberon will not have cast his spell to cuckold himself' (The Arden Shakespeare, p. cxv, n. 1). During the Restoration, however, self-cuckoldom was a highly developed conceit, almost a fixation among several playwrights, particularly Otway and Southerne. Surprisingly, the textual emendations in Q1692 do little to intensify the latent eroticism of the adoration; in fact, Titania's most salacious line is removed: 'To have my love to bed, and to arise' (III.i.164). The third scene of Act III continues as in the *Dream*, except that Demetrius's entreaties to Hermia (III.ii.43–87) are played in dumb show, while the episode ends with a masque inspired by the beginning of Shakespeare's Act IV and representing Titania's adoration of Bottom. This gloriously ironic scene, the central lyrical part of the opera, dwells on Oberon's self-cuckoldom, sending shock waves through much of the remaining music.

Act IV. The adoring masque displaces most of Shakespeare's III.ii into the fourth act of *The Fairy-Queen*; yet except for one long cut (III.ii.197–242) the entanglement among the pairs of lovers is largely intact. After bringing the amorous sub-plot up to date, Q1692 then devotes the rest of the fourth act to the reunion of Oberon and Titania, based on the original IV.i.64ff. The dance of royal reconciliation is replaced by a masque in cele-

---

[12] Leveridge's dates from 1716 and Lampe's from 1745: see Roger Fiske, *English Theatre Music in the Eighteenth Century* (London: Oxford Univ. Press, 1973), pp. 59, 157–8.

bration of the sunrise and, metaphorically as the seasonal renewal of life, the curing of the fairy queen's infatuation with the Indian boy. Through remarkably judicious editing, the adapter has achieved the seemingly impossible tasks of removing the Lamentable Comedy from Act V and inserting three long masques into Acts II–IV, while preserving most of the action of the mortals, fairies, and artisans.

Act V. Turning to the second part of Shakespeare's fourth act (IV.i. 102ff), the opera brings the mortals' story to a close. The mechanicals make a last appearance, the only major deviation from the original text being Snug's report of what might have been: 'O Masters! the Duke's going to the Temple! the Lords and the Ladies are to be Married this Morning. If our Play had gone forward, we had been all made Men.' The final scene begins as in V.i of the *Dream*, with Theseus superciliously rejecting the lovers' fantastic stories of the preceding night in the forest. A short symphony heralds the arrival of Oberon, Titania, Puck, and all the fairies. The fairy king announces to an astonished Theseus a masque 'To cure your Incredulity'; the duke feebly responds, 'does my sence inform me right? / Or is my hearing better than my sight?'

Before regarding the mingling of mortals and fairies as the last straw, one should pause to reflect. Until this point no one could deny that the adaptation preserves the spirit and to a large extent the letter of the original. One may abhor the changes, but *The Fairy-Queen* is still *A Midsummer Night's Dream*. Thus having fulfilled what they apparently regarded as an obligation to tell Shakespeare's story essentially as he wrote it, Purcell and his collaborator felt free to exercise their fancy. Another facet of their underlying design now emerges. The masques have been an entertainment for Titania, Bottom, and Oberon, in that order. The culminating show draws the mortals, now fully conscious, into the fantasy world, a *coup de théâtre* that resurrects the heart of the Stuart masque: the revels, during which masquers and audience met in a phantasmagoric dance, a fusion of the real and the representational. None of the speaking characters sings or dances in the final entertainment, yet the protagonists are no longer mere observers; they have themselves become a part of the dream.

The Fairy-Queen was a costly production. Narcissus Luttrell reports that the Theatre Royal sank £3,000 in it, and Downes the prompter writes that while the 'Court and Town were wonderfully satisfy'd with it. . . the Company got very little by it'.[13] And the preface to Q1692, which begins as if it were going to be a probing discussion of the aesthetics of music drama, digresses to a rambling plea for money to support opera in London, 'considering what a Sum we must Yearly lay out among Tradesmen for the fitting out so great a work'. The opera's gestation appears to

---

[13] *A Brief Historical Relation of State Affairs*, II, 435; *Roscius Anglicanus*, p. 43.

have been unusually long, even for a work of this kind. The play-book was entered in the Stationers' Register on 2 November 1691, and *The Gentleman's Journal* for January 1692 states that production was imminent, a claim repeated in the March issue. In April the same journal reports the banning of Dryden's *Cleomenes*, adding that the expected semi-opera 'will be hasten'd upon this account'. The première finally came on 2 May, and if one can believe the newspaper gossip even this performance may have been rushed, despite preparations begun at least seven months earlier.

The opera was revived in February of the following year, 'With Alterations, Additions, and several new Songs', as announced on the title-page of the 1693 play-book (hereinafter called Q1693). Perhaps the revision was intended to recoup some of the loss incurred by the extraordinarily expensive original production; at least I can see no artistic reason for the changes made in Q1693, all of which damage the fragile but ingenious union of Shakespeare's play and Purcell's music outlined above. Furness's description of the opera, upon which many later scholars have relied, is based on Q1693, from which one might well draw the conclusion that the *Dream* has been truly ravished.[14] The major disfigurements are the addition of new music for the fairies and a skit for a drunken poet, both at the end of Act I. These necessitated the removal of the entire first scene, thereby rendering the mortals' plot incomprehensible to anyone unfamiliar with the play. Roger Savage believes the omission of the scene to be a 'printing-house convenience', adding that 'I am sure it was never performed without it' ('The Shakespeare–Purcell *Fairy Queen*', p. 209, n. 19). But the following alteration, previously unnoticed by scholars, shows that the 1693 production was almost certainly acted without the first scene. It will be recalled that in Q1692 all references to Theseus and Hippolyta's wedding are removed, since the Amazon herself is omitted.

Shakespeare

Quince. Here is the scroll of every man's name which is thought fit through all
  Athens to play in our interlude before the Duke and the Duchess, on his wedding-
  day at night (I.ii.4–6).

Q1692	*Q1693*
Quince. Here is the Scrowl of every Man's Name, who is thought fit through all the Town to play in our Enterlude before the Duke, at the Marriage of *Lysander* and *Hermia*, or *Demetrius* and *Hermia*, no matter which.	Quince. Here is the Scrowl of every Man's Name, who is thought fit through all the Town to play in our Enterlude before the Duke, on his Wedding-Day.

[14] *A New Variorum Edition*, p. 340: 'The Opera opens with the Second Scene of the Comedy's First Act, when the Clowns have assembled to arrange for the Play.'

In Q1693 the names of the pairs of lovers are suppressed, since they have yet to appear. The other changes in the revival production are minor by comparison: a song 'Ye gentle spirits of the air' is added to the third-act masque; and the famous Plaint, 'O let me weep', is inserted after Juno's song in the fifth act. Both lyrics are printed on separate sheets bound into a re-issue of Q1692.[15]

The Sources

By a great stroke of luck a theatre score of *The Fairy-Queen* prepared under Purcell's supervision and partly autograph survives in the Royal Academy of Music (MS 3). In 1701 the managers of the Theatre Royal placed an advertisement in two London newspapers, the following appearing in *The Flying Post* 9–11 October:

The Score of Musick for the Fairy Queen, set by the late Mr. Henry Purcel, and belonging to the Patentees of the Theatre-Royal in Covent-Garden, London, being lost upon his Death: Whoever shall bring the said Score, or a true Copy thereof, first to Mr. Zachary Baggs, Treasurer of the said Theatre, shall have twenty Guinea's for the same.

Apparently drawing no response, the notice was run again in the 16–20 October issue of *The London Gazette*, with the following postscript: '. . . twenty Guinea's reward, or proportional for any act or acts there of'. Scholars have assumed that these appeals netted some result, but not the lost full score, since only one act of the opera was performed at Drury Lane on 1 February 1703.[16] The theatre score remained hidden until J. S. Shedlock discovered it in virtually mint condition at the library of the Royal Academy of Music about 1900. Its disappearance during the period when the company might profitably have revived the opera probably saved it from the wear and tear that undoubtedly destroyed other theatre copies.

As it includes all the music added to Act I as well as 'Ye gentle spirits of the air' in the third-act masque, Royal Academy MS 3 was prepared for the 1693 version. It is by far the most complete manuscript of any Purcell semi-opera, recording even the act music. Of the lyrics required in Q1693 it omits only the Plaint and 'When I have often heard' in Act III (both discussed below), as well as three instrumental pieces that have not been recovered: at the end of Act I, a blank folio was left for a 'Dance' with a key signature of one flat (fol. 20); in Act III after the dialogue for Coridon and Mopsa, space was set aside for a 'Dance for a Clown' in G major (fol. 47v); and after the masque in Act IV, there is ample room for a 'Dance for the 4

---

[15] Between pp. 30 and 31, and 48 and 49. Only the first act was reset to complete Q1693. See Paul S. Dunkin, 'Issues of *The Fairy Queen*, 1692', *The Library*, 4th ser., Transactions of the Bibliographical Society, 26 (1946), 297–304.

[16] With a cut-down version of *Marriage A-la-Mode*; see *The London Stage*, Part 2, p. 31.

seasons of the year' (fols. 79v–81).[17] The missing music implies that the score was made in haste before the February 1693 revival. But rare is the manuscript of late seventeenth-century English theatre music that includes all the dances required by the play-books.[18] The Royal Academy score does not otherwise give the impression of having been hurriedly copied, and I should guess that it was prepared after the event for the library of the Theatre Royal, passing from Purcell's hands before he could write in the dances.

The score is mainly the work of an unidentified copyist (scribe A), while the first three pages are in a second hand (scribe B), and the 'Dance for Chinese Man & Woman' entered at the back of the inverted volume was copied by a third person (scribe C). Sections in Purcell's autograph are found throughout:

page[19]	piece	comment	Royal Academy MS
1	first music, prelude	1st violin and bass parts of bar 4, beats 3–4	fol. 1v
4	first music, hornpipe	viola, bar 4, last three crotchets	2v
6–7	second music, air	all parts, bars 6–20	3–3v
8–9	second music, rondeau	all parts	3v–4
10	beginning of overture	trumpets, bars 1–3; 1st violin, bars 1–2; 2nd violin, bars 3–4	4
34–5	first act tune	complete	20v
65	Dance for the Followers of Night	rubric '4 in 2' in Purcell's hand	35v
102–3	third act tune	complete	54v
141–3	'See my many colour'd fields'	autograph begins in strings, bar 25, and in all other parts from bar 33, except the text, which starts in bar 38	76v–77v
147	fourth act tune	1st violin part and bass only in autograph, as well as all accidentals	81v
149–51	'Thrice happy'	opening recitative completely autograph, except clefs; voice part, bars 45–6, corrected by Purcell	82v–83
185–90	'Sure the dull god'	autograph begins at last quaver of bar 5	97–100

The composer also supervised or at least proof-read the bulk of the work of the other copyists. The airs of the first and second music are very faulty, and he seems to have taken over from scribe B in the middle of the piece on fol. 3, as if exasperated. After beginning the overture, he left by far the

[17] Other gaps include blank staves for second violin and viola parts in the 'Dance for hay makers' in Act III, fol. 47, and beginning on fol. 48 a vacant staff with a bass clef was left in the countertenor air 'A thousand, thousand ways'.
[18] See my article 'Restoration Stage Fiddlers and Their Music', pp. 316–17.
[19] In Purcell Society Edition, XII (rev. Anthony Lewis) (1968).

largest share of the work to the generally reliable scribe A. As mentioned in earlier chapters, Purcell was meticulous about accidentals, and his own sharps and flats are sprinkled throughout the manuscript, heavily in those pieces written by scribes B and C. In the Preludio (fol. 1v), for example, the composer has marked nearly every accidental with laborious redundancy, as he has done in those pieces in his own hand. An even more cautious editorial procedure is seen in the chaconne for the Chinese man and woman, in which Purcell, obviously having instructed the perhaps inexperienced scribe C to omit the sharps and flats, added all the chromatics after the piece was copied. His obsession with this aspect of notation demands that one accept the readings of the Royal Academy manuscript literally, something its editors have not always done. The two commonest misinterpretations are adding chromatics where Purcell wrote none, and assuming incorrectly that accidentals hold throughout the bar.

The Royal Academy score, while clearly the best source for *The Fairy-Queen*, is not the earliest. Shortly after the première in 1692, Purcell published *Some Select Songs, as they are Sung in the Fairy Queen*, which includes nine airs and the popular dialogue for Coridon and Mopsa. Some of these differ significantly from the versions in the Royal Academy manuscript. The only other major sources are *Ayres for the Theatre* (1697), *Orpheus Britannicus* (1698, 1702) and a manuscript in the British Council Library, OP. 45, which dates from after 1700. The latter, the largest single source after the Royal Academy score, includes less than half the total music in the opera. Margaret Laurie's collation of the variants is of the utmost importance in evaluating the differences between the 1692 and 1693 productions; her findings are summarized in Figure 3.[20] Despite its late date, the British Council manuscript includes only music from the original production, and it agrees more closely with *Some Select Songs* than with the Royal Academy score. Laurie also notes that the pieces in *Orpheus Britannicus* have a greater affinity with the British Council manuscript than with the partial autograph, implying that they too may be survivors from the first production. The act music in *Ayres for the Theatre* closely resembles that in Purcell's hand in the Royal Academy manuscript. Since the full score was mislaid in 1695 and therefore was unavailable to Purcell's widow when she assembled the instrumental suites for publication in *Ayres for the Theatre* two years later, the incidental music probably existed in a separate autograph from which the composer himself copied when preparing the 1693 full score.[21] The original score, or parts of it, must have survived until at least 1702, when it was tapped for the second book of *Orpheus Britannicus*. Another confirmation that the Royal Academy manuscript was out of circulation after 1695 is that the anthology reprints

[20] The variants are discussed in detail in 'Purcell's Stage Works', pp. 108–18.
[21] The overture presents a special problem discussed below.

Fig. 3

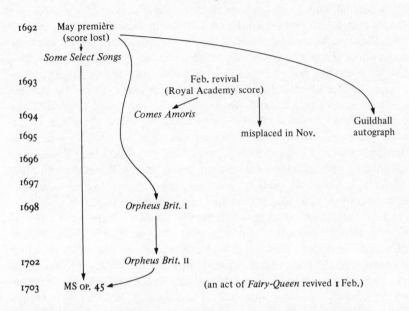

the reading of the duet 'Come, let us leave the town' published in *Comes Amoris*, v (1694), rather than the one in the full score. Purcell made yet another version of some of the songs and duets in *The Fairy-Queen* in the Guildhall Library song-book, which was not used as the source for *Orpheus Britannicus* or for any other manuscript; that the Guildhall manuscript is more closely related to the British Council score than to the Royal Academy one is probably a coincidence rather than the result of linear descent. To summarize Laurie's classification, the sources fall into three groups: *Some Select Songs*, *Orpheus Britannicus*, and the British Council manuscript are remnants of the lost score of the 1692 production; the Royal Academy manuscript was prepared for the 1693 revival; and the revised pieces in the Guildhall Library song-book, probably assembled for teaching purposes, were never sung in a production of the opera, nor were they subsequently published.

The major difference between the music for the two productions is the greater number of songs and ensembles for sopranos in the Q1692 sources. For example, the voice parts of the echo duet in Act II, 'May the god of wit inspire', are in alto, tenor, and bass clefs in the Royal Academy score, while in British Council MS OP. 45 the upper parts are placed an octave higher in the treble clef. One may wonder whether in the latter manuscript voice parts are written indiscriminately in the treble clef, as is often the case in the printed song-books; even *Orpheus Britannicus* sometimes gives alto and tenor parts an octave too high. But the appearance in both *Some Select Songs* and MS OP. 45 of airs in the alto clef – such as 'A thousand, thousand ways we'll find', which is known to have been sung by the counter-tenor Freeman – adds weight to the authority of the Q1692 sources. Nine pieces in all seem to have been transferred from female to male voices in the 1693 theatre score.[22] But one must not automatically assume that Purcell made these changes. An unsettling aspect of MS OP. 45 is that several of the treble airs designated for alto or tenor in the Royal Academy manuscript are too high for the normal soprano range. For instance, the first song in Act II, 'Come all ye songsters' in C major, often touches top A in the soprano version, a pitch that Purcell uses sparingly elsewhere. In fact, when he later arranged this piece for treble voice in the Guildhall Library song-book, he moved it down a tone to B♭ major. A similar trans-position occurs in the music for Act IV. The British Council version of the duet 'Let the fifes and the clarions' is for sopranos in C major, while in the Royal Academy manuscript it is in D for altos. But in its British Council form the piece badly disrupts the key scheme for the masque, the duet being surrounded by music in D major.

The British Council manuscript should be treated with caution, and I doubt that it is a copy of the original version of the opera. Most of its con-tents closely resemble the pieces published in *Some Select Songs* and *Orpheus Britannicus*, even with respect to variations in melodic detail. In fact the score includes only three pieces that an enterprising copyist, hoping to claim a proportion of the twenty guineas' reward offered for the recovery of the Theatre Royal manuscript, could not have found in the London music shops: the choruses 'May the god of wit inspire' and 'Sing while we trip it on the green', both in Act II, and 'Thus wildly we live' in Act V. The first two are unique to MS OP. 45 and are of doubtful authenticity. 'May the god of wit' duplicates the trio of the same title, putting the alto up an octave to serve as soprano and using the original tenor part as the alto, while the choral tenor part is new. This produces a very un-Purcellian texture, with sopranos and altos moving for the most part in parallel tenths rather than the more typical thirds and sixths, while the tenors and basses muddy the waters by crossing frequently. Furthermore, the soprano part lies impossibly high, reaching a B♭ in the second strain, a pitch unprece-dented in the composer's other theatrical choruses (see Example 1). The choral version of 'Sing while we trip it' is even more suspect, because it is simply taken from the four-part song-tune published in *Ayres for the Theatre*, with the alto an octave below the second violin and the tenor doubling the viola. This also produces some topsy-turvy part-writing. The

---

[22] In addition to 'May the god of wit inspire', these include 'Come all ye songsters', 'Now the maids and the men', 'Let the fifes and the clarions', 'When a cruel long winter', 'Here's the summer', 'See my many colour'd fields', 'Thus the gloomy world', and 'Yes, Dafne'.

Example 1. *The Fairy-Queen*: 'May the god of wit inspire' (British Council MS version), bars 29–36 (strings omitted)

fifth-act chorus 'Thus wildly we live' has been similarly altered, probably from the instrumental version also found in *Ayres for the Theatre*.

I should not hesitate to dub the British Council manuscript a fake except that it preserves the complete version of the D major trumpet overture, which was not in print at the time the volume was copied. This piece is imperfect even in Purcell's own manuscript, as the trumpet parts break off after the first three bars. *Ayres for the Theatre* also omits these parts, but this does not prove that they were unavailable in 1697, since the collection mindlessly reduces all orchestral pieces with winds and drums to a four-part string format. The trumpet parts in the British Council manuscript's overture are undoubtedly authentic; and a significant variant in the viola near the beginning might be interpreted as a genuine revision rather than an unauthorized emendation. As shown in Example 2, the viola in both the Royal Academy score and *Ayres for the Theatre* rests in bar 4, entering with the semiquaver countersubject in the next. The statement of the main subject in the viola in bar 4 (in the British Council copy) is con-

Example 2. *The Fairy-Queen*: Overture, bars 1–6

335

sistent with the previous entries, but all other appearances of the counter-subject are preceded by rests. The version in the Royal Academy score is a subtle refinement. To sum up the British Council manuscript, I believe that, except for the overture and the botched choruses mentioned above, it was copied entirely from printed sources shortly after the publication of the second book of *Orpheus Britannicus* in 1702, perhaps in conjunction with the Theatre Royal revival of an act of *The Fairy-Queen* in 1703.

The Music

The music in *The Fairy-Queen* is of consistently higher quality than that in any of the other dramatic operas. No vacuous choruses or tedious dialogues of the sort one occasionally hears in *Dioclesian* and *King Arthur* are to be found in the original version of this splendid score. While the opera lacks moments of dramatic intensity characteristic of the later music for *Don Quixote* and *The Indian Queen*, it is unmistakably *A Midsummer Night's Dream*. Despite the lack of a sub-plot running through the highly varied masques, the distinctive quality of the music pervades even the act tunes. Dennis Arundell puts a finger on the special aura when he writes that 'Purcell's music takes the place of [Shakespeare's] descriptive poetry'.[23] Titania's foul-weather speech and Puck's flights of fancy are elliptical moments of repose that transport the playgoer into a scintillating reverie. Purcell's music has much the same effect. To give one example, the masque of sleep in Act II, a hugely expanded induction into the queen's dream, suspends the action with ever softer and sweeter music. But instead of numbing our senses, the airs and choruses grow richer, and the scene ebbs to a close with the highly abstracted, almost painfully dissonant dance for the followers of Night.

Although not directly affecting the theme of the original play, the music does, I feel, vitiate its topicality in a manner literary critics have not noticed. Few of them would challenge the supposition that the *Dream* was designed to grace a wedding. And central to the vast literature on the play is the theme of love in relation to marriage (see the Arden edition, p. lxxxix). Furness even looked to *The Fairy-Queen* to support this thesis: 'Although we have no record whatsoever that the Opera was intended to celebrate any nuptials, yet its appropriateness to such a celebration is as marked as in *A Midsummer Night's Dream*, if not even more emphatically marked – a fact which I humbly commend to the consideration of those who contend for this interpretation of Shakespeare's play.'[24] While the 1692 play-book offers this impression, the music is not consistent in its support. On the contrary, I believe that Purcell viewed the impending

[23] Introduction to *The Fairy Queen . . . as Performed at the New Theatre, Cambridge* (Cambridge: Cambridge Univ. Press, 1931), p. ix.
[24] *A New Variorum Edition*, pp. 342–3; see also pp. xix–xx.

weddings and especially the fairy monarchs' rocky marriage with virulent cynicism. In the masques of Acts III–V the original theme of 'love in relation to marriage' is twisted into 'sex in relation to adultery'. The text of the opera retains much of the play's romantic spirit, but the music undermines it with a healthy dose of late seventeenth-century irony.

Because it was not part of the original design, the first-act masque should be considered separately from the others. However fine the music, the scene badly disfigures the drama. After the artisans are heard planning the Lamentable Comedy, Titania enters attended by fairies and leading the Indian boy. The setting is unspecified, though the queen says 'we glide from our abodes, / To Sing, and Revel in these Woods'. Apparently overlooking the humble origins of her beloved boy, she commands that no mortal be admitted while the 'Fairy Coire' entertain him. The opening music, 'Come, let us leave the town', a duet for soprano and bass, urges a retreat from urban din. This might have been an appropriate serenade for the eloping Lysander and Hermia, but since the fairy queen and her courtiers are already in the 'gloomy Grove' it is redundant. Perhaps the most notable feature of the C minor duet is its rhythm; with frequent shifts of accent from triple to duple metre and straitening imitation between the voices, it conveys a hasty exit from the town. But it is only a prelude to the main attraction of the first masque, the tormenting of the drunken poet.

According to stage directions in Q1693, *'three Drunken Poets, one of them Blinded'* (blindfolded?), are led in. Purcell reduced the number to one, whom the fairies pinch until he confesses to being 'a scu- scu- scu- scu- scurvy, scurvy Poet' – the composer, not the librettist, providing the stammering. This has long been considered a satire of the similarly afflicted Durfey, who self-mockingly owned that 'the Town may da- da- da-m me as a poet, but they sing my songs for all that'.[25] I think, however, the attack is broader. Durfey was not the only stuttering poet in the public eye; Elkanah Settle was ridiculed for the same affliction.[26] And would Purcell have poked such cruel fun at one of his chief collaborators? I wonder whether the peculiar declamation, generally thought to represent a stammer, might not be an attempt to depict the poet's drunken state, a condition in which Durfey is said rarely to have found himself. And the confession extracted by physical punishment might be an allusion to Dryden's Rose Alley cudgelling in 1679, supposedly at the hands of Rochester's hired thugs. Roger Savage offers yet another interpretation, viewing the

[25] *Dictionary of National Biography*, s.v. Durfey, Thomas, p. 25. See also Day, *The Songs of Thomas D'Urfey*, p. 6.

[26] In criticizing *The Empress of Morocco*, Crowne, Shadwell, and Dryden notice that the king has 'a strange infirmity in his Speech, and like some other Fools . . . is perpetually stammering. Perhaps our Author thinks it an Ornament; no wonder if he makes such ridiculous Characters when he Copies himself' (*Notes and Observations on the Empress of Morocco*, pp. 8–9). See also Downes, *Roscius Anglicanus*, p. 35.

drunken poet as the 1692 adapter himself, who 'does penance in advance in his own libretto' by accepting blame for the doggerel he has inflicted upon Shakespeare ('The Shakespeare–Purcell *Fairy Queen*', p. 211). Considering Purcell's merciless ridicule, I should think this improbable, but the implication of the poet's final couplet cannot be ignored: 'And as I hope to wear the Bays, / I'll write a Sonnet in thy Praise'. Perhaps the sonnet is the sizeable libretto added near the end of each of the succeeding acts.

There is nothing subtle about this scene except the fairy choruses, each of which is a gem of taut motifs and clean, impelling harmonies, above which the scribbler's discordant protests are heard. His cries of pain are uncomfortably realistic, but the episode is dramatically incongruous and is introduced clumsily. One should recall that it was played to an audience already well acquainted with the opera; as explained below, its coarseness accords well with other novelties of the 1693 production. Despite Savage's refreshing interpretation, the first act of Q1692, which includes no music, should probably be restored in modern revivals, a sacrifice that will benefit the whole.

The second-act masque, the first vocal music of the 1692 version, begins the adventure in fairyland. Titania is preparing for bed, but before falling asleep she requests an entertainment. While a brisk C major symphony strikes up, the scene is transformed from '*a Wood, by Moon-light*' to a prospect of flowery grottos, in which voices and instruments imitate the sounds of birds. The trio 'May the god of wit inspire' is closely related to Locke's 'Great Psyche shall find no such pleasure', since both have double echoes – loud, soft, softer – in which the final repetition is half the length of the original phrase. The air and chorus 'Sing while we trip it', though also in C major, mark the turning point from diversion to drowsiness. As Night approaches, the fairy music becomes harmonically lusher and occasionally bittersweet. One of Purcell's favourite forms in his large stage works is the coupled air and chorus, in which the second is a four-part arrangement of the song. But the hallmark of *The Fairy-Queen* is that the choruses are so ingeniously reharmonized that they virtually become new pieces. The solo version of 'Sing while we trip it', performed at the première by Mrs Ayliff, is routinely diatonic, beguiling but not profound. The chorus, however, takes on a dark hue, an effect achieved with the usual array of clashes and cross-relations. But two devices in particular help give the piece a special poignancy: the abandoned or spoilt cadence, in which the dominant chord is made suddenly minor just before resolving; and the 'augmented' dominant triad – both devices shown in Example 3. The impressionistic effect is achieved almost entirely by the alto and tenor parts, since the outer voices merely duplicate the jolly air. There is also a nearly independent second violin line, a certain sign that Purcell desired the richest possible chords.

Example 3. *The Fairy-Queen*: 'Sing while we trip it', bars 31–7

The augmented dominant, described anachronistically as a dominant thirteenth, pervades the opera as no other Purcell theatre work. In certain contexts it is extremely pungent, and editors are inclined to soften it. For instance, in the excerpt given as Example 4, from the Preludio of the first music, to which Purcell himself added most of the accidentals in the Royal

Example 4. *The Fairy-Queen*: Preludio, bars 11–12

Academy manuscript, an E♭ is clearly wanted in the second violin on the second beat of bar 12. And in the Entry Dance published in *Ayres for the Theatre* an equally stinging C♯ is shown in the second violin part in bar 25 (see Example 5), though the accidental is not in the Royal Academy score.

Example 5. *The Fairy-Queen*: Entry Dance, bars 24–6

As explained below, this is an intensely expressive chord for Purcell, and its high concentration in the choral version of 'Sing while we trip it' obviously foreshadows Titania's erotic dream, despite her courtiers' promise that 'nothing will offend' her slumber.

340

The singing to sleep of Titania is one of the greatest scenes in opera. Rather than write miniature songs and choruses for Q1693's added verses (thirty-five lines compared to Shakespeare's fifteen), Purcell lingers here with soft symphonies and frequent word repetition until time seems to stand still. The opening air for Night, 'See, even Night herself', accompanied by muted strings without bass or continuo, epitomizes the conflict between Titania's desire for a peaceful sleep and the uxorious Oberon's plan to give her disturbing dreams. A glance at the white, minim-covered page suggests a soporific blandness, but closer inspection reveals writhing harmonies and jarring tone clusters, as in Example 6. The famous countertenor air 'One charming night' is especially rich in augmented triads, in which the added minor sixths are resolved as appoggiaturas. The song is the first piece in the score to establish a clear link between the distinctive sonority and sexual passion.

Example 6. *The Fairy-Queen*: 'See, even Night herself', bars 23–9

The final vocal music of the scene is Sleep's bass aria 'Hush, no more, be silent all', during which Titania finally nods off. The gentle chains of suspensions in the violins are punctuated by frequent rests, while the chorus repeats the verse, adding the most sophisticated harmonies encountered thus far. Compare the parallel passages shown in Example 7: the new upper parts of the choral version produce a modulation more Brahmsian than baroque. To enhance the image of drifting into sleep, Purcell wisely declined to set the final line of the lyric, 'Rest till the Rosie Morn's uprise', a blunder by the librettist that would have sent the music off in the wrong direction. This is one of the composer's few emendations to the 1692 text.

The drama of the music has reached its most mysterious moment. Titania slumbers, but the air tingles with anticipation. Her dream begins with a dance for the followers of Night, arguably the most bizarre piece Purcell ever wrote. It is a double canon, as the composer notes in the rubric

Example 7. *The Fairy-Queen*: 'Hush, no more' (a) bars 11–13 and (b) bars 33–5

'4 in 2', and was surely inspired by the final act tune of Locke's *Tempest* music, which is also 'A Canon 4 in 2'. The contrapuntal strait-jacket produces some very peculiar progressions, but the dance possesses the same tang of augmented triads that permeates much of the rest of the score – a splendidly perverse demonstration that these supercharged chords are not the accidental products of the canons. I wonder, therefore, if the obvious homage to Locke goes beyond the borrowed technique. Augmented chords are even more numerous in the earlier composer's act tune. Both pieces verge on musical unintelligibility, but the progressions contained are all to be found in their less esoteric counterpoint. Purcell's debt to Locke should never be underestimated.

Titania's adoration of the braying Bottom in the third-act masque is launched by the *Dream*, IV.i.1–44. Framed by two G minor masterpieces, this episode is strewn with the emblems of metaphorical death, making explicit what Shakespeare leaves ambiguous. The soprano air 'If Love's a sweet passion' belongs to the small number of Purcell's songs often described as perfect, though its enveloping prelude and chorus of dryads and naiads are so plastic, so casually dissonant that one supposes the composer could have hit upon half a dozen equally stunning harmonizations. Again, the augmented dominant is important, especially in the chorus, where it depicts the torment of love. The four-part symphony is already richly adorned with suspensions and appoggiaturas; and when the choral parts are added to it, after the song, the alternate octave and unison doublings of second violin by tenor and viola by alto, in their several permutations, as well as the occasional touch of genuine five-part writing, produce a treacly, supersaturated texture – an excursion to the limits of tastefulness that wonderfully complements Titania's infatuation.

But the entertainment is for Bottom and, as in the *Dream*, his interests after acquiring the ass-head are more bestial than romantic. While 'If Love's a sweet passion' is performed, two swans are seen gliding on a river '*at a great distance*'. They swim forward to the accompaniment of a G minor French overture in which the canzona has been foreshortened, presumably for choreographic reasons; they turn themselves into fairies, and dance to a lithe tune in the parallel major. The antimasque is completed by four savages (called 'green men' in the Royal Academy score) who frighten away the fairies with a grotesque dance.

At this point in Q1692 follows the famed rustic dialogue 'Now the maids and the men'. But in the second production it was preceded by the long aria 'Ye gentle spirits of the air', in D minor. Like the other 1693 accretions, the soprano song is superfluous to the drama, a faint shadow of the far more impressive 'Thrice happy lovers' in Act V: that is, in the opening declamatory section, a rhythmically pointed motto theme is briefly imitated by the voice, which then wanders off in dreamy, time-breaching melismas. Both are striking departures from Purcell's usual recitative style, but unlike 'Thrice happy lovers' the novel structure of the song added to Act III is not dictated by the drama. 'Ye gentle spirits' is one of the composer's few fully developed *da capo* arias; besides 'Thus the gloomy world' in Act V, the only later one is 'Return revolting rebels' in *Timon of Athens*.[27]

The dialogue of Coridon and Mopsa stands in stark – some would say indecorous – contrast to the elegant music surrounding it. Yet this is Bottom's treat, and in some measure 'Now the maids and the men' is Purcell's answer to 'the tong and the bones'. Two versions survive, the earlier one, in F major, published in *Some Select Songs* (1692) and sung by Mrs Ayliff and the bass Reading.[28] For the 1693 revival, Purcell recast it in G major for alto and bass, presumably Pate and Reading, since they are named as the singers on a single-sheet engraving issued in 1695 (see Zimmerman, *An Analytical Catalogue*, p. 326). One can easily guess why it was altered. The dialogue is extremely funny, Mopsa's coy denial of the 'clown' being a lampoon of prudery; Coridon's boorish shift to the minor mode (bar 49) and his mock-lament (bars 51–4) will draw laughter from the stuffiest audience, regardless of whether or not they realize that Purcell is poking fun at his own chromatic laments. But even a good joke pales upon repetition, and Pate's appearance in drag as Mopsa at the 1693 revival must have been a hilarious parody of the parody.

The different versions of the dialogue raise questions about the sequence of keys in the masque, the two productions of which may be compared thus:

1692				1693
			g	prelude
If Love's a sweet passion	g	{	g	If Love's a sweet passion
			g	I press her hand gently (chorus)
			g	overture for the swans
			G	dance for the fairies
			G	dance for the green men
	?	⟵	d	Ye gentle spirits
Now the maids and the men	F		G	Now the maids and the men
When I have often heard	C		—	[deleted]
			G	dance for the haymakers
A thousand, thousand ways	g		g	A thousand, thousand ways

The tonal organization of the 1693 production is a classic example of Purcell's usual block-like scheme. Only 'Ye gentle spirits', which was added

[27] 'Ye gentle spirits' is incomplete in the Royal Academy manuscript, and more than seventy bars of the missing bass part have been filled in by a late eighteenth-century hand, apparently copying from *Orpheus Britannicus*, II.

[28] In the earliest sources of the original – *Orpheus Britannicus*, I, and *Some Select Songs* – both voice parts are given in the treble clef, as they are also in Purcell's second revision in the Guildhall Library autograph. Only *Orpheus Britannicus* names Mrs Ayliff and Reading as singers. See Laurie, 'Purcell's Stage Works', p. 112.

to the revival, falls outside the sequence. But in the original the shift to F major for the dialogue, assuming that the instrumental pieces preceding it were also in G major or minor, is awkward – a tonal relationship found in none of Purcell's other major stage works. Note, however, that the key of 'When I have often heard' in Q1692 makes a smooth bridge back to G minor through the subdominant. The C major song was dropped from the 1693 production – at least it is not in the Royal Academy manuscript – perhaps because the rustic dialogue had been transposed to G major, therefore eliminating the need for a linking piece. In this light, I wonder if 'Ye gentle spirits' may have been added to the original production after the 1692 play-book was published, since it makes a neat transition from the G major/minor dances to the F major dialogue.

According to *Some Select Songs*, 'When I have often heard', an unpretentious strophic air, was sung by Mrs Butler, fresh from her successful portrayal of Philidel and Cupid in *King Arthur*. She is the only singing actress known to have performed in *The Fairy-Queen*. Cibber reports that about the time of the 1693 revival she asked the managers of the Theatre Royal to increase her salary from forty to fifty shillings a week (*An Apology*, p. 94). They refused, and she left London for Dublin, beginning to act there during the 1694–5 season (see *A Biographical Dictionary*, II, 449). Her departure might therefore explain why Purcell cut the song from the second production, but, as Laurie notes, 'Thus the ever grateful Spring' in the fourth-act masque, also written for her, was retained ('Purcell's Stage Works', p. 113). One might suppose that her emigration was a blow to Purcell, but I find it striking that most of the airs for Mrs Ayliff, Mrs Dyer, and the other professional sopranos are far more substantial than either of those sung by the actress. In terms of sheer vocal technique, *The Fairy-Queen* is something of a breakthrough for Purcell.[29]

He obviously took great pains with the final piece in the third-act masque, 'A thousand, thousand ways'. The highly imitative countertenor air includes contrasting passages that leap up by octaves or down by triads, and intervening phrases that descend more gradually, while the panting quavers convey urgency. The attached chorus, perhaps the most intricate piece of the entire score, is no mere four-part harmonization of the air. The mould is broken as early as the second bar, when the soprano rises a diminished octave as the alto descends the by-now-familiar augmented triad (see Example 8). The rest is an orgy of cross-relations and augmented chords; by the closing bars, given as Example 9, the dissonant triad has finally established itself as a true dominant thirteenth, the pungent B♭ resolving directly to the tonic rather than acting as an appoggiatura to A.[30]

[29] Cf. Spink, *English Song*, p. 226.
[30] Notice a similar cadence in the fourth bar of 'If Love's a sweet passion', at the word 'torment'.

Example 8. *The Fairy-Queen*: 'A thousand, thousand ways', bars 23–4 (strings omitted)

Explicit symbolism must be left to the imagination, but at the very least this distinctive chord is emblematic of Titania's passion for Bottom. And we have not heard the last of it.

Example 9. *The Fairy-Queen*: 'A thousand, thousand ways', bars 46–7 (strings omitted)

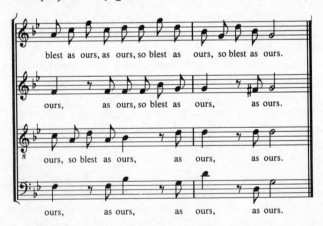

Purcell and his collaborator understood *A Midsummer Night's Dream* well enough to realize that Titania's infatuation with the Indian boy and its strain on the fairy monarchs' marriage is a metaphor of the strife disrupting all earthly order and fertility. Accordingly, the opera expands the queen's reconciliation with Oberon, after being cured of her doting, into a glorious three-fold celebration of renewal: a spacious six-movement symphony of trumpets, drums, and strings accompanies the sunrise; the fairy courtiers then salute Oberon on his birthday;[31] finally, Phoebus descends to ruminate on the process of regeneration in the masque of seasons. The apparent superfluity on both literal and figurative levels is too consistent a feature of Purcell's semi-operas to be shrugged off as careless construction. In *Dioclesian* the fifth-act masque is a summary of musical ideas presented earlier in the play. The fourth act of *King Arthur* is simply a variation of the preceding one. And in *The Fairy-Queen* each lyric in the masque of sleep in Act II merely rearranges the images of the one before it, while the music becomes ever more abstract. The fourth-act masque carries the technique a step further. Purcell strips away the gaudy foliage of pomp and celebration to expose the root cause of the monarchs' marital strife, thereby paving the way for the restoration of order among the mortal lovers. And the music becomes more sophisticated as the drama retraces its steps.

The fourth-act masque begins with another scenic transformation, judging by the detailed description provided in the oft-quoted stage direction, probably the most elaborate in the opera. The garden of fountains, the marble columns, the stairs rising '*to the top of the House*', and so on were paint-and-canvas illusions that no amount of scholarly inquiry will ever recapture; but one need only hear the Italianate symphony to realize that Betterton and his scene-painters must have created a feast for the eyes.

The air and chorus 'Now the night is chas'd away' are built on a striding two-bar ground that is putty in Purcell's hands; transposed to the dominant here and extended by half a bar there, the bass is never allowed to hobble the soaring vocal lines. The soprano soloist moves joyously through the first two lines, 'Now the Night is chac'd away, / All salute the rising Sun', and is answered by a brief choral interjection.[32] When she takes up the next lines, ''Tis the happy, happy Day, / The Birth-Day of King Oberon', the ground, after only six appearances in the tonic, veers off into B minor, and the sudden modulation, shown in Example 10,

Example 10. *The Fairy-Queen*: 'Now the night is chas'd away', bars 15–16

---

[31] The *Dream* makes no mention of the king's birthday.

[32] Bars 13–14 on p. 116 of the Purcell Society revised edition do not appear in the Royal Academy manuscript. Moore (*Henry Purcell & the Restoration Theatre*, p. 114) incorrectly states that there is a cadence in the mediant at the end of the first phrase.

produces a jolting clash. The bass soon recovers its D major composure, but the choral repetition, first avoiding the conflict, recalls it with a vengeance two bars later (see Example 11). One may wish to regard this passage simply as an example of cavalier part-writing where Purcell chose the clash over the hollow octave between soprano and bass if the leading-note had been left unsharped. But notice that the sour chord is the familiar augmented triad from Acts II and III, spelled enharmonically D-F♯-A♯. The two passages barely ruffle the regal splendour of the piece, and only the performer might notice that something is amiss; nevertheless, the clashes are needling reminders of Titania's night of debauchery that puncture Oberon's 'happy day' with more than a hint at cuckoldom.

Example 11. *The Fairy-Queen*: 'Now the night is chas'd away', bars 24–7

The most cerebral music of the score – or of any of the major stage works, for that matter – is the masque of seasons. Avoiding obvious rhetorical devices such as stylized birdsong for spring or shivering frost music for winter, Purcell created a series of four diminutive masterpieces in which seasonal change is suggested by the subtlest of means. Each phase of the year is represented by an air – for soprano, countertenor, tenor, and bass – in a different key: B minor, Spring; G major, Summer; E minor, Autumn; and A minor, Winter. Completing the cycle of related tonalities is the flanking chorus in D major, 'Hail! great parent of us all', a welcome ode for Phoebus. But first, in yet another instance of fecund redundancy, the whole process of renewal is anticipated by the god in the declamatory air 'When a cruel long winter has frozen the earth'. The song is in Winter's key, A minor, and the modulation to C major at the words "Tis I who give life' is one of the warmest moments in all of Purcell. For the most part, however, Phoebus dwells on infertility and 'Nature Imprison'd'. A sense of barrenness is clearly conveyed, especially in the abandonment of the domi-nant after imperfect cadences (see Example 12), which occurs throughout

Example 12. *The Fairy-Queen*: 'When a cruel long winter has frozen the earth', bars 14–19

349

the masque proper, except in Summer. Purcell's genius for capturing emotion in his word-setting is manifest, but the poignancy of this passage resides in the deceptively simple parts for the accompanying violins.

The upper strings are called upon again to provide a symphony for 'Thus the ever grateful Spring'. The choice of B minor, an unusual key in the theatre music, allows the conflict arising from the abandoned dominant to fall prominently on A♯ and A♮, last heard clanging together in Oberon's birthday ode. Purcell momentarily resorts to the old-fashioned practice of crossing the violin parts to permit the contentious pitches to appear in the same voice (see Example 13). Of the songs for the seasons,

Example 13. *The Fairy-Queen*: 'Thus the ever grateful Spring', bars 1–3 (bass omitted)

only 'Here's the Summer, sprightly, gay' is untroubled by these tonal arcana, the countertenor air being in G major, the key of the central part of Bottom's masque, and recalling the guileless charm of 'Now the maids and the men'.

The most impressive piece in the sequence is Autumn's 'See my many colour'd fields', a tenor air in which the composer explores in depth the relationship between minor dominant and tonic. Again, the violins play an important role. Many of the accidentals are very odd, and in Example 14 the D in the bass at bar 43 is sharped in both *Orpheus Britannicus* and the British Council manuscript, while Purcell himself left the leading-note unsigned here and in three analogous places, thereby sapping the strength of the voice after its otherwise triumphant arrival on the dominant. To summarize the paradox expressed in the verse, Autumn's bounty is the fruit of dying things, a sacrifice to the god of day. That a late seventeenth-century composer should have invented musical symbols to express such a conceit may be difficult to believe, but even a plodding analysis would record that the spoiling of dominant chords is carried to extremes in the following piece, 'Next Winter comes slowly'. It bears little resemblance to the far better-known frost music in *King Arthur*, and despite the lines 'trembling with Age, and then quiv'ring with Cold; / Benum'd with hard Frosts, and with Snow cover'd o're', winter is conjured entirely by chromatic counterpoint; special tricks of declamation are avoided, and the voice part, which duplicates the bass except for an occasional flourish, is

Example 14. *The Fairy-Queen*: 'See my many colour'd fields', bars 38–46 (violins omitted)

melodically indistinguishable from the others. Dominant after dominant is sounded, only to be consumed by the relentlessly drooping lines, and the final chord serves as a minor dominant to the returning chorus 'Hail! great parent', thereby completing the tonal cycle.

Above I suggest the masque may have been designed to some extent as a replacement for Titania's foul-weather speech, cut from the adaptation. Roger Savage takes this notion a step further, proposing that 'when Oberon and Titania are reconciled under the benediction of the rational and enlightening Phoebus, the seasons have their true liveries restored them and the world's perplexities are soothed' ('The Shakespeare–Purcell *Fairy Queen*', p. 213). Yet what strikes me most about these four songs is an underlying unity, despite their different keys, different singers, and varying degrees of chromatic complexity. Each is subdued; the voice parts are pale and retiring, often deferring to the violins for expressive highlights. Their rich colours seem to fade into a monochrome, as if a shadow had been cast over all the year. If these songs were performed instrumentally without the soloists, could the listener match each with its correct season? The masque is the musical nucleus of the opera, a core of mystery encased in the hard shell of a homophonic choral paean to Phoebus.

351

Despite the theme of renewal, the four songs do little to resolve the central conflict of the drama.

Purcell's reluctance to ratify a tension-less dénouement by glossing over the fundamental causes of Titania and Oberon's strife and its allegorical implications for the mortal lovers is also detectable in the fifth-act masque, an initially tepid celebration of marriage and purity of mind. As in *Dioclesian*, the final entertainment is a pot-pourri of music, dance, and spectacle in which the adapter loosens, if not frees, his reins on the drama. The composer also imposes a far less strict organization on the miscellaneous collection of pieces; the key sequence, to take just one aspect, wanders much more than in the previous masques, and I can find no unifying motif or preponderant sonority. As with the patriotic finale of *King Arthur*, it is probably pointless to look for an ingenious design. 'Thrice happy lovers' sets the equivocal tone. Cautioning the lovers not to let jealousy invade their happiness, the lyric is sung by Juno, who has had much experience in these matters. The unusual declamatory style of the first half results entirely from a slavish attention to the text:

> Thrice happy Lovers, may you be
> For ever, ever free,
> From that tormenting Devil, Jealousie.

The song begins as if built on a sprightly ground, but the steady rhythm gives way to recitative, an apparent reflection of 'free'. Momentum is lost just after the arrival on yet another minor dominant, shown in Example 15, a chilling reminder of Titania and Oberon's formerly sterile marriage.

Example 15. *The Fairy-Queen*: 'Thrice happy lovers', bars 1–9

Example 15 (cont.)

may you be for ev-er

The voice will not be coaxed back to the original motto by two subsequent false starts of the 'ground'. Jealousy has reared its ugly head, and the music dwells for ten long bars on the 'anxious Care and Strife,/That attends a married Life'. Purcell takes licence with the text by repeating the opening two lines at the end of the first section, thereby implying that lovers can only be happy if they are free, a wry jest reinforced by the nervous outburst on the operative word (see Example 16). The aria proper, 'Be to one another true', is by comparison dramatically tame and conventionally contrapuntal.

Example 16. *The Fairy-Queen*: 'Thrice happy lovers', bars 20–4

Thrice happy, thrice happy, thrice hap - py, hap - py, hap - py,

hap - - - py, hap - py hap - py__ lov-ers__

At this point in Q1693, Oberon asks to hear the Plaint, 'O let me weep', which Dent describes as 'so singularly inappropriate to its surroundings that we can have no doubt that it was already known as a favourite song and was inserted simply for the benefit of a favourite singer' (*Foundations*, p. 226). Dent passes no judgement on the music itself, but another writer calls it 'one of Purcell's finest' pieces, even comparable to Dido's Lament (Spink, *English Song*, p. 229). Savage acknowledges that it is unmotivated, but defends its inclusion because 'it helps to humanize the rather sinister Oberon. Among its listeners are Helena and Hermia, who have very

353

recently experienced the same desolations and desertions as' the singer
('The Shakespeare–Purcell *Fairy Queen*', p. 217). I believe Dent comes
much nearer the mark. The Plaint is not found in the first production, and
Purcell did not include it in the full score of the 1693 version; nor did he
even leave space for it to be copied in later. Not published until 1698 (in
Orpheus Britannicus), and then with no indication that it originated in
The Fairy-Queen, the song is an over-indulgence; interminable, especially
in the slow tempo at which it is usually performed, it has for me none of
the pathos of Dido's final aria. The free treatment of the ground bass,
which is much admired by some critics, fails to exploit the dramatic possibilities of its two basic forms – one chromatic and the other diatonic.
And the maudlin obbligato violin part is never really integrated with the
voice. The interior recitative 'He's gone, he's gone', for which the turgid
bass finally comes to rest, is admittedly moving, but it is an oasis found too
late in a journey too long.

The climax of the fifth-act masque is Oberon's call for another rehearsal
of the passage from dreams to consciousness, already thrice accomplished
in the preceding acts as celebrations of sunrise, birth, and seasonal change.
The stage is darkened, then suddenly illuminated to reveal a strange new
world, a Chinese garden as it happens, though no one would guess the
locale from the music. Perhaps the librettist was making some profound
philosophical statement – a vision of unobtainable purity, for instance –
but, as the lampoon of this transformation and similar 'world-of-the-
moon' scenes in *The Female Wits* reveals, cynical members of the audience
saw the chinoiserie for what it was: another diversion.[33] But by taking 'care
of the Songish part . . . after a great Man', the adapter secured immortality
for this silly scene, because the 'new Transparent World' was ushered in by
the greatest of all trumpet songs, 'Thus the gloomy world at first began to
shine', sung by a Chinese man. Like 'His yoke is easy' in *Messiah*, the piece
embodies an airy exaltation that beggars attempts at description, being
simply Purcell at his purest and, considering the brassy medium, least belligerent. The middle section of this full-fledged *da capo* aria, a form suggested by the composer not the lyricist, could hardly stand in greater contrast to what surrounds it: the ground bass ceases (though it is replaced by
another repeating pattern); the trumpet gives way to a pair of violins; and
the metre changes from duple to triple. But the feeling of emerging lightness is never lost.

In the rest of the masque one can identify at least four more masterpieces, 'Hark! how all things with one sound rejoice', 'Hark! the echoing
air', 'Turn then thy eyes', and the chaconne for the Chinese man and

[33] *The Female Wits* is discussed in Chapter 7. For thoughts on the topicality of the Chinese
scene as well as a possible antecedent, see Savage, 'The Purcell–Shakespeare *Fairy Queen*',
p. 217, n. 35, and Moore, *Henry Purcell & the Restoration Theatre*, pp. 128–9.

woman, a feat of eleventh-hour show-stopping unmatched in any of the other major stage works. But none of the pieces is very effective in knitting together the thin strands of the music drama. The rambling entry of Hymen, however, at least ties off the rather frayed theme of 'love in relation to marriage'. Reluctant to appear because he hates to wait 'on loose dissembled Vows . . . Where hardly Love out-lives the Wedding-Night', the god sings in Autumn's key of E minor, a symbol of the sickly flame of his wedding torch. To fuse once and for all the parallel images of seasonal renewal and the rebirth of love in Titania and the mortal lovers, Hymen ignites his torch from the orange trees that sprout from China porcelain vases, and moves to C major, the prevailing key of celebration.

The chaconne for the Chinese man and woman, though only a terminal flourish of general rejoicing, nevertheless adds another dimension to the peculiar manner in which the dominant is treated throughout *The Fairy-Queen*. The ground, which is the hardly original configuration of rising fifths and falling fourths, is unusual for Purcell in one respect: the eight-bar pattern has alternating endings, one an imperfect and the other a perfect cadence, much like the first and second endings of the opening strain of a binary dance.[34] This scheme produces an abundance of dominant and secondary-dominant chords that more than makes up for their relative dearth earlier in the score. The most striking variation, shown in Example 17, is in the parallel minor. The ground is unchanged, except for being divided between the viola and bass parts, but the principal chords of the first six bars are now all minor, and the passing dominants in bars 66-8 are resolved deceptively. Except for the authentic cadence in bars 72-3, the harmony of this variation is sinister in its remoteness from the tonal idiom, yet when one realizes that the bass has ignored the cloud of dark chords passing above it, the 'modulation' to C minor becomes but one more illusion.

As in all semi-operas, music does not have the last word. After the grand chorus 'They shall be as happy as they're fair', Oberon and Titania come forward to speak an enchanting benediction that begins with lines reminiscent of Shakespeare's V.i.387ff: 'At Dead of Night we'll to the Bride-bed come, / And sprinkle hallow'd Dew-drops round the Room'. But the fairy monarchs gradually shed their fantastic personas to become a pair of cynical Dorset Garden players, and the final page of dialogue unravels into a topical epilogue. The beautifully written conclusion, which alone should cause us to take the entire adaptation more seriously, is the last transformation; any remaining cobwebs of the illusion that began with the masque

[34] Manfred Bukofzer points out that this is essentially the same ostinato as the C major air on a ground published in *Ayres for the Theatre*; see *Music in the Baroque Era* (New York: Norton, 1947), p. 211. Anthony Lewis also notices this connection as well as a similarity between the air and a ground by Blow; see 'Purcell and Blow's "Venus and Adonis"', *Music & Letters*, 44 (1963), 266-9.

Example 17. *The Fairy-Queen*: Dance for the Chinese Man and Woman (Chaconne), bars 65–74

of sleep in Act II are swept away. The music and the fairies have disappeared, and the drama moves finally into the light of reality.

According to the dubious evolutionary history of seventeenth- and eighteenth-century English music drama outlined in the first chapter of this study, both the masque and play with interpolated music were progressing inexorably toward 'perfect' or all-sung opera, a development stunted by the death of Purcell and then completely halted by the arrival of Handel and Italianate opera fifteen years later. This ascent to the operatic Parnassus supposedly followed two parallel tracks. One lay through the self-contained school masques, or 'chamber operas' as Dent calls them, miniatures such as *Venus and Adonis* and *Dido and Aeneas*, needing only to be bolstered with *secco* recitative and *da capo* arias to attain a length suitable for the professional stage. Eccles and Congreve's *Semele* does indeed bear these characteristics, though it was never performed, and any link with the earlier private masques is at best tenuous. The second path to true English opera, the one favoured by some drama historians, would have replicated the French triumph of the seventies. In this quest for the baroque ideal, the native play with music was to have metamorphosed into lyrical tragicomedy, wherein the protagonists would sing their own songs, entertainments would advance plots, and the 'interlocutions' would finally be converted into recitative. This theory is strongest when applied to the increasingly operatic plays produced by the Duke's Company in the mid-seventies – *Macbeth*, *The Tempest*, *Psyche*, and *Circe*. Dryden and Purcell, too, seem to have taken up the torch with *King Arthur*, which, when compared to *Dioclesian*, is a decisive step toward the desired goal. But *The Fairy-Queen*, the grandest of Purcell's major stage works, is a jolting detour on the road to pure opera. The singing and speaking casts are completely segregated and the main musical entertainments do not appreciably advance the plot. The choice of play is itself anathema to the idea of a steady progression towards all-sung opera, because the peculiar structure of *A Midsummer Night's Dream* encouraged the separation rather than the integration of music and spoken dialogue. By eschewing the innate operatic features of the play in favour of new, self-contained masques, Purcell was able to build upon the lyricism of the drama without having to stand forever in Shakespeare's shadow.

List of Works Cited

The following includes only modern books, articles, and editions of plays and music. For a list of printed and manuscript sources of music consulted, see Franklin B. Zimmerman, *Henry Purcell 1659–1695: An Analytical Catalogue of His Music*, Appendices III and IV.

Adams, Henry Hitch. 'A Prompt Copy of Dryden's *Tyrannick Love*'. *Studies in Bibliography*, 4 (1951–2), 170–4.

Alssid, Michael. 'The Impossible Form of Art: Dryden, Purcell and *King Arthur*'. *Studies in the Literary Imagination*, 10 (Spring 1977), 125–44.

Altieri, Joanne. 'Baroque Hieroglyphics: Dryden's *King Arthur*'. *Philological Quarterly*, 61 (1982), 431–51.

Arundell, Dennis. *The Critic at the Opera*. 1957; rpt New York: Da Capo, 1980.

Baker, David Erskine. *The Companion to the Play-House*. 2 vols. London: T. Becket, 1764.

Baldwin, Olive and Thelma Wilson. 'A Purcell Problem Solved'. *The Musical Times*, 122 (1981), 445.

_____. 'Purcell's Sopranos'. *The Musical Times*, 123 (1982), 602–9.

_____. 'Richard Leveridge, 1670–1758, I: Purcell and the Dramatic Operas'. *The Musical Times*, 111 (1970), 592–4.

Brinkley, Roberta Florence. *Arthurian Legend in the Seventeenth Century* (Johns Hopkins Monographs in Literary History, III). Baltimore: Johns Hopkins Press, 1932.

Brown, F. C. *Elkanah Settle: His Life and Works*. Chicago: Univ. of Chicago Press, 1910.

Brown, Laura. 'Restoration Drama Criticism: Revisions and Orthodoxies'. In *Drama, Dance and Music* (Themes in Drama, 3), ed. James Redmond. Cambridge: Cambridge Univ. Press, 1981, pp. 191–201.

Buelow, George J. 'An Evaluation of Johann Mattheson's Opera *Cleopatra* (Hamburg, 1704)'. In *Studies in Eighteenth-Century Music*, ed. H. C. Robbins Landon and Roger E. Chapman. New York: Oxford Univ. Press, 1970, pp. 98–104.

_____. 'The *Loci Topici* and Affect in Late Baroque Music: Heinichen's Practical Demonstration'. *The Music Review*, 27 (1966), 161–76.

Bukofzer, Manfred. *Music in the Baroque Era*. New York: Norton, 1947.

Burney, Charles. *A General History of Music*. 1776–89; 2 vols., rpt New York: Dover, 1957.

Buttrey, John. 'Dating Purcell's Dido and Aeneas'. *Proceedings of the Royal Musical Association*, 94 (1967–8), 51–62.

_____. 'The Evolution of English Opera between 1656 and 1695: A Re-investigation'. Diss. Cambridge 1967.

Chan, Mary. 'The Witch of Endor and Seventeenth-Century Propaganda'. *Musica Disciplina*, 34 (1980), 205–14.

Charlton, David, '*King Arthur*: Dramatick Opera'. *Music & Letters*, 64 (1983), 183–92.

Charteris, Richard. 'Some Manuscript Discoveries of Henry Purcell and His Contemporaries in the Newberry Library, Chicago'. *Notes*, 37 (1980), 7–13.

Cibber, Colley. *A Brief Supplement to Colley Cibber, An Apology*, ed. Robert W. Lowe. 1889; rpt New York: AMS, 1966.

———. *An Apology for the Life of Colley Cibber*, ed. B. R. S. Fone, Ann Arbor: Univ. of Michigan Press, 1968.

A Comparison between the Two Stages. 1702; ed. Staring B. Wells. Princeton: Princeton Univ. Press, 1942.

Craven, Robert R. 'Nahum Tate's Third *Dido and Aeneas*: The Sources of the Libretto to Purcell's Opera'. *The World of Opera*, 1 (1979), 65–78.

Day, Cyrus L. *The Songs of John Dryden*. Cambridge, Mass.: Harvard Univ. Press, 1932.

———. *The Songs of Thomas D'Urfey*. Cambridge, Mass.: Harvard Univ. Press, 1933.

———, and Eleanore Boswell Murrie. *English Song-Books 1651–1702*. London: Bibliographical Society, 1940. (Cited in the text as 'D&M')

Dean, Winton. *Handel's Dramatic Oratorios and Masques*. London: Oxford Univ. Press, 1972.

Dennis, John. *The Musical Entertainments in the Tragedy of Rinaldo and Armida*. 1699; rpt in *Theatre Miscellany*, ed. C. H. Wilkinson. Oxford: Blackwell, 1953.

Dennison, Peter. '[Purcell:] The Stylistic Origins of the Early Church Music'. In *Essays on Opera and English Music*. Oxford: Blackwell, 1975, pp. 44–61.

Dent, Edward J. *Foundations of English Opera*. 1928; rpt New York: Da Capo, 1965.

———. *Mozart's Operas*. 2nd edn. London: Oxford Univ. Press, 1947.

Downes, John. *Roscius Anglicanus*. 1708; ed. Montague Summers. London: Fortune, [1928].

Dryden, John. *The Letters of John Dryden*, ed. Charles E. Ward. Durham, N.C.: Duke Univ. Press, 1942.

———. *Dryden: The Dramatic Works*, ed. Montague Summers. 6 vols. London: Nonesuch, 1931–2

———. *The Works of John Dryden*, ed. Edward N. Hooker, H. T. Swedenberg, Jr et al. Berkeley and Los Angeles: Univ. of California Press, 1956–.

Dunkin, Paul S. 'Issues of *The Fairy Queen*, 1692'. *The Library*, 4th ser. Transactions of the Bibliographical Society, 26 (1946), 297–304.

Eccles, John. *Eight Songs by John Eccles*, ed. Michael Pilkington. London: Stainer & Bell, 1978.

Einstein, Alfred. *A Short History of Music*. New York: Vintage, 1954.

Falle, G. G. *Three Restoration Comedies*. Toronto: Macmillan, 1964.

Fiske, Roger. *English Theatre Music in the Eighteenth Century*. London: Oxford Univ. Press, 1973.

Freehafer, John. 'The Formation of the London Patent Companies in 1660'. *Theatre Notebook*, 20 (1966), 6–30.

Fuller Maitland, J. A. 'Purcell's "King Arthur"'. In *Studies in Music by Various Authors*, ed. Robin Grey. London: Simpkin, Marshall, Hamilton, Kent, 1901.

Genest, John. *Some Account of the English Stage from the Restoration in 1660 to 1830*. 10 vols. Bath: H. E. Carrington, 1832.

Gray, Thomas, et al. *The Correspondence of Gray, Walpole, West and Ashton*, ed. Paget Toynbee. 2 vols. Oxford: Clarendon, 1915.

Guffey, George Robert, *After The Tempest*. Los Angeles: Augustan Reprint Society, 1969.

Haley, K. H. D. *The First Earl of Shaftesbury*. Oxford: Clarendon, 1968.

Ham, Roswell G. 'Dryden's Dedication for *The Music of the Prophetesse*, 1691'. *Publications of the Modern Language Association*, 50 (1935), 1065-75.

Harris, Ellen T. *Handel and the Pastoral Tradition*. London: Oxford Univ. Press, 1979.

Hawkins, Sir John. *A General History of the Science and Practice of Music*. 1776; 2 vols., rpt New York: Dover, 1963.

Hazlitt, W. Carew. *Bibliographical Collections and Notes on Early English Literature*. 2nd ser. London: B. Quaritch, 1882.

Highfill, Philip H. Jr, Kalman A. Burnim, and Edward A. Langhans. *A Biographical Dictionary of Actors, Actresses, Musicians, Dancers, Managers, and Other Stage Personnel in London, 1660-1800*. 16 vols. in progress. Carbondale: Southern Illinois Univ. Press, 1973-.

Historical Manuscripts Commission Seventh Report. Part 1. London, 1879.

Holland. Peter. *The Ornament of Action*. Cambridge: Cambridge Univ. Press, 1979.

Holman, Peter. 'Continuo Realizations in a Playford Songbook'. *Early Music*, 6 (1978), 268-9.

Hume, Robert D. *The Development of English Drama in the Late Seventeenth Century*. Oxford: Clarendon, 1976.

_____. 'Manuscript Casts for Revivals of Shadwell's *The Libertine* and *Epsom-Wells*'. *Theatre Notebook*, 31 (1977), 19-22.

_____. 'The Satiric Design of Nat. Lee's *The Princess of Cleve*'. *Journal of English and Germanic Philology*, 75 (1976), 117-38.

_____. 'Studies in English Drama 1660-1800'. *Philological Quarterly*, 55 (1976), 451-87.

Kerman, Joseph. *Opera as Drama*. New York: Vintage, 1956.

Lafontaine, Henry Cart de. *The King's Musick*. 1909; rpt New York: Da Capo, 1973.

Laurie, A. Margaret. 'Did Purcell Set *The Tempest*?' *Proceedings of the Royal Musical Association*, 90 (1963-4), 43-57.

_____. 'Purcell's Stage Works'. Diss. Cambridge 1961.

Lenneberg, Hans. 'Johann Mattheson on Affect and Rhetoric in Music (II)'. *Journal of Music Theory*, 2 (1958), 193-236.

Lewis, Anthony. 'Purcell and Blow's "Venus and Adonis"'. *Music & Letters*, 44 (1963), 266-9.

The London Stage 1660-1800. Part 1 (1660-1700), ed. William Van Lennep, Emmett L. Avery, and Arthur H. Scouten. Part 2 (1700-1729), ed. Emmett L. Avery. Carbondale: Southern Illinois Univ. Press, 1965, 1960.

Luckett, Richard. 'Exotick but Rational Entertainments: The English Dramatick Operas'. In *English Drama: Forms and Development*, ed. Marie Axton and Raymond Williams. Cambridge: Cambridge Univ. Press, 1977, pp. 123-41, 232-4.

Luttrell, Narcissus. *A Brief Historical Relation of State Affairs*. 6 vols. Oxford: Oxford Univ. Press, 1857.

McCutcheon, R. P. 'Dryden's Prologue to *The Prophetess*'. *Modern Language Notes*, 39 (1924), 123-4.

McFadden, George. *Dryden the Public Writer*. Princeton: Princeton Univ. Press, 1978.

Milhous, Judith. *Thomas Betterton and the Management of Lincoln's Inn Fields 1695-1708*. Carbondale: Southern Illinois Univ. Press, 1979.

_____, and Robert D. Hume. 'Dating Play Premières from Publication Data, 1660-1700', *Harvard Library Bulletin*, 22 (1974), 374-405.

_____, and Robert D. Hume. 'Attribution Problems in English Drama, 1660-1700', *Harvard Library Bulletin*, 31 (1983), 5-39.

Moore, Robert E. *Henry Purcell & the Restoration Theatre*. Cambridge, Mass.: Harvard Univ. Press, 1961.

Nicoll, Allardyce. *A History of English Drama 1660-1900*. 6 vols. Rev. edn Cambridge: Cambridge Univ. Press, 1952-9.

North, Roger. *Roger North on Music*, ed. John Wilson. London: Novello, 1959.

Novak, Maximillian E., ed. *The Empress of Morocco*. Los Angeles: Augustan Reprint Society, 1968.

Oliver, H. J. *Sir Robert Howard*. Durham, N.C.: Duke Univ. Press, 1963.

Pirrotta, Nino. *Music and Theatre from Poliziano to Monteverdi*, trans. Karen Eales. Cambridge: Cambridge Univ. Press, 1982.

Price, Curtis A. 'Music as Drama'. In *The London Theatre World, 1660-1800*, ed. Robert D. Hume. Carbondale: Southern Illinois Univ. Press, 1980, pp. 210-35.

_____. *Music in the Restoration Theatre*. Ann Arbor, Mich.: UMI Research Press, 1979.

_____. 'Restoration Stage Fiddlers and Their Music'. *Early Music*, 7 (1979), 315-22.

_____. 'The Songs for Katherine Philips' *Pompey* (1663)'. *Theatre Notebook*, 33 (1979), 61-6.

Raddadi, Mongi. *Davenant's Adaptations of Shakespeare*. Studia Anglistica Upsaliensia, 36 (Uppsala, 1979).

Rolland, Romain. 'L'Opéra anglais au xviie siècle'. *Encyclopédie de la musique*, ed. Albert Lavignac. Vol. 1. Paris: Delagrave, 1913.

Rosand, Ellen. 'The Descending Tetrachord: An Emblem of Lament'. *The Musical Quarterly*, 65 (1979), 346-59.

Rothstein, Eric. *Restoration Tragedy*. Madison: Univ. of Wisconsin Press, 1967.

Saslow, Edward L. 'Dryden in 1684'. *Modern Philology*, 72 (1975), 248-55.

Savage, Roger. 'Producing *Dido and Aeneas*'. *Early Music*, 4 (1976), 393-406.

_____. 'The Shakespeare-Purcell *Fairy Queen*'. *Early Music*, 1 (1973), 201-21.

Simpson, Claude M. *The British Broadside Ballad and Its Music*. New Brunswick, N.J.: Rutgers Univ. Press, 1966.

Sorelius, Gunnar. 'The Early History of the Restoration Theatre: Some Problems Reconsidered'. *Theatre Notebook*, 33 (1979), 52-61.

_____. *'The Giant Race before the Flood': Pre-Restoration Drama on the Stage and in the Criticism of the Restoration*. Studia Anglistica Upsaliensia, 4 (Uppsala, 1966).

Southerne, Thomas. *Oroonoko*, ed. Maximillian E. Novak and David Stuart Rodes. Lincoln: Univ. of Nebraska Press, 1976.

_____. *The Wives Excuse*, ed. Ralph R. Thornton. Wynnewood, Pa.: Livingston, 1973.

Spencer, Christopher, ed. *Five Restoration Adaptations of Shakespeare*. Urbana: Univ. of Illinois Press, 1965.

Spencer, Hazelton. *Shakespeare Improved*. Cambridge, Mass.: Harvard Univ. Press, 1927.

Spink, Ian. *English Song Dowland to Purcell*. London: Batsford, 1974.

Sprague, Arthur C. *Beaumont and Fletcher on the Restoration Stage*. Cambridge, Mass.: Harvard Univ. Press, 1926.

Squire, William Barclay. 'Purcell's Dramatic Music'. *Sammelbände der Internationalen Musikgesellschaft*, 5 (1903–4), 489–564.

_____. 'An Unknown Autograph of Henry Purcell'. *The Musical Antiquary*, 3 (1911–12), 5–17.

Summers, Montague. *The Restoration Theatre*. London: Kegan Paul, 1934.

Tilmouth, Michael. 'A Calendar of References to Music in Newspapers Published in London and the Provinces (1660–1719)'. *R.M.A. Research Chronicle*, No. 1 (1961), *passim*. No. 2 (1962), 1–15.

Villiers, George, Second Duke of Buckingham. *The Rehearsal*, ed. Montague Summers. Stratford-upon-Avon: The Shakespeare Head Press, 1914.

Virgil. *The Aeneid of Virgil*, trans. C. Day Lewis. London: Hogarth, 1952.

Westrup, Jack A. *Purcell*, rev. Nigel Fortune. London: Dent, 1980.

White, Eric Walter. 'New Light on "Dido and Aeneas"'. In *Henry Purcell 1659–1695*, ed. Imogen Holst. London: Oxford Univ. Press, 1959, pp. 14–34.

Whittaker, W. Gillies. 'Some Observations of Purcell's Harmony'. *The Musical Times*, 75 (1934), 887–94.

Zaslaw, Neal. 'An English "Orpheus and Euridice" of 1697'. *The Musical Times*, 118 (1977), 805–8.

Zimmerman, Franklin B. *Henry Purcell*. New York: Macmillan, 1967.

_____. *Henry Purcell 1659–1695: An Analytical Catalogue of His Music*. New York: St Martin's Press, 1963.

Index

Dramatic works are indexed under both playwright and composer. Titles refer the reader to playwright and, for discussions of a given work not covered under the author entry, to composer. Main discussions are indicated by bold-face type.

Index

'Take not a woman's anger ill', 76
'Tell me no more I am deceived',
    180-2 (ex.)
'Tell me why', 283, 285-6 (ex.),
    316
'Their necessary aid you use', 101
    (ex.)
'There's not a swain', 146n., 203
'There's nothing so fatal as
    woman', 157
'They shall be as happy as they're
    fair', 355
'They tell us that you mighty
    powers above', 128, 131, 141-2
    (ex.)
'Thou doting fool, forbear', 305
'Though you make no return to
    my passion', 177
'Thousand, thousand ways we'll
    find, A', 330n., 333, 344,
    345-6 (exx.)
'Thrice happy lovers', 330, 343-4,
    352-3 (exx.)
'Thus the ever grateful Spring',
    345, 350 (ex.)
'Thus the gloomy world', 280,
    333n., 344, 354
'Thus to a ripe consenting maid',
    183, 184
'Thus wildly we live', 334
'Thy hand, Belinda', 241, 258, 261
'Thy genius, lo!' (first setting), 21,
    60-1 (ex.), 64; (second setting),
    21, 61-4 (exx.)
''Tis death alone', 158
'To arms, heroic prince', 114
'To arms, to arms', 123 (ex.)
'To celebrate his so much wished
    return', 241n.
'To the hills and the vales', 250
    (ex.)
'To Urania and Caesar', 242n.
'Triumph victorious Love', 282,
    286-7 (ex.)
'Turn then thine eyes', 219, 354
''Twas within a furlong of
    Edinboro' town' (attr.), 146n.,
    200-1
'Two daughters of this aged
    stream', 219, 283, 308, 309 (ex.)
'Wake, wake Quevira', 133

'We come to sing great Zempoal-
    la's story', 130
'We have sacrificed', 299-300
'We must assemble by a sacrifice',
    101, 299
'We the spirits of the air', 130,
    139, 140
'What flatt'ring noise is this', 134,
    242n.
'What ho! thou genius of this
    isle', 304
'What power thou art', 303-6
    (ex.), 318
'What shall I do to show how
    much I love her', 273, 278-9,
    284, 288
'What! what can pomp or glory
    do?', 33-4 (ex.)
'When a cruel long winter', 333n.,
    349-50 (ex.)
'When first I saw the bright
    Aurelia's eyes', 278-9
'When I am laid in earth', 219,
    246, 250, 253, 254, 256, 257,
    258-9 (ex.), 285, 352
'When I have often heard', 329,345
'When monarchs unite', 229, 244
    (ex.)
'When the world first knew crea-
    tion', 214
'Whilst I with grief did on you
    look', 86, 87-8 (ex.), 215
'Who can resist such mighty
    charms', 91-3 (ex.)
'Why should men quarrel?', 133,
    134, 142
'With dances and songs', 121, 276
    (ex.)
'With drooping wings', 259-60
    (ex.), 260-1 (ex.)
'With this sacred charming wand',
    214-15
'Woden, first to thee', 306
'Ye blust'ring brethren of the
    skies', 313
'Ye gentle spirits of the air', 329
    (2), 343-4, 345
'Yes, Dafne', 333n.
'You say, 'tis Love', 316
'You twice ten hundred deities',
    102-3, 128-30 (ex.), 135-6, 228

375